# Voice Over!
## Seiyu Academy

6

## Vol.6
### Story & Art by
# Maki Minami

TECHNICAL ADVISORS
Yoichi Kato, Kaori Kagami, Ayumi Hashidate,
Ayako Harino and Touko Fujitani

Voice Over! Seiyu Academy

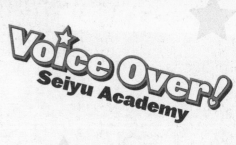

Vol. 6

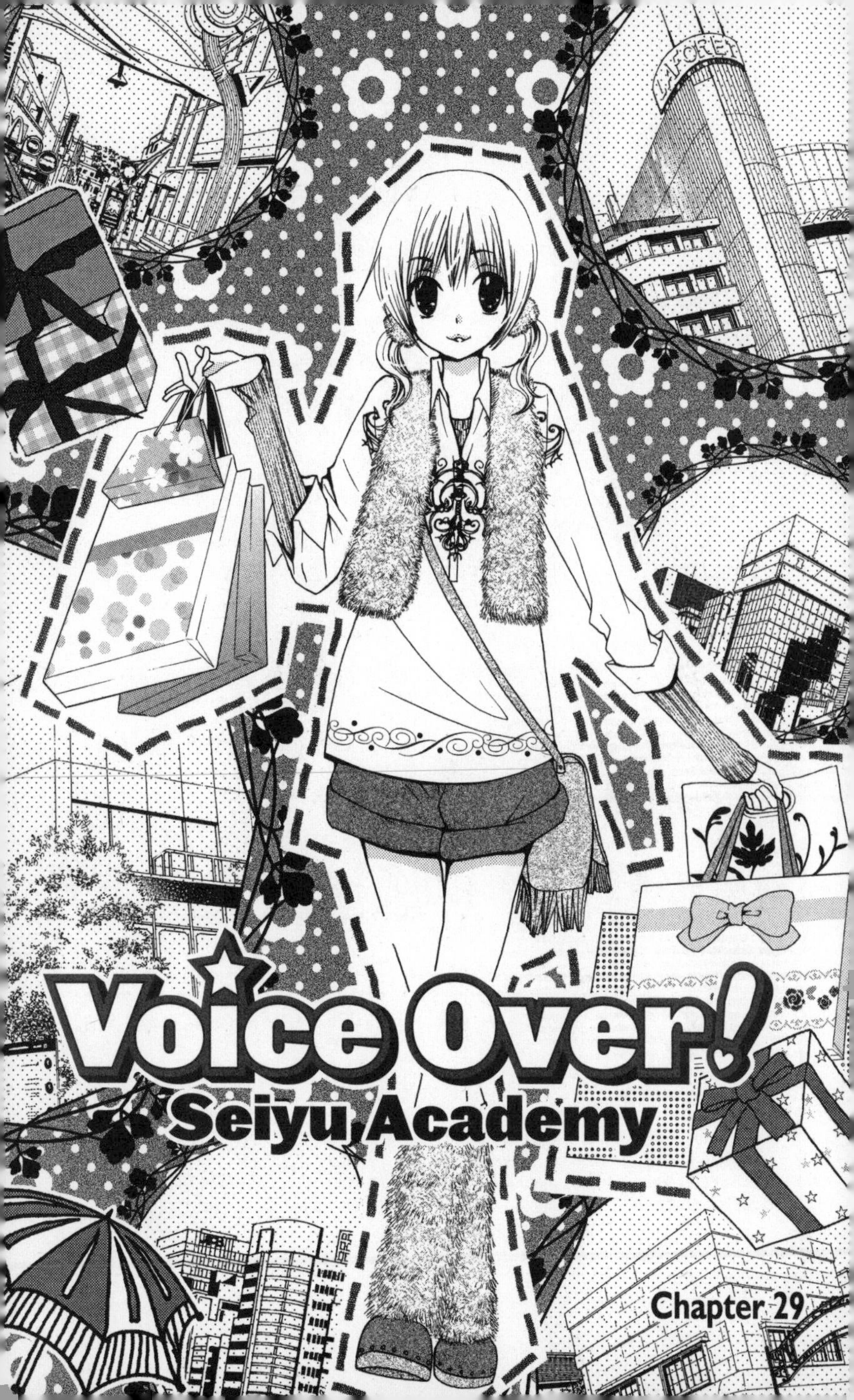
Voice Over!
Seiyu Academy
Chapter 29

SO...

HUH?

IT'S A SECRET THAT I'M WORKING AS...

...A MALE VOICE ACTOR NAMED SHIRO. ☆

Same per-son ♡

Cover & Various Things

The cover this time shows Tsukino and Ume. Two girls! I love drawing girls! ☺

Ever since Shiro showed up, it's been nothing but guys, so when the ladies show up, I have fun drawing them. But I always have trouble figuring out how to color their long hair...

Where should I color and how?!

①

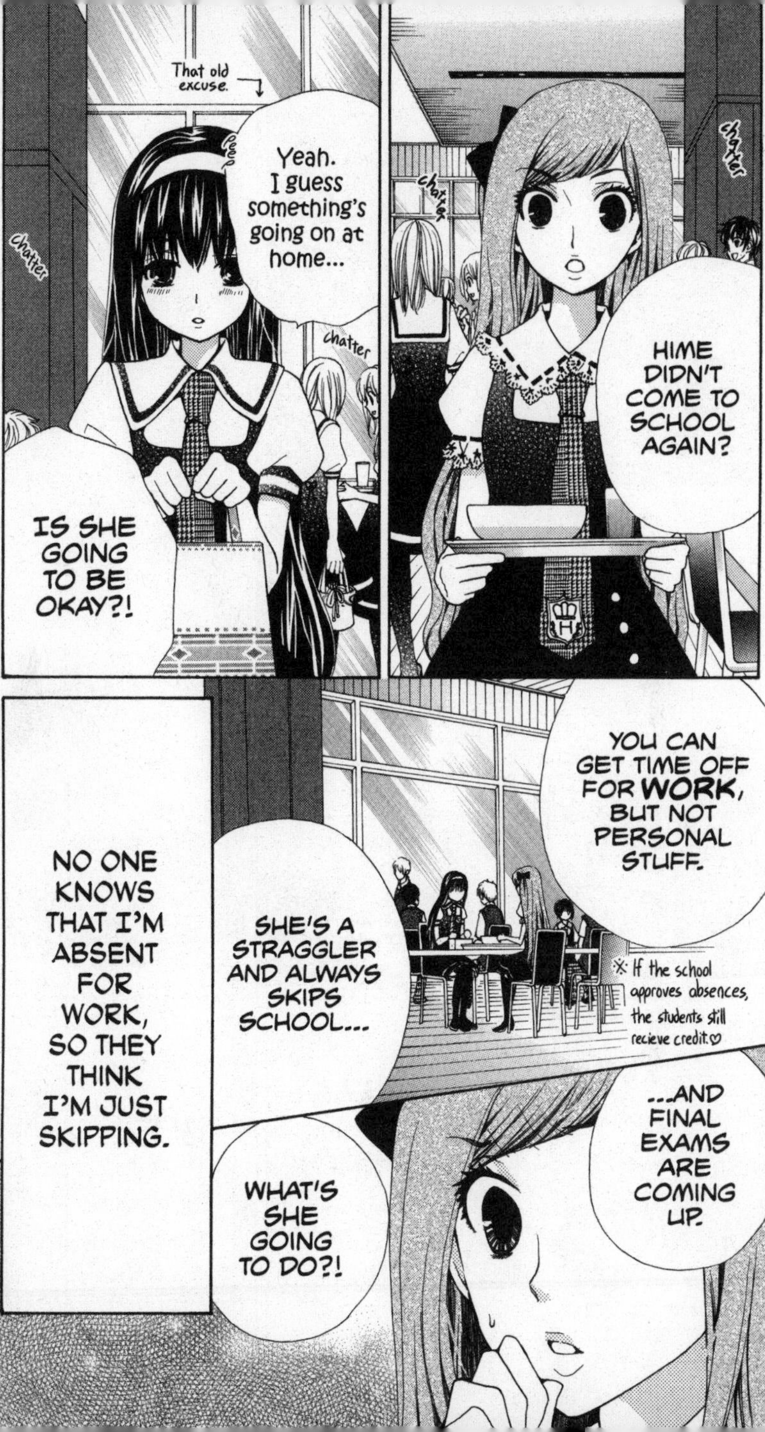
chatter
chatter
HIME DIDN'T COME TO SCHOOL AGAIN?
That old excuse.
peep
Yeah. I guess something's going on at home...
chatter
chatter
IS SHE GOING TO BE OKAY?!
YOU CAN GET TIME OFF FOR WORK, BUT NOT PERSONAL STUFF.
※ If the school approves absences, the students still recieve credit.♡
SHE'S A STRAGGLER AND ALWAYS SKIPS SCHOOL...
...AND FINAL EXAMS ARE COMING UP.
WHAT'S SHE GOING TO DO?!
NO ONE KNOWS THAT I'M ABSENT FOR WORK, SO THEY THINK I'M JUST SKIPPING.

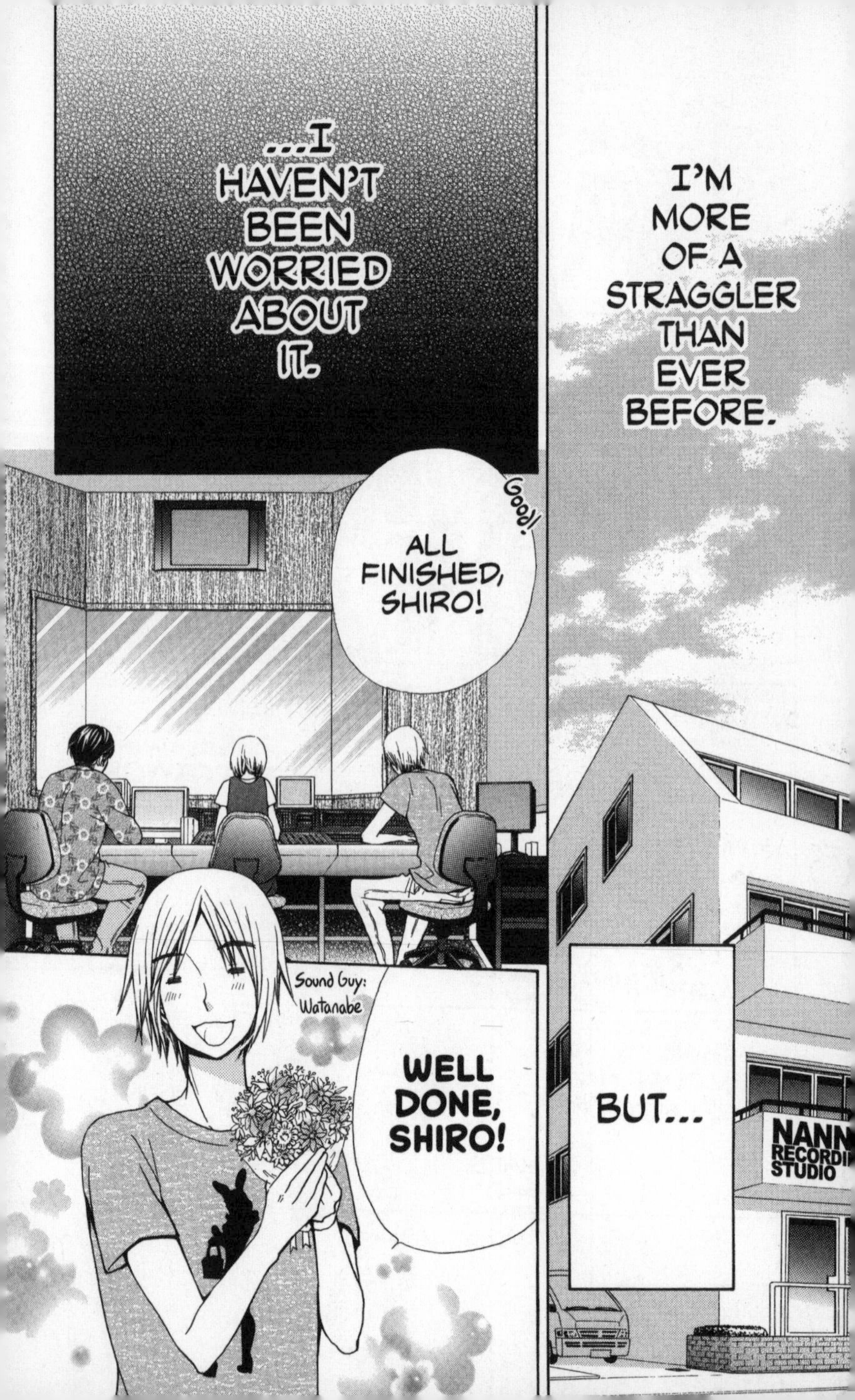
I'M MORE OF A STRAGGLER THAN EVER BEFORE.
BUT...
NANN
RECORDI
STUDIO
...I HAVEN'T BEEN WORRIED ABOUT IT.
Good!
ALL FINISHED, SHIRO!
Sound Guy: Watanabe
WELL DONE, SHIRO!

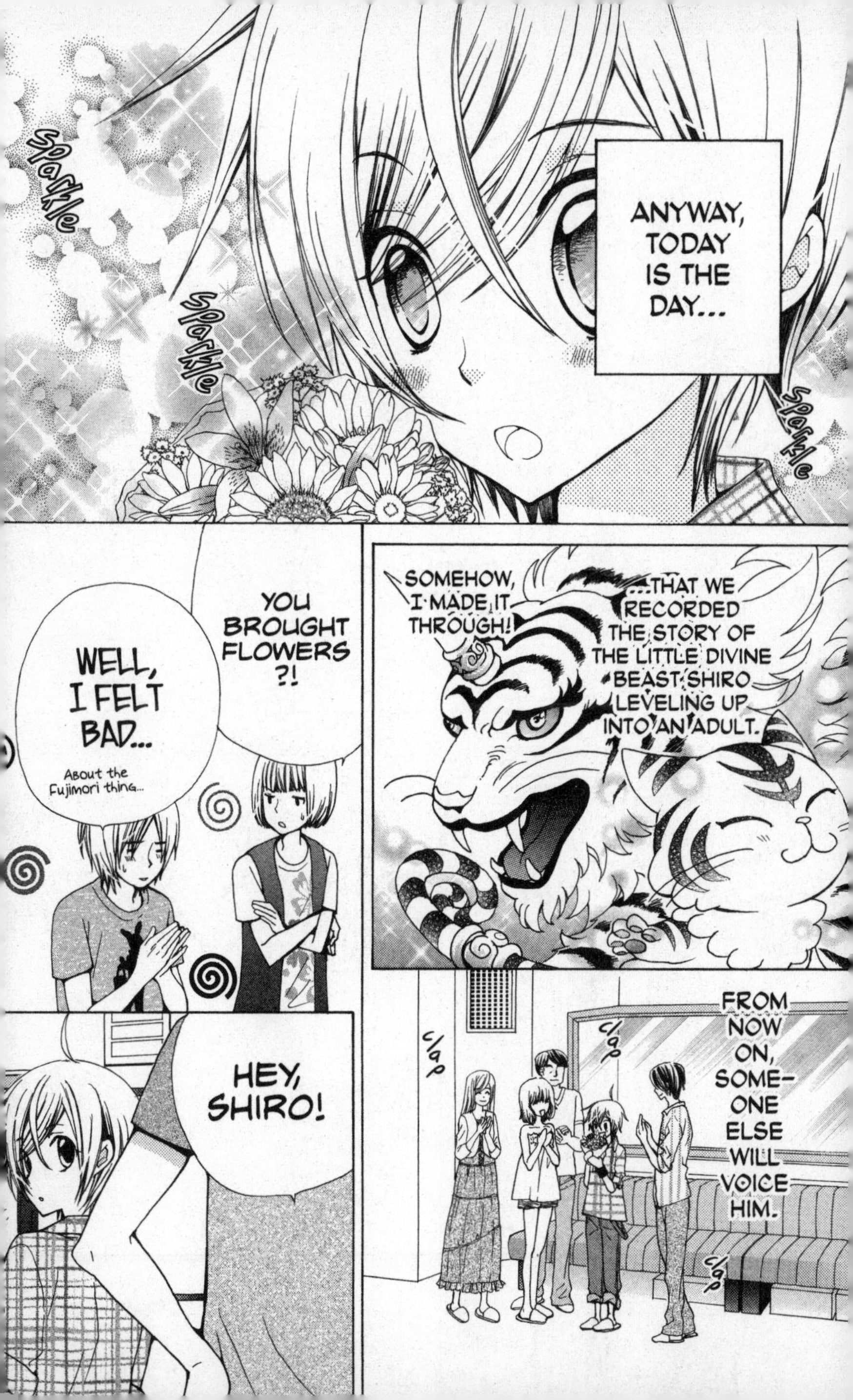
ANYWAY, TODAY IS THE DAY...
Sparkle
Sparkle
Sparkle
...THAT WE RECORDED THE STORY OF THE LITTLE DIVINE BEAST SHIRO LEVELING UP INTO AN ADULT.
SOMEHOW, I MADE IT THROUGH!
YOU BROUGHT FLOWERS?!
WELL, I FELT BAD...
About the Fujimori thing...
FROM NOW ON, SOME-ONE ELSE WILL VOICE HIM.
clap
clap
clap
HEY, SHIRO!

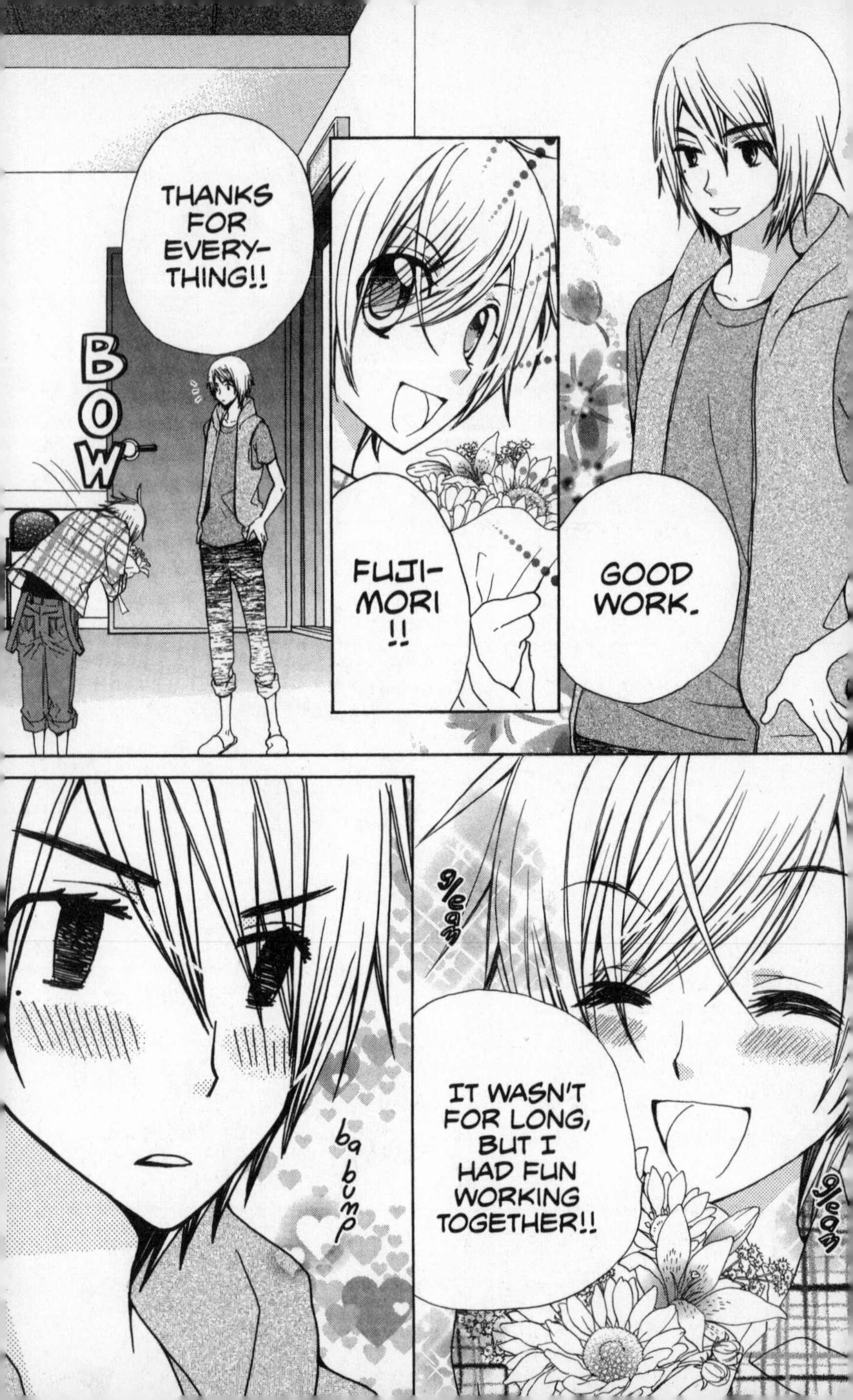
GOOD WORK.
FUJI-MORI!!
THANKS FOR EVERY-THING!!
BOW
gleam
gleam
IT WASN'T FOR LONG, BUT I HAD FUN WORKING TOGETHER!!
ba bump

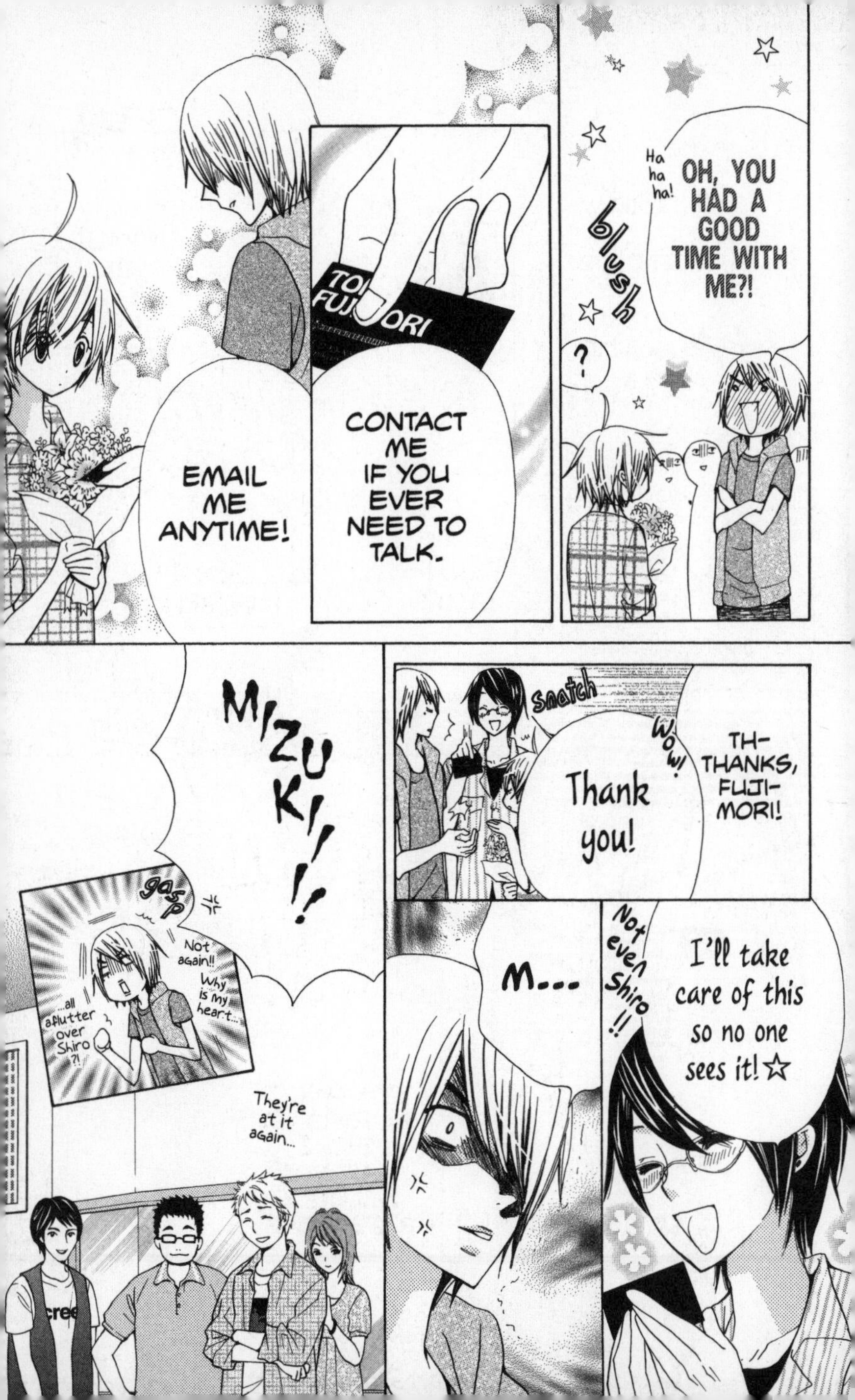
Ha ha ha!
OH, YOU HAD A GOOD TIME WITH ME?!
blush
?
CONTACT ME IF YOU EVER NEED TO TALK.
EMAIL ME ANYTIME!
TH-THANKS, FUJIMORI!
Wow!
Thank you!
snatch
I'll take care of this so no one sees it!☆
Not even Shiro!!
M...
MIZUKI!!!
gasp
Not again!!
Why is my heart...
...all aflutter over Shiro?!
They're at it again...

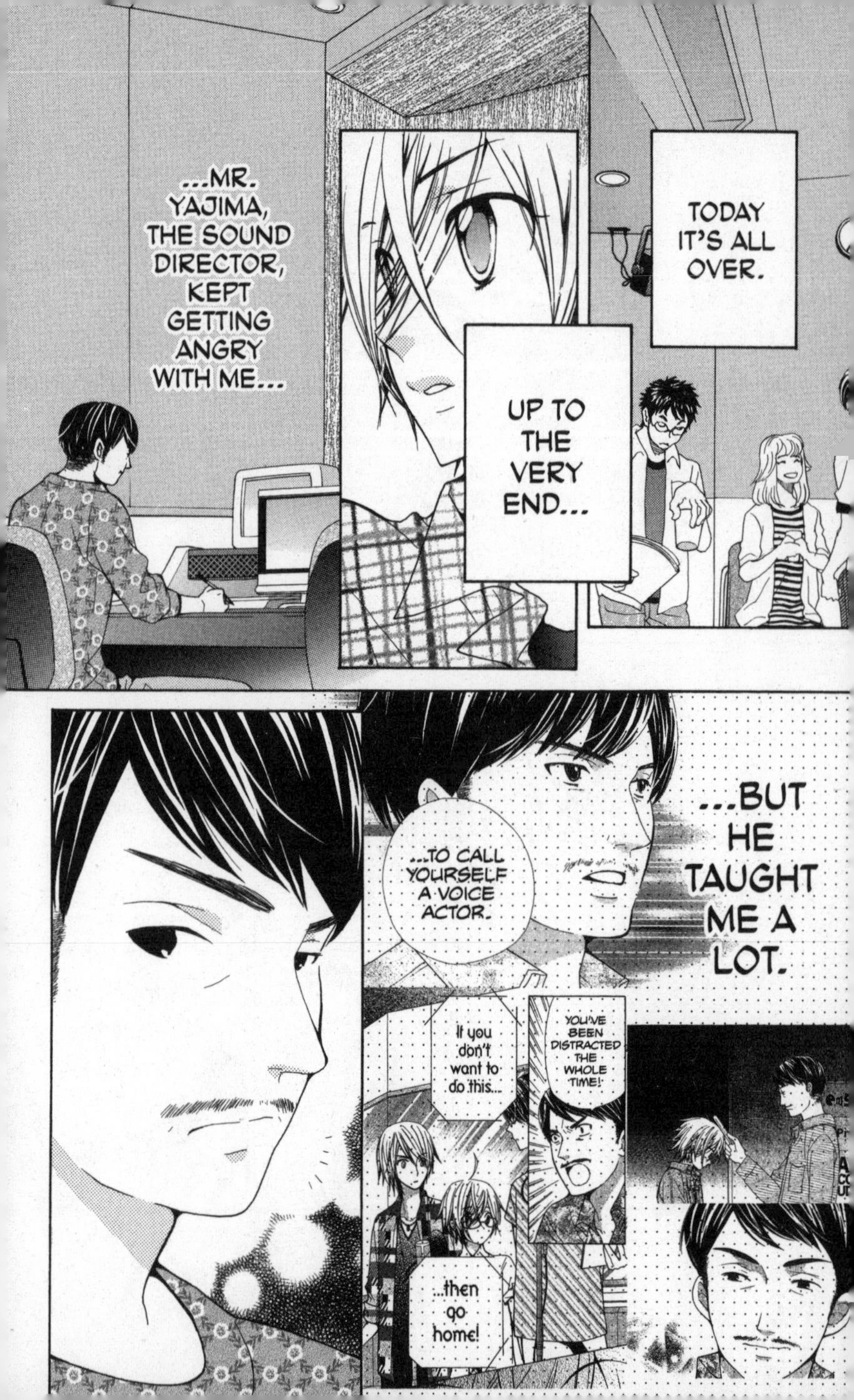
TODAY IT'S ALL OVER.
UP TO THE VERY END...
...MR. YAJIMA, THE SOUND DIRECTOR, KEPT GETTING ANGRY WITH ME...
...BUT HE TAUGHT ME A LOT.
...TO CALL YOURSELF A VOICE ACTOR.
YOU'VE BEEN DISTRACTED THE WHOLE TIME!
If you don't want to do this...
...then go home!

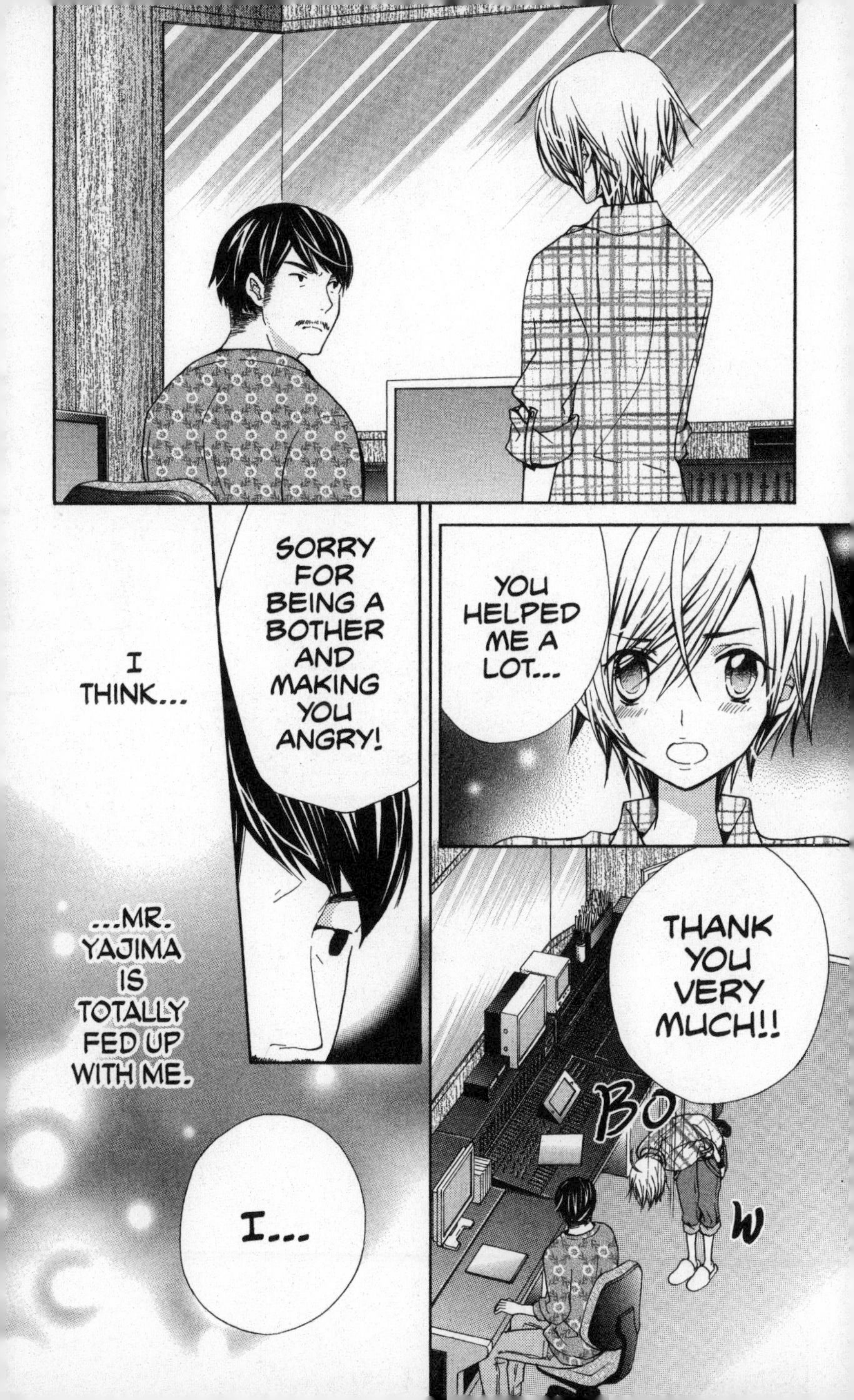
YOU HELPED ME A LOT...
SORRY FOR BEING A BOTHER AND MAKING YOU ANGRY!
THANK YOU VERY MUCH!!
BOW
I THINK...
...MR. YAJIMA IS TOTALLY FED UP WITH ME.
I...

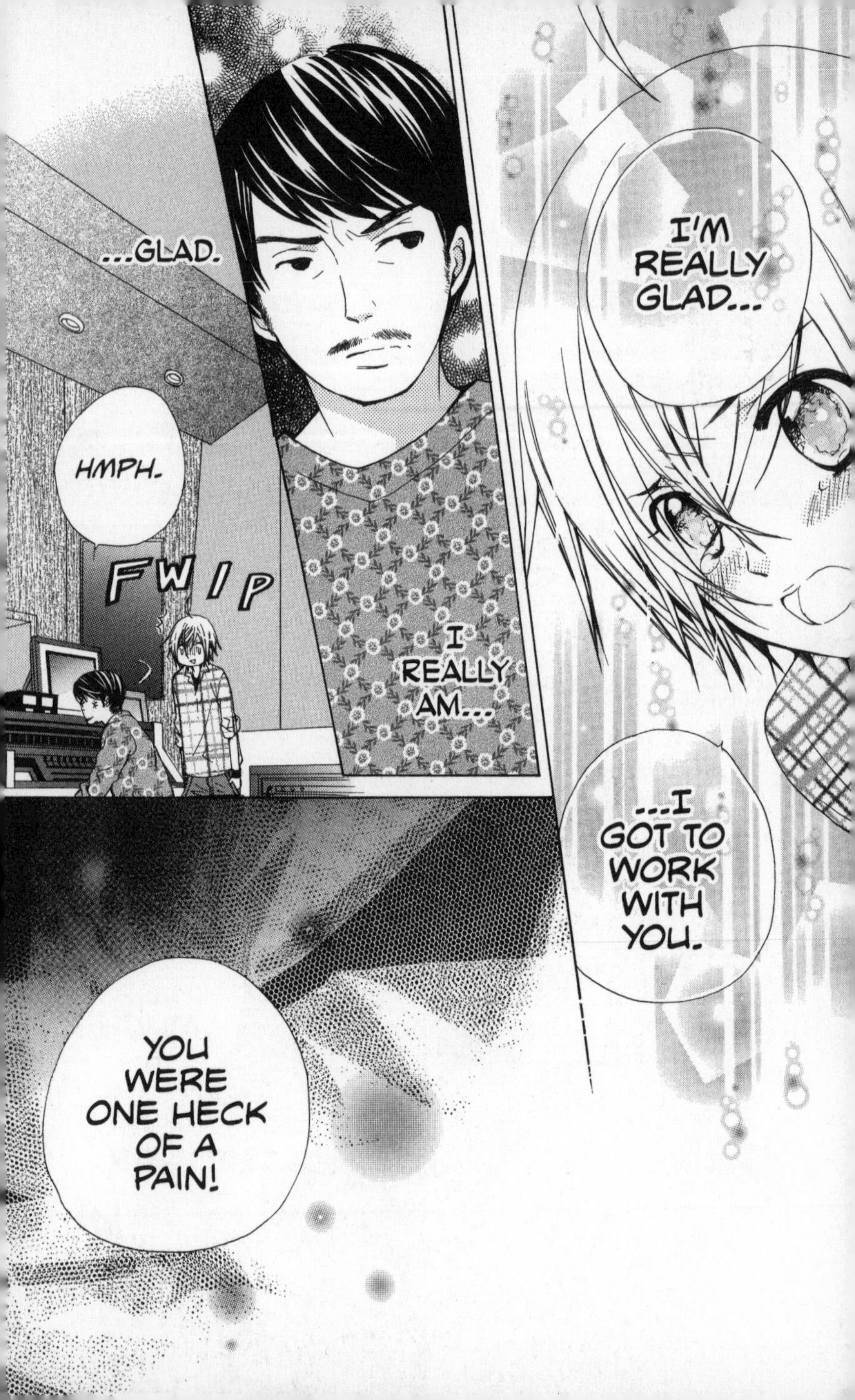
I'M REALLY GLAD...
...I GOT TO WORK WITH YOU.
I REALLY AM...
...GLAD.
HMPH.
FWIP
YOU WERE ONE HECK OF A PAIN!

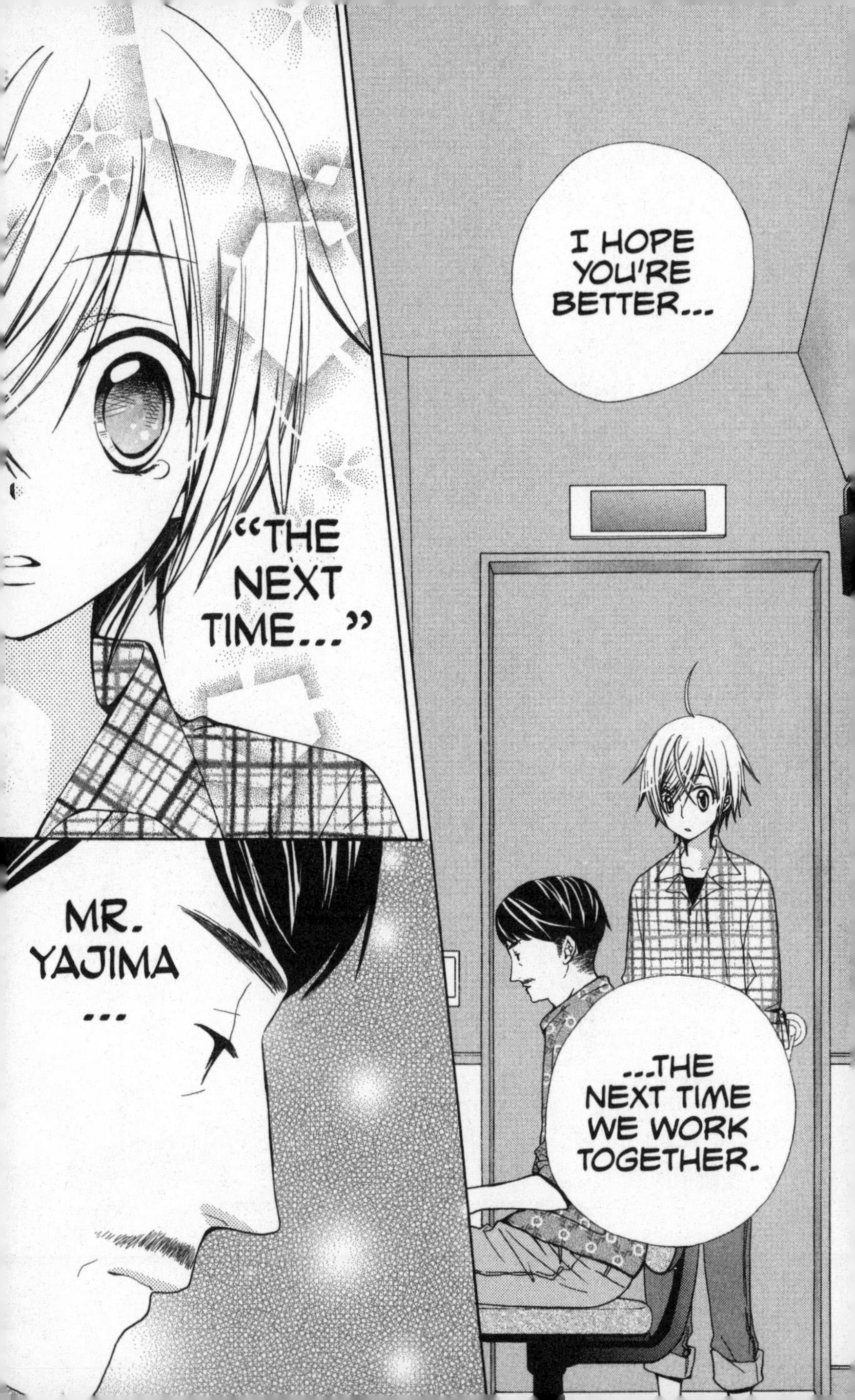
I HOPE YOU'RE BETTER...
...THE NEXT TIME WE WORK TOGETHER.
"THE NEXT TIME..."
MR. YAJIMA ...

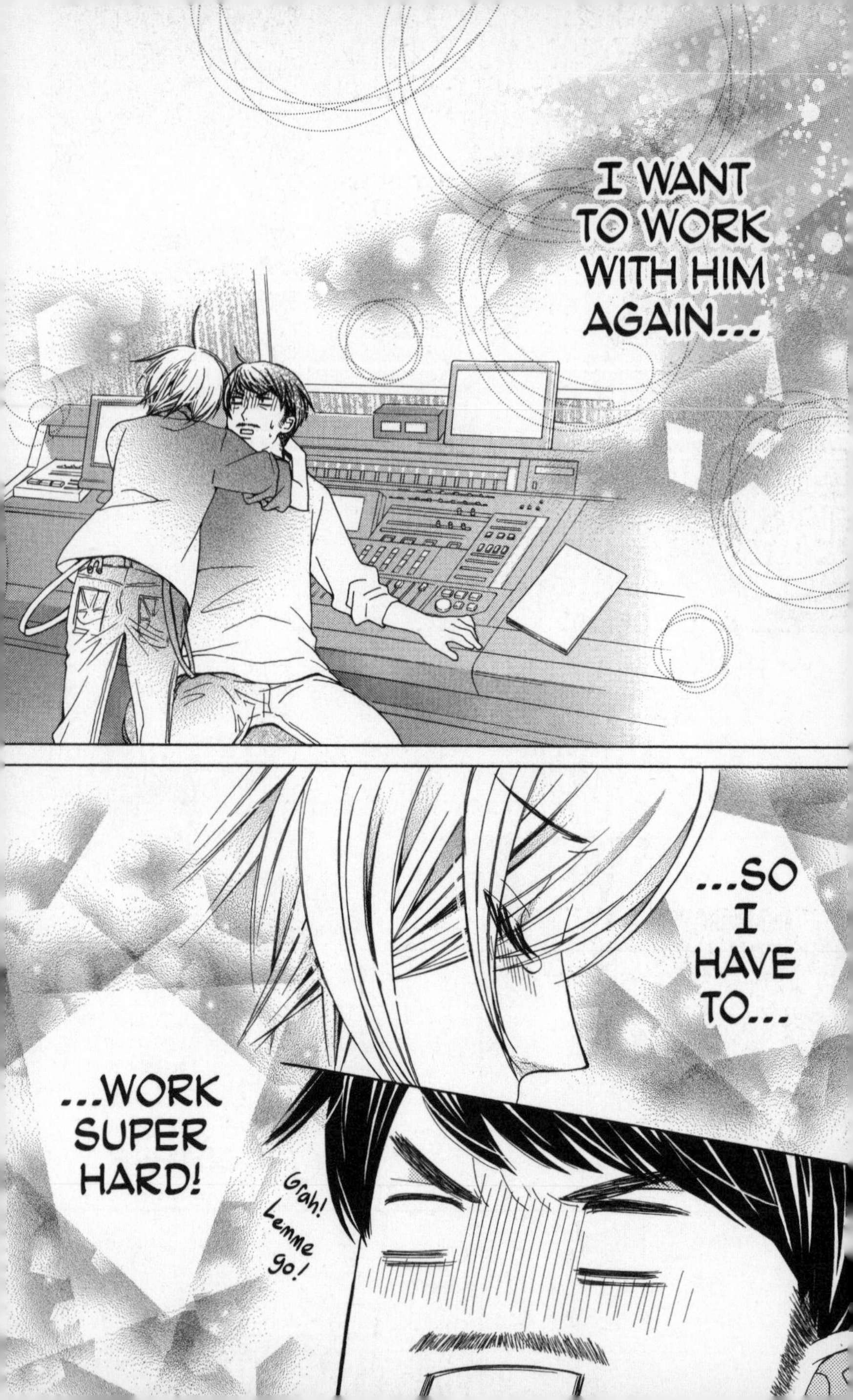
I WANT TO WORK WITH HIM AGAIN...
...SO I HAVE TO...
...WORK SUPER HARD!
Grah! Lemme go!

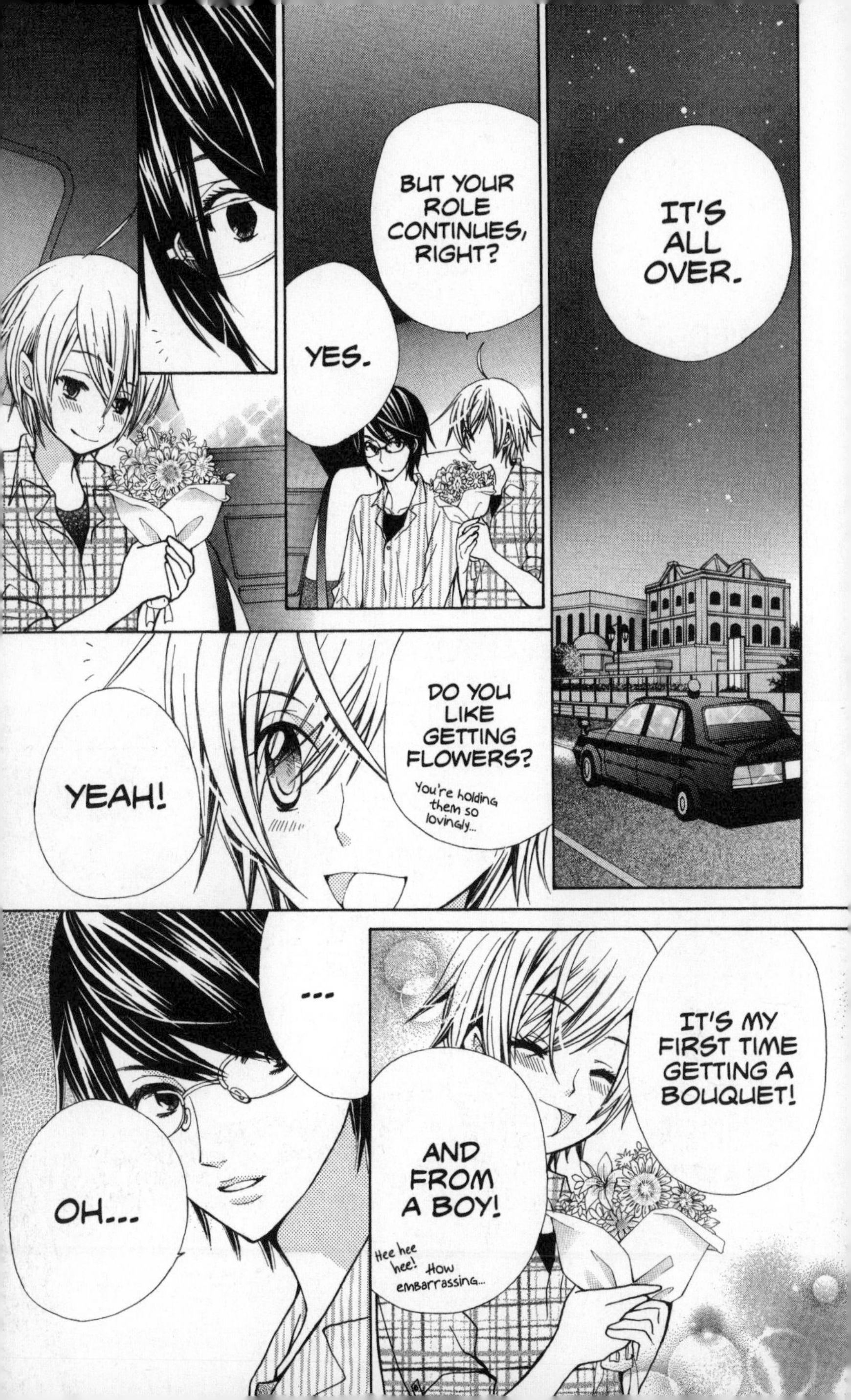
IT'S ALL OVER.
BUT YOUR ROLE CONTINUES, RIGHT?
YES.
DO YOU LIKE GETTING FLOWERS?
You're holding them so lovingly...
YEAH!
IT'S MY FIRST TIME GETTING A BOUQUET!
AND FROM A BOY!
Hee hee hee! How embarrassing...
...
OH...

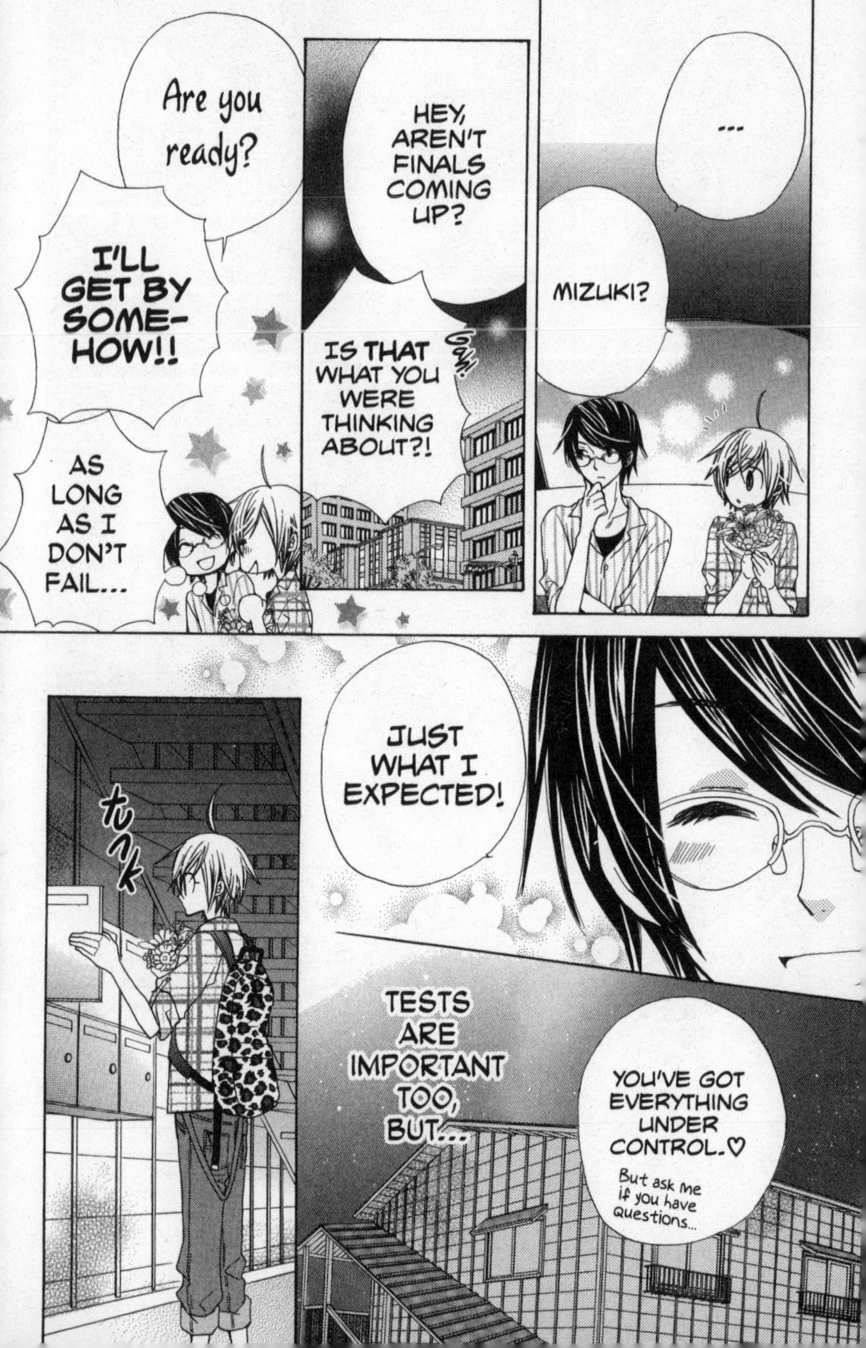
...
MIZUKI?
HEY, AREN'T FINALS COMING UP?
IS THAT WHAT YOU WERE THINKING ABOUT?!
Are you ready?
I'LL GET BY SOME-HOW!!
AS LONG AS I DON'T FAIL...
JUST WHAT I EXPECTED!
TESTS ARE IMPORTANT TOO, BUT...
YOU'VE GOT EVERYTHING UNDER CONTROL.♡
But ask me if you have questions...

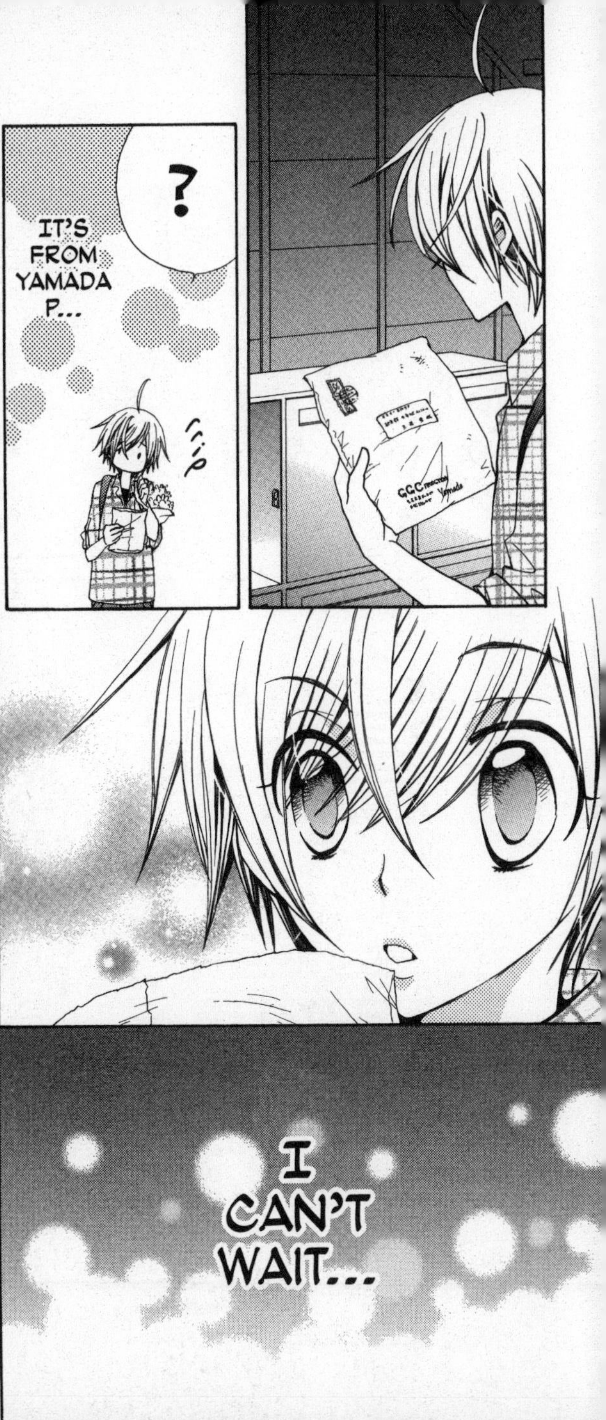
?
IT'S FROM YAMADA P...
rip
I CAN'T WAIT...

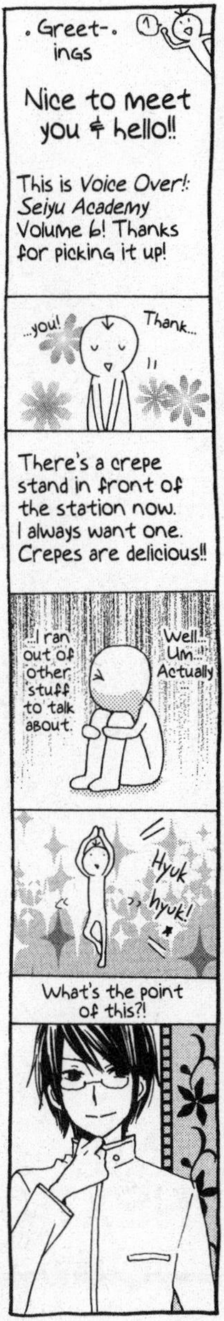
. Greet- . ings
1
Nice to meet you & hello!!
This is *Voice Over!: Seiyu Academy* Volume 6! Thanks for picking it up!
Thank...
...you!
There's a crepe stand in front of the station now. I always want one. Crepes are delicious!!
Well... Um... Actually
...I ran out of other stuff to talk about.
Hyuk hyuk!
What's the point of this?!

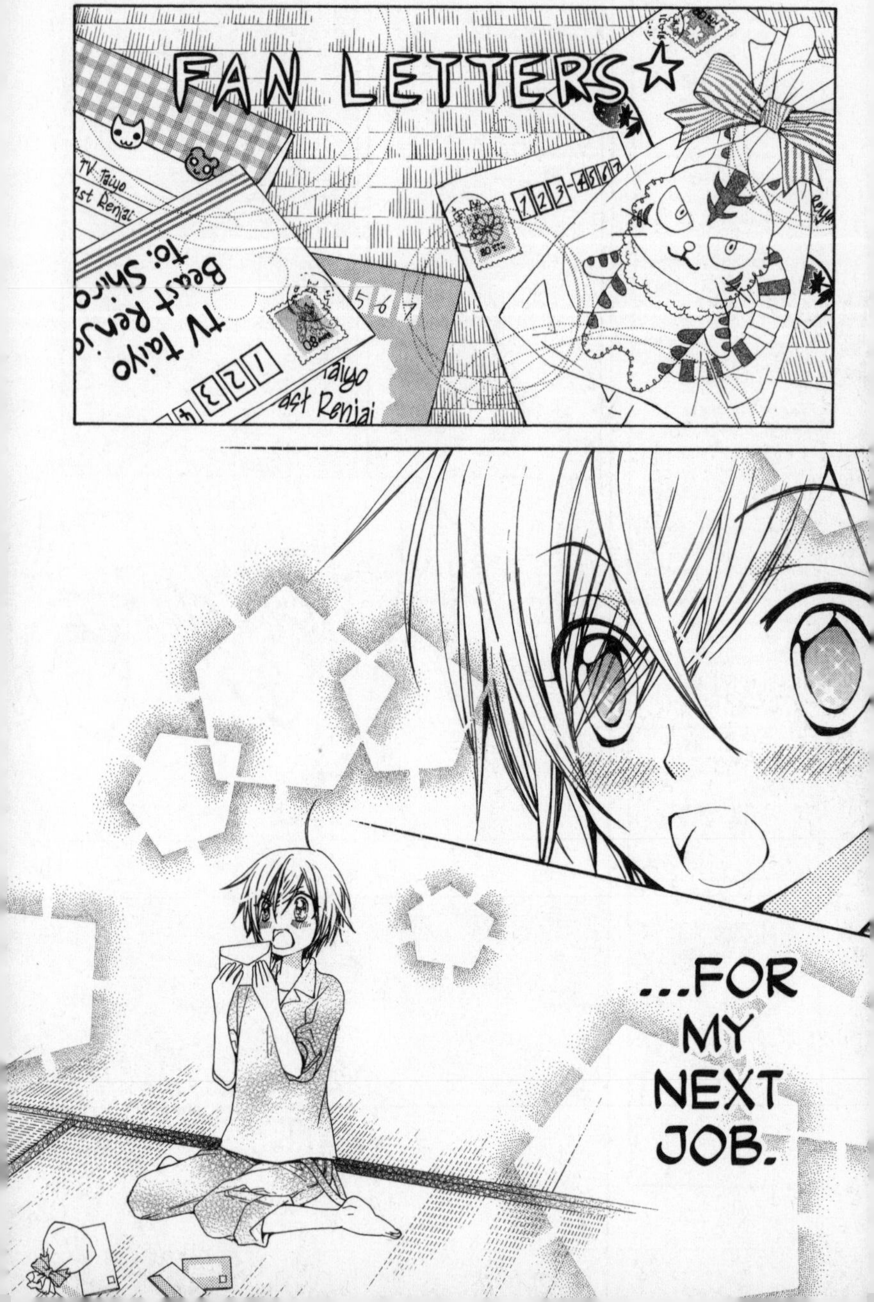
FAN LETTERS☆
TV Taiyo Beast Renjai to: Shiro
...FOR MY NEXT JOB.

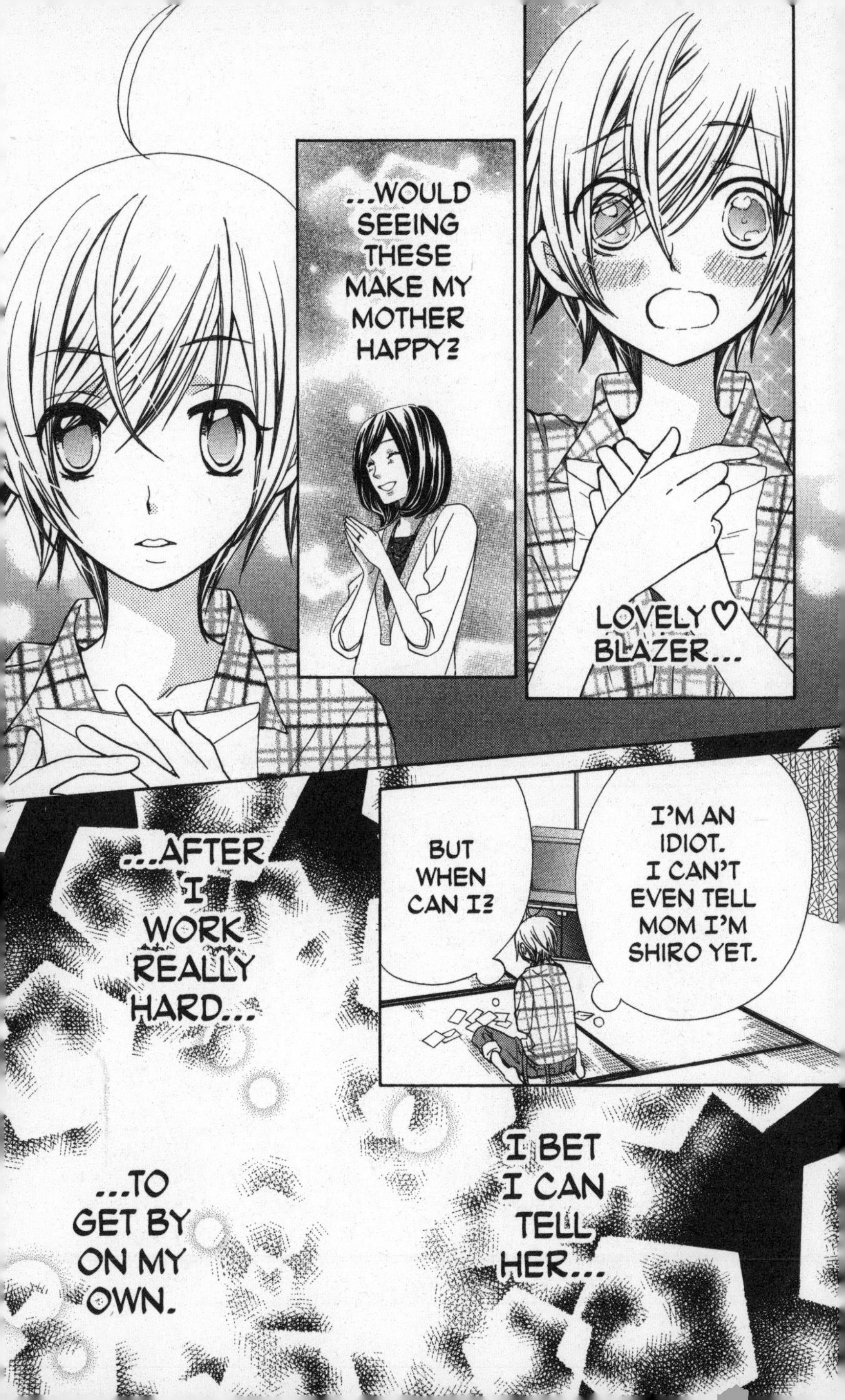
LOVELY♡ BLAZER...
...WOULD SEEING THESE MAKE MY MOTHER HAPPY?
I'M AN IDIOT. I CAN'T EVEN TELL MOM I'M SHIRO YET.
BUT WHEN CAN I?
...AFTER I WORK REALLY HARD...
I BET I CAN TELL HER...
...TO GET BY ON MY OWN.

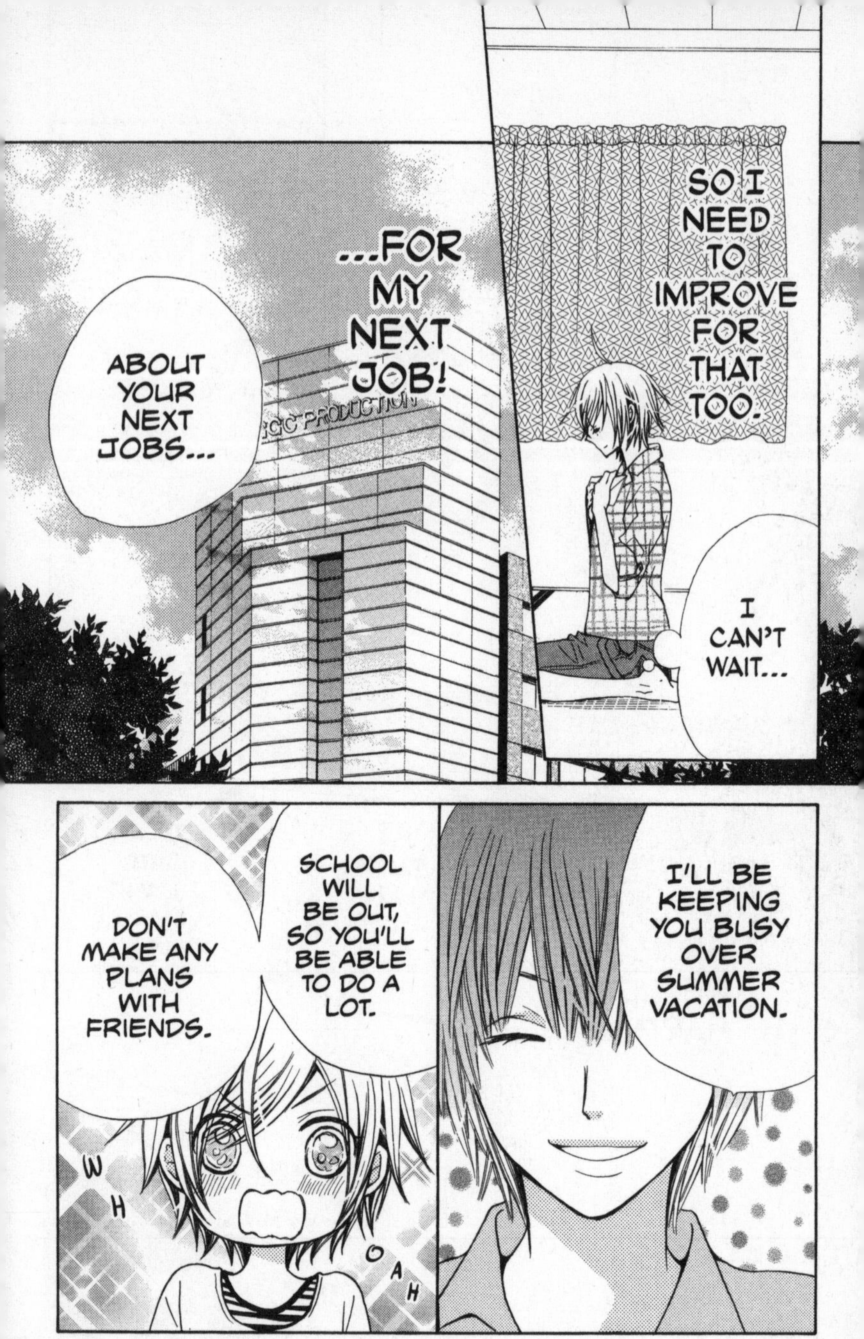
SO I NEED TO IMPROVE FOR THAT TOO.
I CAN'T WAIT...
...FOR MY NEXT JOB!
ABOUT YOUR NEXT JOBS...
I'LL BE KEEPING YOU BUSY OVER SUMMER VACATION.
SCHOOL WILL BE OUT, SO YOU'LL BE ABLE TO DO A LOT.
DON'T MAKE ANY PLANS WITH FRIENDS.
WH
OAH

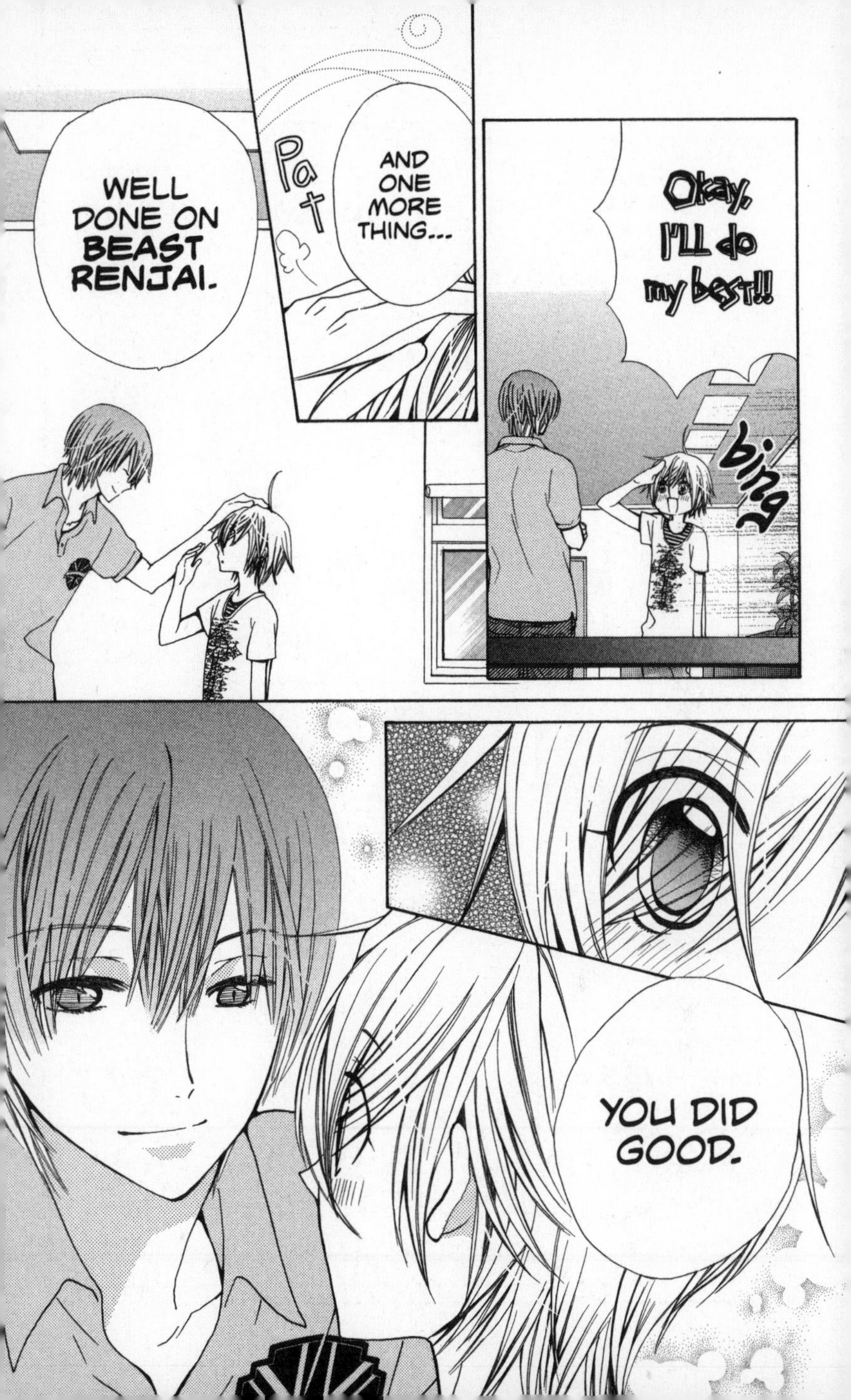
Okay, I'll do my best!!
bing
Pat
AND ONE MORE THING...
WELL DONE ON BEAST RENJAI.
YOU DID GOOD.

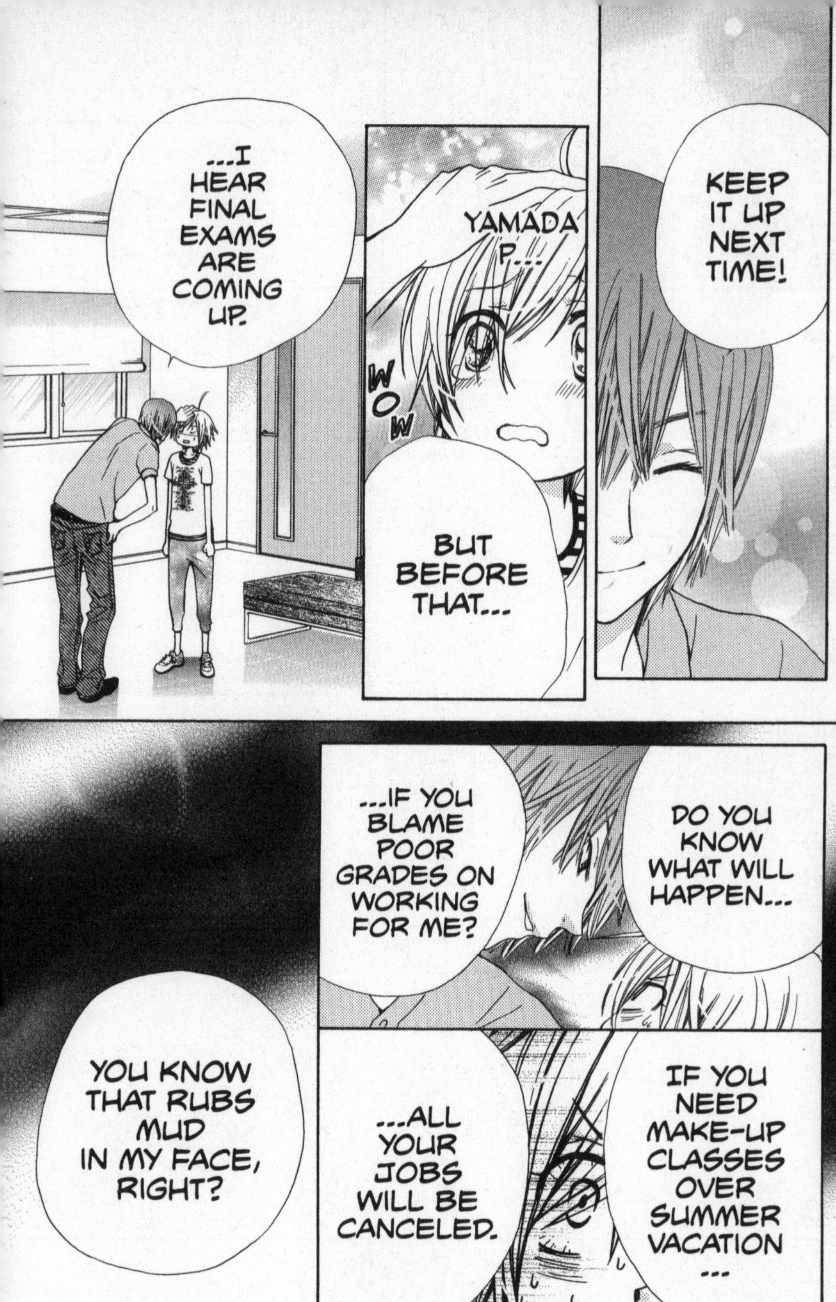
KEEP IT UP NEXT TIME!
YAMADA P...
WOW
BUT BEFORE THAT...
...I HEAR FINAL EXAMS ARE COMING UP.
DO YOU KNOW WHAT WILL HAPPEN...
...IF YOU BLAME POOR GRADES ON WORKING FOR ME?
IF YOU NEED MAKE-UP CLASSES OVER SUMMER VACATION...
...ALL YOUR JOBS WILL BE CANCELED.
YOU KNOW THAT RUBS MUD IN MY FACE, RIGHT?

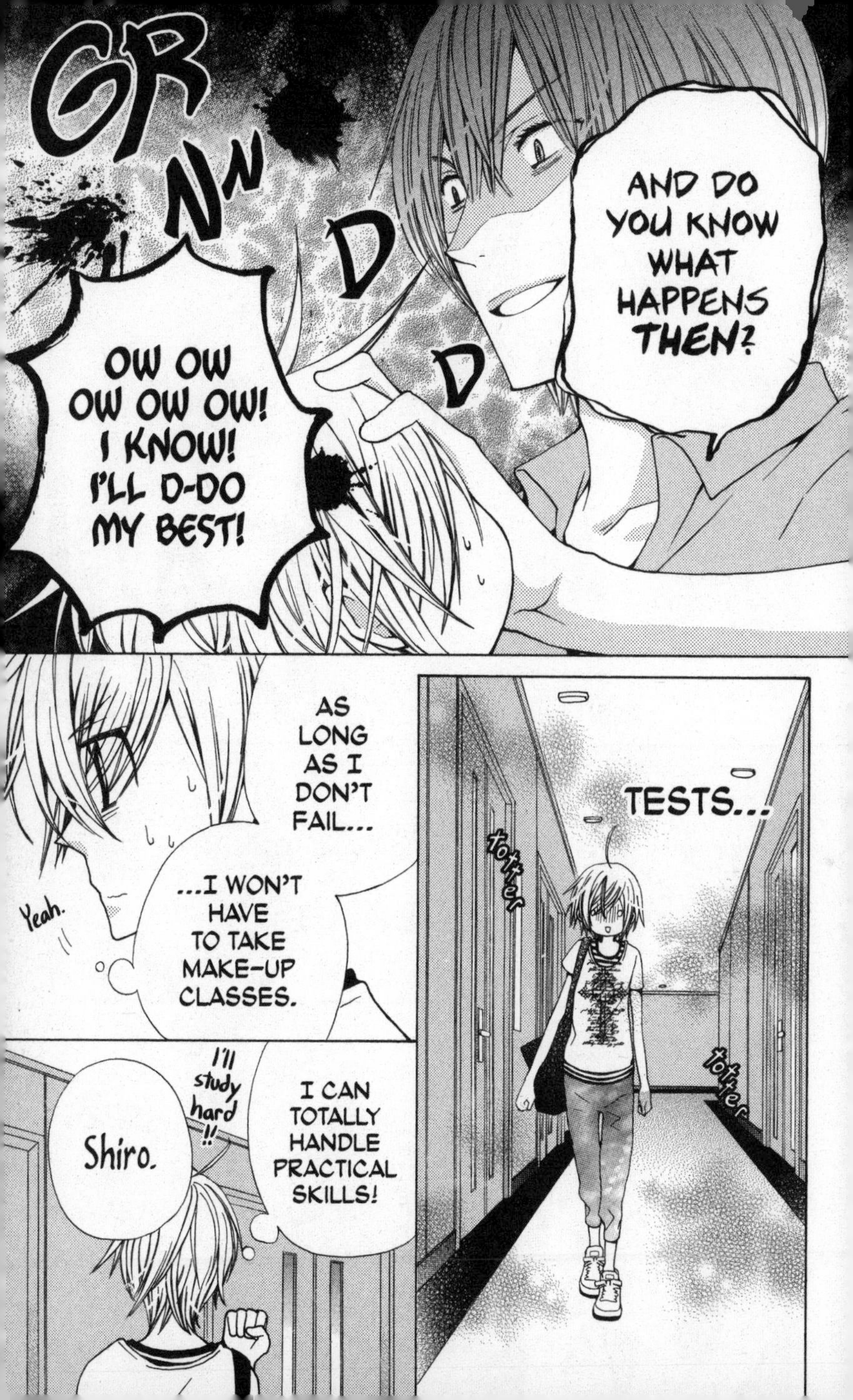
AND DO YOU KNOW WHAT HAPPENS THEN?
GRNND
OW OW OW OW OW! I KNOW! I'LL D-DO MY BEST!
TESTS...
totter
totter
AS LONG AS I DON'T FAIL...
...I WON'T HAVE TO TAKE MAKE-UP CLASSES.
Yeah.
I CAN TOTALLY HANDLE PRACTICAL SKILLS!
I'll study hard!!
Shiro.

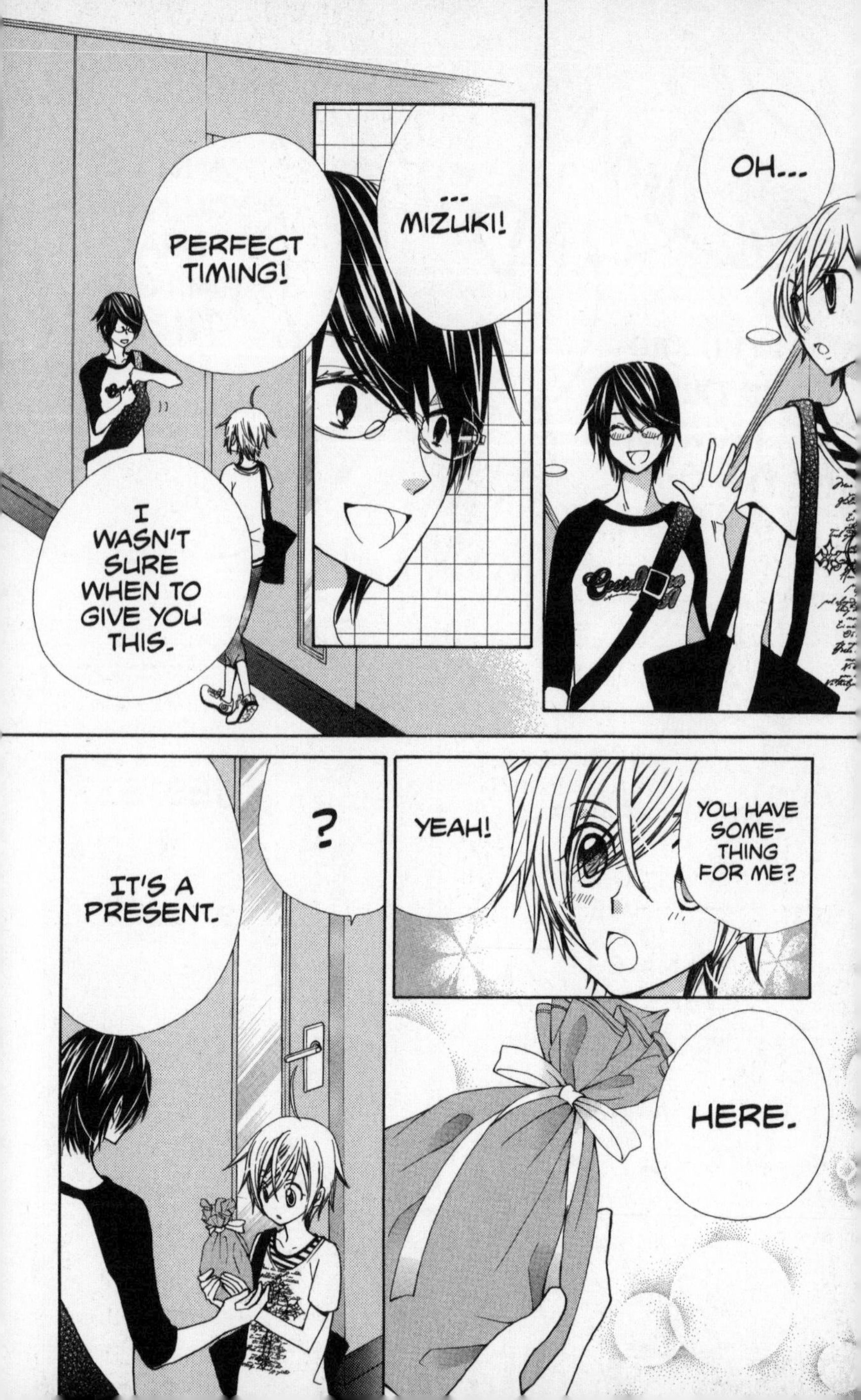
OH...
...MIZUKI!
PERFECT TIMING!
I WASN'T SURE WHEN TO GIVE YOU THIS.
YOU HAVE SOME-THING FOR ME?
YEAH!
HERE.
?
IT'S A PRESENT.

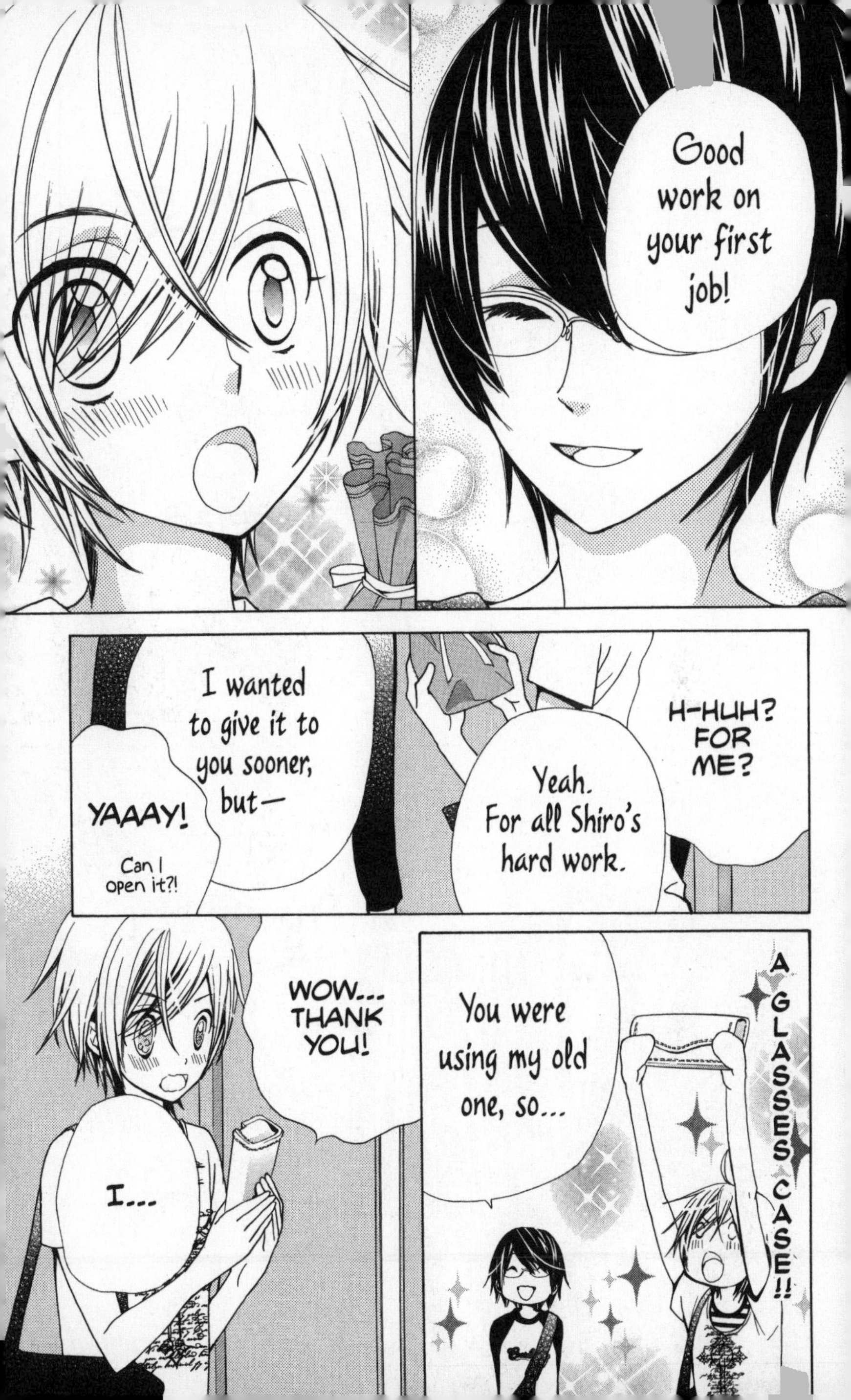
Good work on your first job!
H-HUH? FOR ME?
Yeah. For all Shiro's hard work.
I wanted to give it to you sooner, but—
YAAAY!
Can I open it?!
A GLASSES CASE!!
You were using my old one, so...
WOW... THANK YOU!
I...

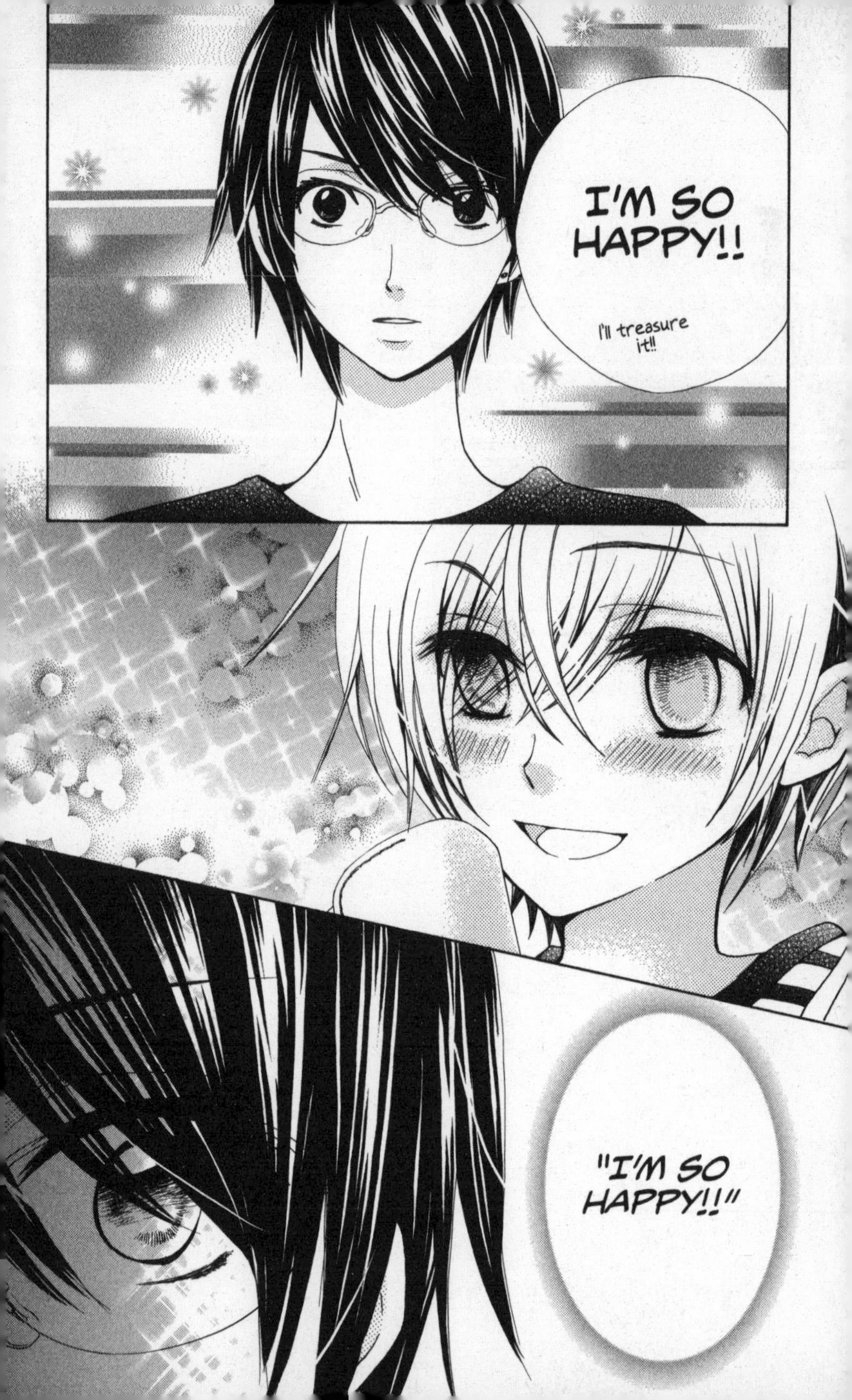
I'M SO HAPPY!!
I'll treasure it!!
"I'M SO HAPPY!!"

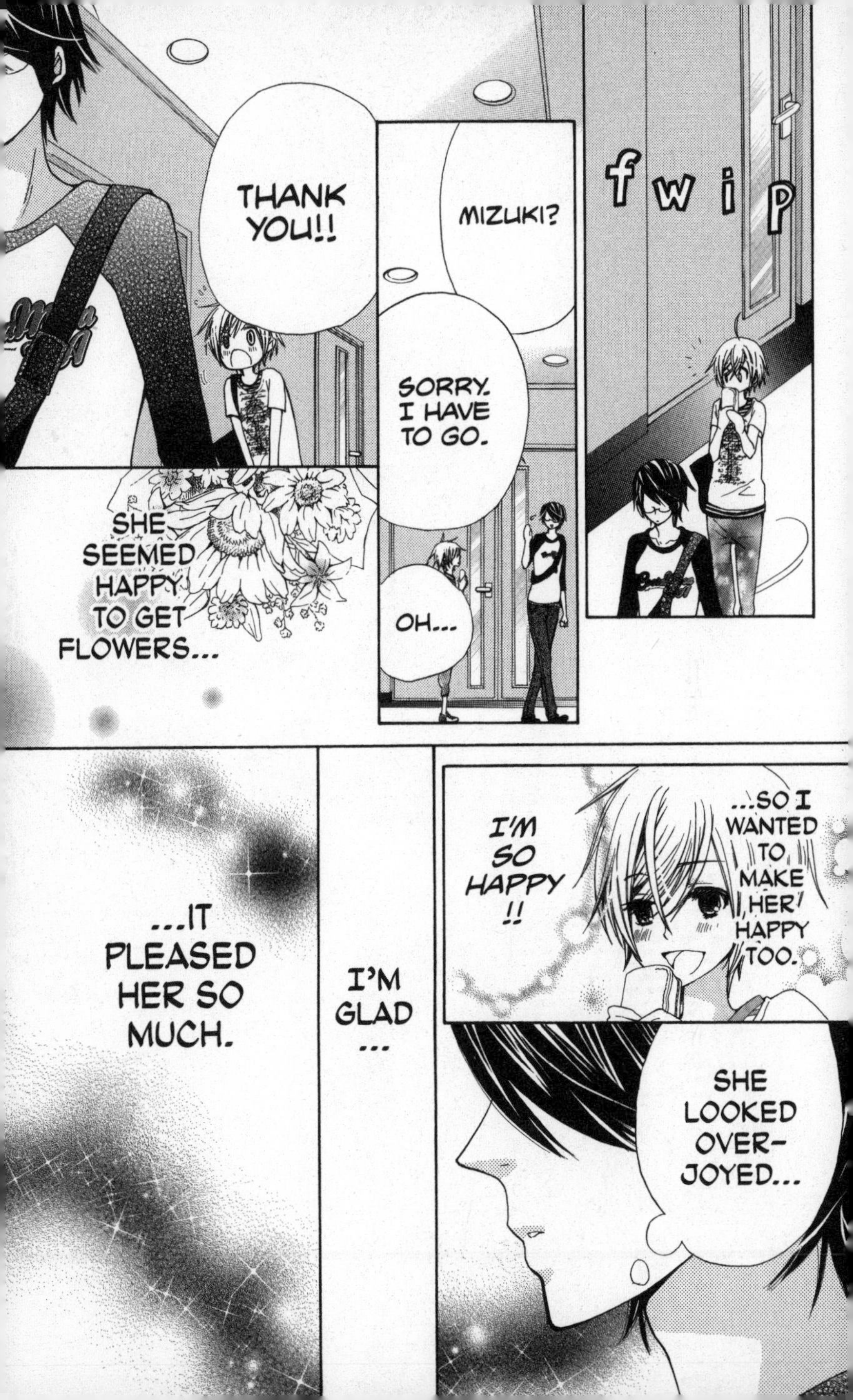
fwip
MIZUKI?
SORRY. I HAVE TO GO.
OH...
THANK YOU!!
SHE SEEMED HAPPY TO GET FLOWERS...
...SO I WANTED TO MAKE HER HAPPY TOO.
I'M SO HAPPY!!
SHE LOOKED OVER-JOYED...
I'M GLAD...
...IT PLEASED HER SO MUCH.

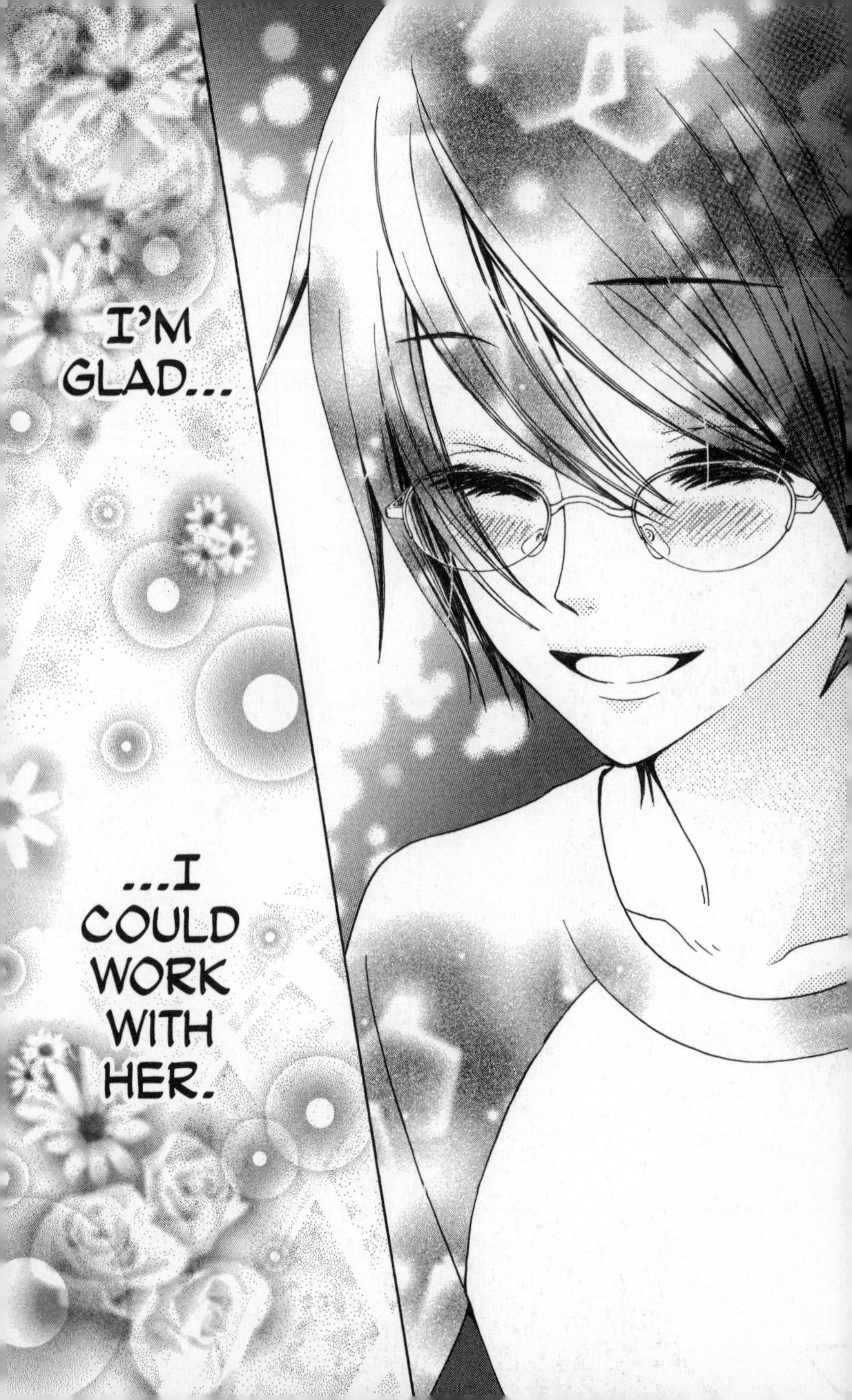
I'M GLAD...
...I COULD WORK WITH HER.

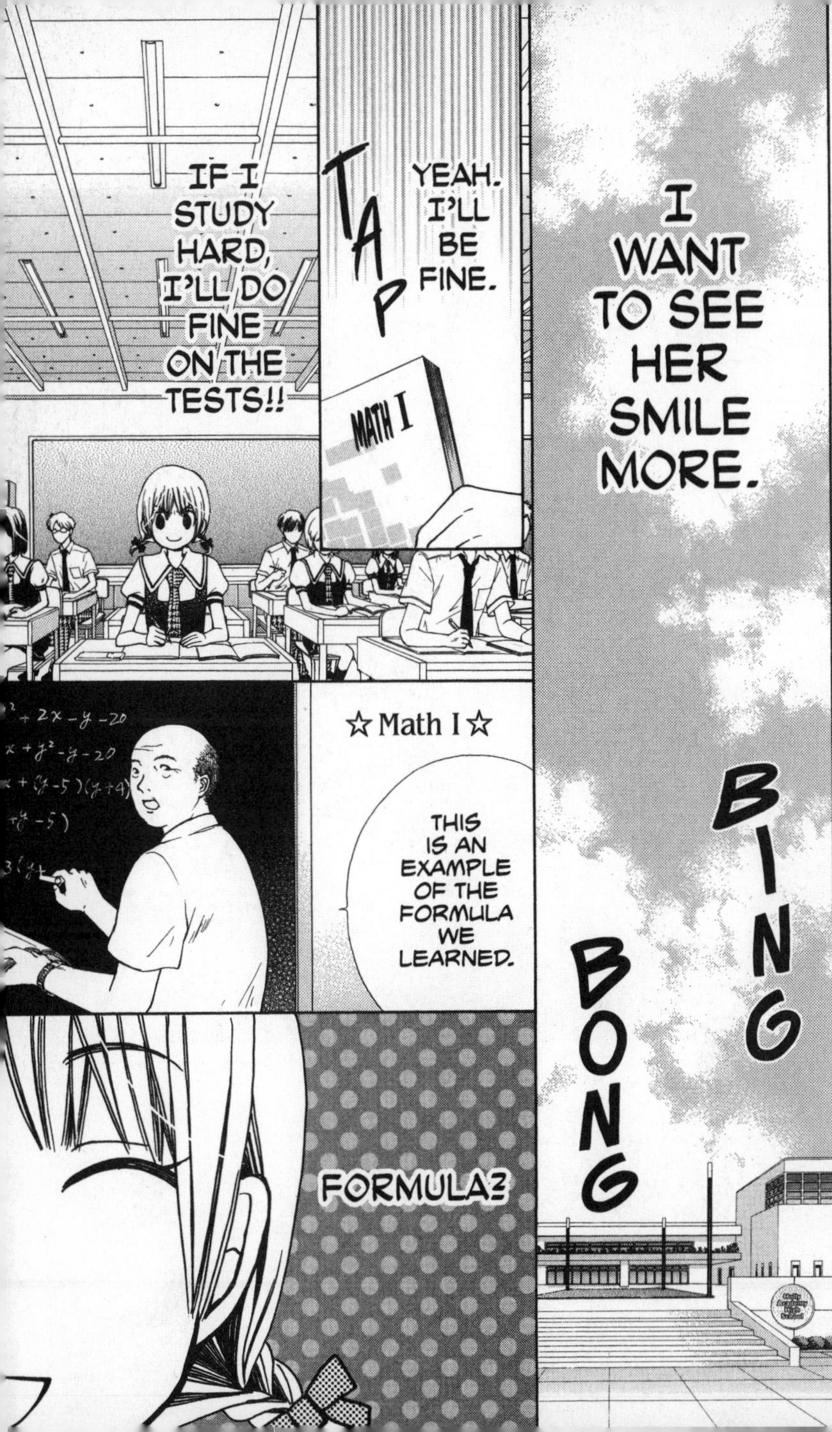
I WANT TO SEE HER SMILE MORE.
BING
BONG
TAP
YEAH. I'LL BE FINE.
MATH I
IF I STUDY HARD, I'LL DO FINE ON THE TESTS!!
☆ Math I ☆
THIS IS AN EXAMPLE OF THE FORMULA WE LEARNED.
FORMULA?

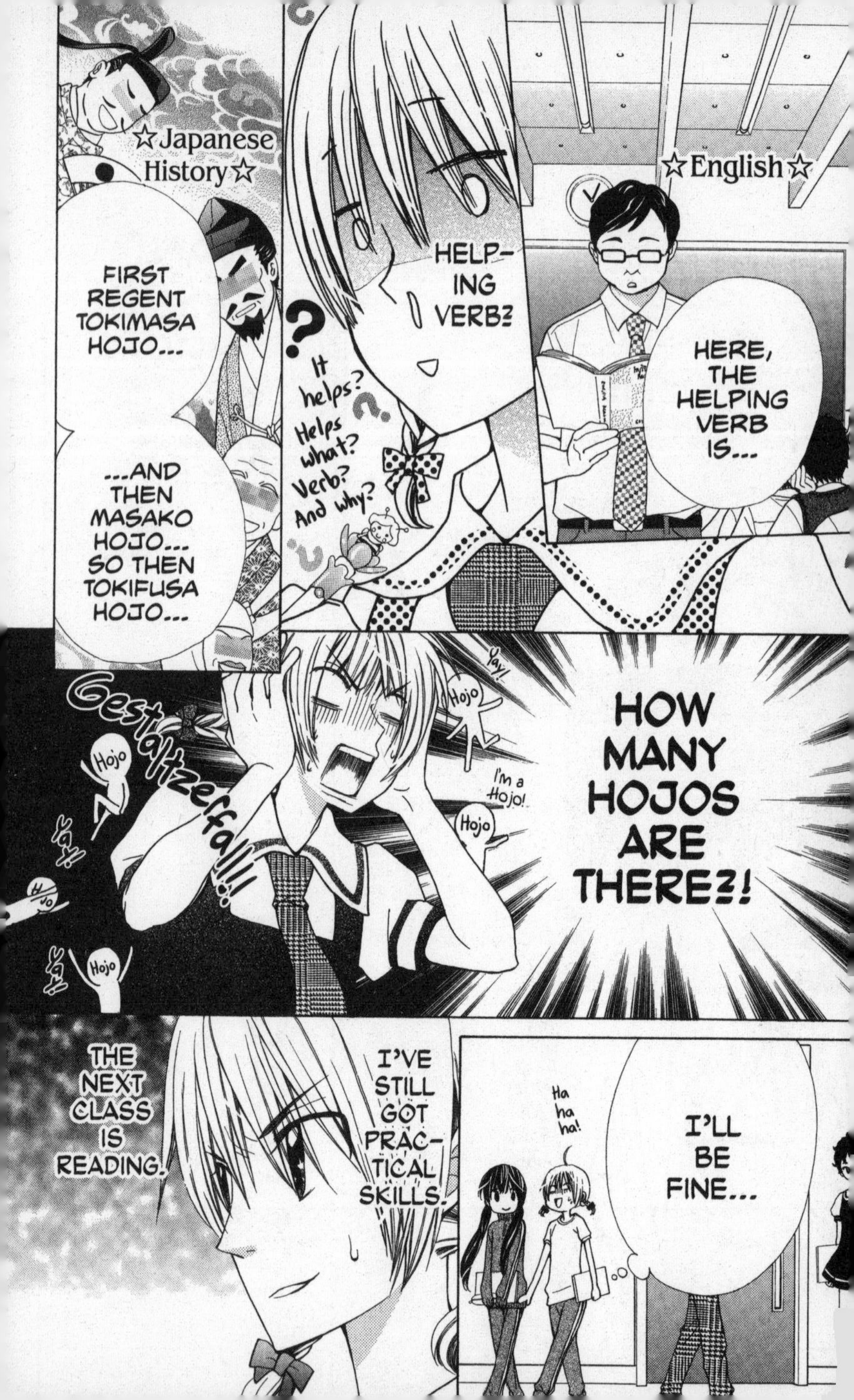

☆English☆
HERE, THE HELPING VERB IS...
HELPING VERB?
It helps? Helps what? Verb? And why?
☆Japanese History☆
FIRST REGENT TOKIMASA HOJO...
...AND THEN MASAKO HOJO... SO THEN TOKIFUSA HOJO...
HOW MANY HOJOS ARE THERE?!
Yay!
Hojo
I'm a Hojo!
Hojo
Gestaltzerfall!!
Hojo
Yay!!
Hojo
Yay!!
Hojo
I'LL BE FINE...
Ha ha ha!
I'VE STILL GOT PRACTICAL SKILLS.
THE NEXT CLASS IS READING!

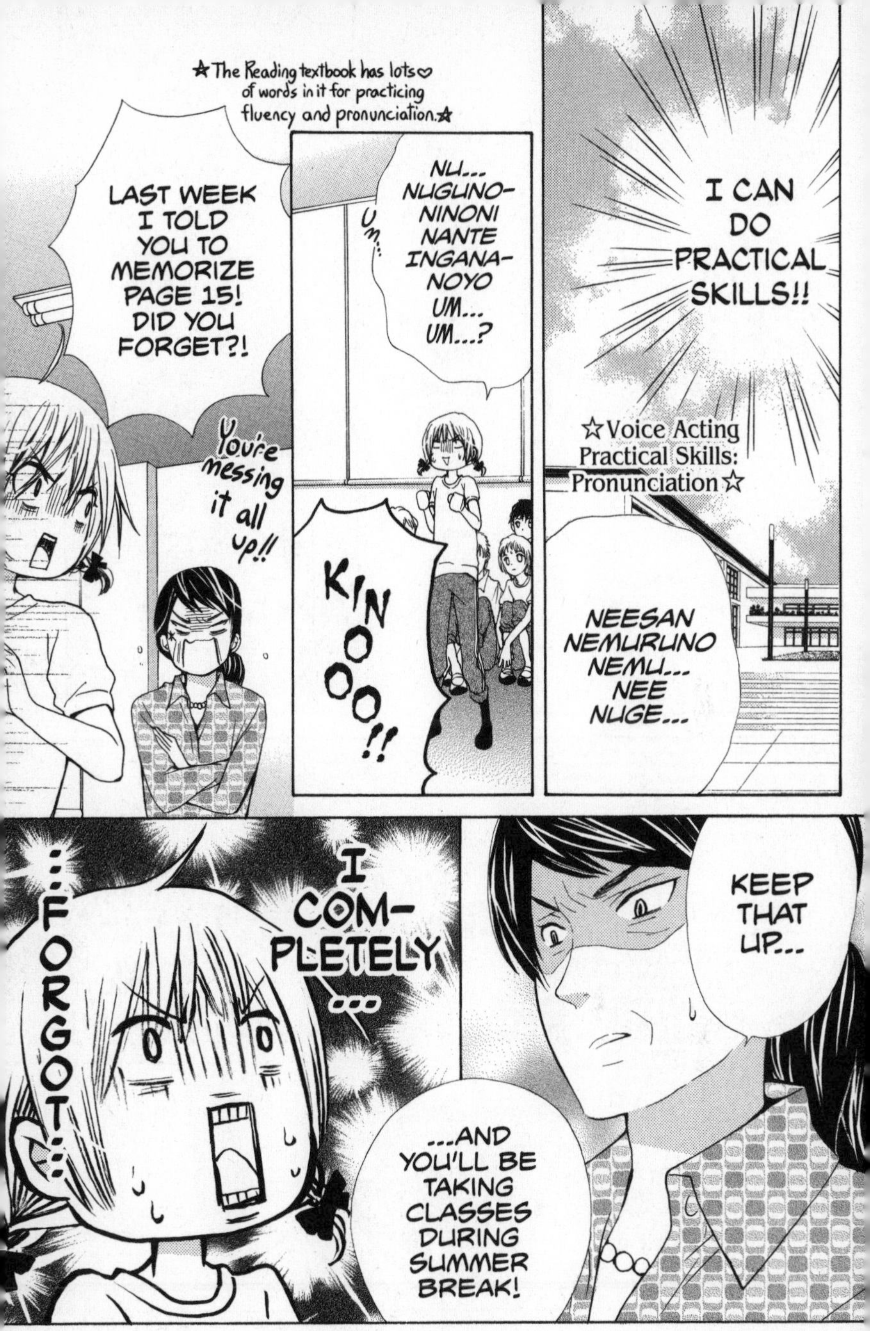
I CAN DO PRACTICAL SKILLS!!
☆Voice Acting Practical Skills: Pronunciation☆
NEESAN NEMURUNO NEMU... NEE NUGE...
NU... NUGUNO-NINONI NANTE INGANA-NOYO UM... UM...?
Um...
KINOOO!!
★The Reading textbook has lots of words in it for practicing fluency and pronunciation.★
LAST WEEK I TOLD YOU TO MEMORIZE PAGE 15! DID YOU FORGET?!
You're messing it all up!!
KEEP THAT UP...
...AND YOU'LL BE TAKING CLASSES DURING SUMMER BREAK!
I COM-PLETELY...
...FORGOT...

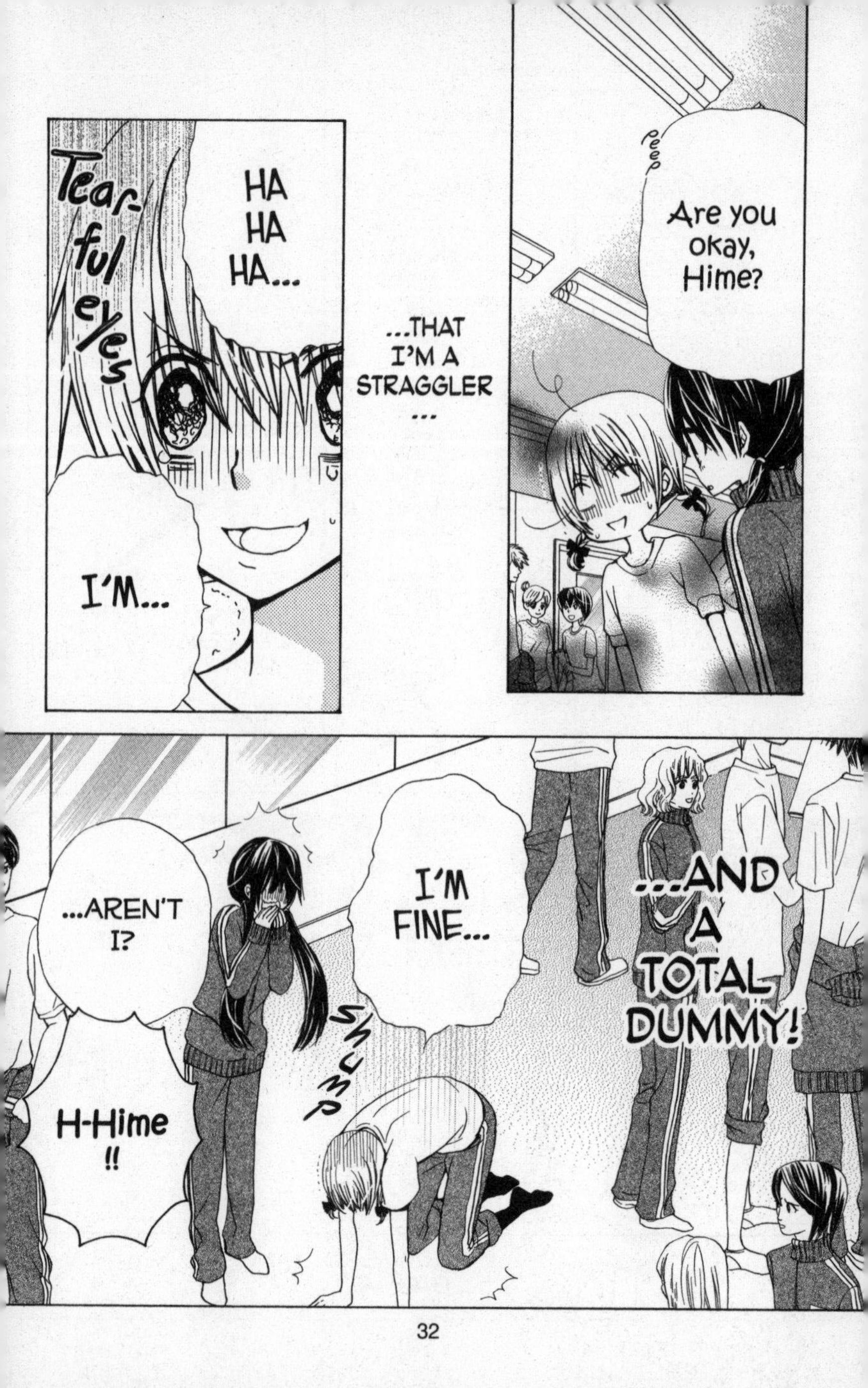
peep
Are you okay, Hime?
...THAT I'M A STRAGGLER ...
HA HA HA...
Tearful eyes
I'M...
...AND A TOTAL DUMMY!
I'M FINE...
SHUMP
...AREN'T I?
H-Hime !!

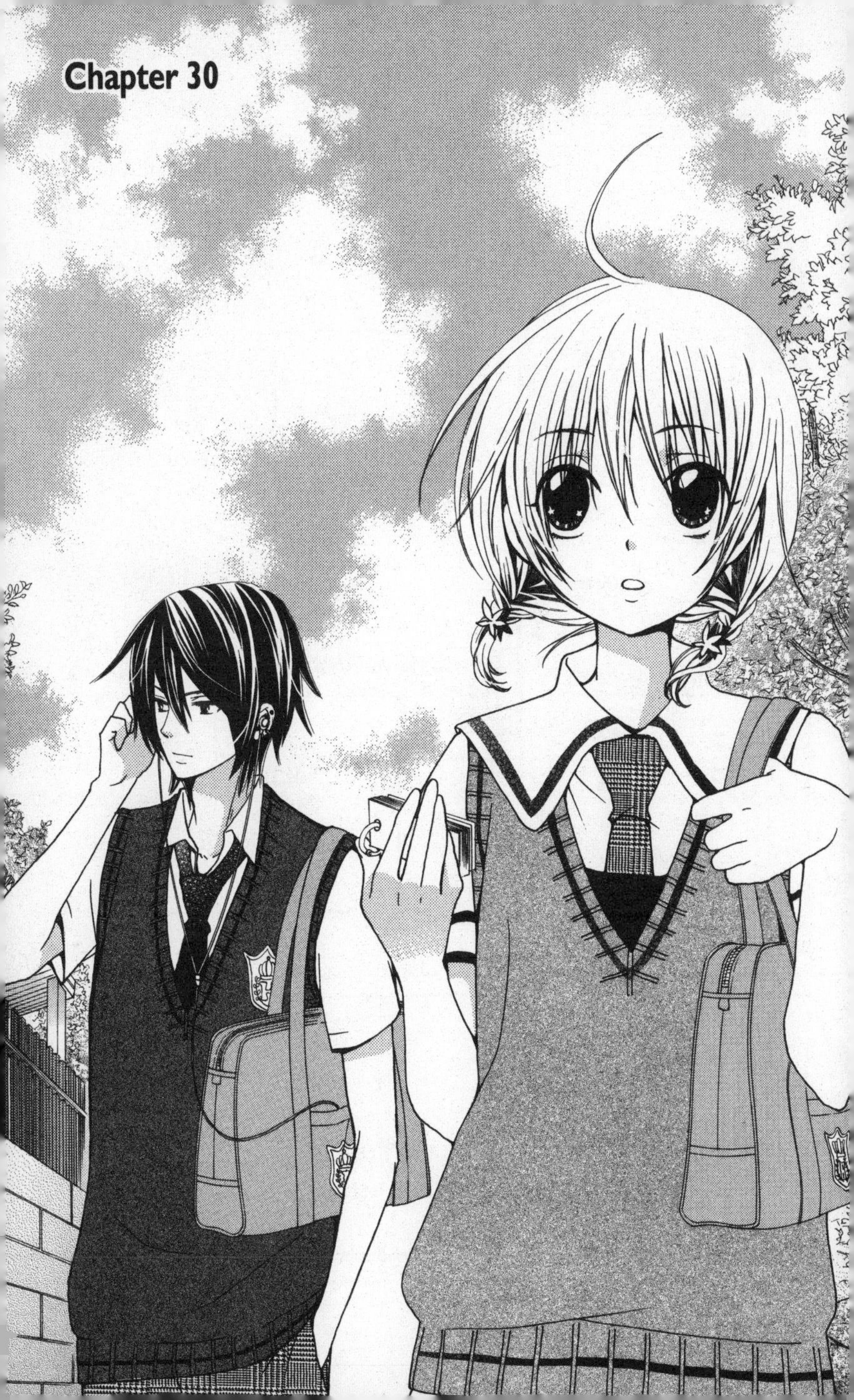
Chapter 30

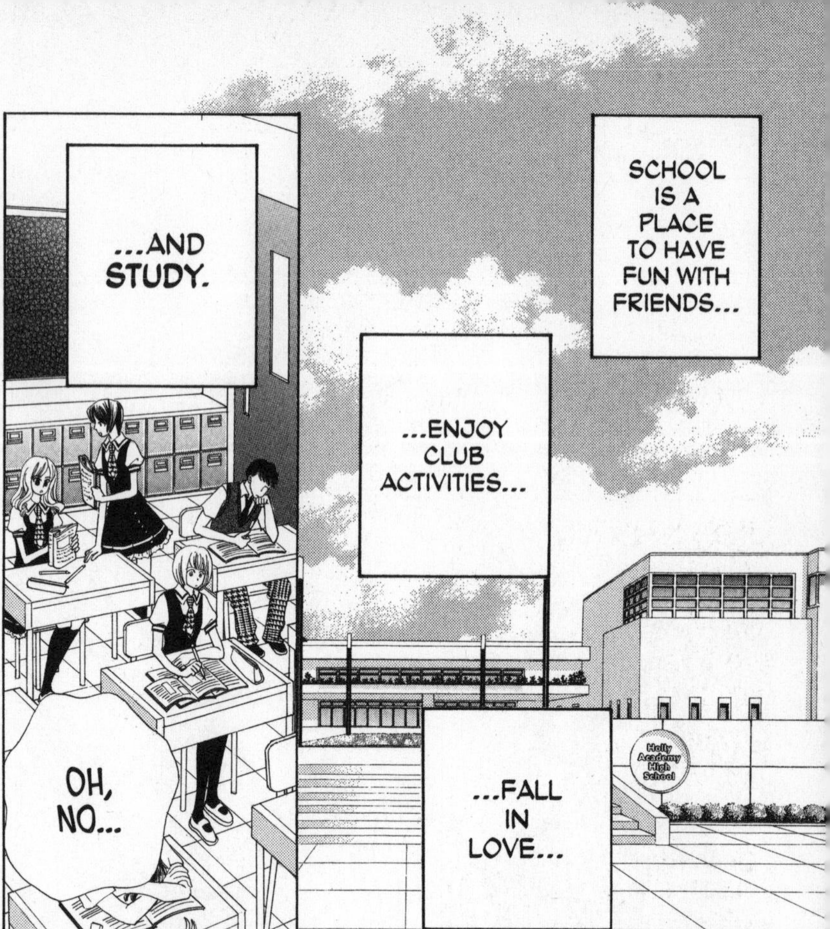
SCHOOL IS A PLACE TO HAVE FUN WITH FRIENDS...
...ENJOY CLUB ACTIVITIES...
Holly Academy High School
...FALL IN LOVE...
...AND STUDY.
OH, NO...

Introducing the assistants... ①

Assistants who always help me out!

I-san

A super assistant who knows all and has been with me the longest. She'll draw anything. She's really good. And she's extra good at older men! She fills in black, glossy areas for me. And she proofreads! She's great at teasing people. And she has allergies.

②

K-san

Loves BL & rice!

I can leave all the screentone effects to her and she does an awesome job! And what's more, she draws great flowers and food and stuff! And she does backgrounds. She's good at cooking. Her little brother's a chef. And she's the one who told me there's nothing embarrassing about buying something that's being sold!

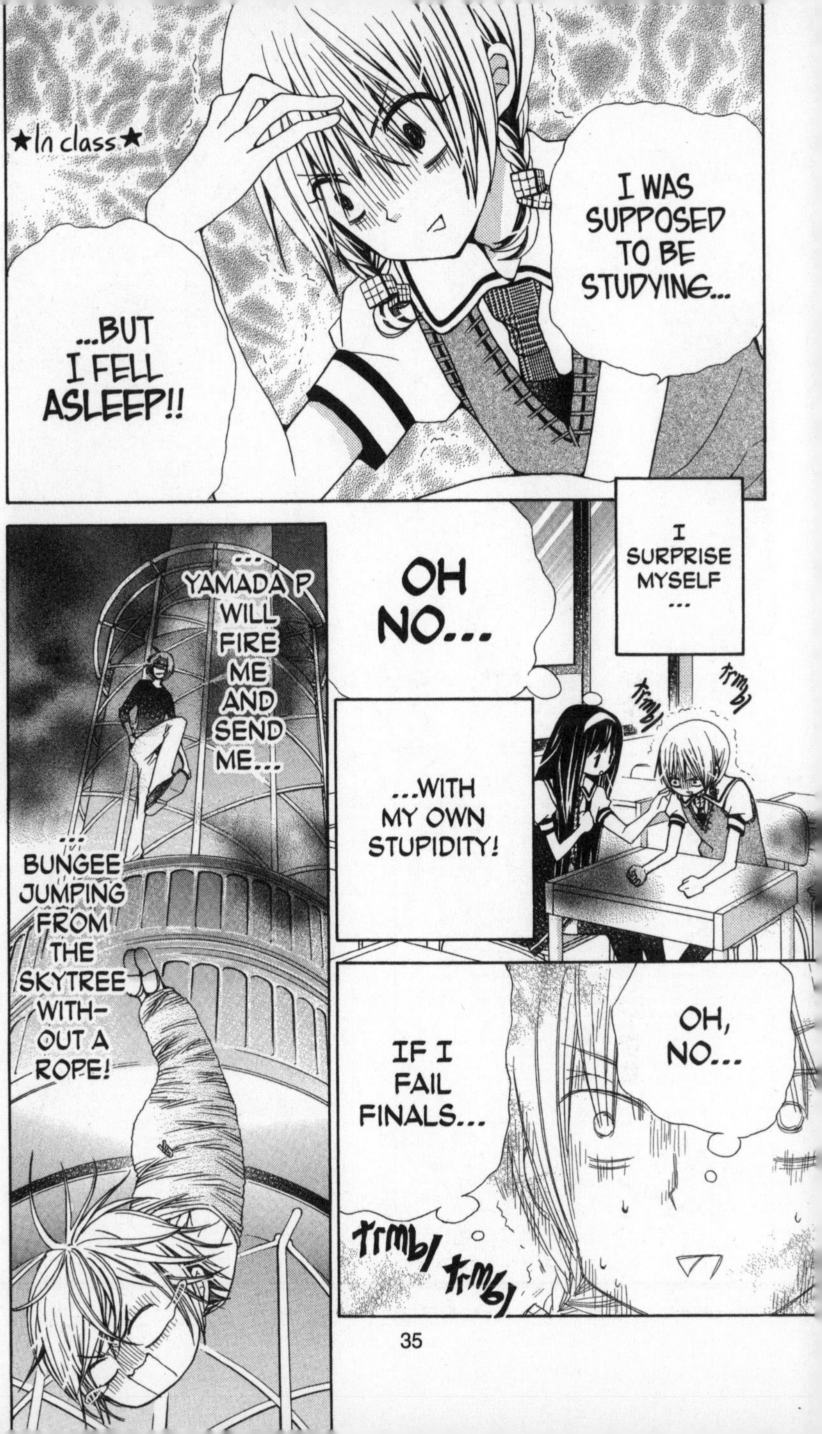
★In class★
I WAS SUPPOSED TO BE STUDYING...
...BUT I FELL ASLEEP!!
I SURPRISE MYSELF...
OH NO...
...WITH MY OWN STUPIDITY!
trmbl
trmbl
OH, NO...
IF I FAIL FINALS...
trmbl trmbl
...YAMADA P WILL FIRE ME AND SEND ME...
...BUNGEE JUMPING FROM THE SKYTREE WITH-OUT A ROPE!

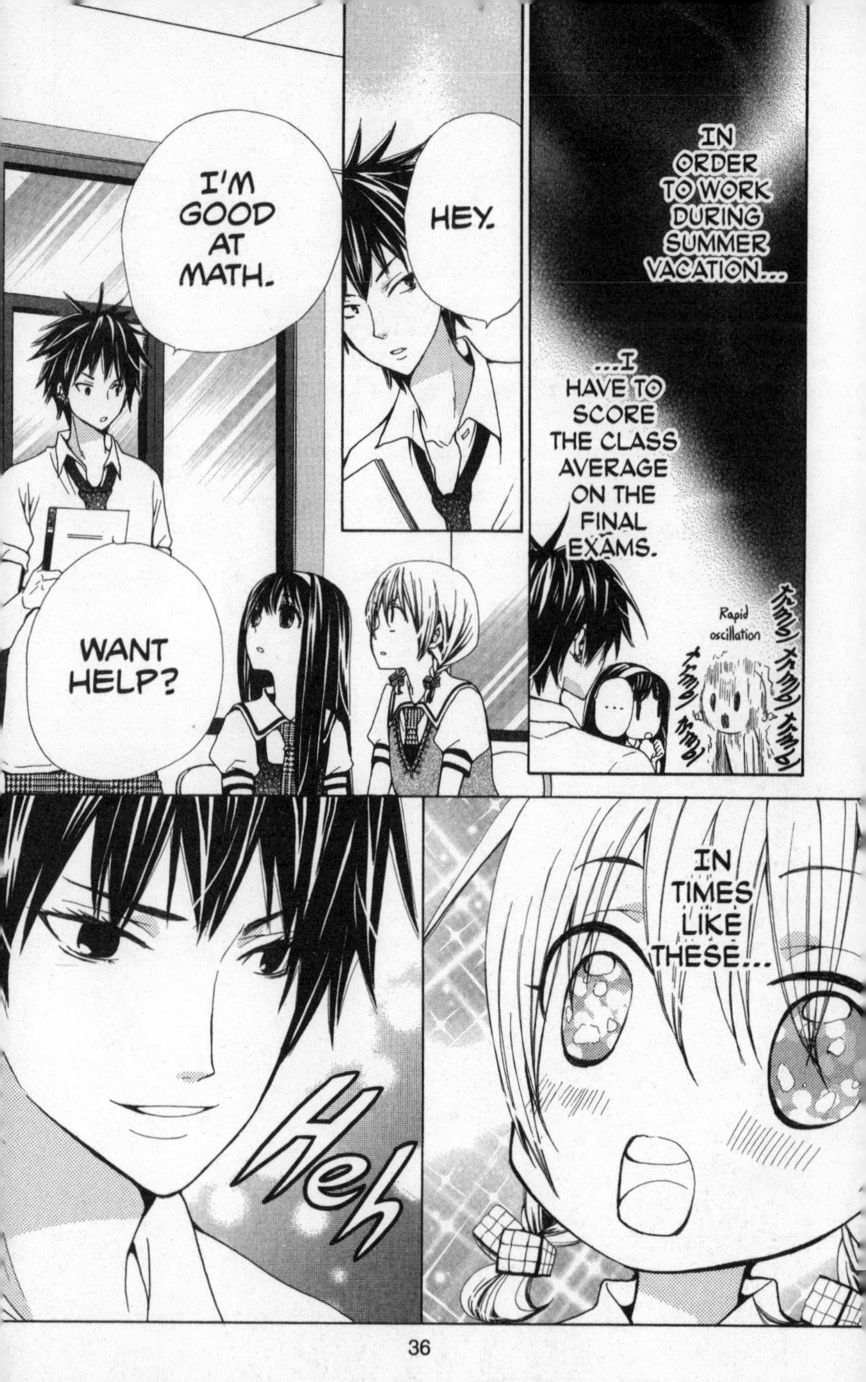
IN ORDER TO WORK DURING SUMMER VACATION...
...I HAVE TO SCORE THE CLASS AVERAGE ON THE FINAL EXAMS.
Rapid oscillation
...
HEY.
I'M GOOD AT MATH.
WANT HELP?
IN TIMES LIKE THESE...
Heh

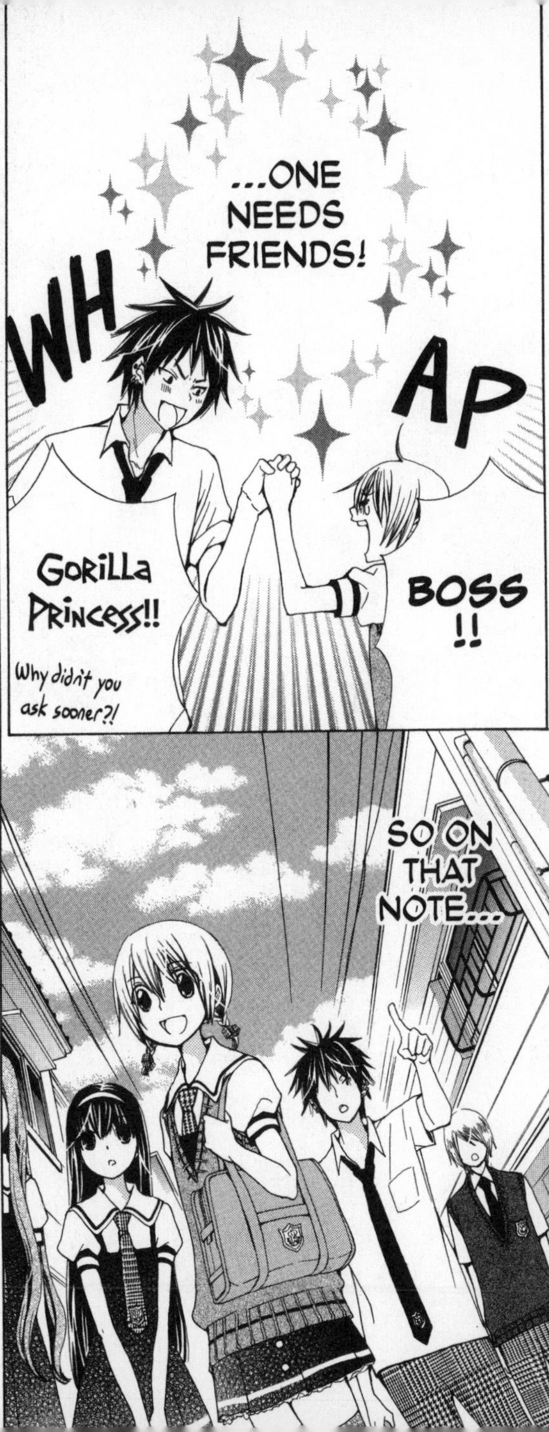
...ONE NEEDS FRIENDS!
WH
AP
BOSS !!
Gorilla Princess!!
Why didn't you ask sooner?!
SO ON THAT NOTE...

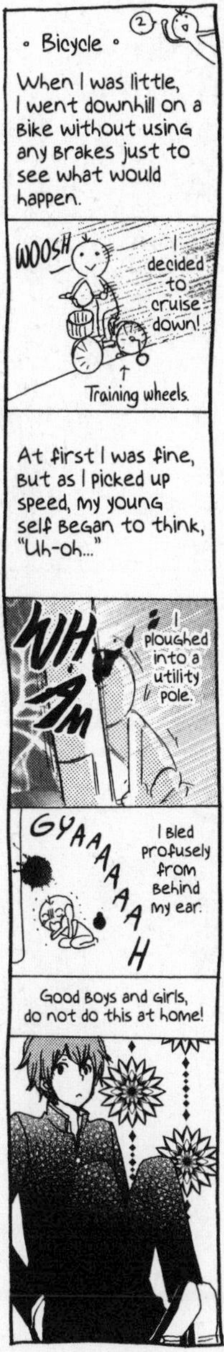
• Bicycle •
2
When I was little, I went downhill on a bike without using any brakes just to see what would happen.
WOOSH
I decided to cruise down!
Training wheels.
At first I was fine, but as I picked up speed, my young self began to think, "Uh-oh..."
WHAM
I ploughed into a utility pole.
GYAAAAAAAH
I bled profusely from behind my ear.
Good boys and girls, do not do this at home!

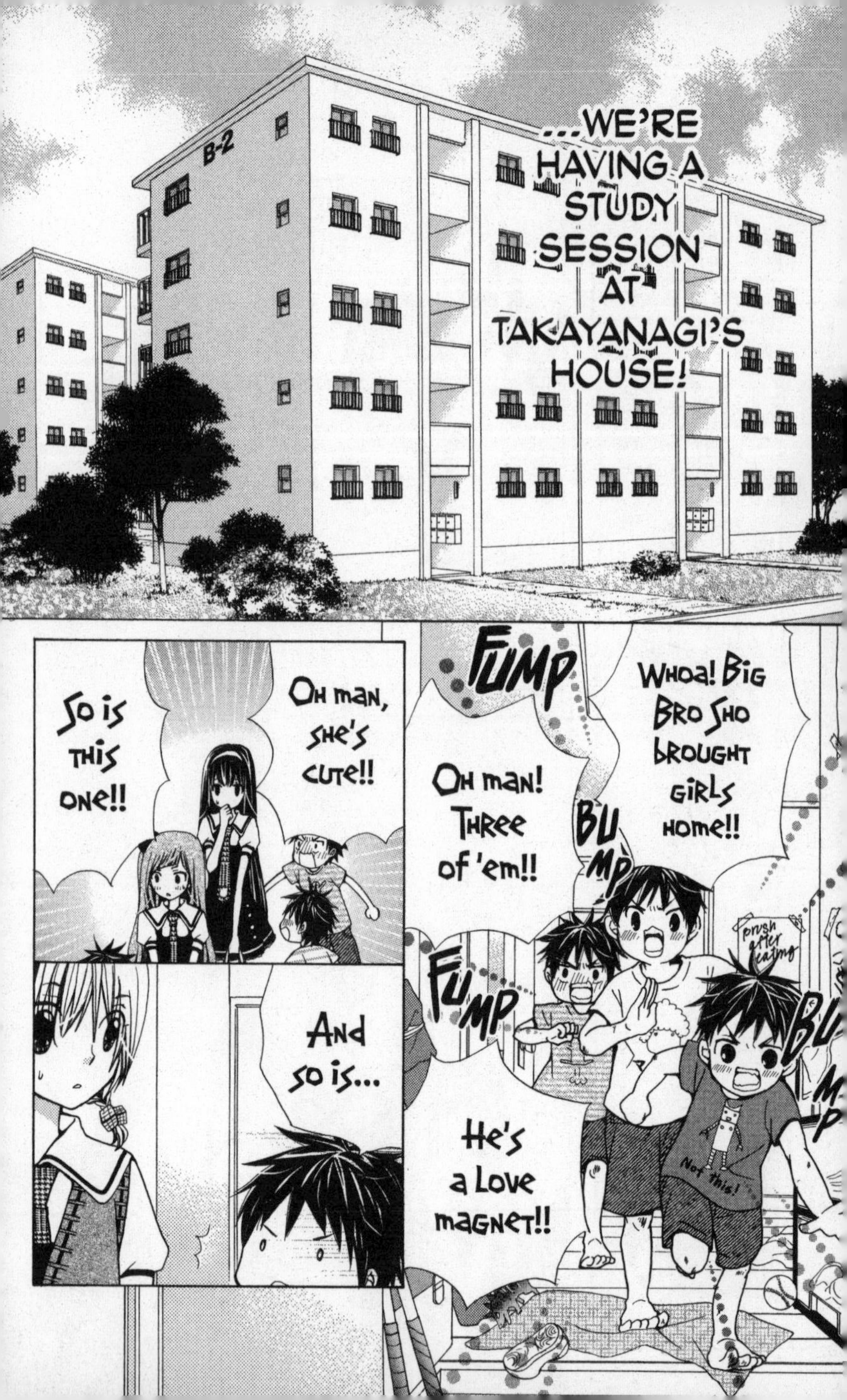
B-2
...WE'RE HAVING A STUDY SESSION AT TAKAYANAGI'S HOUSE!
Whoa! Big Bro Sho brought girls home!!
FUMP
Oh man! Three of 'em!!
BUMP
brush after eating
BUMP
FUMP
He's a love magnet!!
Not this!
Oh man, she's cute!!
So is this one!!
And so is...

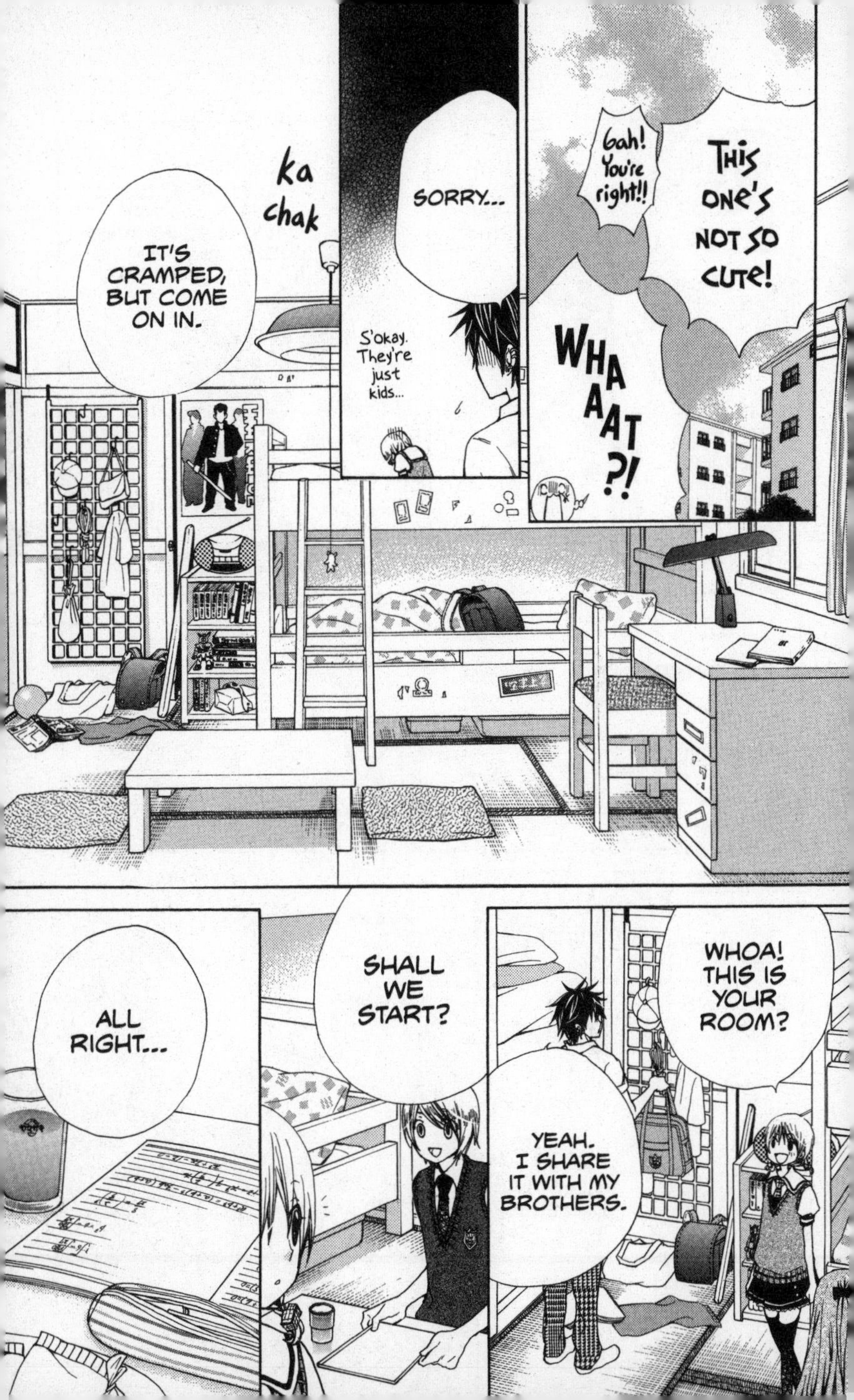
THIS ONE'S NOT SO CUTE!
Gah! You're right!!
WHAAAT?!
SORRY...
S'okay. They're just kids...
ka chak
IT'S CRAMPED, BUT COME ON IN.
WHOA! THIS IS YOUR ROOM?
YEAH. I SHARE IT WITH MY BROTHERS.
SHALL WE START?
ALL RIGHT...

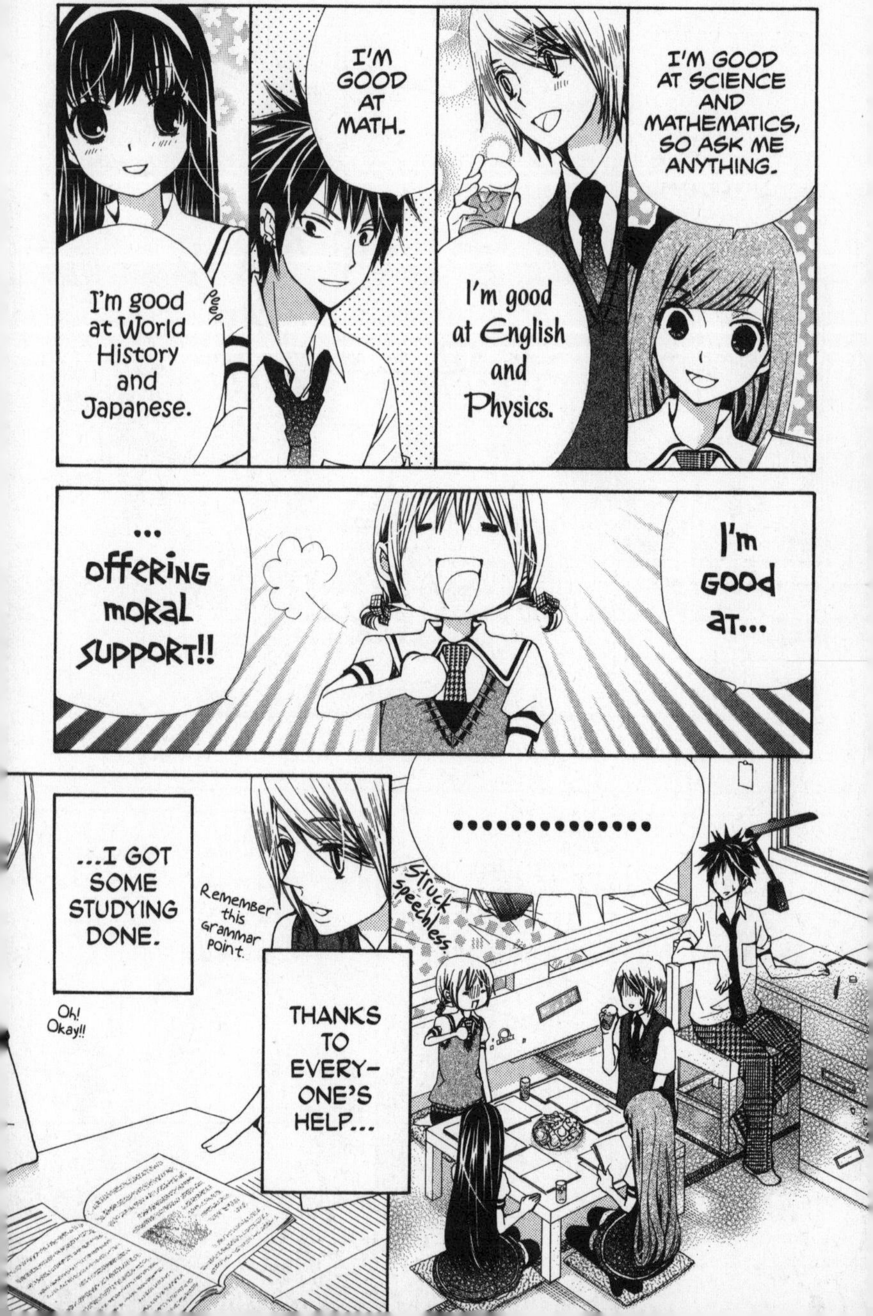
I'M GOOD AT SCIENCE AND MATHEMATICS, SO ASK ME ANYTHING.
I'm good at English and Physics.
I'M GOOD AT MATH.
I'm good at World History and Japanese.
Peep
I'm good at...
...offering moral support!!
...............
Struck speechless.
THANKS TO EVERY-ONE'S HELP...
Remember this Grammar point.
...I GOT SOME STUDYING DONE.
Oh! Okay!!

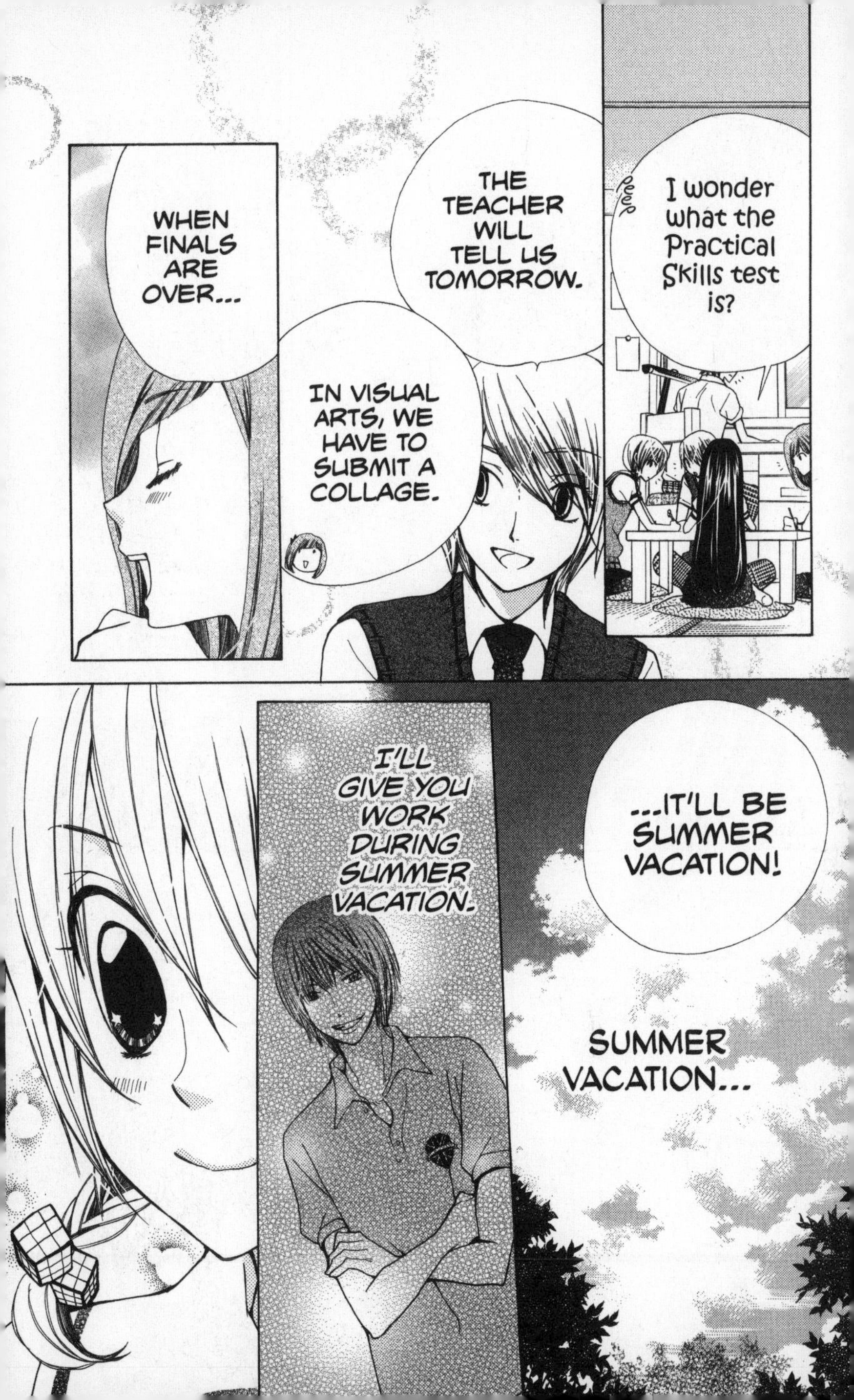
I wonder what the Practical Skills test is?
THE TEACHER WILL TELL US TOMORROW.
IN VISUAL ARTS, WE HAVE TO SUBMIT A COLLAGE.
WHEN FINALS ARE OVER...
...IT'LL BE SUMMER VACATION!
SUMMER VACATION...
I'LL GIVE YOU WORK DURING SUMMER VACATION.

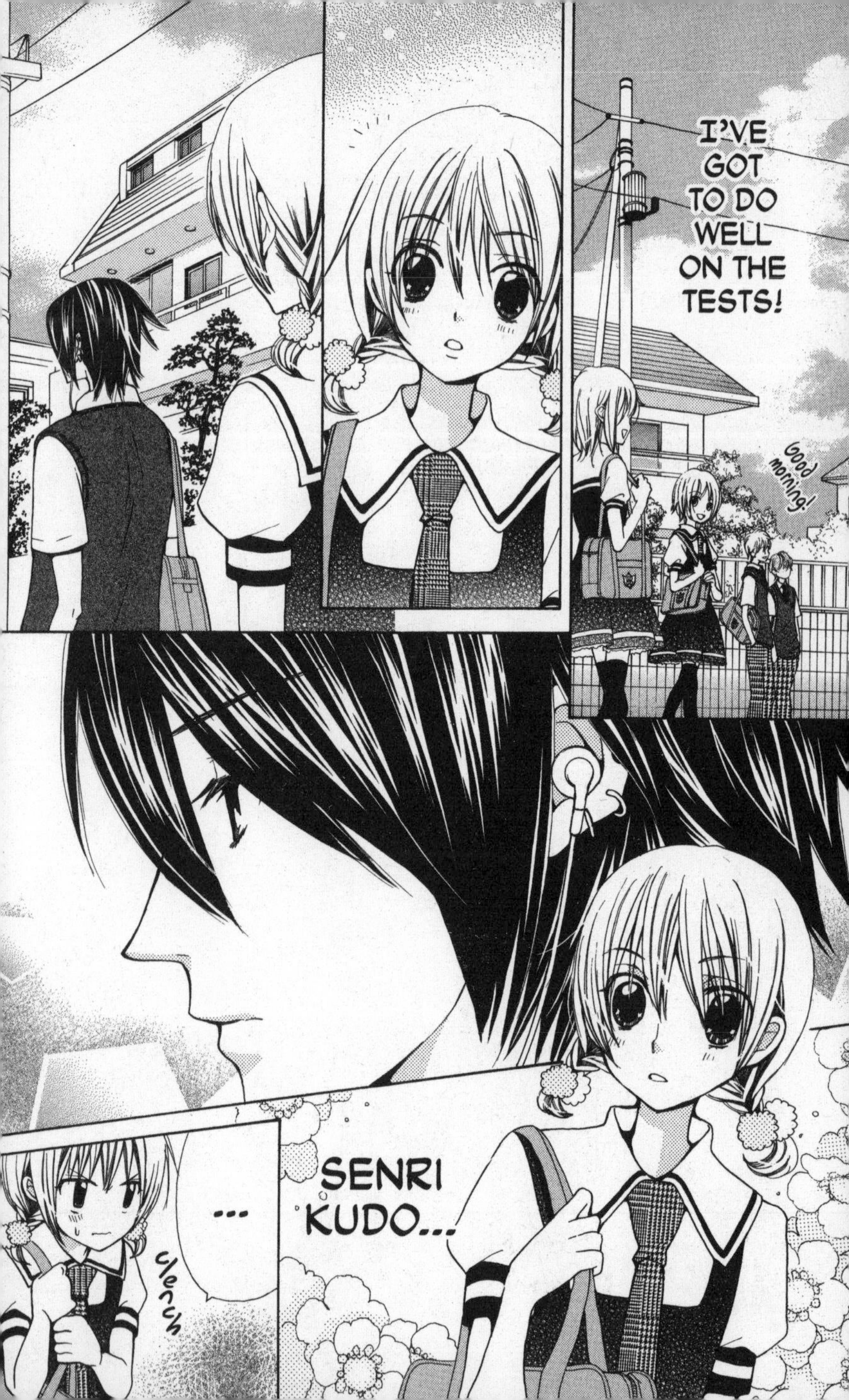
I'VE GOT TO DO WELL ON THE TESTS!
Good morning!
SENRI KUDO...
...
clench

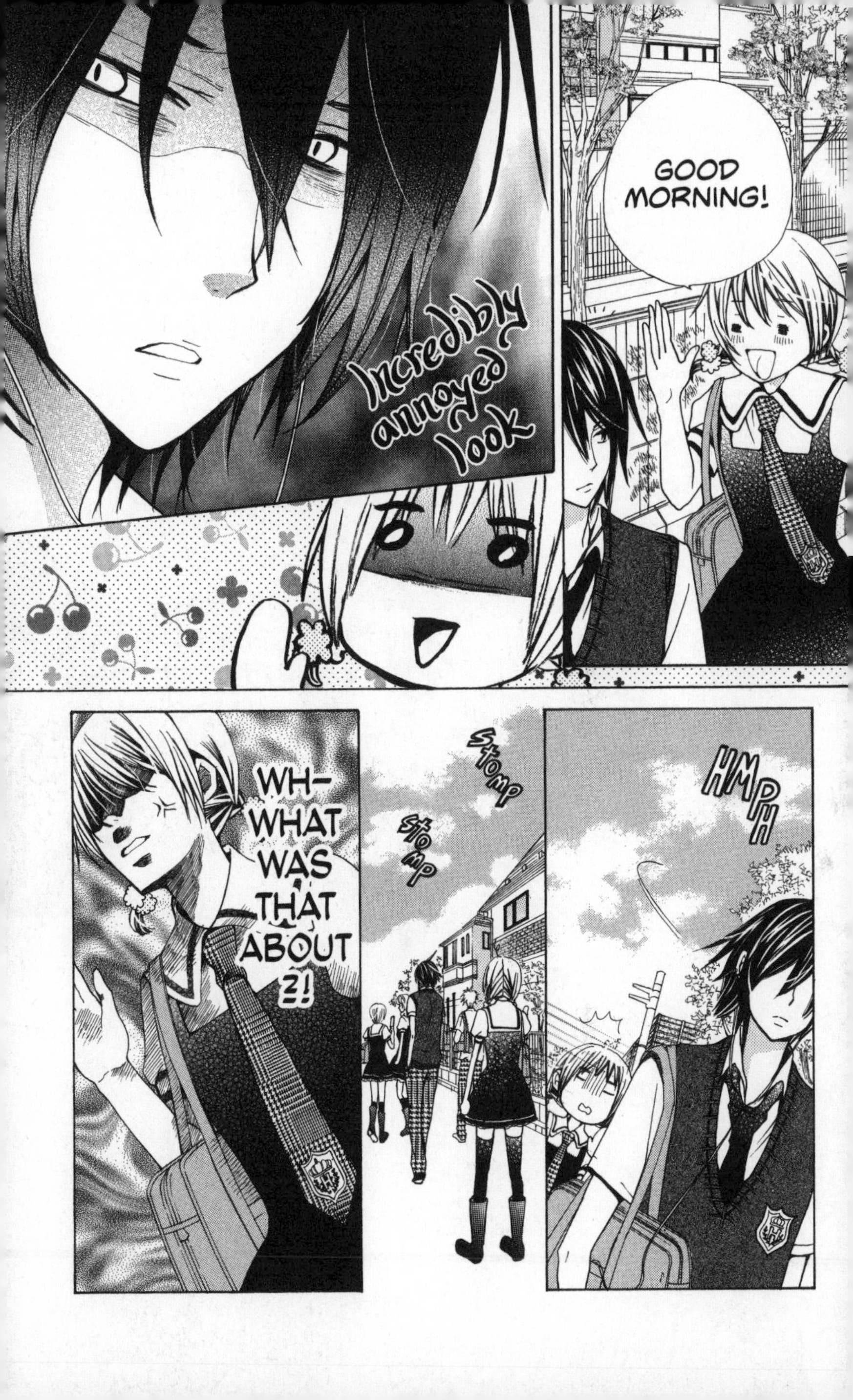
GOOD MORNING!
Incredibly annoyed look
HMPH
Stomp stomp
WH-WHAT WAS THAT ABOUT?!

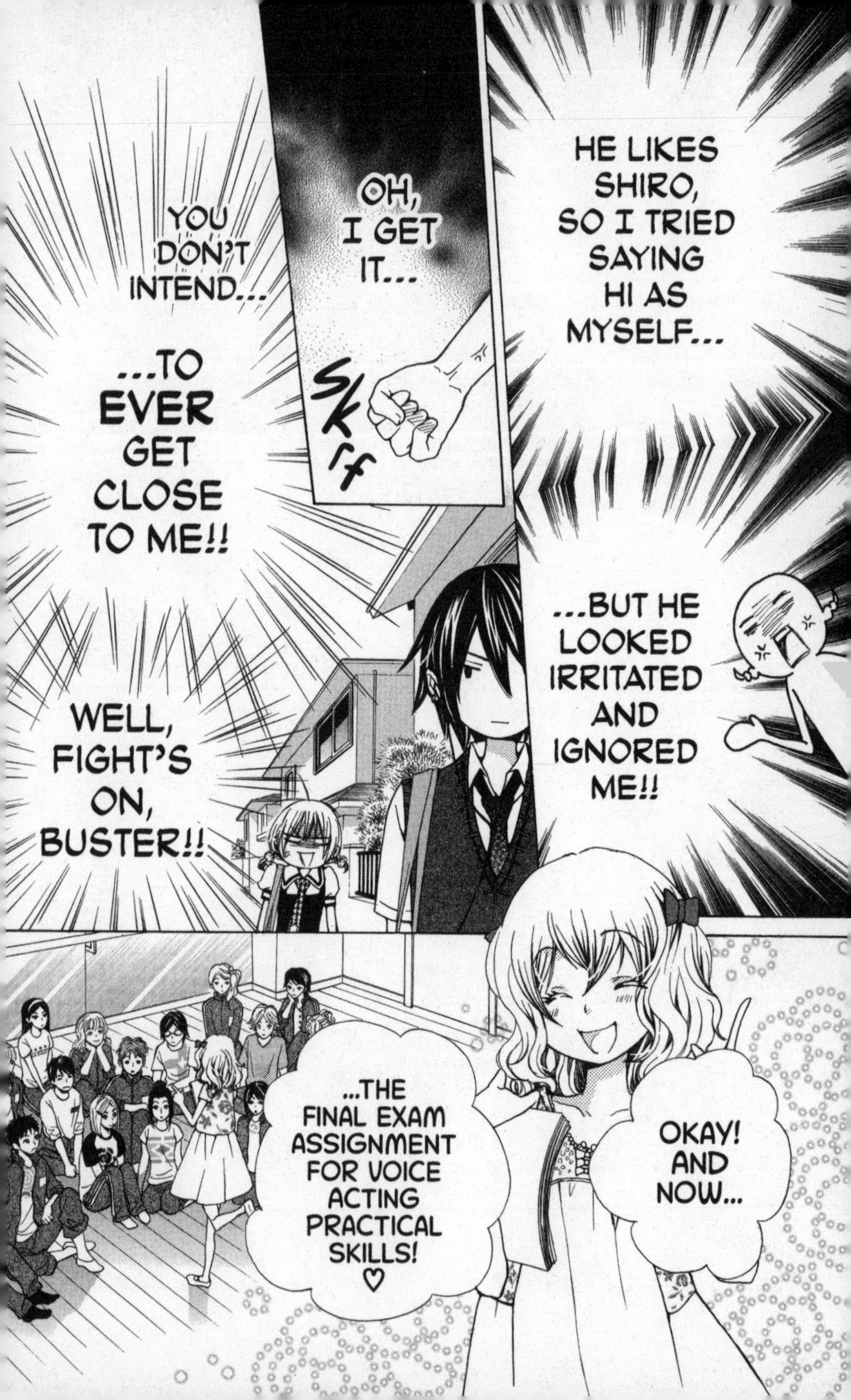
HE LIKES SHIRO, SO I TRIED SAYING HI AS MYSELF...
...BUT HE LOOKED IRRITATED AND IGNORED ME!!
OH, I GET IT...
SKRF
YOU DON'T INTEND...
...TO EVER GET CLOSE TO ME!!
WELL, FIGHT'S ON, BUSTER!!
OKAY! AND NOW...
...THE FINAL EXAM ASSIGNMENT FOR VOICE ACTING PRACTICAL SKILLS! ♡

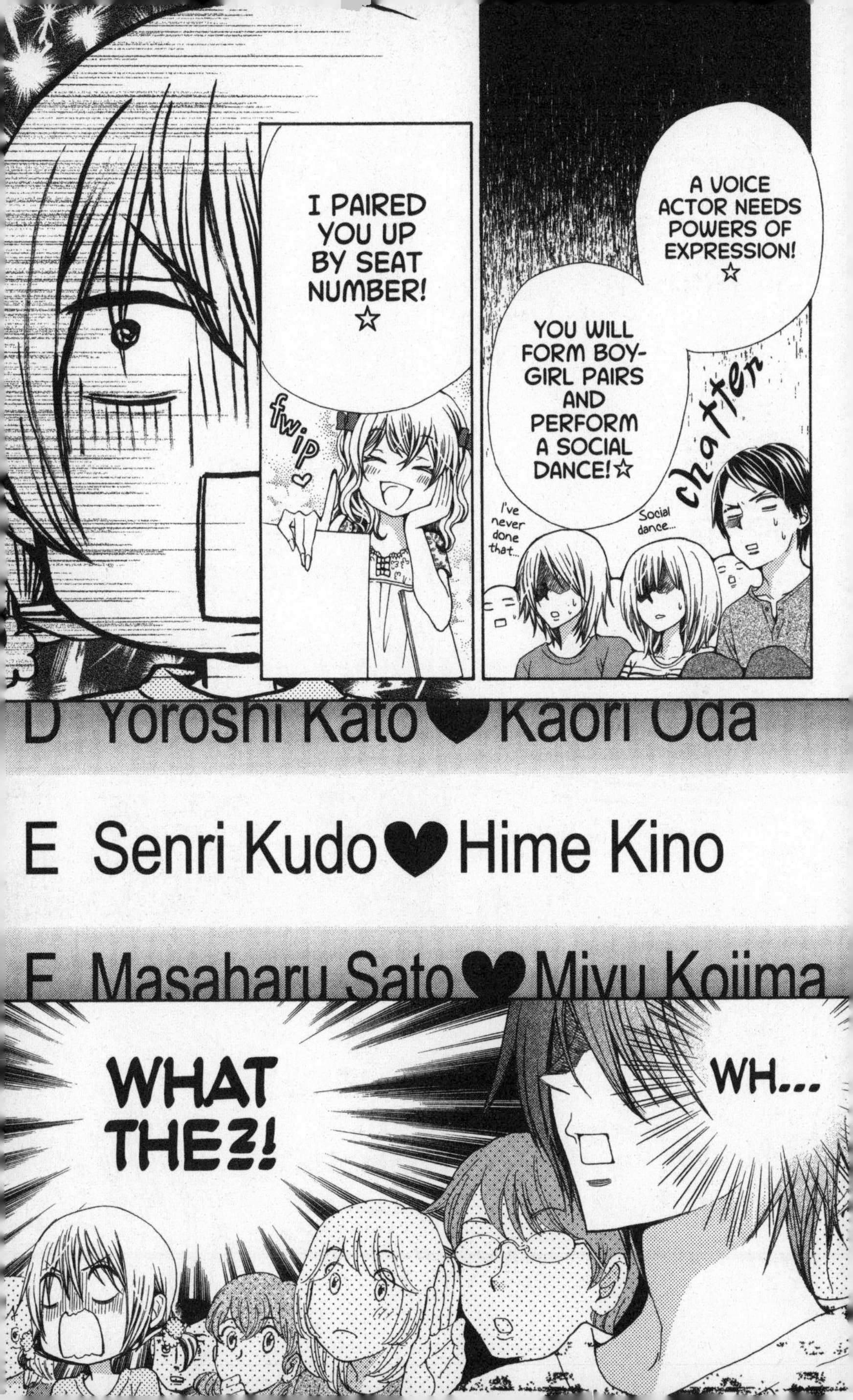
A VOICE ACTOR NEEDS POWERS OF EXPRESSION! ☆
YOU WILL FORM BOY-GIRL PAIRS AND PERFORM A SOCIAL DANCE!☆
chatter
Social dance...
I've never done that...
I PAIRED YOU UP BY SEAT NUMBER! ☆
fwip ♥
D Yoroshi Kato ♥ Kaori Oda
E Senri Kudo ♥ Hime Kino
F Masaharu Sato ♥ Miyu Kojima
WH...
WHAT THE?!

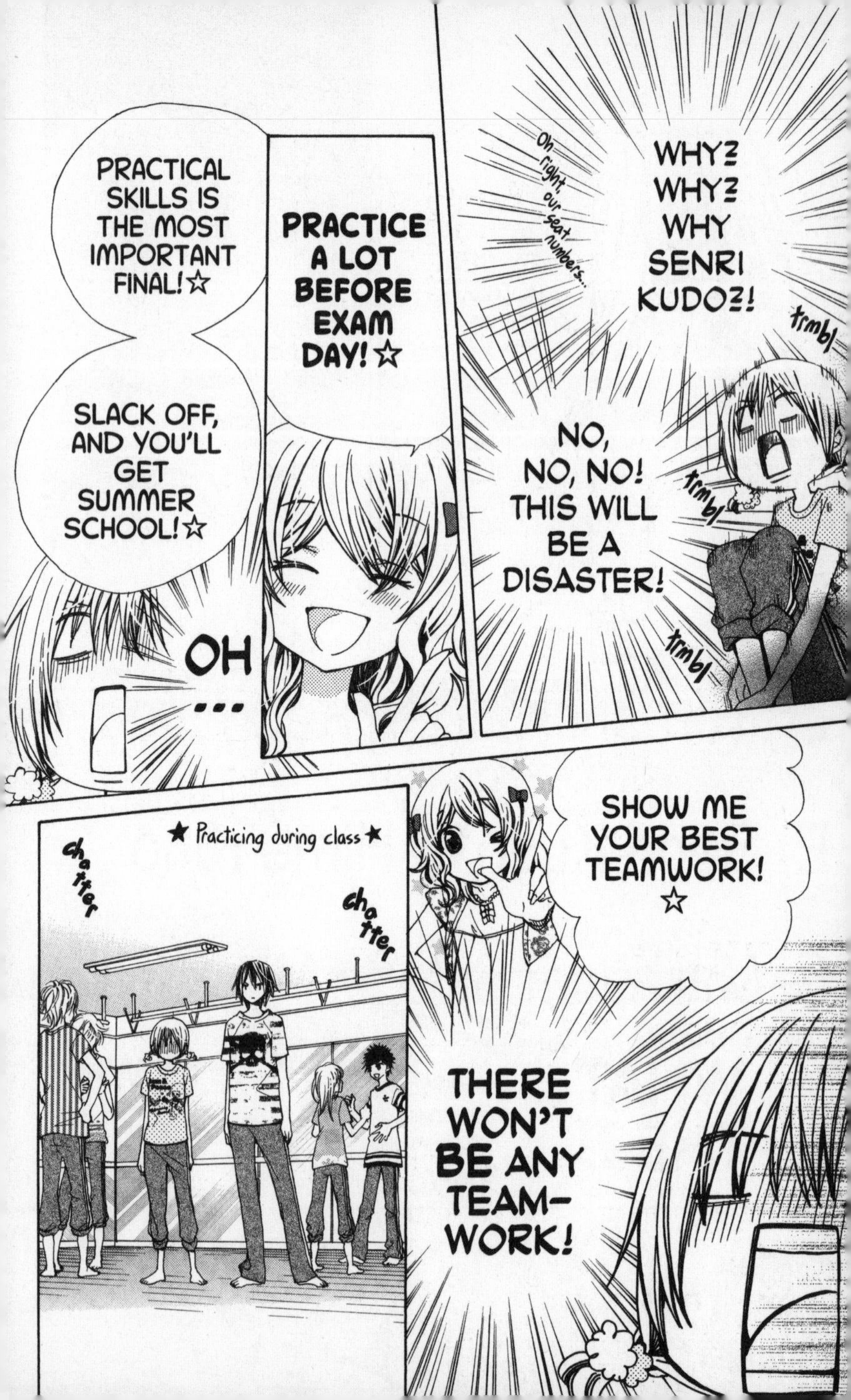
WHY? WHY? WHY SENRI KUDO?!
Oh right, our seat numbers...
trmbl
NO, NO, NO! THIS WILL BE A DISASTER!
trmbl
trmbl
PRACTICE A LOT BEFORE EXAM DAY! ☆
PRACTICAL SKILLS IS THE MOST IMPORTANT FINAL! ☆
SLACK OFF, AND YOU'LL GET SUMMER SCHOOL! ☆
OH ...
SHOW ME YOUR BEST TEAMWORK! ☆
THERE WON'T BE ANY TEAM-WORK!
★ Practicing during class ★
chatter
chatter

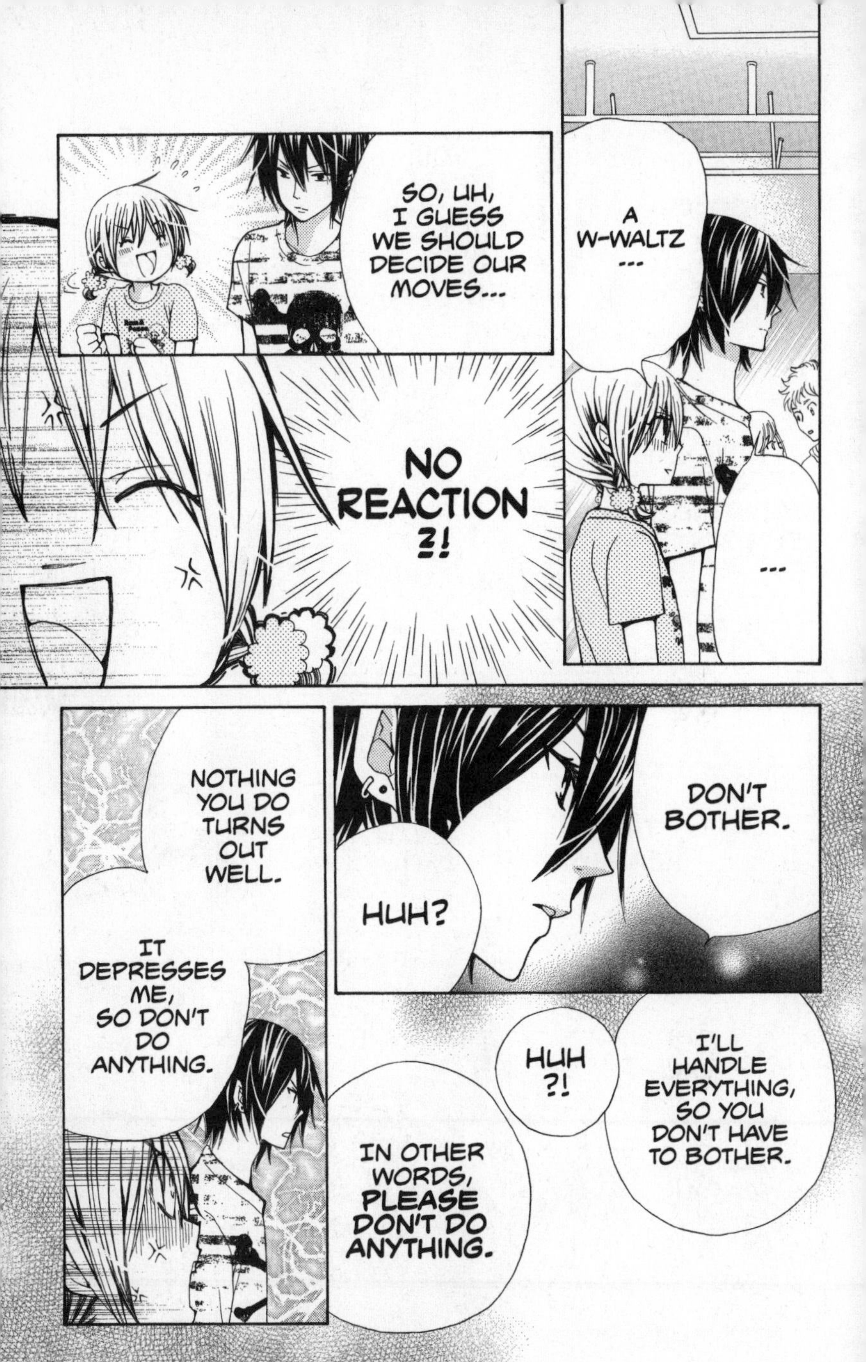
A W-WALTZ ---
...
SO, UH, I GUESS WE SHOULD DECIDE OUR MOVES...
NO REACTION ?!
DON'T BOTHER.
HUH?
I'LL HANDLE EVERYTHING, SO YOU DON'T HAVE TO BOTHER.
HUH ?!
IN OTHER WORDS, PLEASE DON'T DO ANYTHING.
NOTHING YOU DO TURNS OUT WELL.
IT DEPRESSES ME, SO DON'T DO ANYTHING.

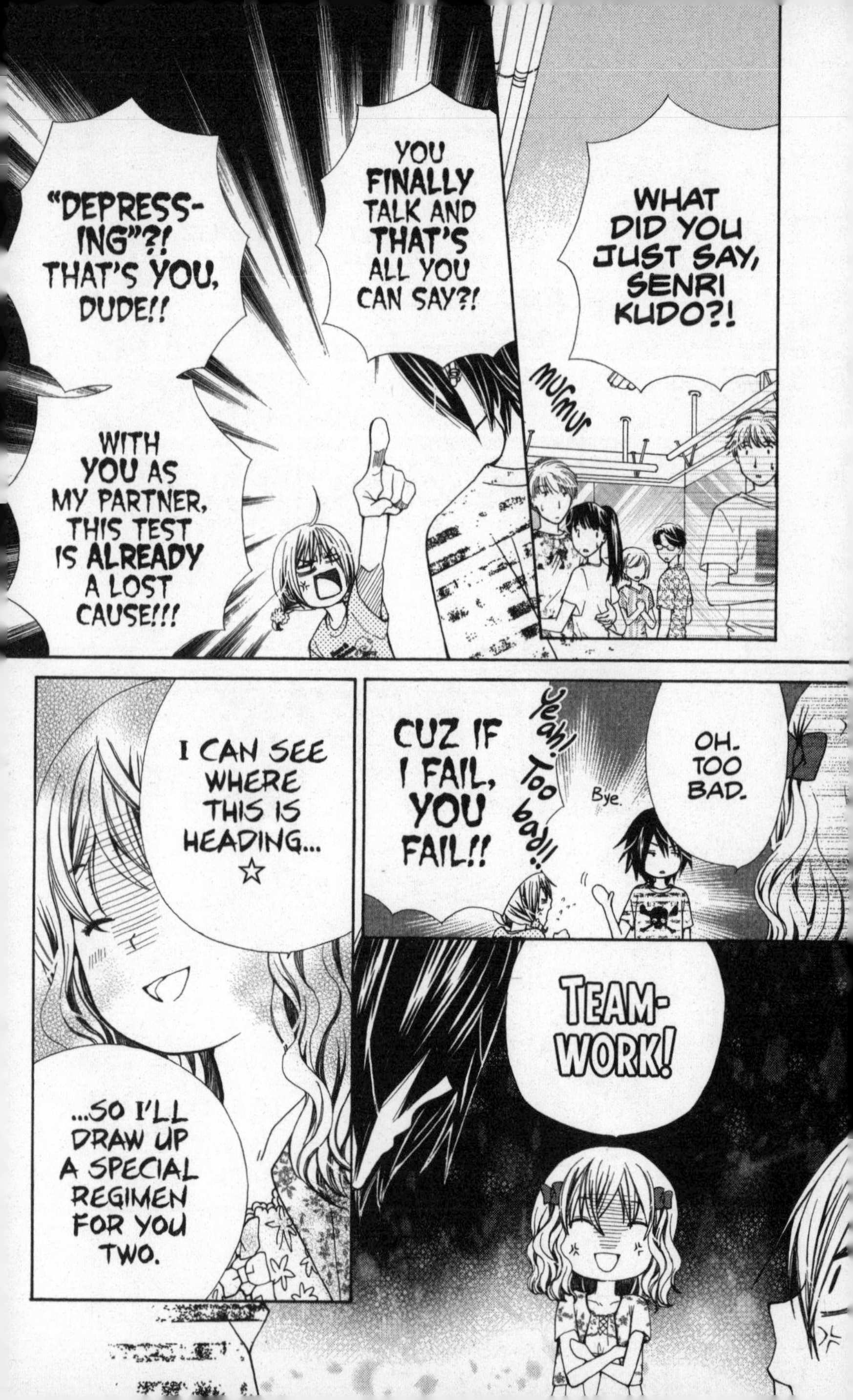
WHAT DID YOU JUST SAY, SENRI KUDO?!
murmur
YOU FINALLY TALK AND THAT'S ALL YOU CAN SAY?!
"DEPRESSING"?! THAT'S YOU, DUDE!!
WITH YOU AS MY PARTNER, THIS TEST IS ALREADY A LOST CAUSE!!!
OH. TOO BAD.
Bye.
Yeah! Too bad!!
CUZ IF I FAIL, YOU FAIL!!
TEAM-WORK!
I CAN SEE WHERE THIS IS HEADING... ☆
...SO I'LL DRAW UP A SPECIAL REGIMEN FOR YOU TWO.

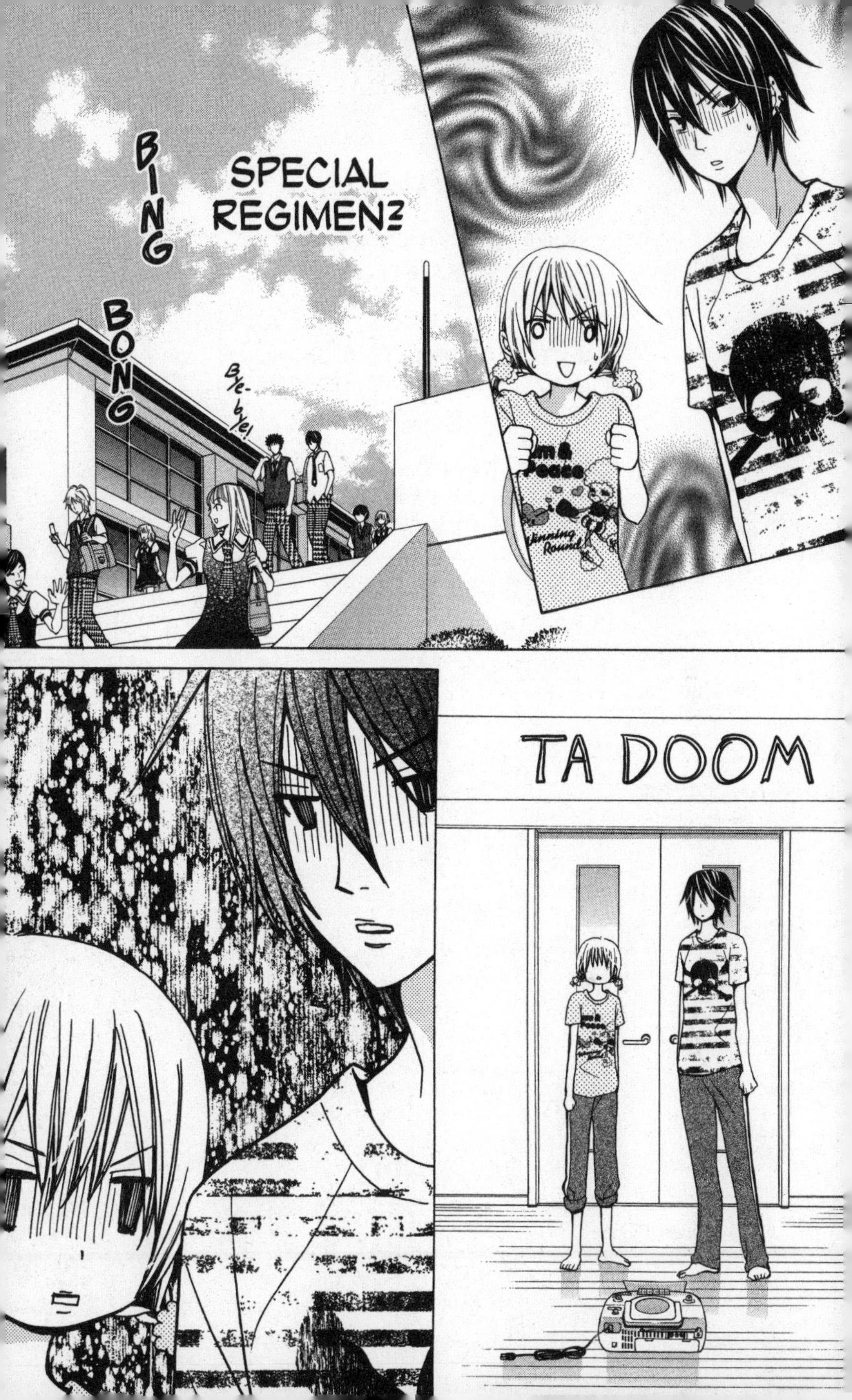
SPECIAL REGIMEN 3
BING BONG
Bye-bye!
TA DOOM

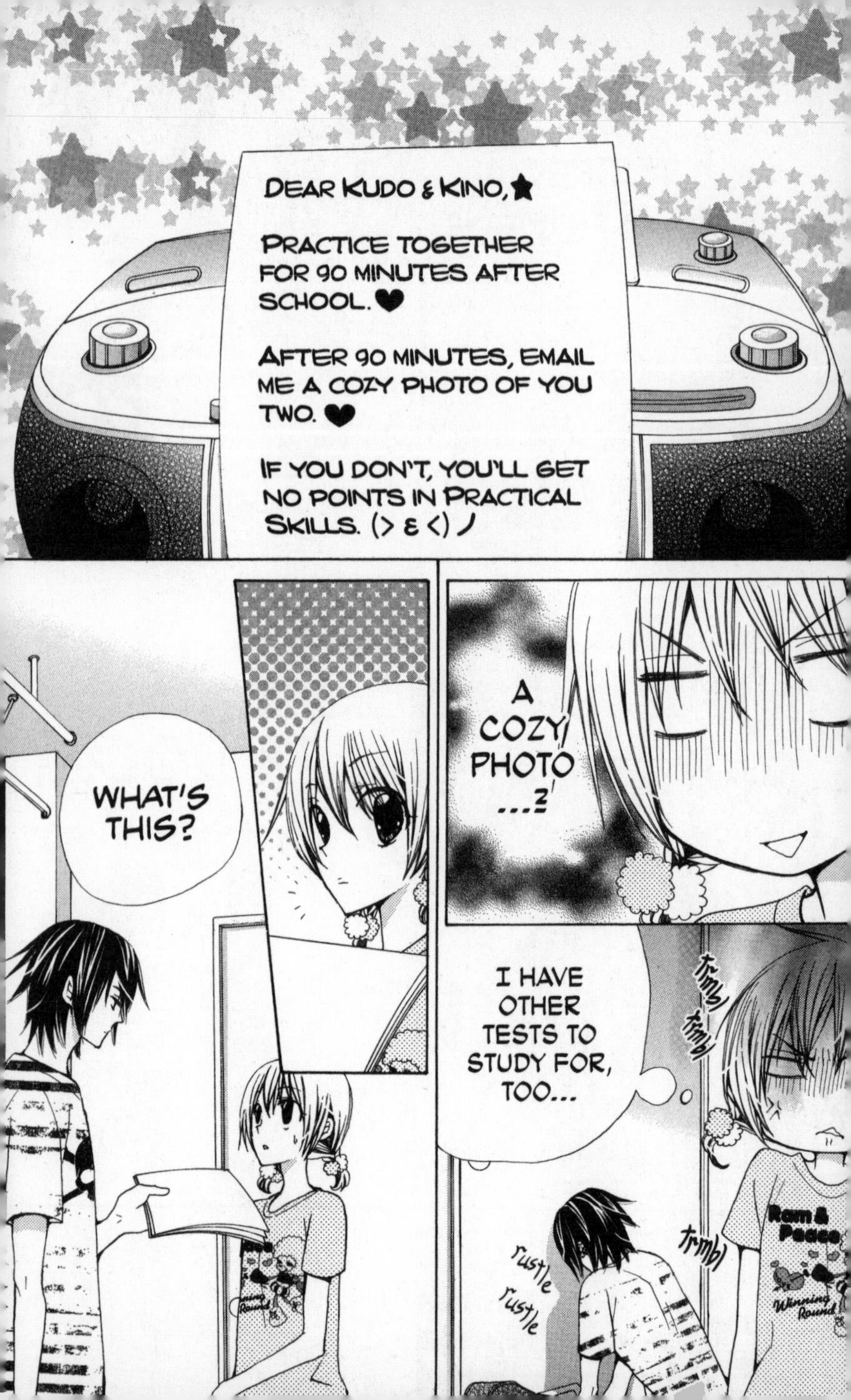
DEAR KUDO & KINO,★
PRACTICE TOGETHER FOR 90 MINUTES AFTER SCHOOL. ♥
AFTER 90 MINUTES, EMAIL ME A COZY PHOTO OF YOU TWO. ♥
IF YOU DON'T, YOU'LL GET NO POINTS IN PRACTICAL SKILLS. (> ε <) ノ
A COZY PHOTO ...?
WHAT'S THIS?
I HAVE OTHER TESTS TO STUDY FOR, TOO...
trmbl trmbl
trmbl
rustle rustle
Ram & Peace
Winning Round

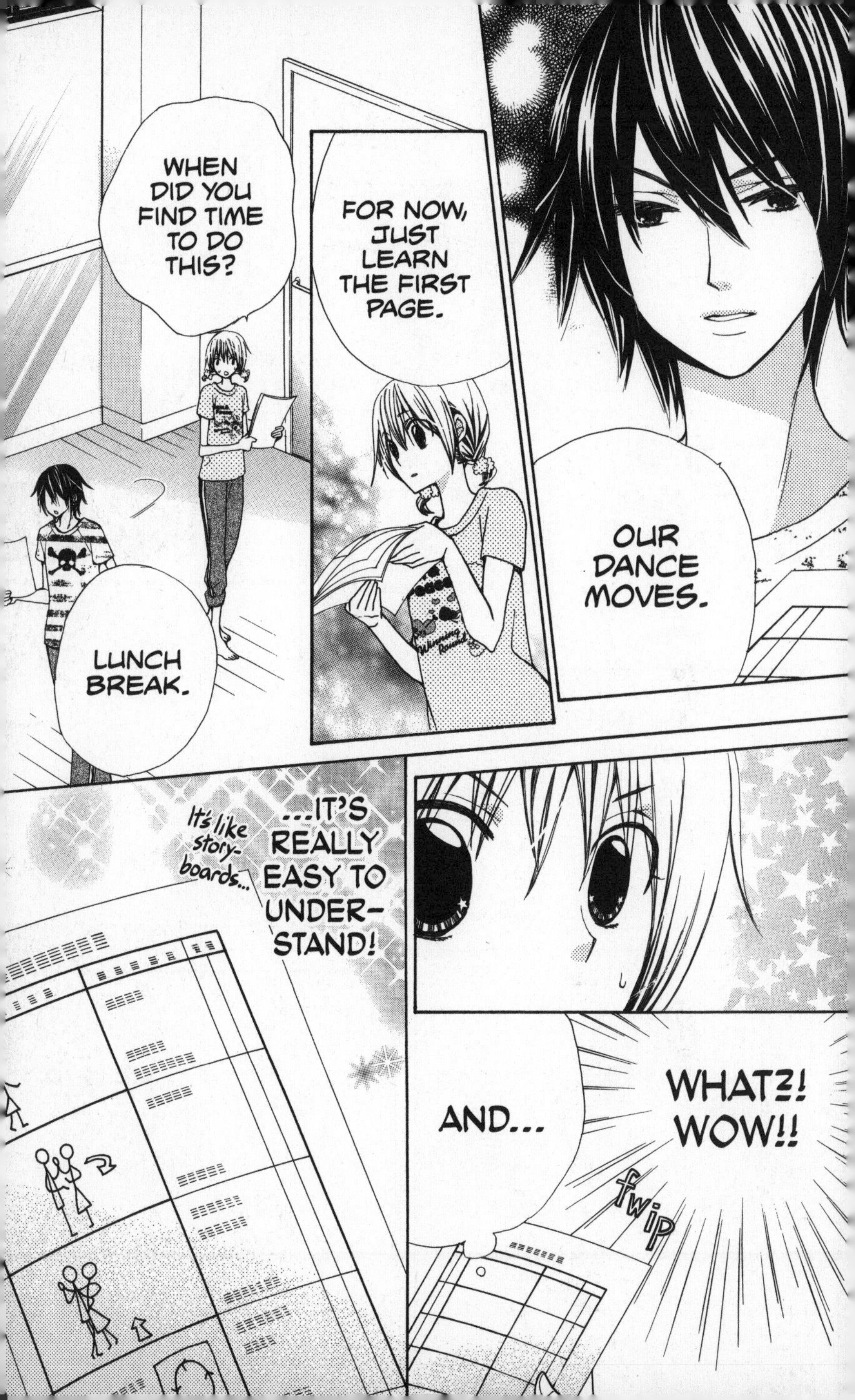
OUR DANCE MOVES.
FOR NOW, JUST LEARN THE FIRST PAGE.
WHEN DID YOU FIND TIME TO DO THIS?
LUNCH BREAK.
WHAT?! WOW!!
AND...
fwip
...IT'S REALLY EASY TO UNDER-STAND!
It's like story-boards...

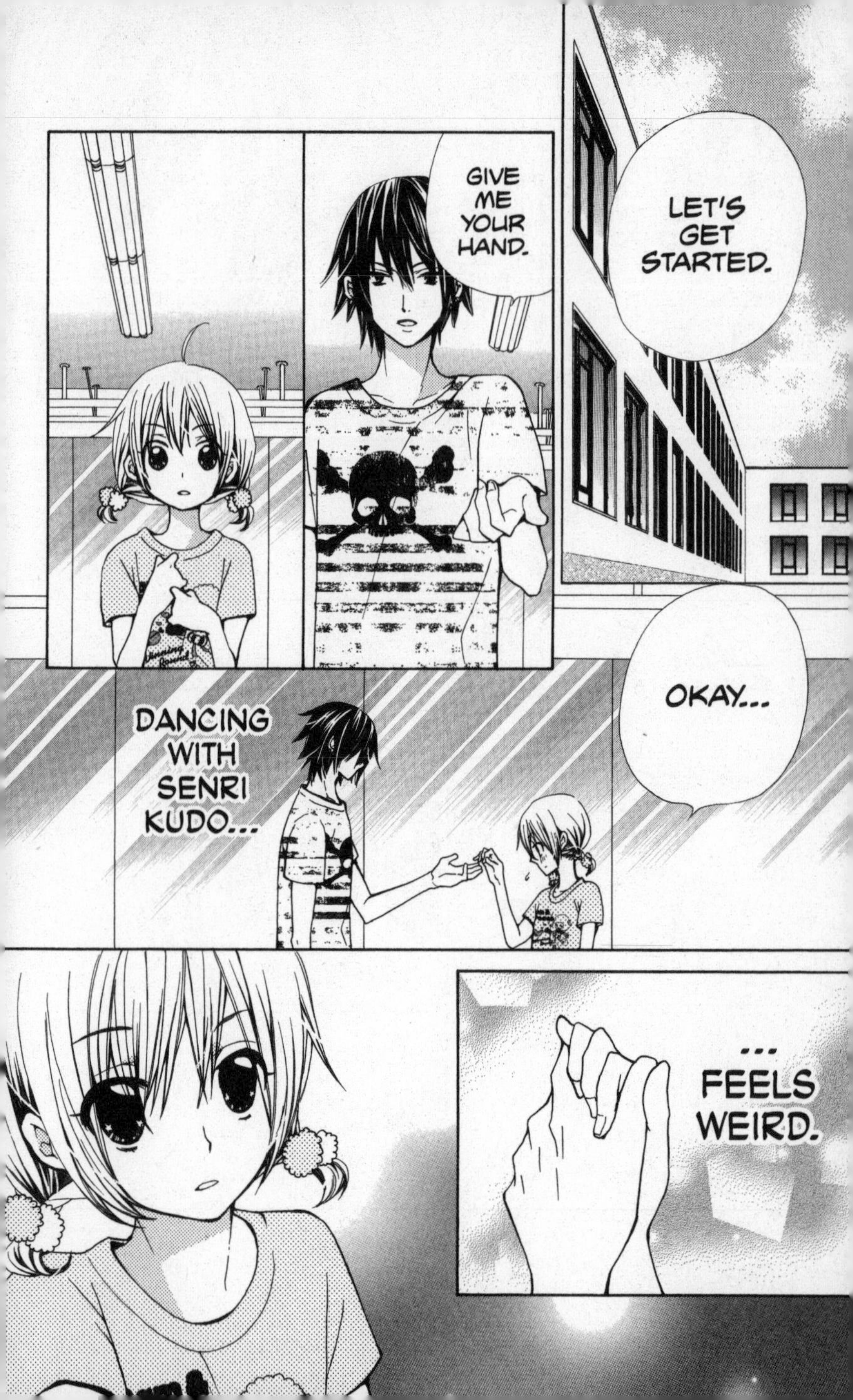
LET'S GET STARTED.
GIVE ME YOUR HAND.
OKAY...
DANCING WITH SENRI KUDO...
...FEELS WEIRD.

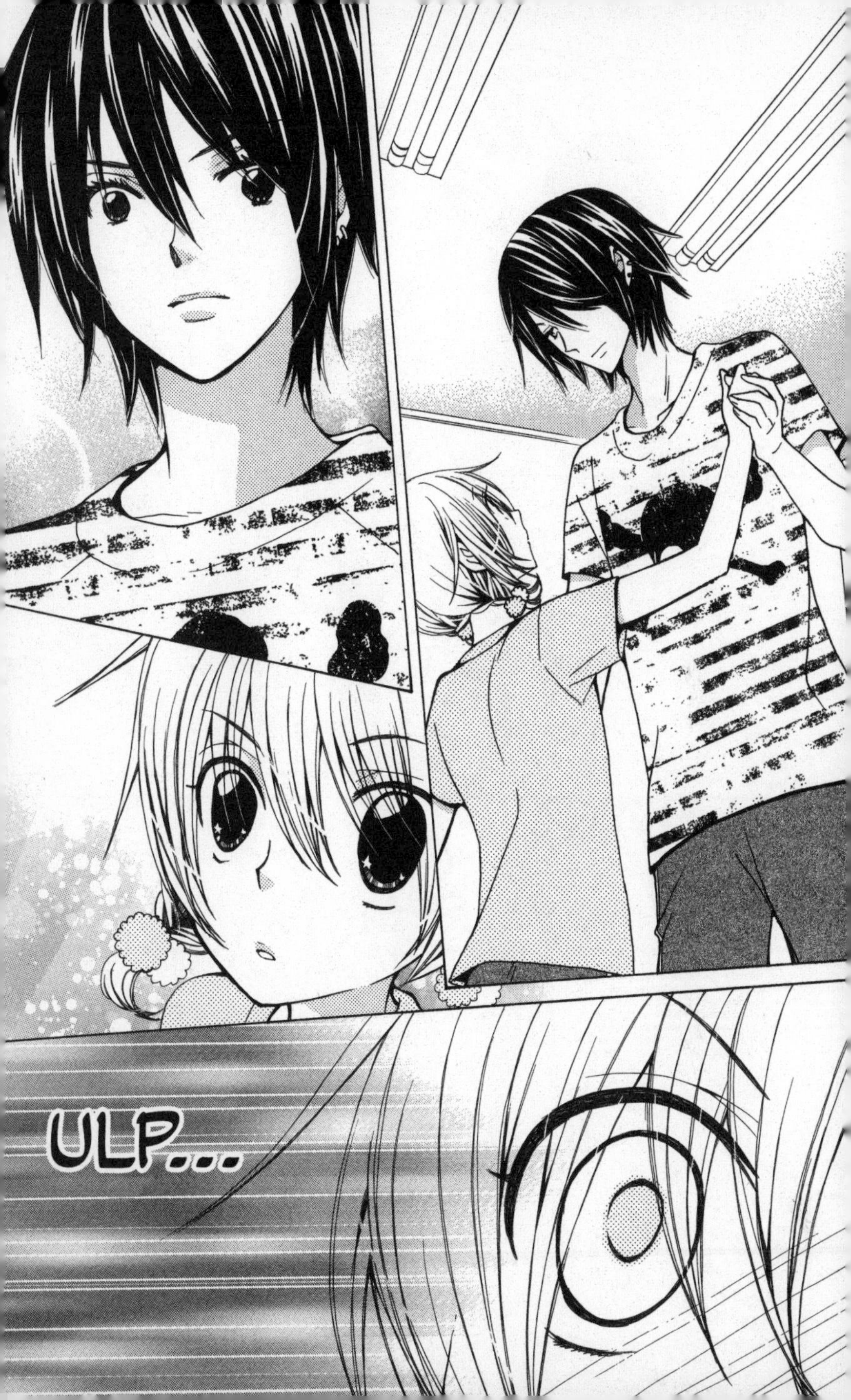
ULP...

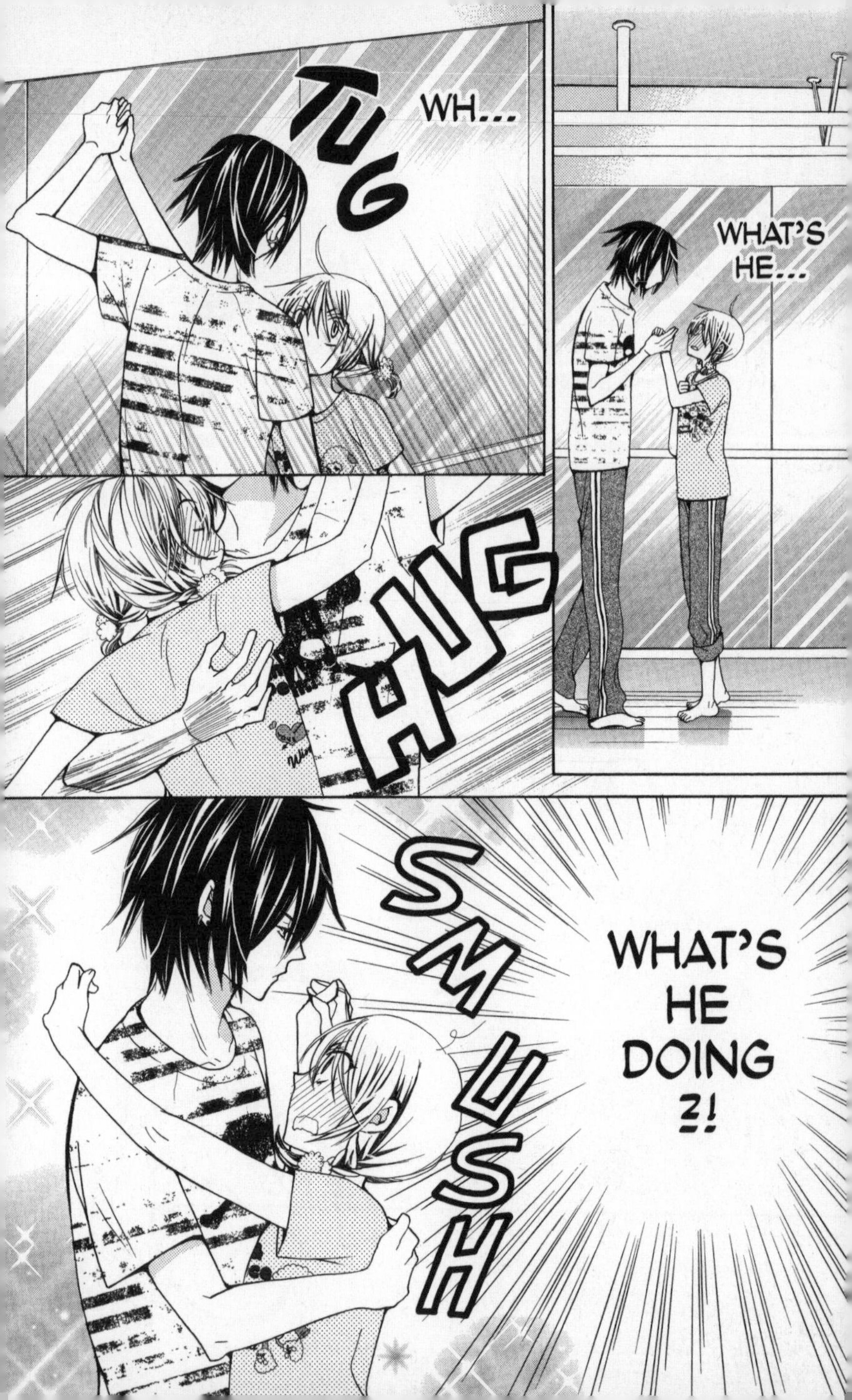
WHAT'S HE...
WH...
TUG
HUG
WHAT'S HE DOING?!
SMUSH

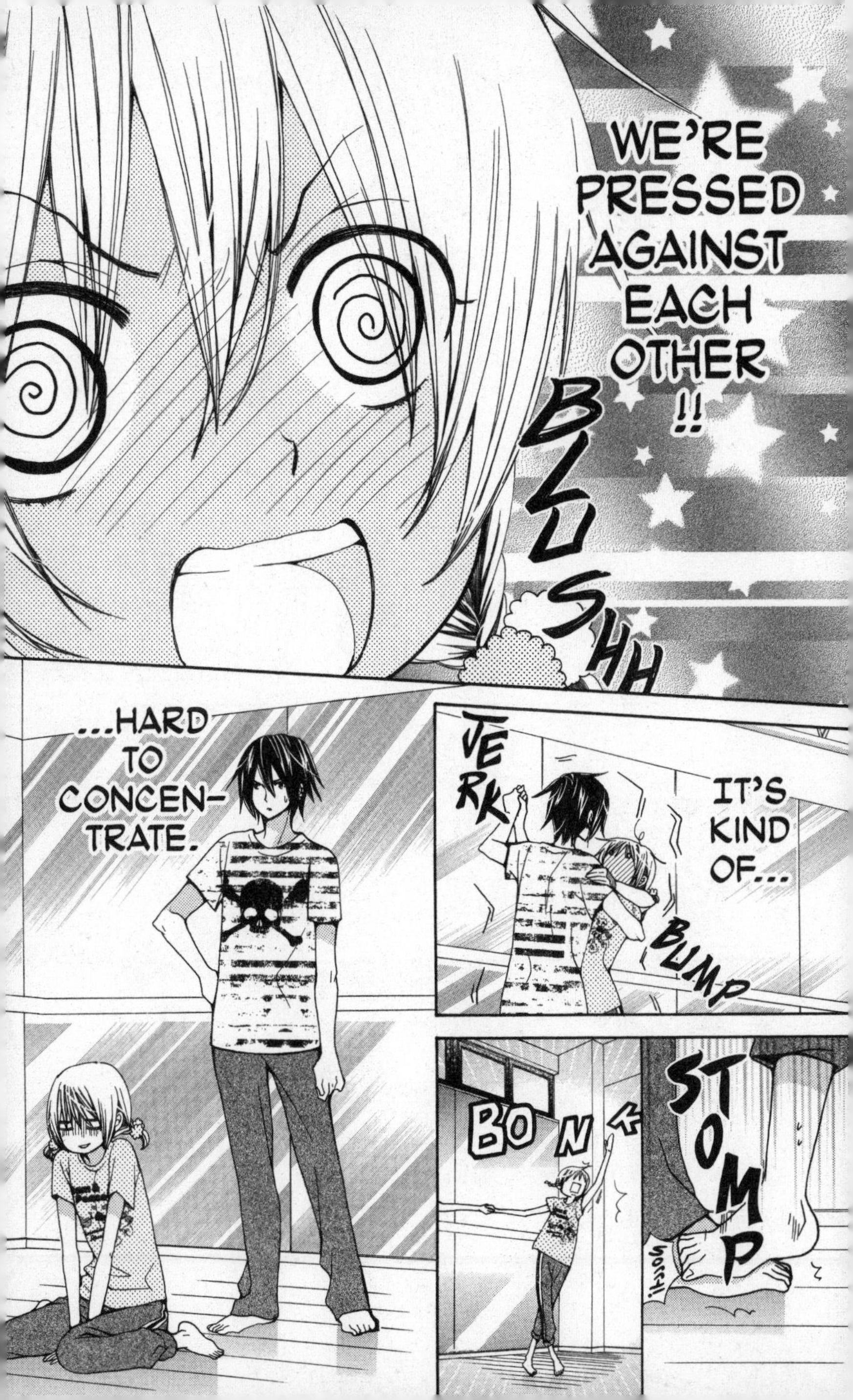
WE'RE PRESSED AGAINST EACH OTHER !!
BLUSHH
JERK
IT'S KIND OF...
BUMP
STOMP
BONK
SORRY!
...HARD TO CONCEN-TRATE.

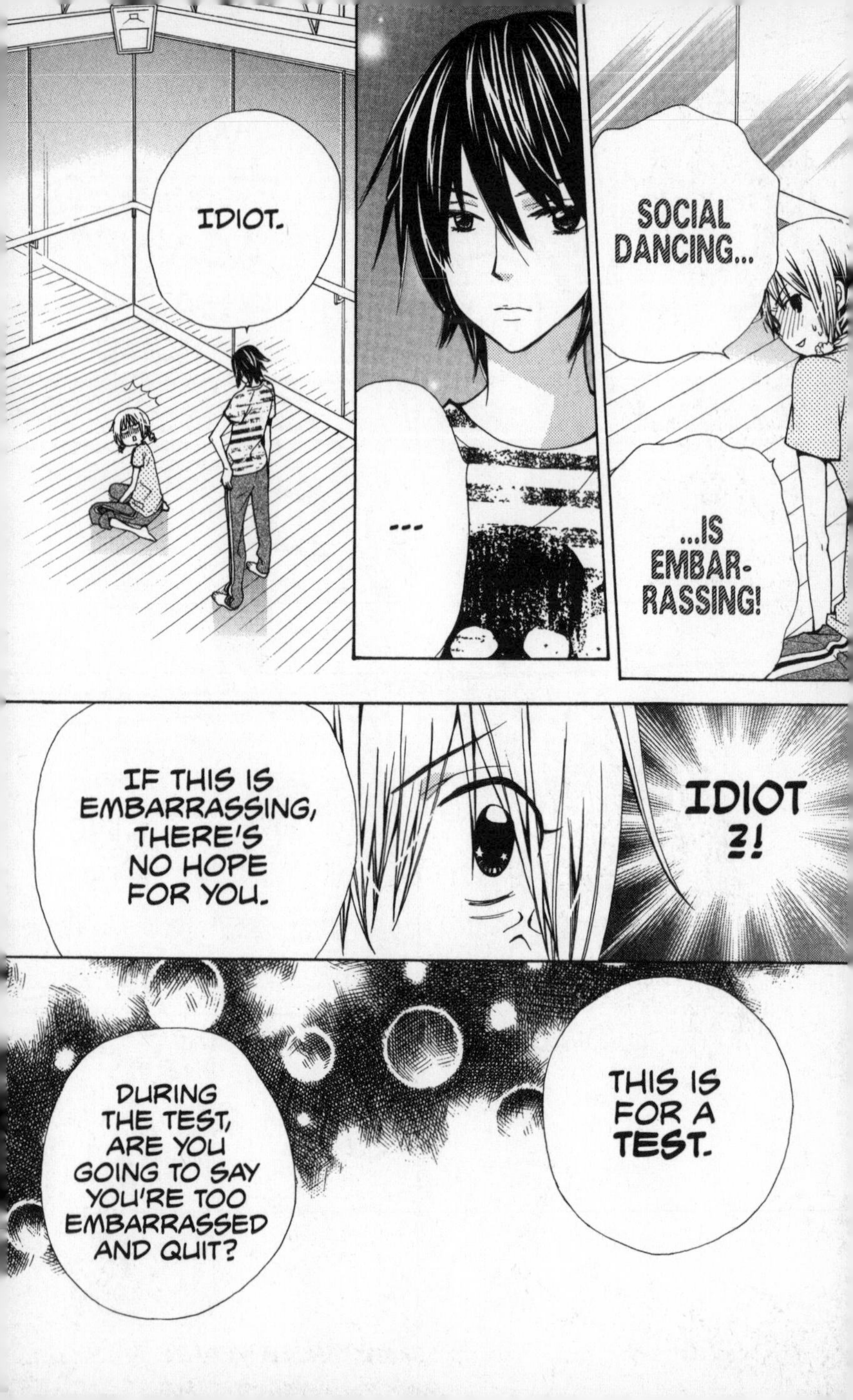
SOCIAL DANCING...
...IS EMBARRASSING!
...
IDIOT.
IDIOT?!
IF THIS IS EMBARRASSING, THERE'S NO HOPE FOR YOU.
THIS IS FOR A TEST.
DURING THE TEST, ARE YOU GOING TO SAY YOU'RE TOO EMBARRASSED AND QUIT?

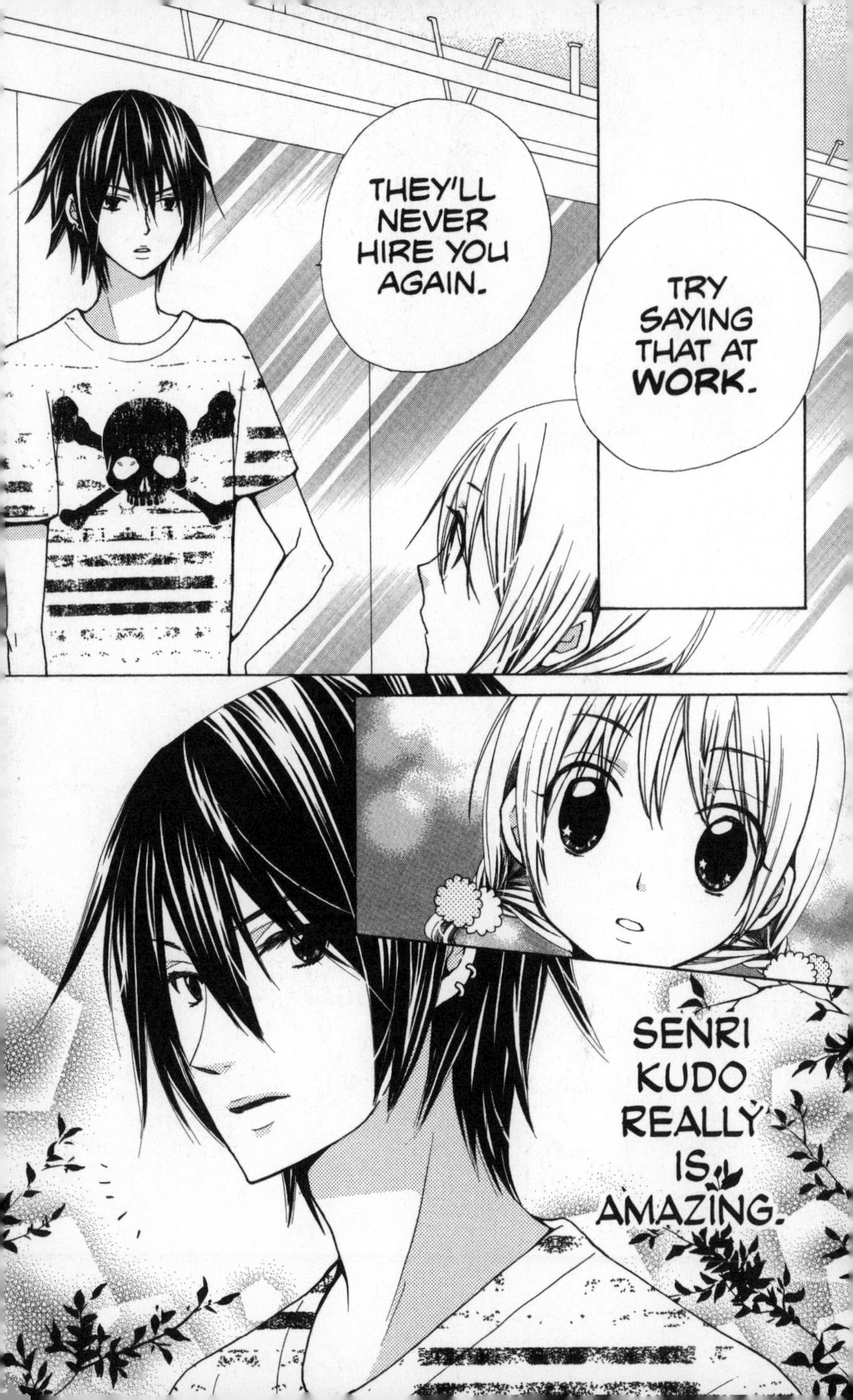
THEY'LL NEVER HIRE YOU AGAIN.
TRY SAYING THAT AT WORK.
SENRI KUDO REALLY IS AMAZING.

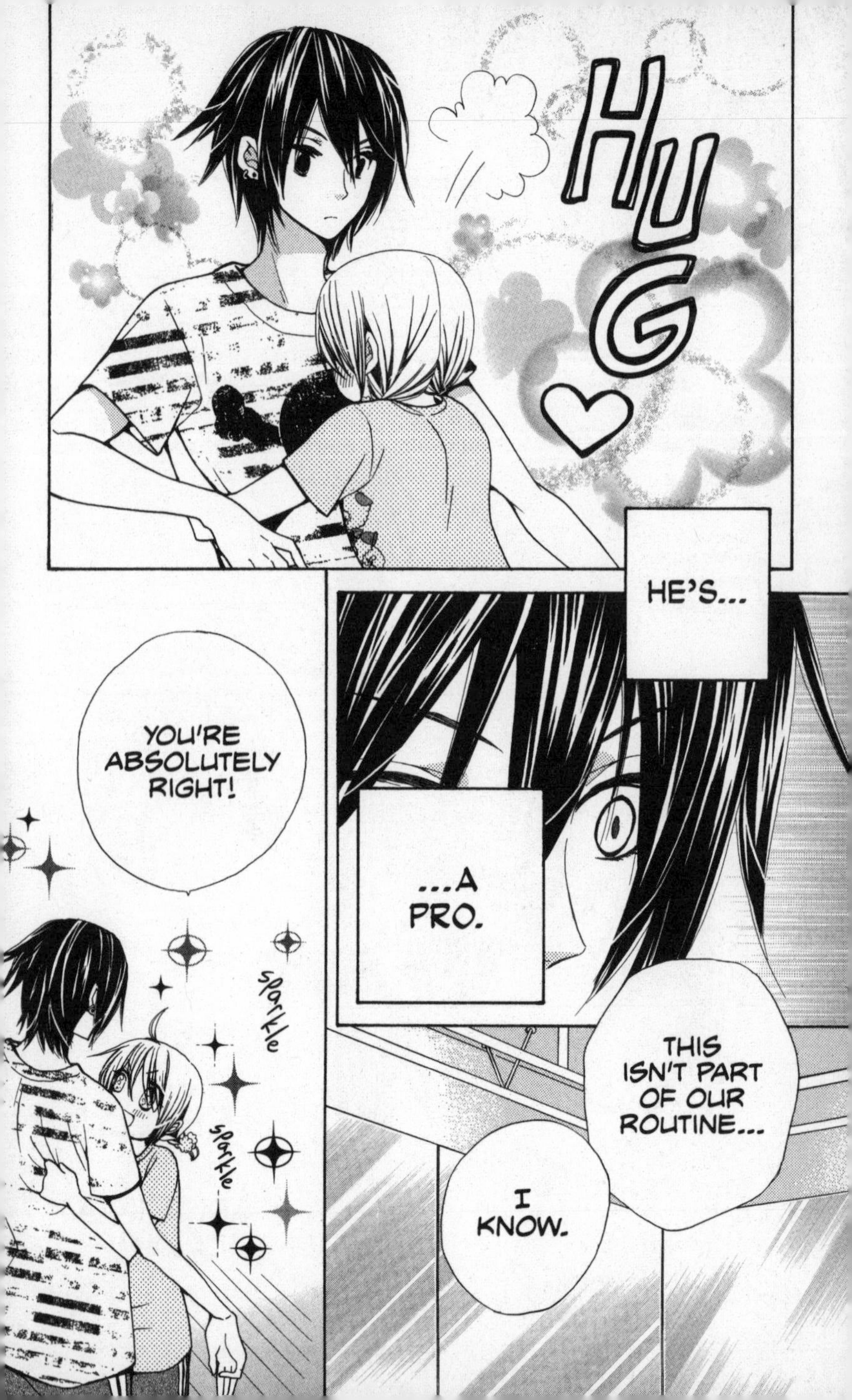
HUG
HE'S...
...A PRO.
THIS ISN'T PART OF OUR ROUTINE...
I KNOW.
YOU'RE ABSOLUTELY RIGHT!
sparkle
sparkle

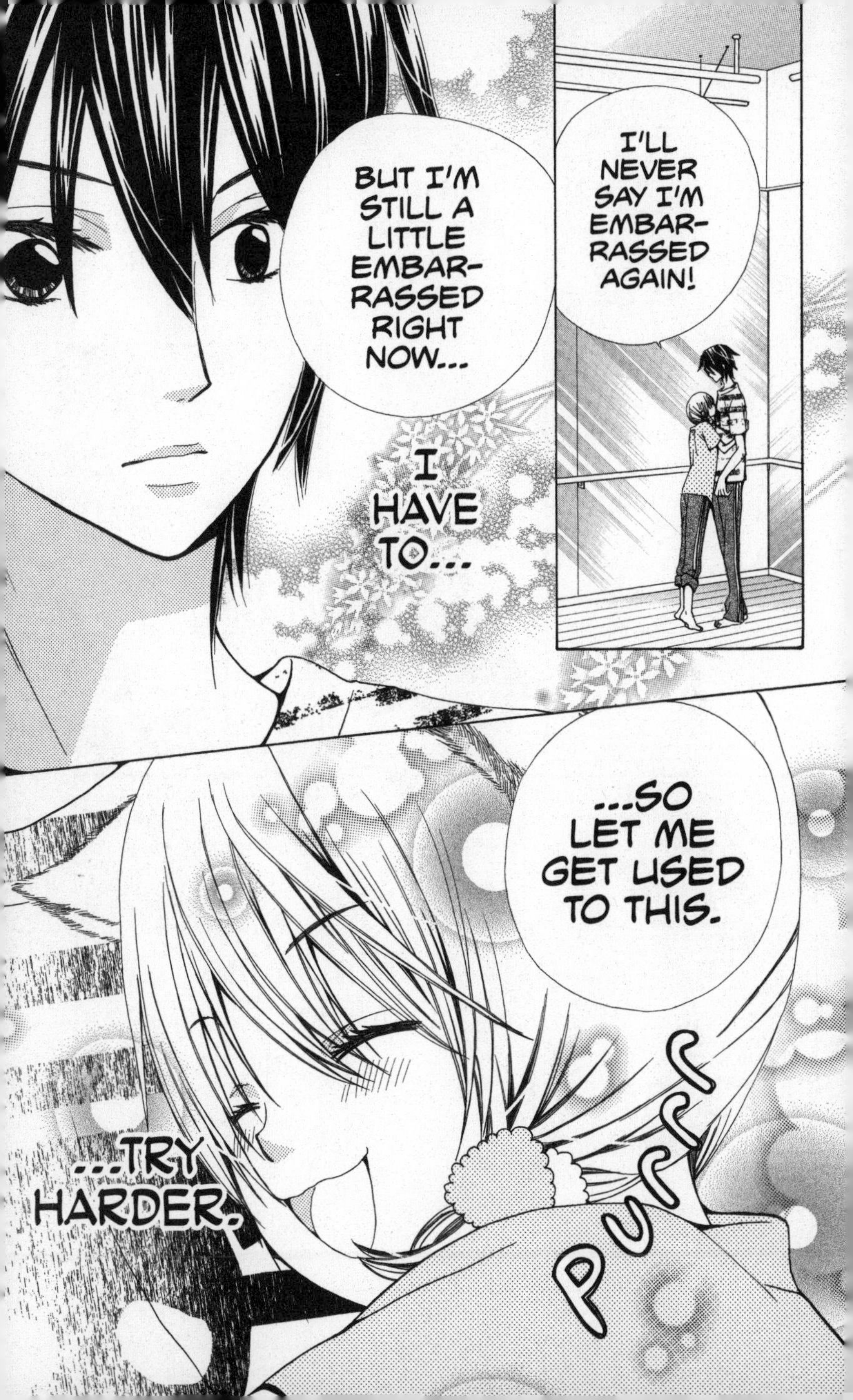
I'LL NEVER SAY I'M EMBARRASSED AGAIN!
BUT I'M STILL A LITTLE EMBARRASSED RIGHT NOW...
I HAVE TO...
...SO LET ME GET USED TO THIS.
PUFF
...TRY HARDER.

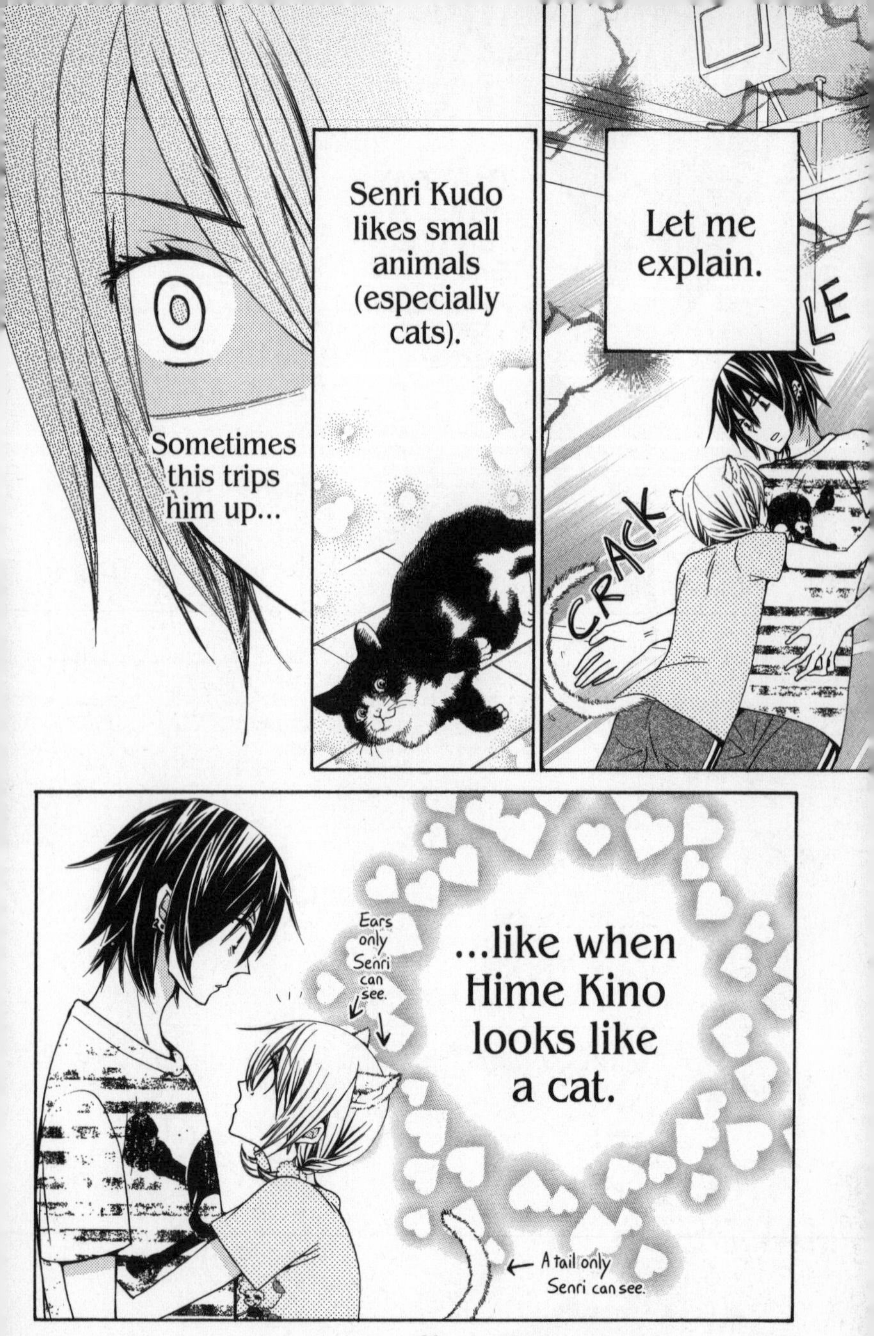
Let me explain.
LE
CRACK
Senri Kudo likes small animals (especially cats).
Sometimes this trips him up...
...like when Hime Kino looks like a cat.
Ears only Senri can see.
A tail only Senri can see.

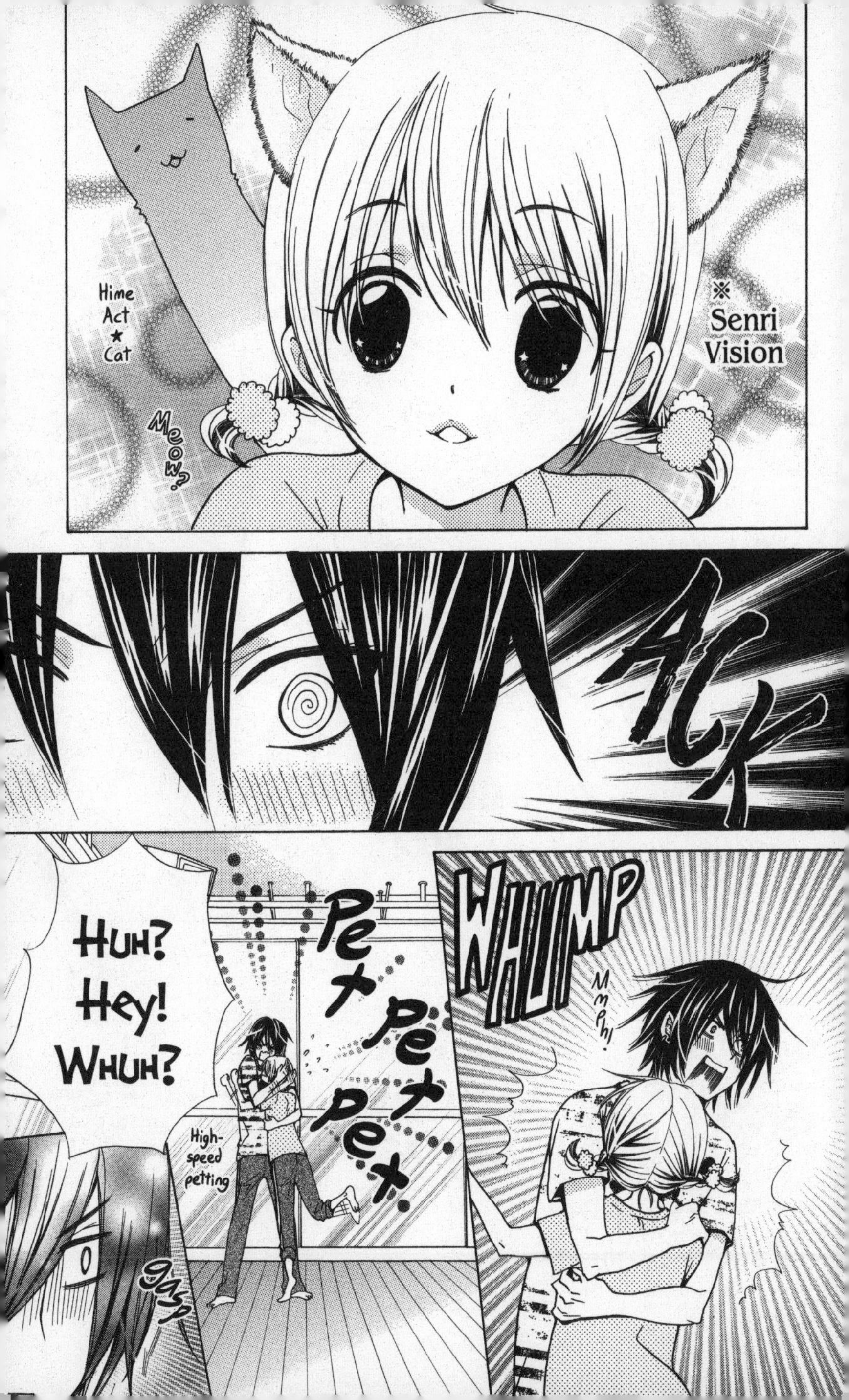
※ Senri Vision
Hime Act ★ Cat
Meow?
ACK
WHUMP
Mmph!
Pet pet pet
High-speed petting
Huh? Hey! Whuh?
gasp

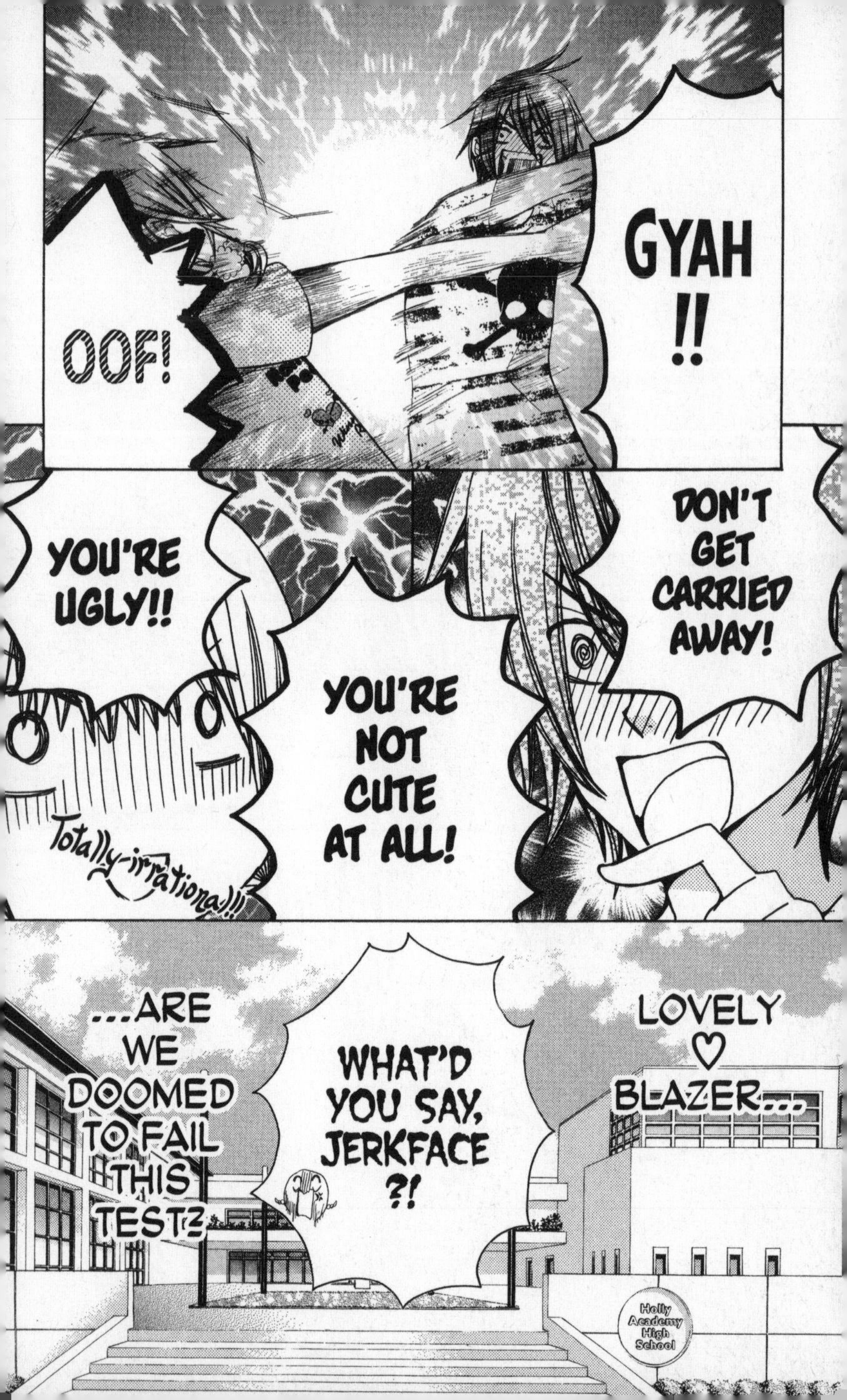
GYAH!!
OOF!
DON'T GET CARRIED AWAY!
YOU'RE NOT CUTE AT ALL!
YOU'RE UGLY!!
Totally-irrational!!!
LOVELY ♡ BLAZER...
Holly Academy High School
WHAT'D YOU SAY, JERKFACE?!
...ARE WE DOOMED TO FAIL THIS TEST?

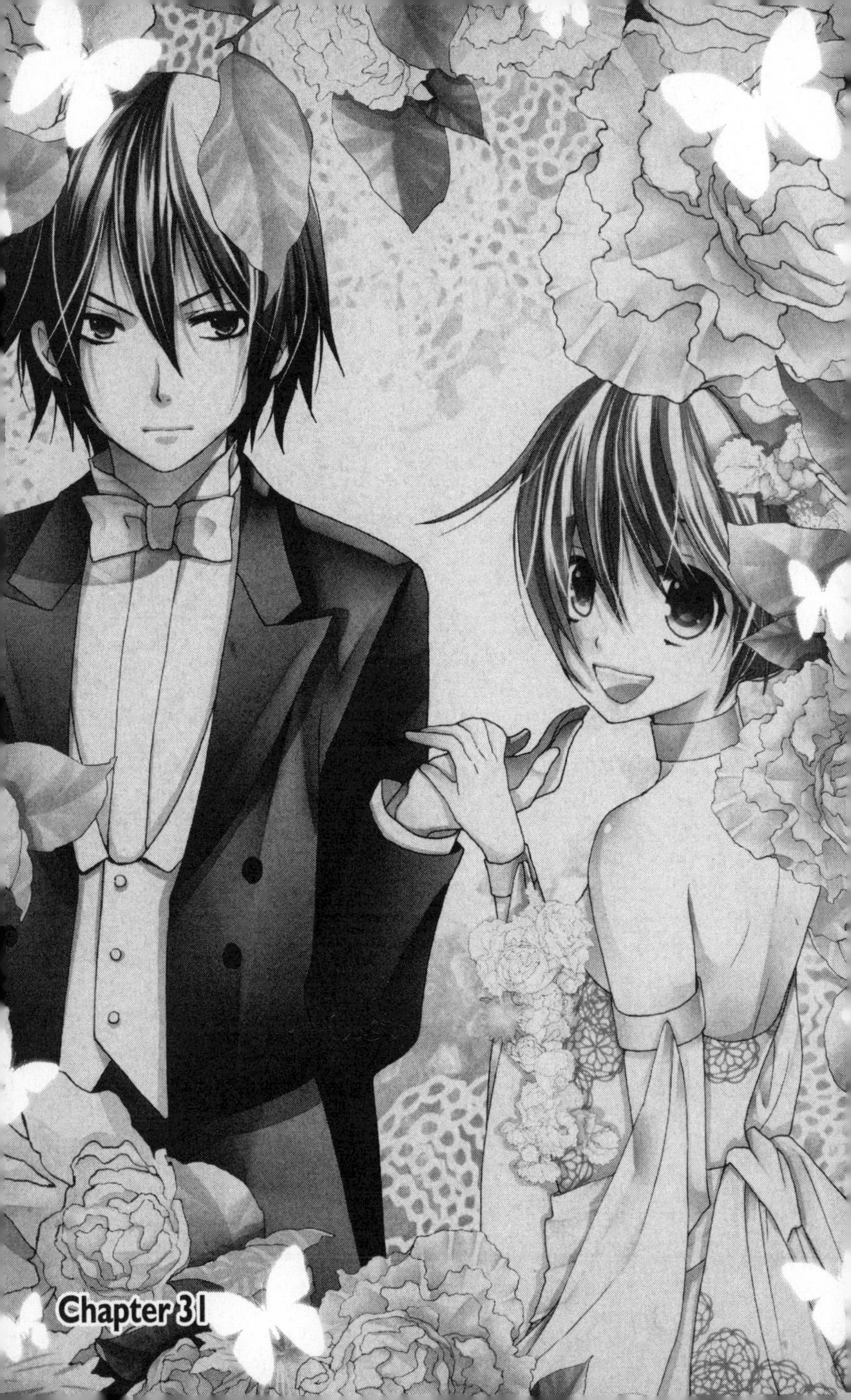
Chapter 31

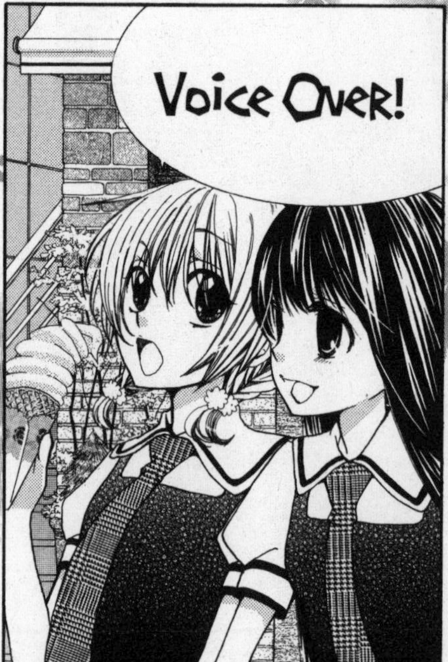
Voice Over!

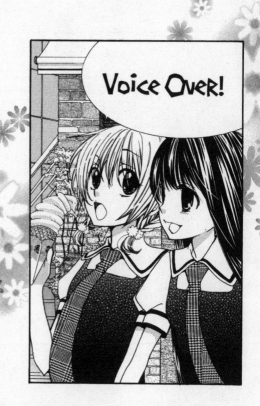

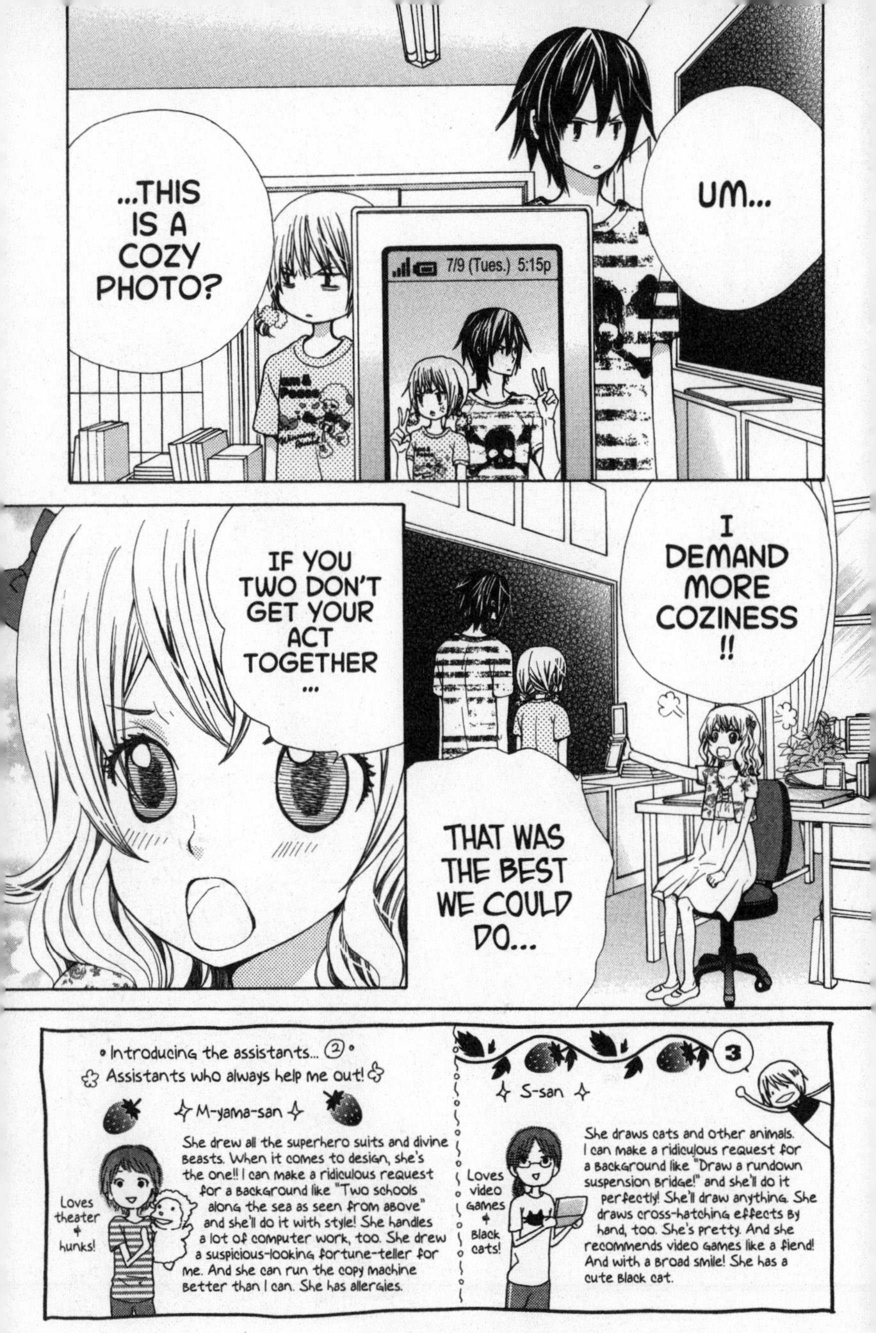
UM...
...THIS IS A COZY PHOTO?
7/9 (Tues.) 5:15p
I DEMAND MORE COZINESS!!
THAT WAS THE BEST WE COULD DO...
IF YOU TWO DON'T GET YOUR ACT TOGETHER...

• Introducing the assistants... ② •

✿ Assistants who always help me out! ✿

✧ M-yama-san ✧

Loves theater + hunks!

She drew all the superhero suits and divine beasts. When it comes to design, she's the one!! I can make a ridiculous request for a background like "Two schools along the sea as seen from above" and she'll do it with style! She handles a lot of computer work, too. She drew a suspicious-looking fortune-teller for me. And she can run the copy machine better than I can. She has allergies.

3

✧ S-san ✧

Loves video games + Black cats!

She draws cats and other animals. I can make a ridiculous request for a background like "Draw a rundown suspension bridge!" and she'll do it perfectly! She'll draw anything. She draws cross-hatching effects by hand, too. She's pretty. And she recommends video games like a fiend! And with a broad smile! She has a cute black cat.

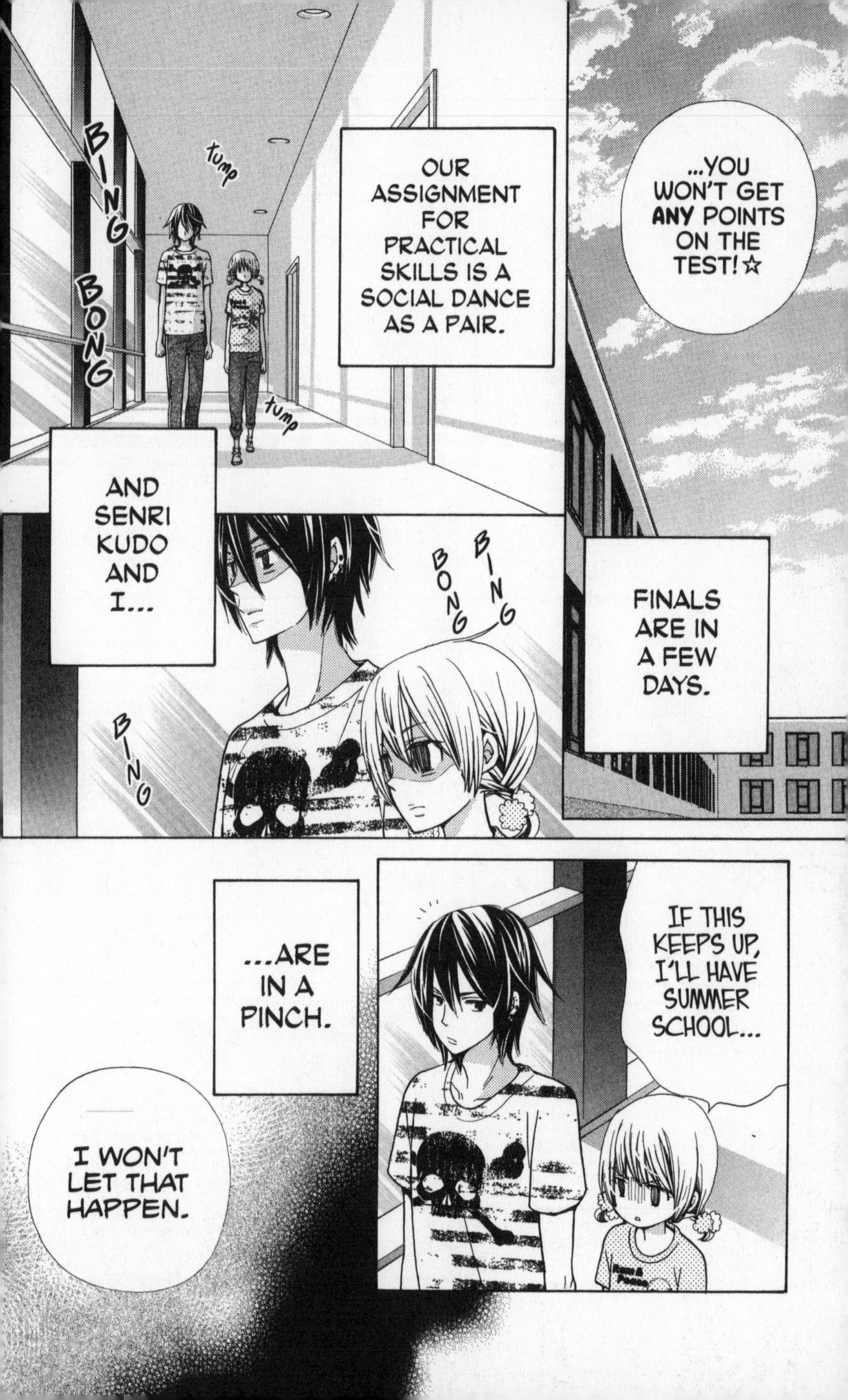
...YOU WON'T GET **ANY** POINTS ON THE TEST!☆
FINALS ARE IN A FEW DAYS.
OUR ASSIGNMENT FOR PRACTICAL SKILLS IS A SOCIAL DANCE AS A PAIR.
tump
BING BONG
tump
BING BONG
AND SENRI KUDO AND I...
BING
IF THIS KEEPS UP, I'LL HAVE SUMMER SCHOOL...
...ARE IN A PINCH.
I WON'T LET THAT HAPPEN.

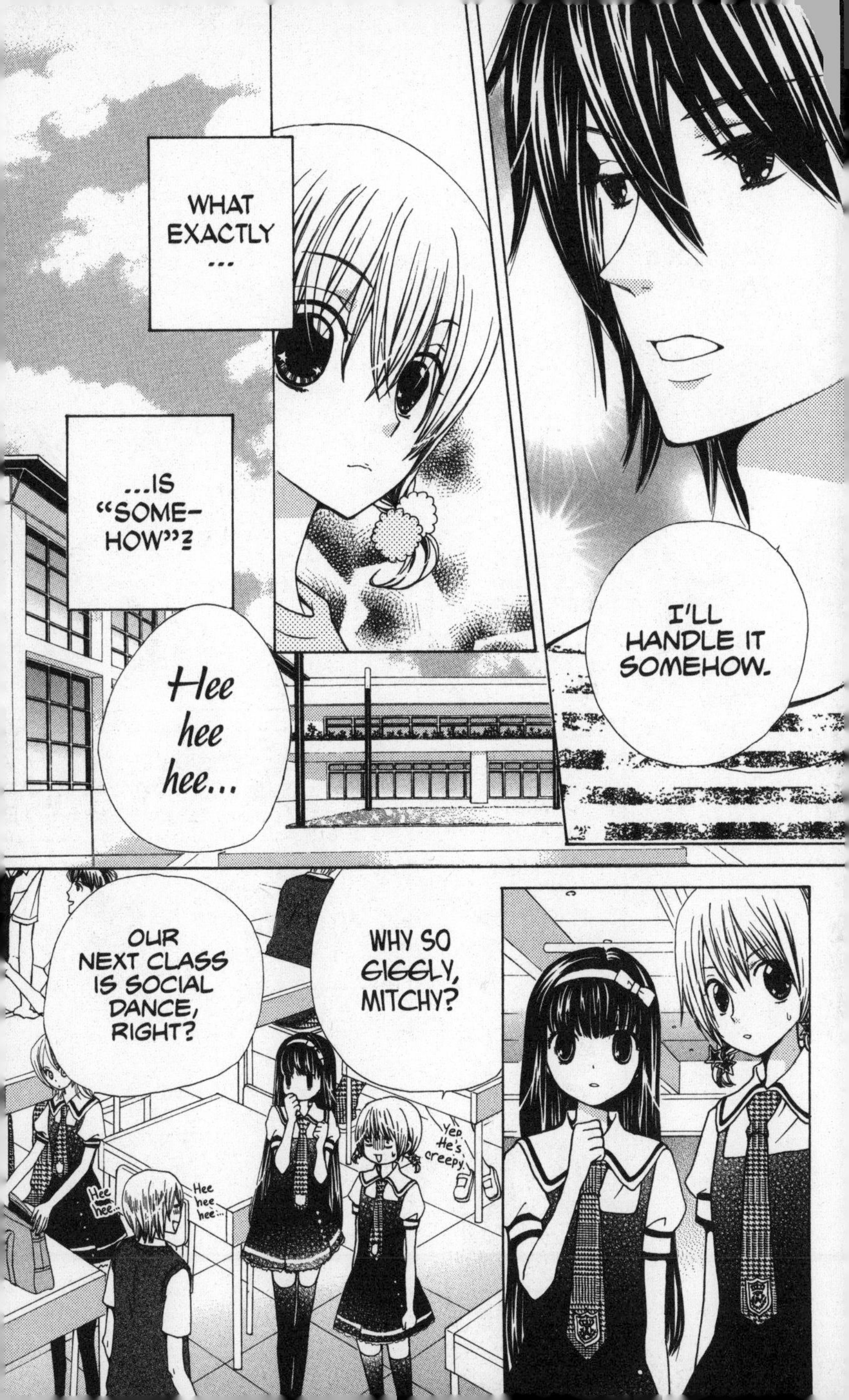
I'LL HANDLE IT SOMEHOW.
WHAT EXACTLY ...
...IS "SOME-HOW"?
Hee hee hee...
WHY SO GIGGLY, MITCHY?
OUR NEXT CLASS IS SOCIAL DANCE, RIGHT?
Yep. He's creepy.
Hee hee hee...
Hee hee...

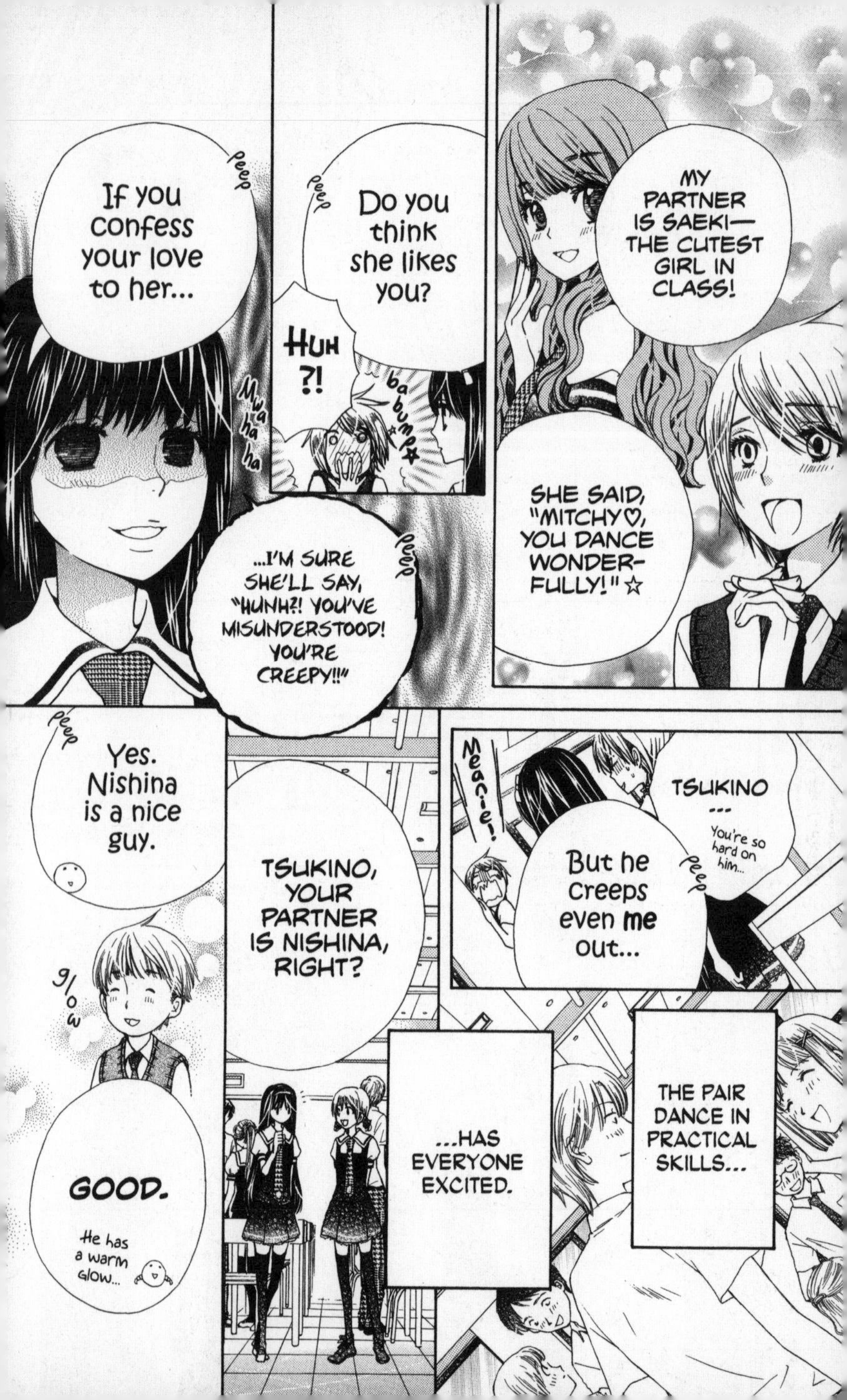
MY PARTNER IS SAEKI— THE CUTEST GIRL IN CLASS!
SHE SAID, "MITCHY♡, YOU DANCE WONDER-FULLY!"☆
peep
Do you think she likes you?
HUH?!
ba bump☆
peep
If you confess your love to her...
Mwa ha ha ha
peep
...I'M SURE SHE'LL SAY, "HUNH?! YOU'VE MISUNDERSTOOD! YOU'RE CREEPY!!"
TSUKINO ---
You're so hard on him...
peep
But he creeps even me out...
Meanie!
THE PAIR DANCE IN PRACTICAL SKILLS...
...HAS EVERYONE EXCITED.
TSUKINO, YOUR PARTNER IS NISHINA, RIGHT?
peep
Yes. Nishina is a nice guy.
glow
GOOD.
He has a warm glow...

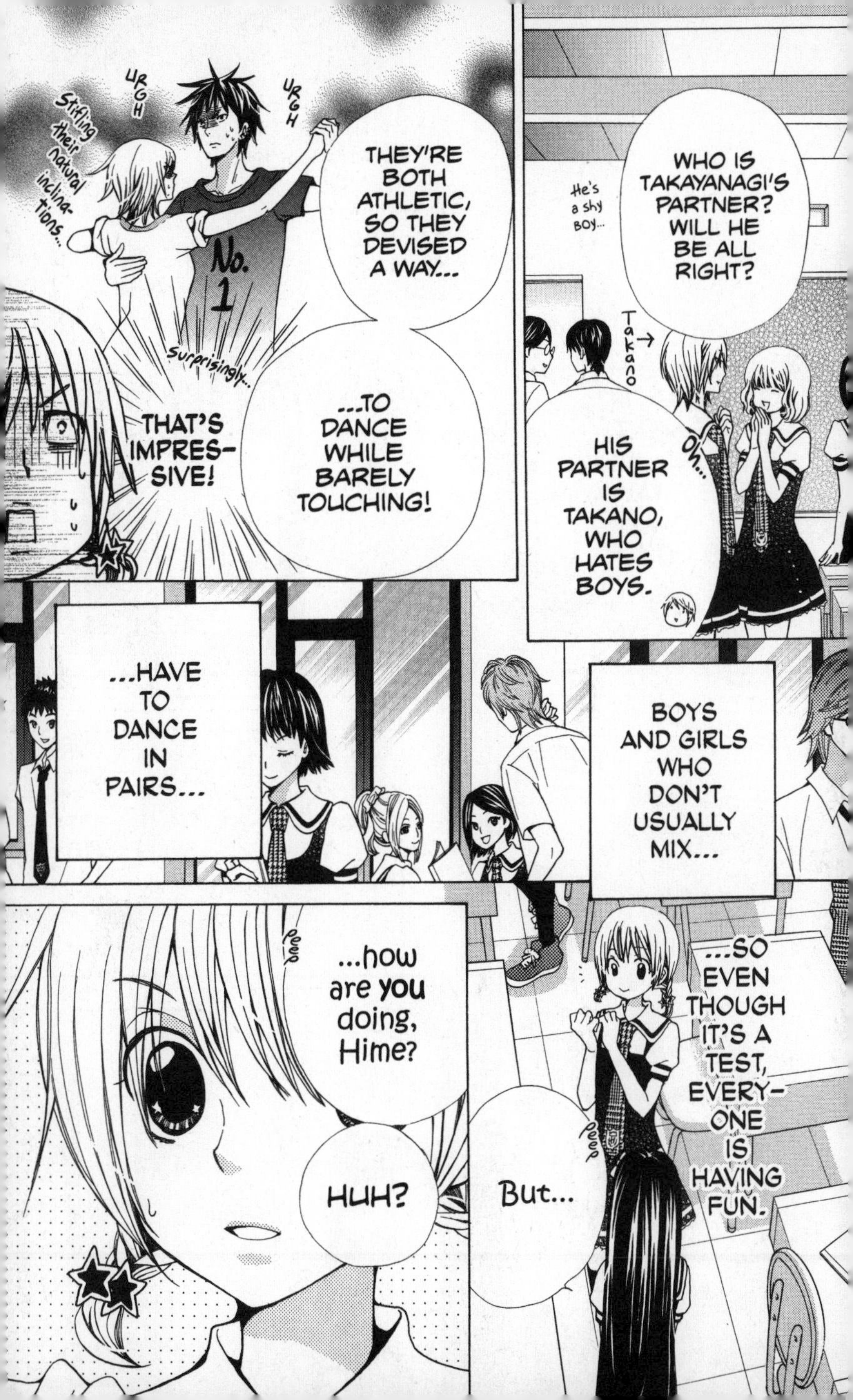
WHO IS TAKAYANAGI'S PARTNER? WILL HE BE ALL RIGHT?
He's a shy boy...
Takano →
Oh...
HIS PARTNER IS TAKANO, WHO HATES BOYS.
URGH
URGH
THEY'RE BOTH ATHLETIC, SO THEY DEVISED A WAY...
Stifling their natural inclinations...
...TO DANCE WHILE BARELY TOUCHING!
Surprisingly...
THAT'S IMPRESSIVE!
No. 1
BOYS AND GIRLS WHO DON'T USUALLY MIX...
...HAVE TO DANCE IN PAIRS...
...SO EVEN THOUGH IT'S A TEST, EVERYONE IS HAVING FUN.
Peep
But...
Peep
...how are you doing, Hime?
HUH?

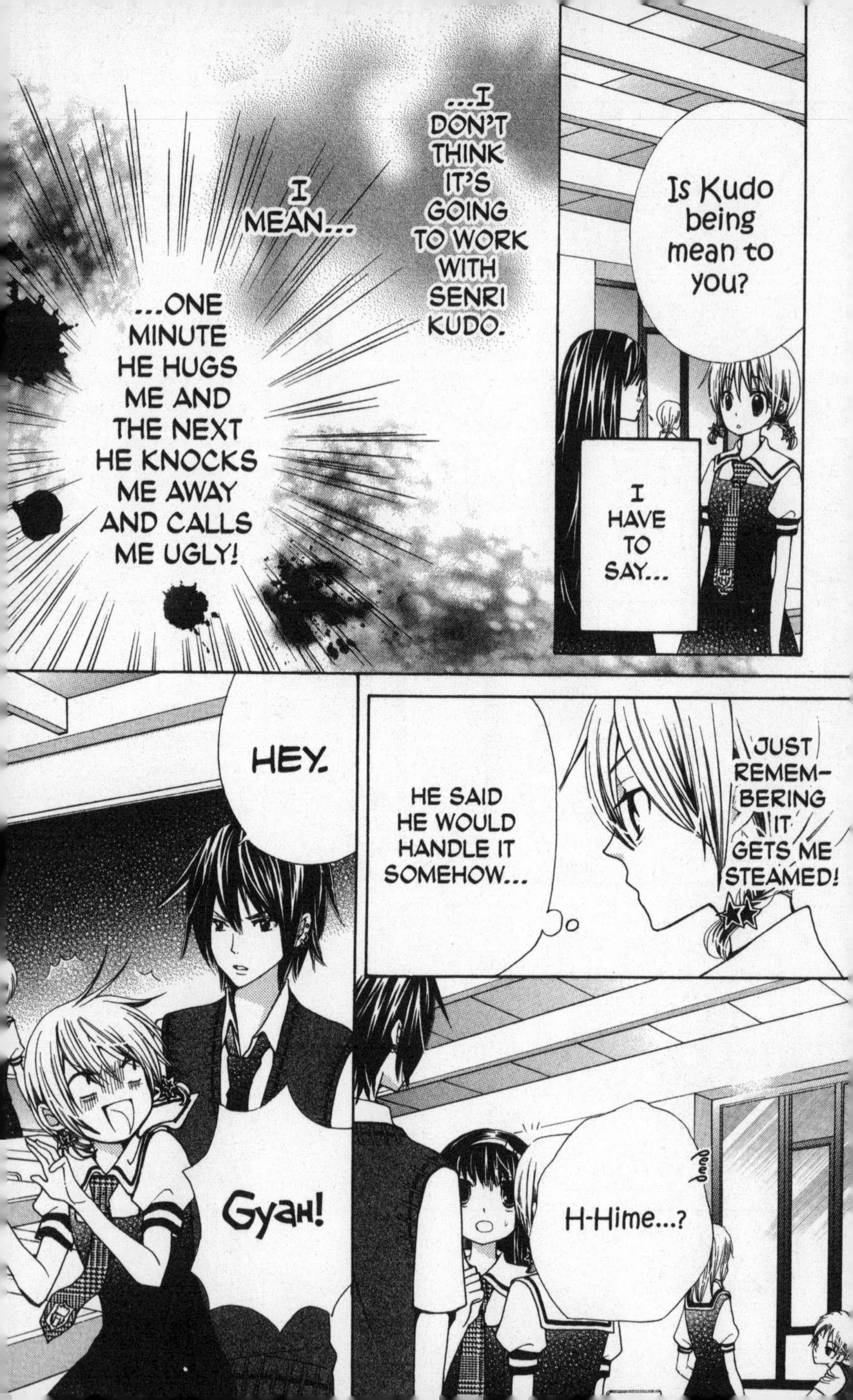
Is Kudo being mean to you?
I HAVE TO SAY...
...I DON'T THINK IT'S GOING TO WORK WITH SENRI KUDO.
I MEAN...
...ONE MINUTE HE HUGS ME AND THE NEXT HE KNOCKS ME AWAY AND CALLS ME UGLY!
JUST REMEMBERING IT GETS ME STEAMED!
HE SAID HE WOULD HANDLE IT SOMEHOW...
H-Hime...?
HEY.
Gyah!

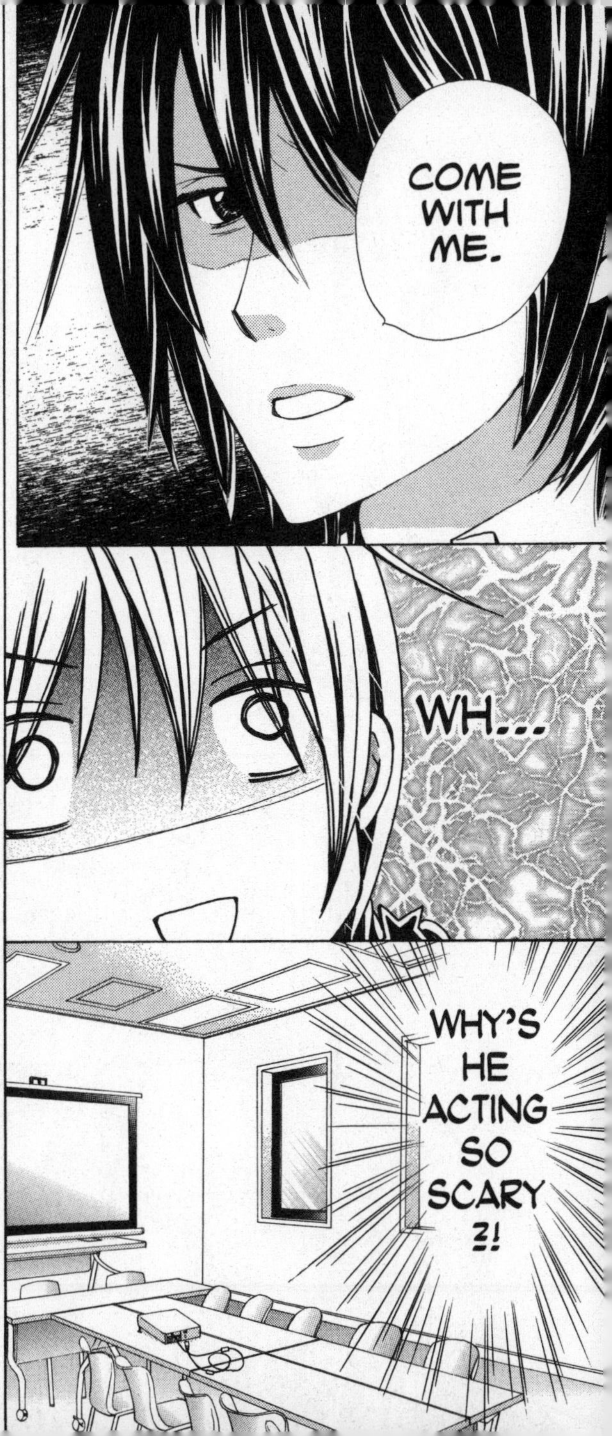
COME WITH ME.
WH...
WHY'S HE ACTING SO SCARY ?!

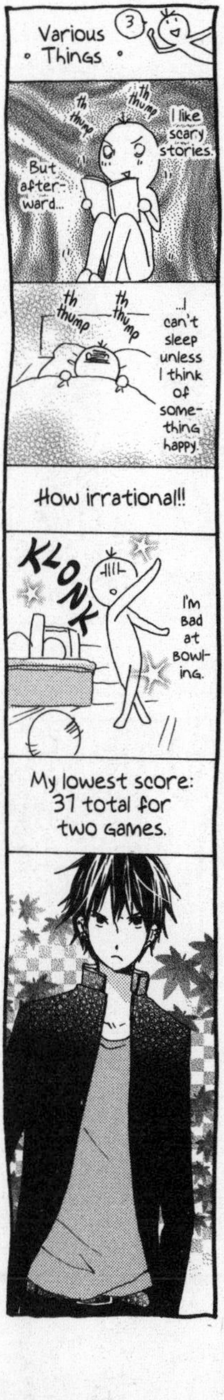
Various Things
3
I like scary stories.
th thump
th thump
But afterward...
th thump
th thump
...I can't sleep unless I think of something happy.
How irrational!!
KLONK
I'm bad at bowling.
My lowest score: 37 total for two games.

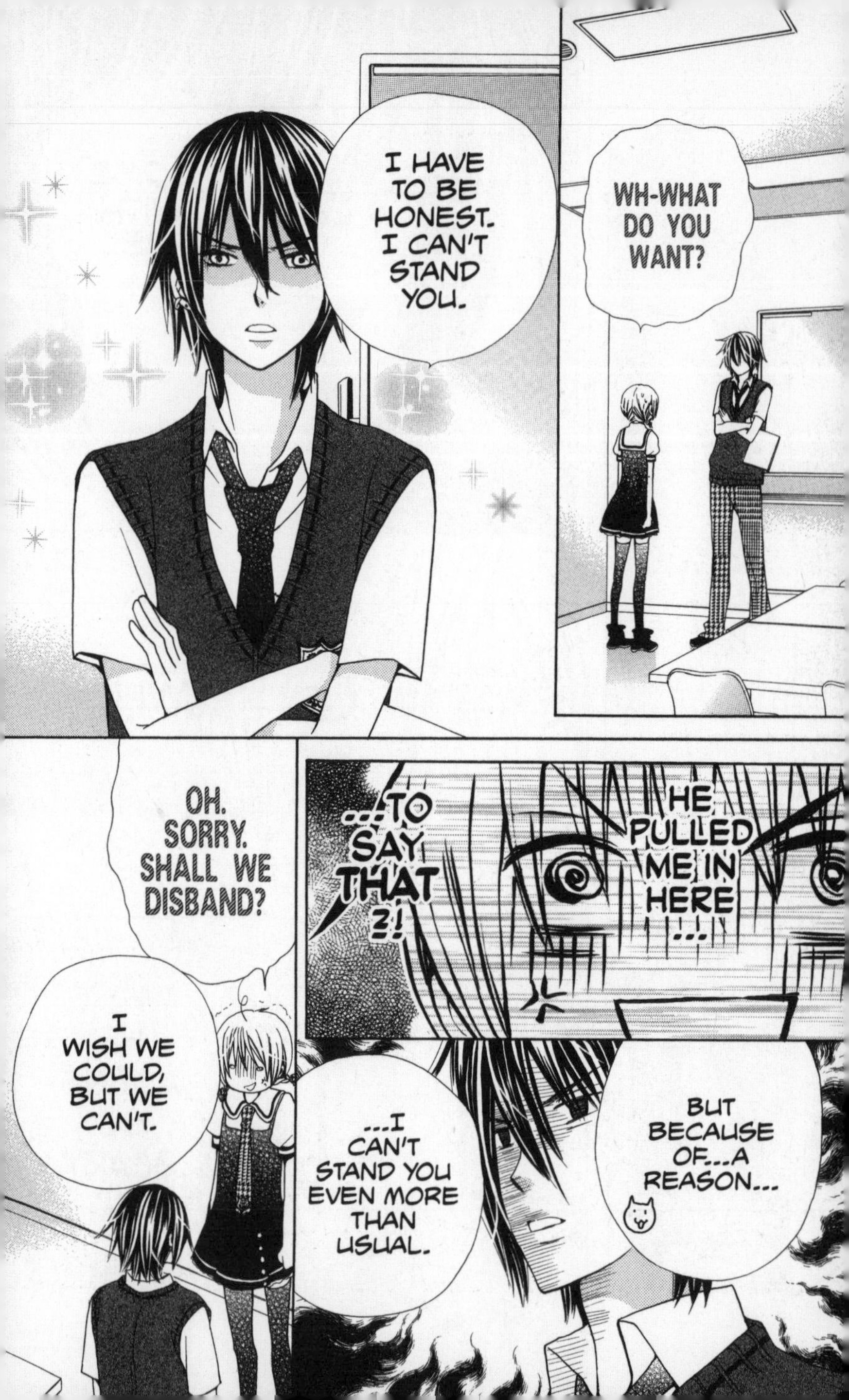
WH-WHAT DO YOU WANT?
I HAVE TO BE HONEST. I CAN'T STAND YOU.
HE PULLED ME IN HERE...
...TO SAY THAT?!
BUT BECAUSE OF...A REASON...
...I CAN'T STAND YOU EVEN MORE THAN USUAL.
OH. SORRY. SHALL WE DISBAND?
I WISH WE COULD, BUT WE CAN'T.

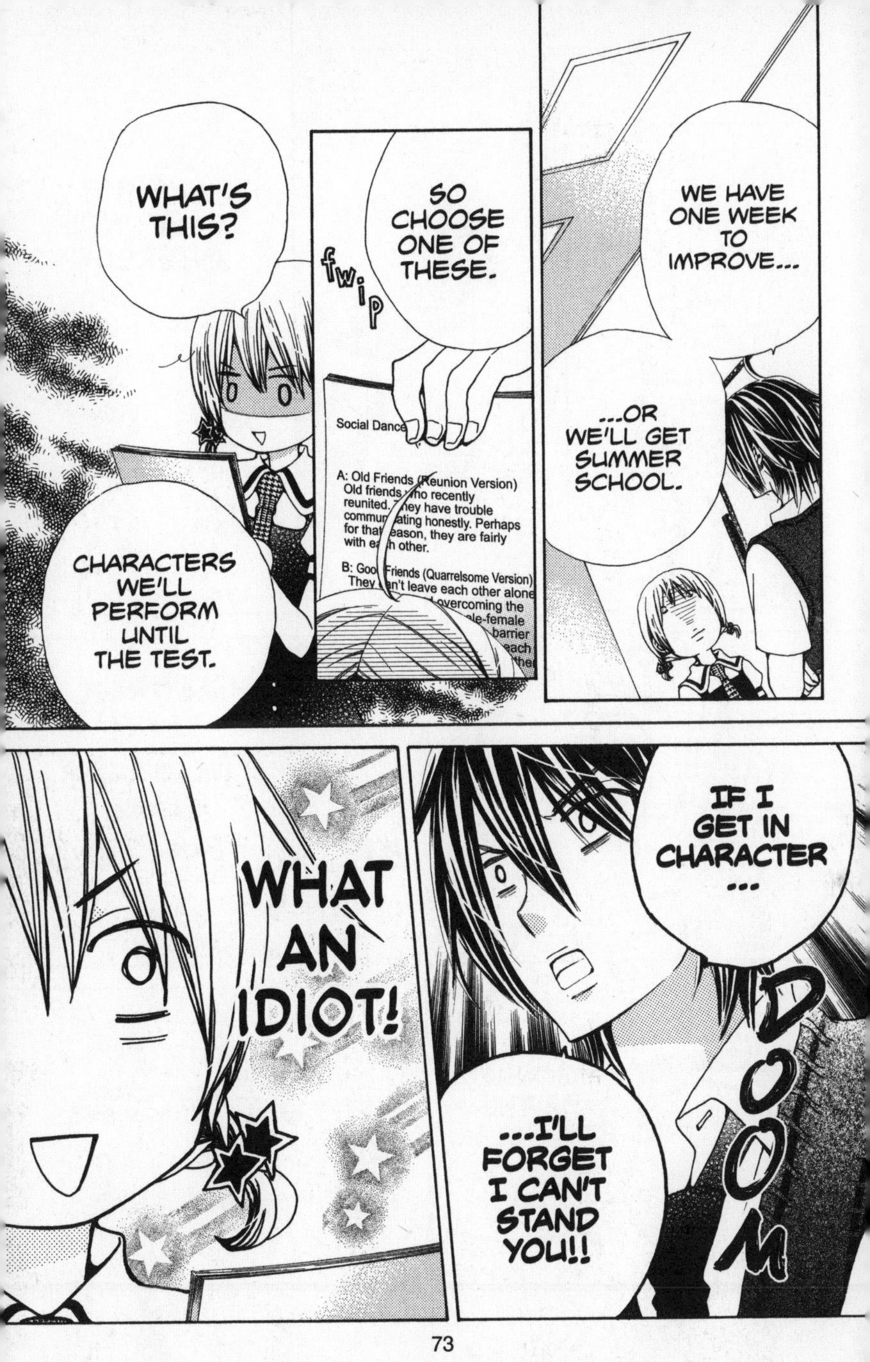
WE HAVE ONE WEEK TO IMPROVE...
...OR WE'LL GET SUMMER SCHOOL.
SO CHOOSE ONE OF THESE.
fwip
Social Dance
A: Old Friends (Reunion Version)
Old friends who recently reunited. They have trouble communicating honestly. Perhaps for that reason, they are fairly with each other.
B: Good Friends (Quarrelsome Version)
They can't leave each other alone
overcoming the
ale-female
barrier
WHAT'S THIS?
CHARACTERS WE'LL PERFORM UNTIL THE TEST.
IF I GET IN CHARACTER...
...I'LL FORGET I CAN'T STAND YOU!!
DOOOM
WHAT AN IDIOT!

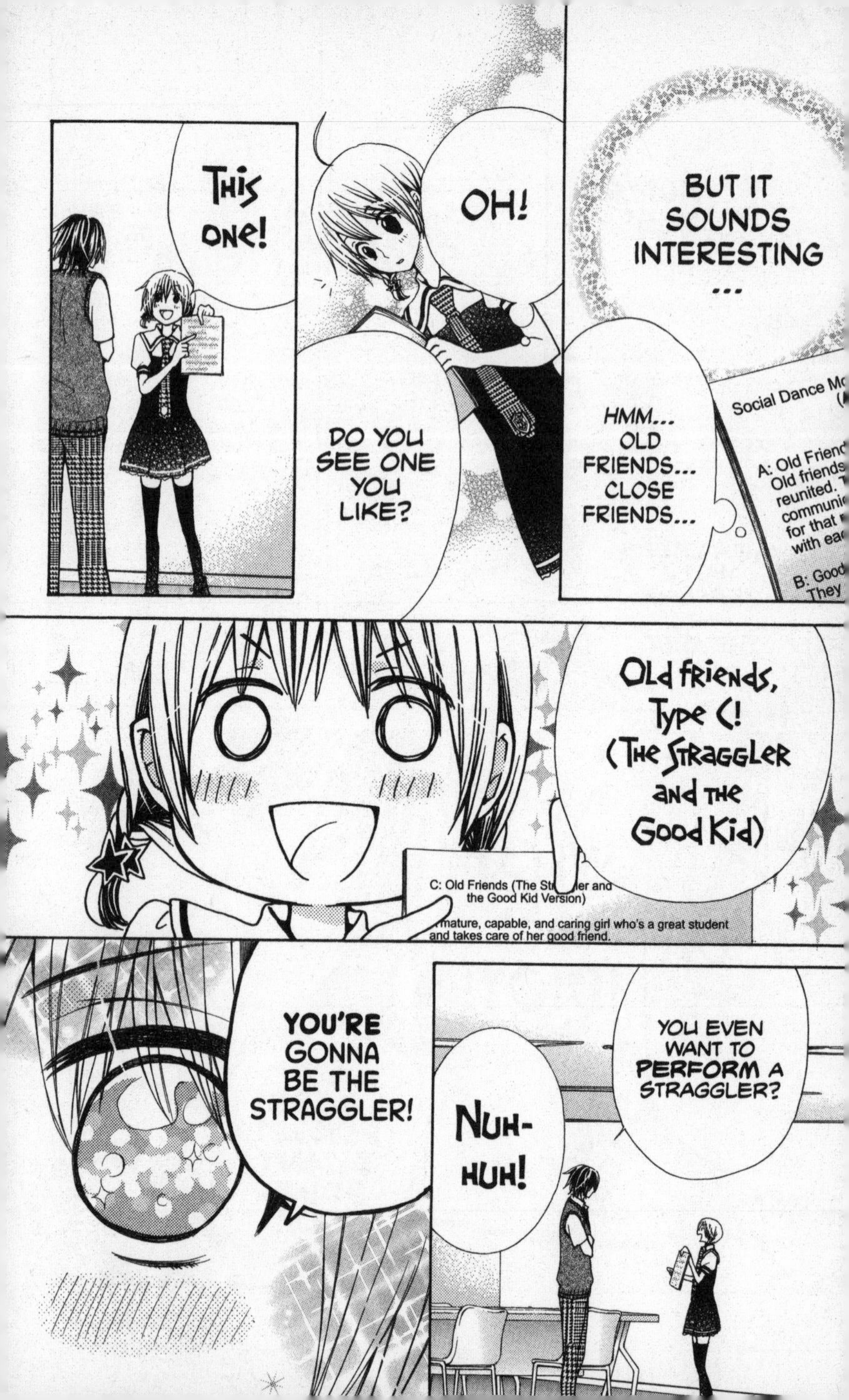
BUT IT SOUNDS INTERESTING...
HMM... OLD FRIENDS... CLOSE FRIENDS...
OH!
DO YOU SEE ONE YOU LIKE?
THIS ONE!
Old friends, Type C! (The Straggler and the Good Kid)
mature, capable, and caring girl who's a great student and takes care of her good friend.
YOU EVEN WANT TO PERFORM A STRAGGLER?
NUH-HUH!
YOU'RE GONNA BE THE STRAGGLER!

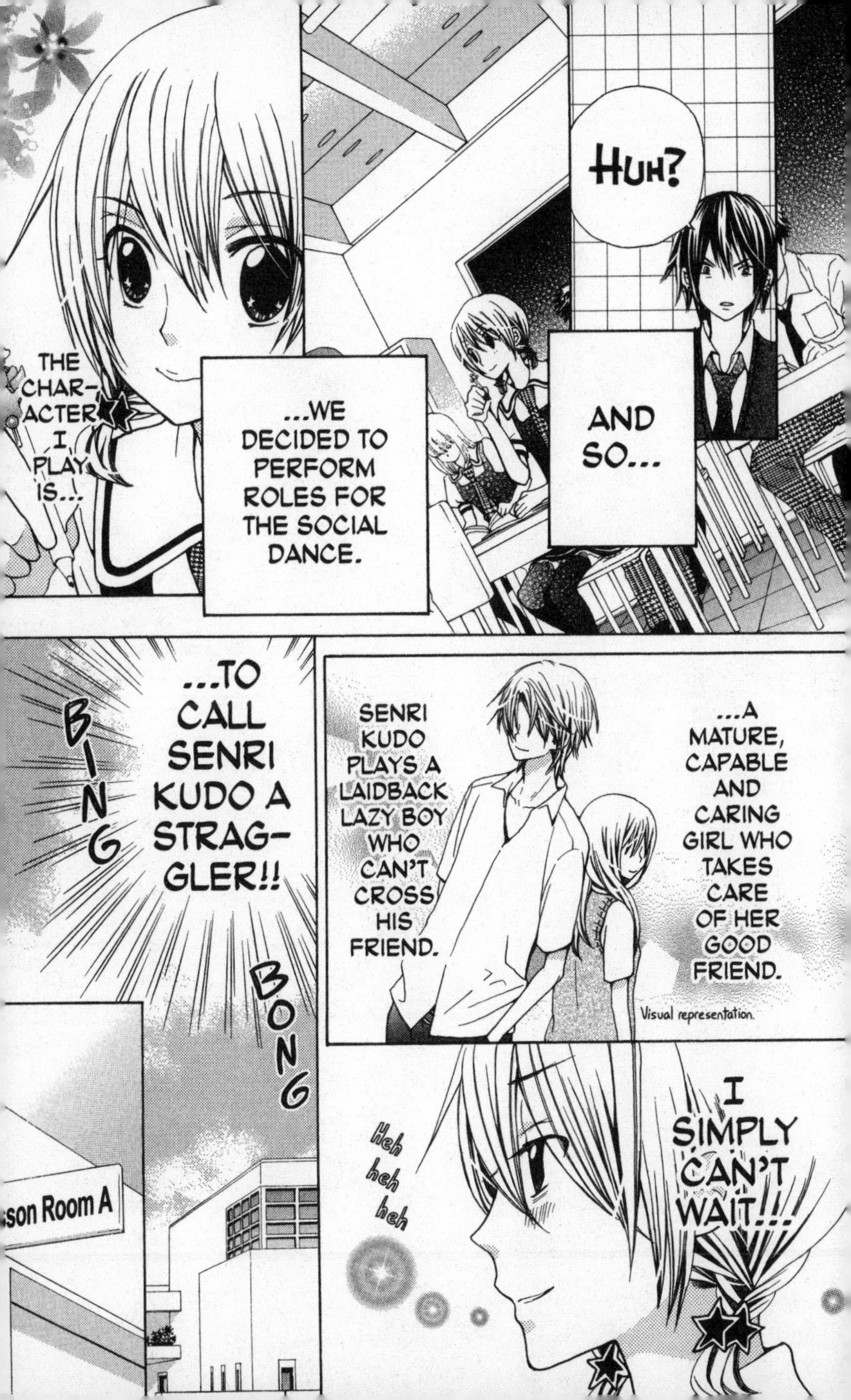
HUH?
AND SO...
...WE DECIDED TO PERFORM ROLES FOR THE SOCIAL DANCE.
THE CHARACTER I PLAY IS...
...A MATURE, CAPABLE AND CARING GIRL WHO TAKES CARE OF HER GOOD FRIEND.
SENRI KUDO PLAYS A LAIDBACK LAZY BOY WHO CAN'T CROSS HIS FRIEND.
Visual representation.
...TO CALL SENRI KUDO A STRAGGLER!!
BING
BONG
I SIMPLY CAN'T WAIT!!
Heh heh heh
sson Room A

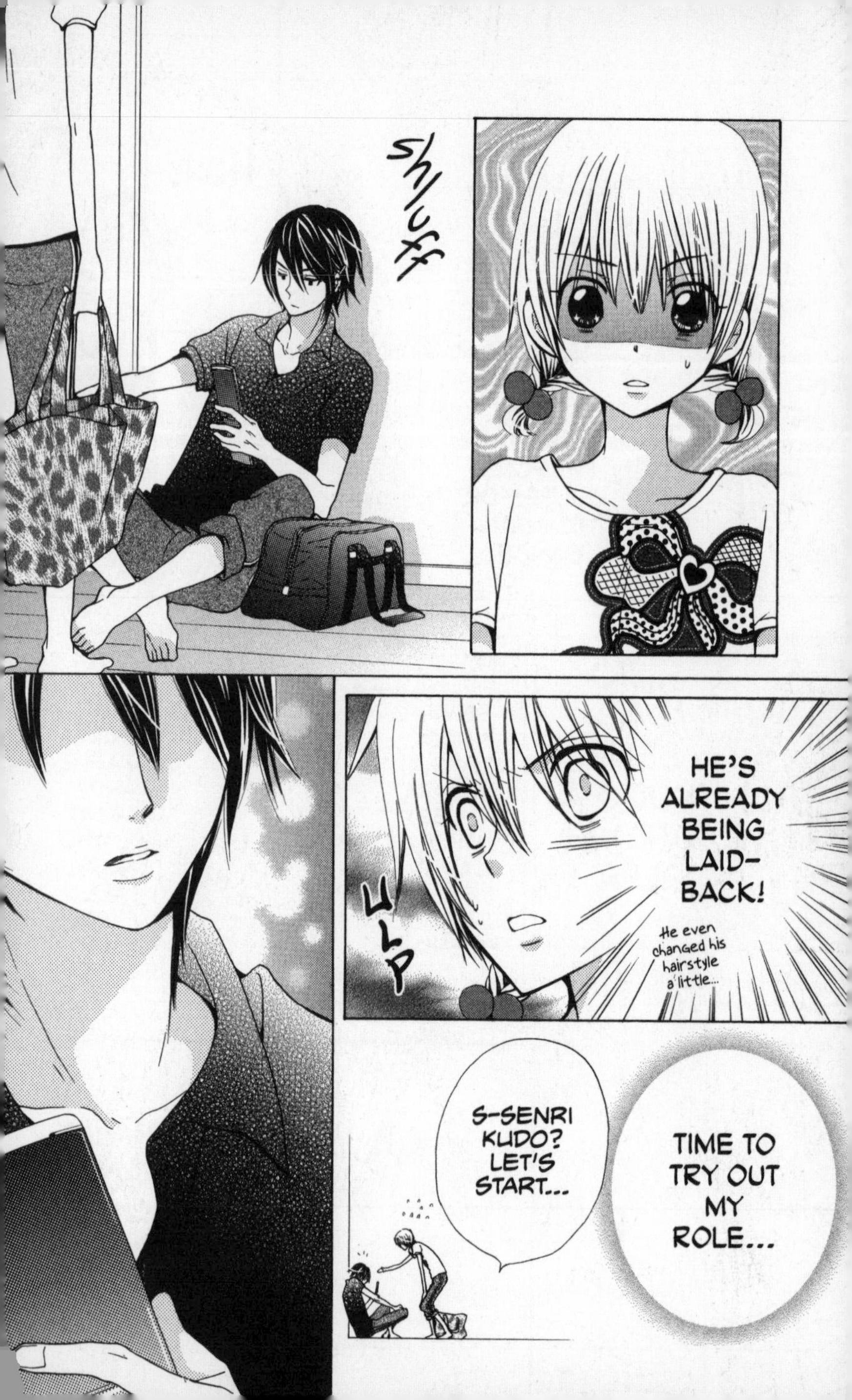
shluff
HE'S ALREADY BEING LAID-BACK!
He even changed his hairstyle a little...
ULP
TIME TO TRY OUT MY ROLE...
S-SENRI KUDO? LET'S START...

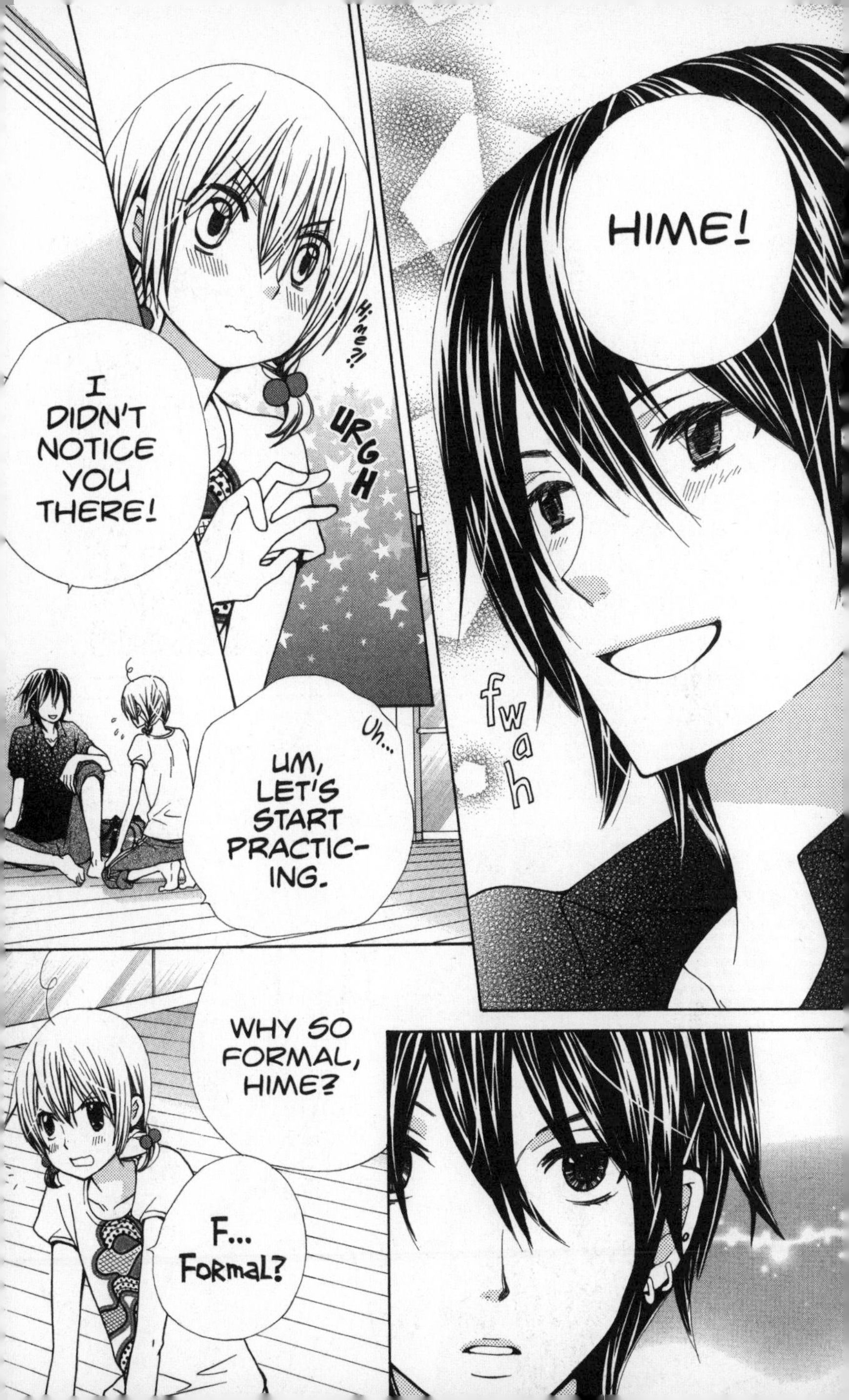
HIME!
fwah
Hime?!
URGH
I DIDN'T NOTICE YOU THERE!
Uh...
UM, LET'S START PRACTICING.
WHY SO FORMAL, HIME?
F... Formal?

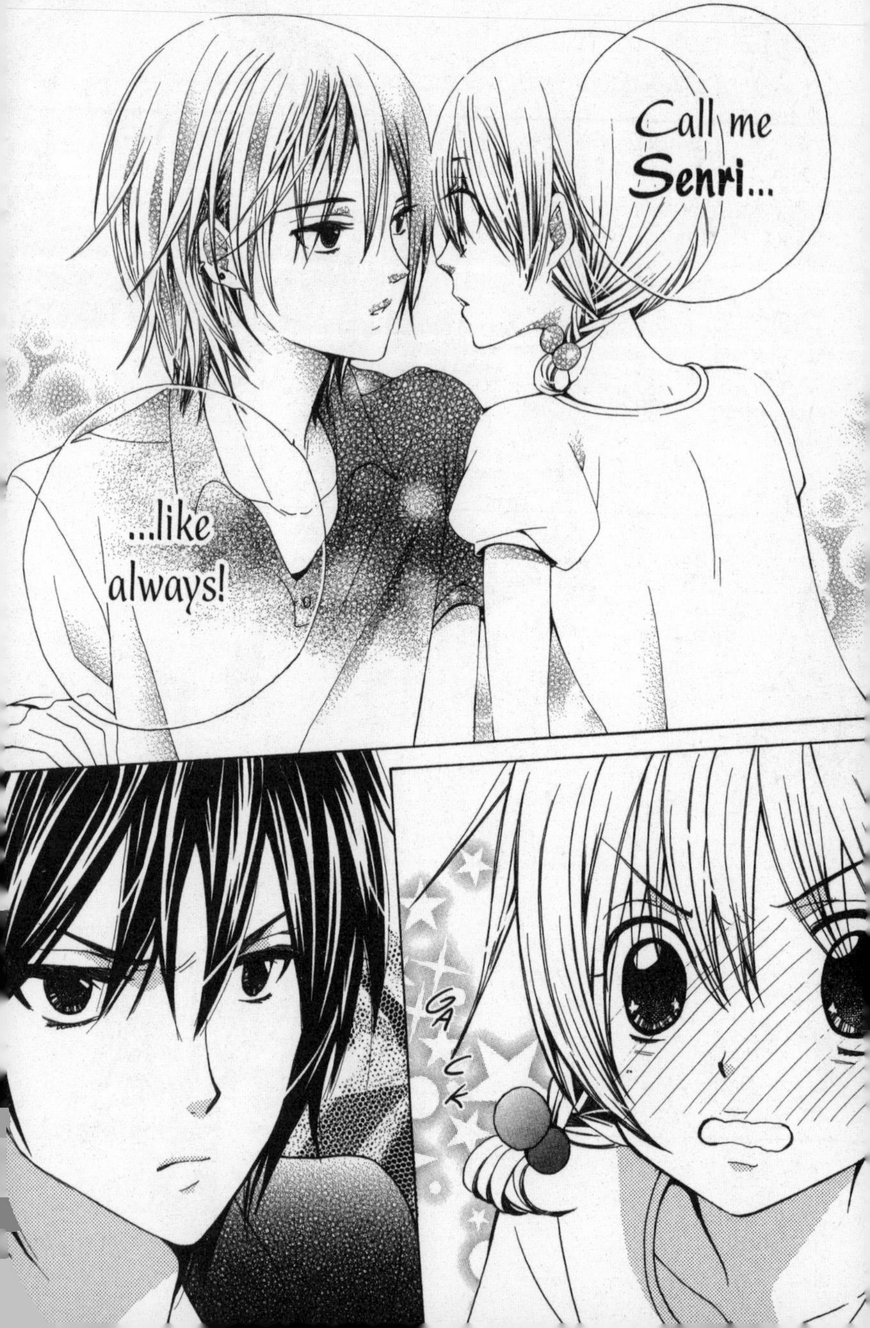
Call me Senri...
...like always!
GACK

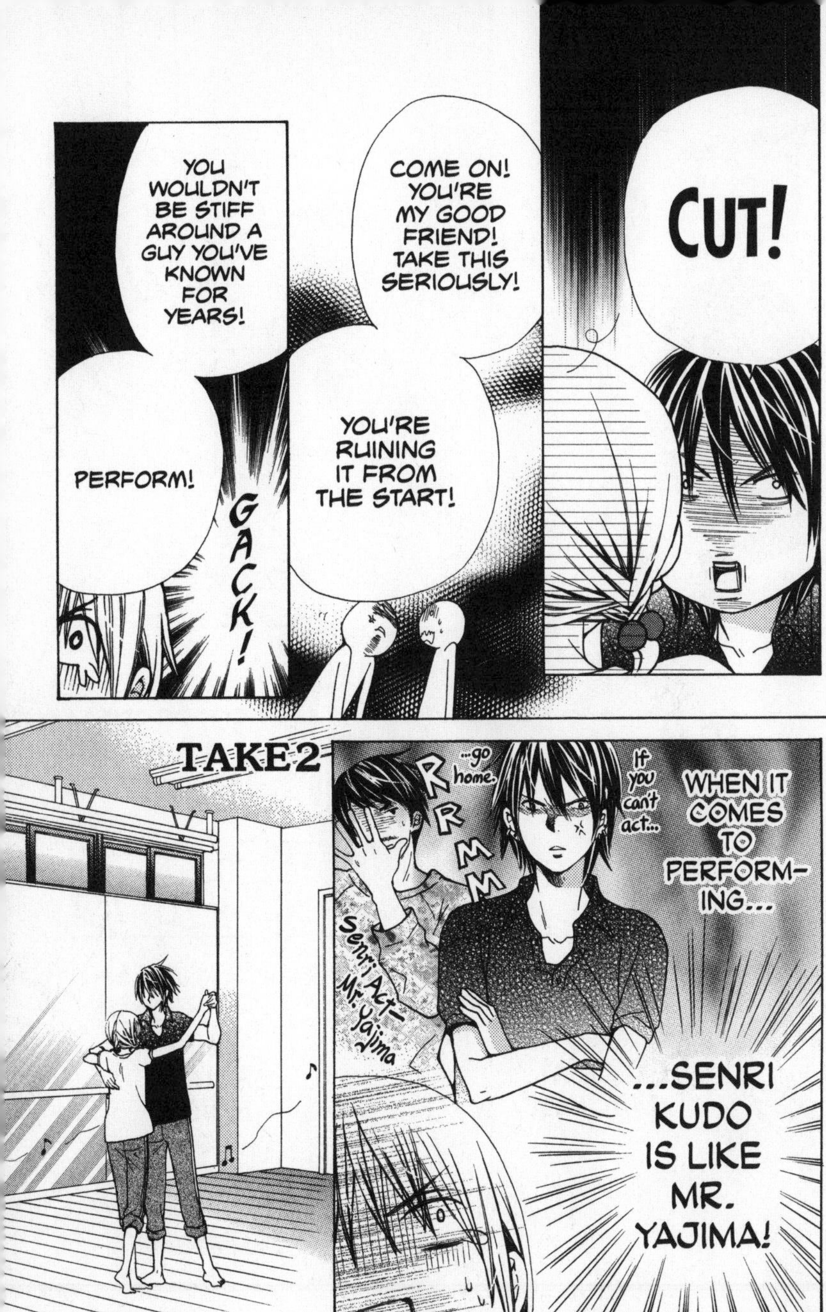
CUT!
COME ON! YOU'RE MY GOOD FRIEND! TAKE THIS SERIOUSLY!
YOU'RE RUINING IT FROM THE START!
YOU WOULDN'T BE STIFF AROUND A GUY YOU'VE KNOWN FOR YEARS!
PERFORM!
GACK!
WHEN IT COMES TO PERFORMING...
If you can't act...
...go home.
RRMMM
Senri Act-Mr. Yajima
...SENRI KUDO IS LIKE MR. YAJIMA!
TAKE 2

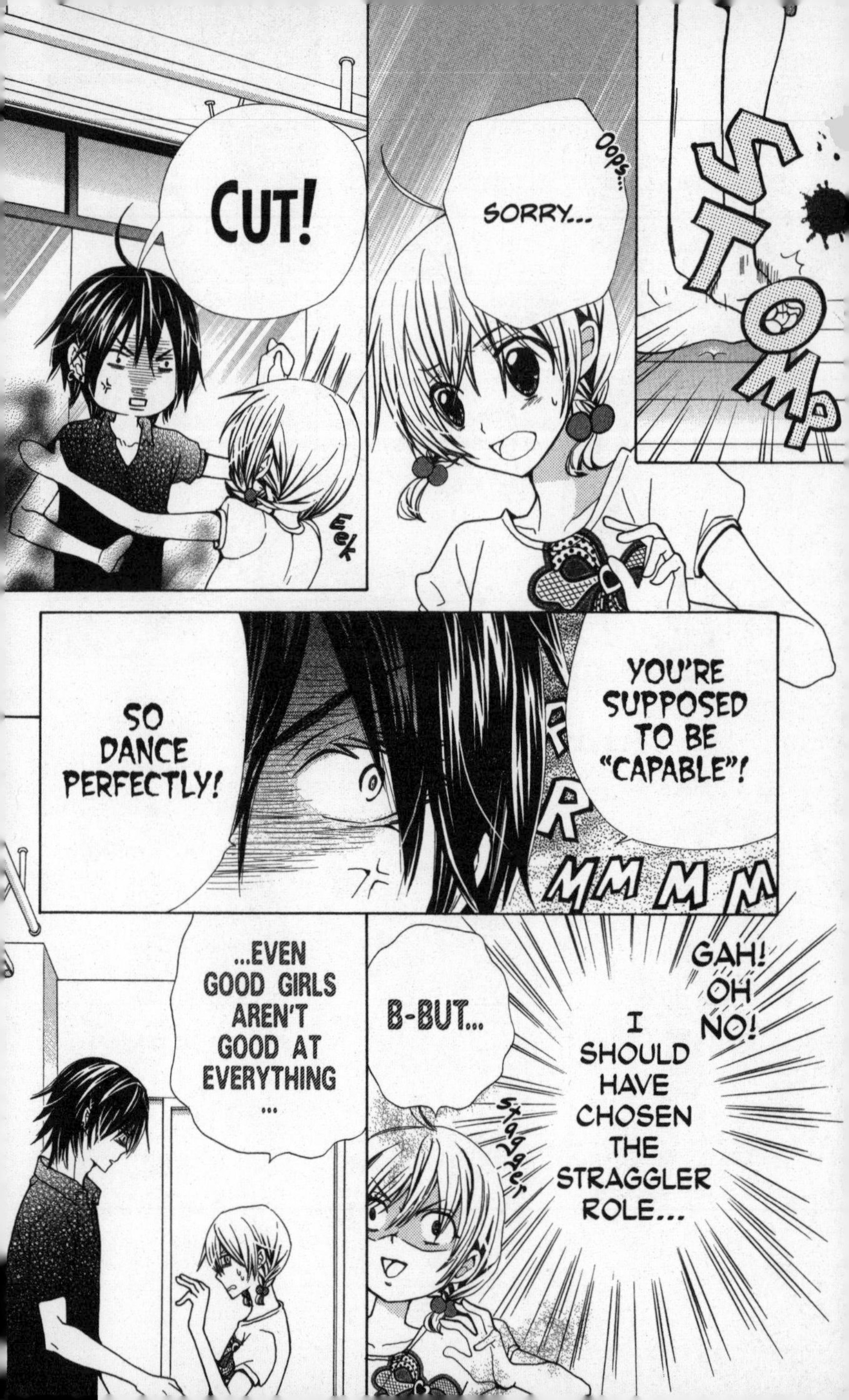
STOMP
Oops...
SORRY...
CUT!
Eek
YOU'RE SUPPOSED TO BE "CAPABLE"!
RRMMMMM
SO DANCE PERFECTLY!
GAH! OH NO!
B-BUT...
I SHOULD HAVE CHOSEN THE STRAGGLER ROLE...
stagger
...EVEN GOOD GIRLS AREN'T GOOD AT EVERYTHING...

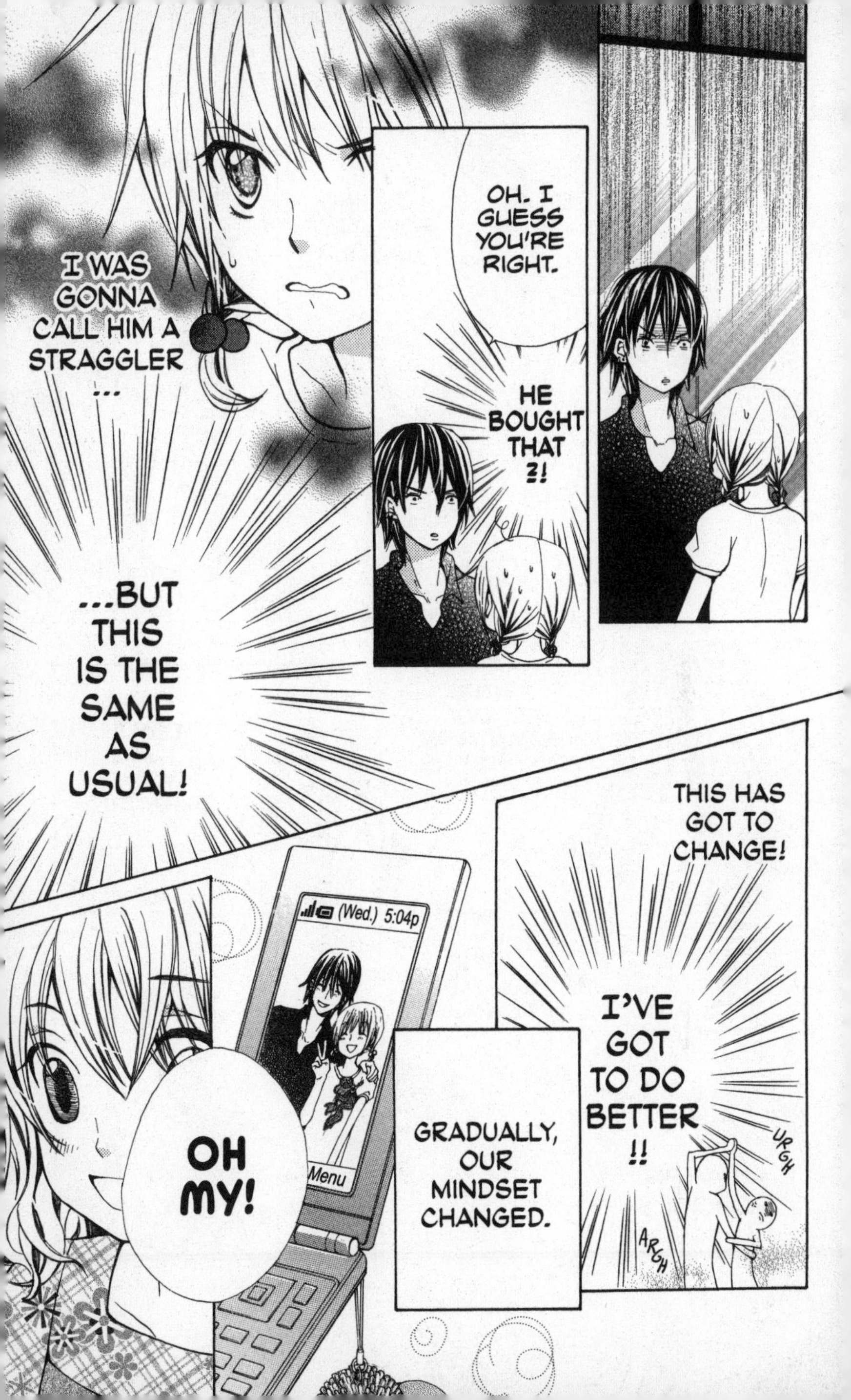
OH. I GUESS YOU'RE RIGHT.
HE BOUGHT THAT ?!
I WAS GONNA CALL HIM A STRAGGLER ...
...BUT THIS IS THE SAME AS USUAL!
THIS HAS GOT TO CHANGE!
I'VE GOT TO DO BETTER !!
URGH
ARGH
GRADUALLY, OUR MINDSET CHANGED.
(Wed.) 5:04p
Menu
OH MY!

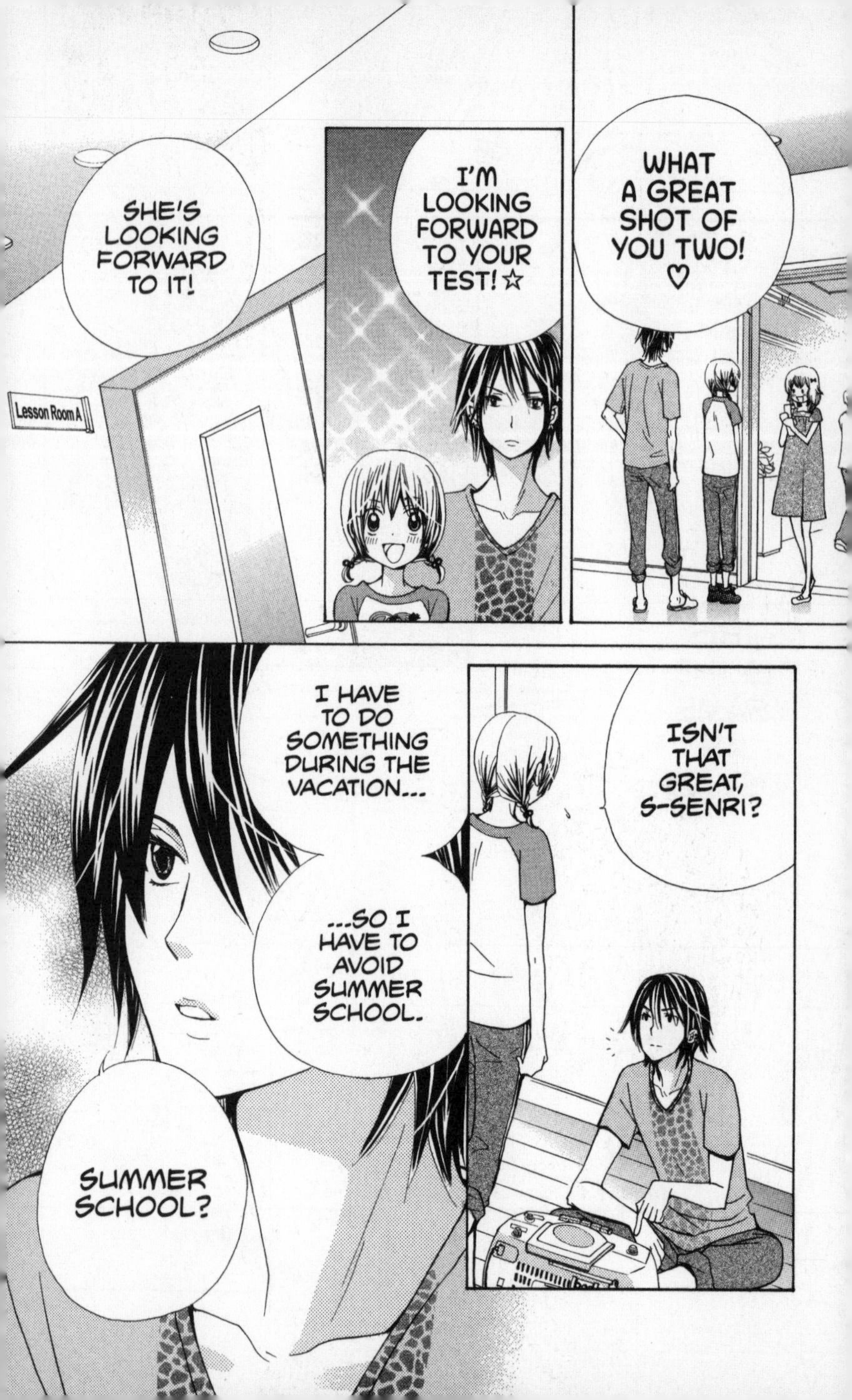
WHAT A GREAT SHOT OF YOU TWO! ♡
I'M LOOKING FORWARD TO YOUR TEST! ☆
SHE'S LOOKING FORWARD TO IT!
Lesson Room A
ISN'T THAT GREAT, S-SENRI?
I HAVE TO DO SOMETHING DURING THE VACATION...
...SO I HAVE TO AVOID SUMMER SCHOOL.
SUMMER SCHOOL?

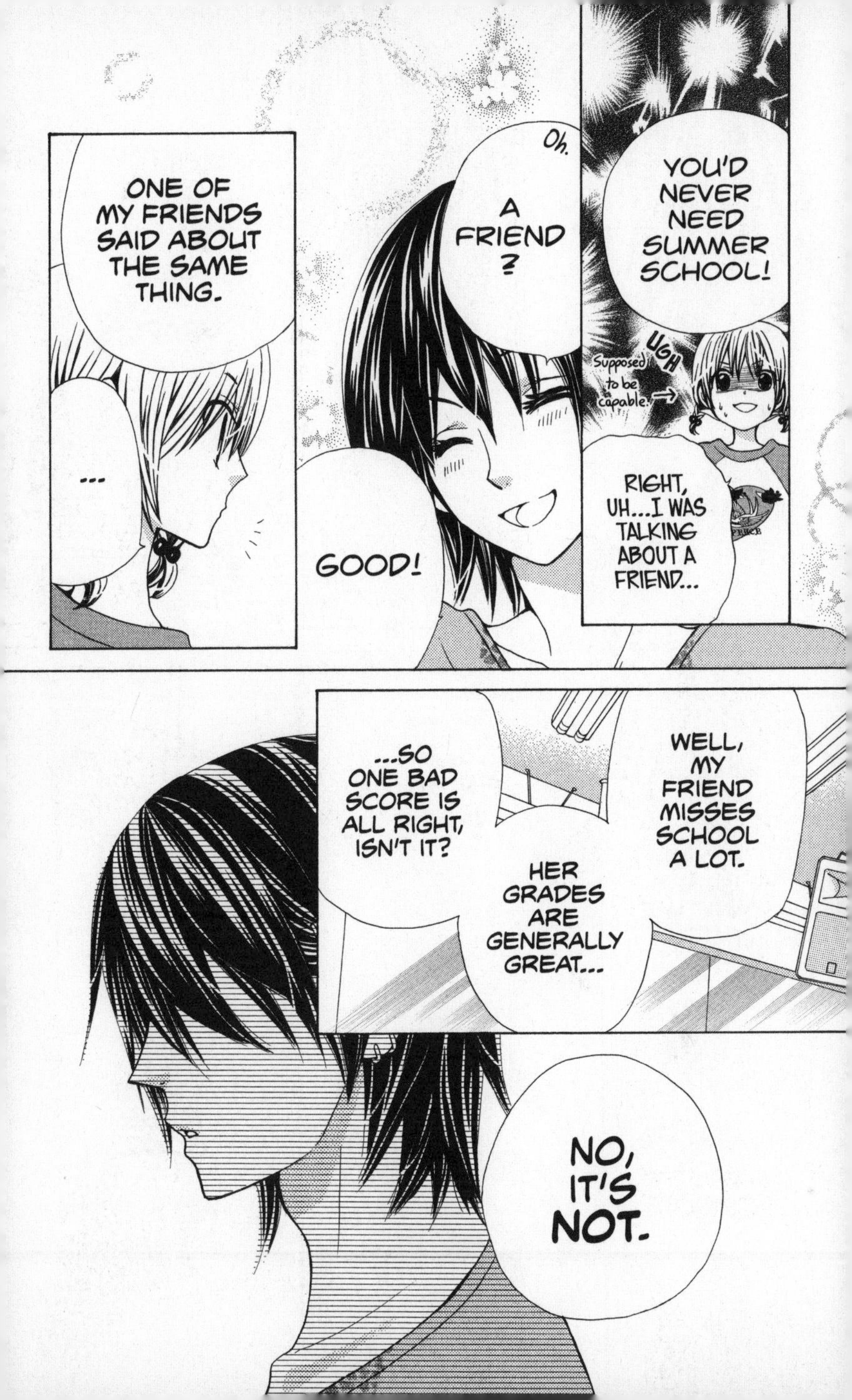
YOU'D NEVER NEED SUMMER SCHOOL!
UGH
Supposed to be capable.
RIGHT, UH...I WAS TALKING ABOUT A FRIEND...
Oh.
A FRIEND?
GOOD!
ONE OF MY FRIENDS SAID ABOUT THE SAME THING.
...
WELL, MY FRIEND MISSES SCHOOL A LOT.
HER GRADES ARE GENERALLY GREAT...
...SO ONE BAD SCORE IS ALL RIGHT, ISN'T IT?
NO, IT'S NOT.

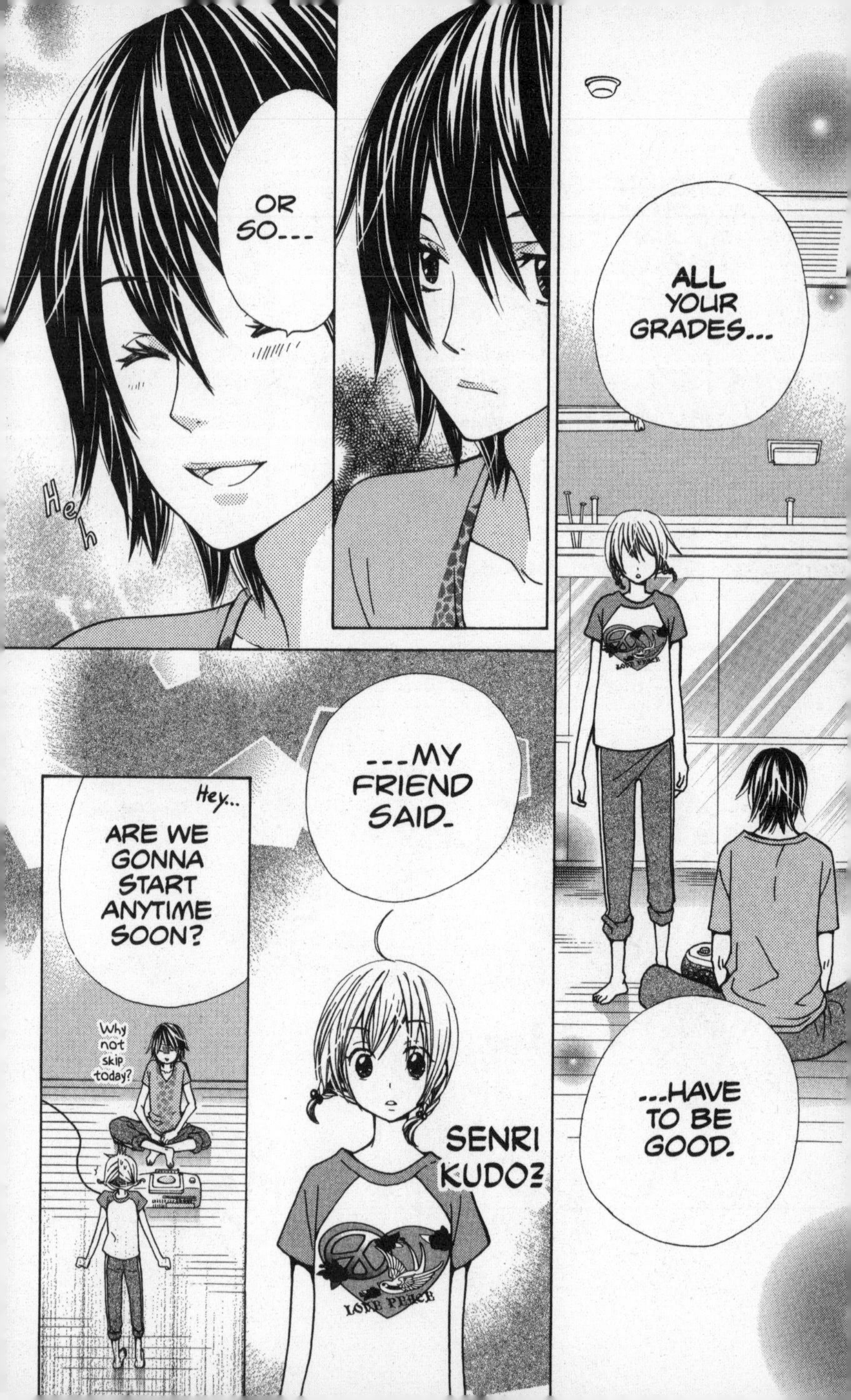
ALL YOUR GRADES...
...HAVE TO BE GOOD.
OR SO...
Heh
...MY FRIEND SAID.
SENRI KUDO?
Hey...
ARE WE GONNA START ANYTIME SOON?
Why not skip today?

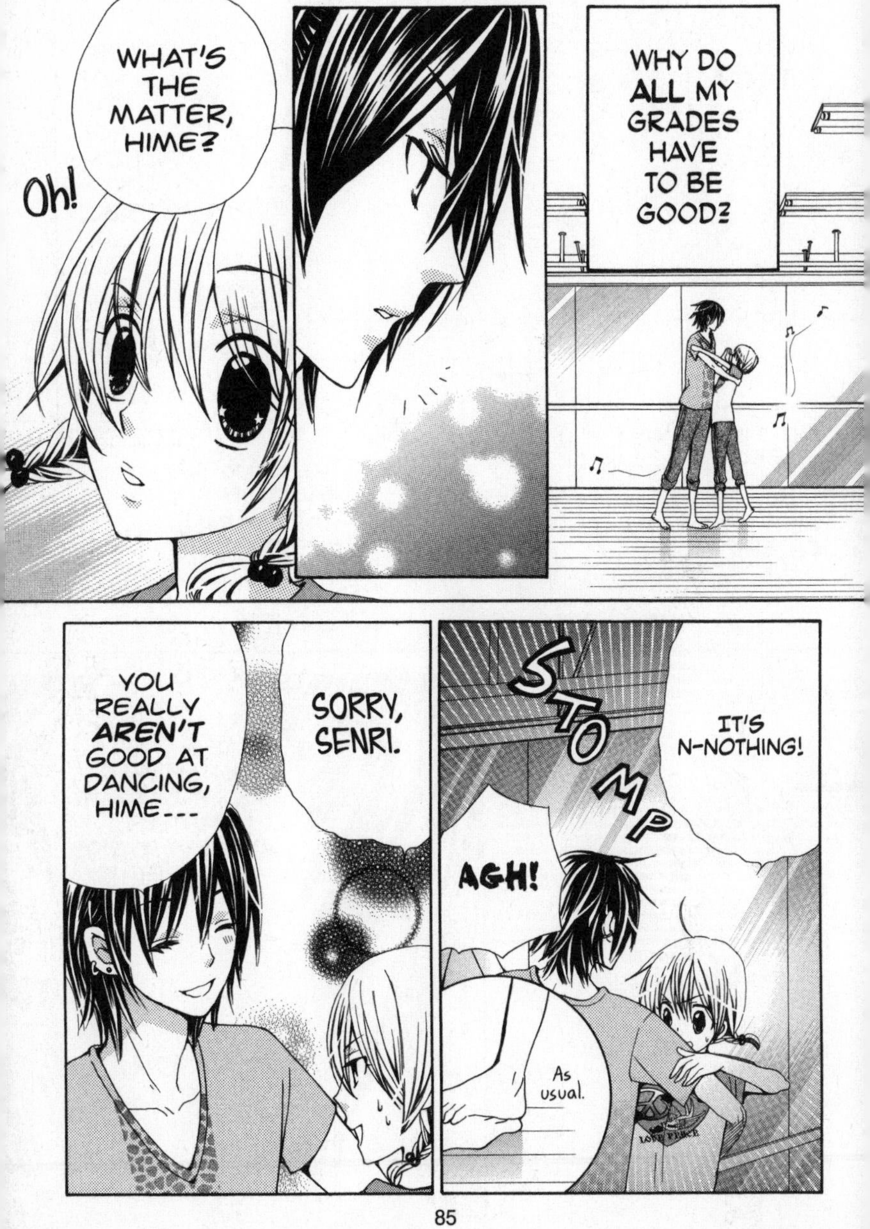
WHY DO ALL MY GRADES HAVE TO BE GOOD?
WHAT'S THE MATTER, HIME?
Oh!
IT'S N-NOTHING!
STOMP
AGH!
As usual.
SORRY, SENRI.
YOU REALLY AREN'T GOOD AT DANCING, HIME...

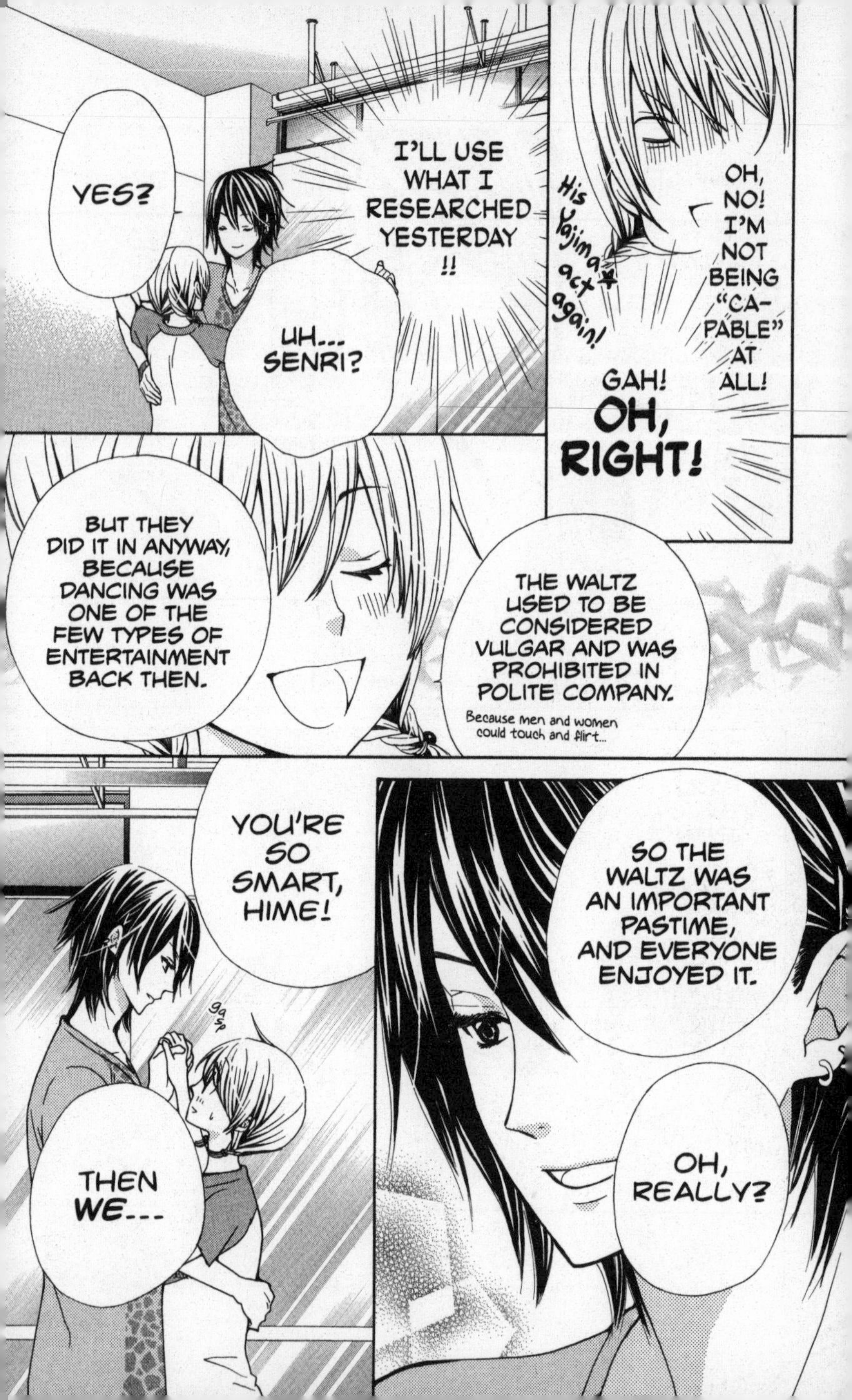
OH, NO! I'M NOT BEING "CAPABLE" AT ALL!
His Yajima act again!
GAH! OH, RIGHT!
I'LL USE WHAT I RESEARCHED YESTERDAY!!
UH... SENRI?
YES?
THE WALTZ USED TO BE CONSIDERED VULGAR AND WAS PROHIBITED IN POLITE COMPANY.
Because men and women could touch and flirt...
BUT THEY DID IT IN ANYWAY, BECAUSE DANCING WAS ONE OF THE FEW TYPES OF ENTERTAINMENT BACK THEN.
SO THE WALTZ WAS AN IMPORTANT PASTIME, AND EVERYONE ENJOYED IT.
OH, REALLY?
YOU'RE SO SMART, HIME!
gasp
THEN WE...

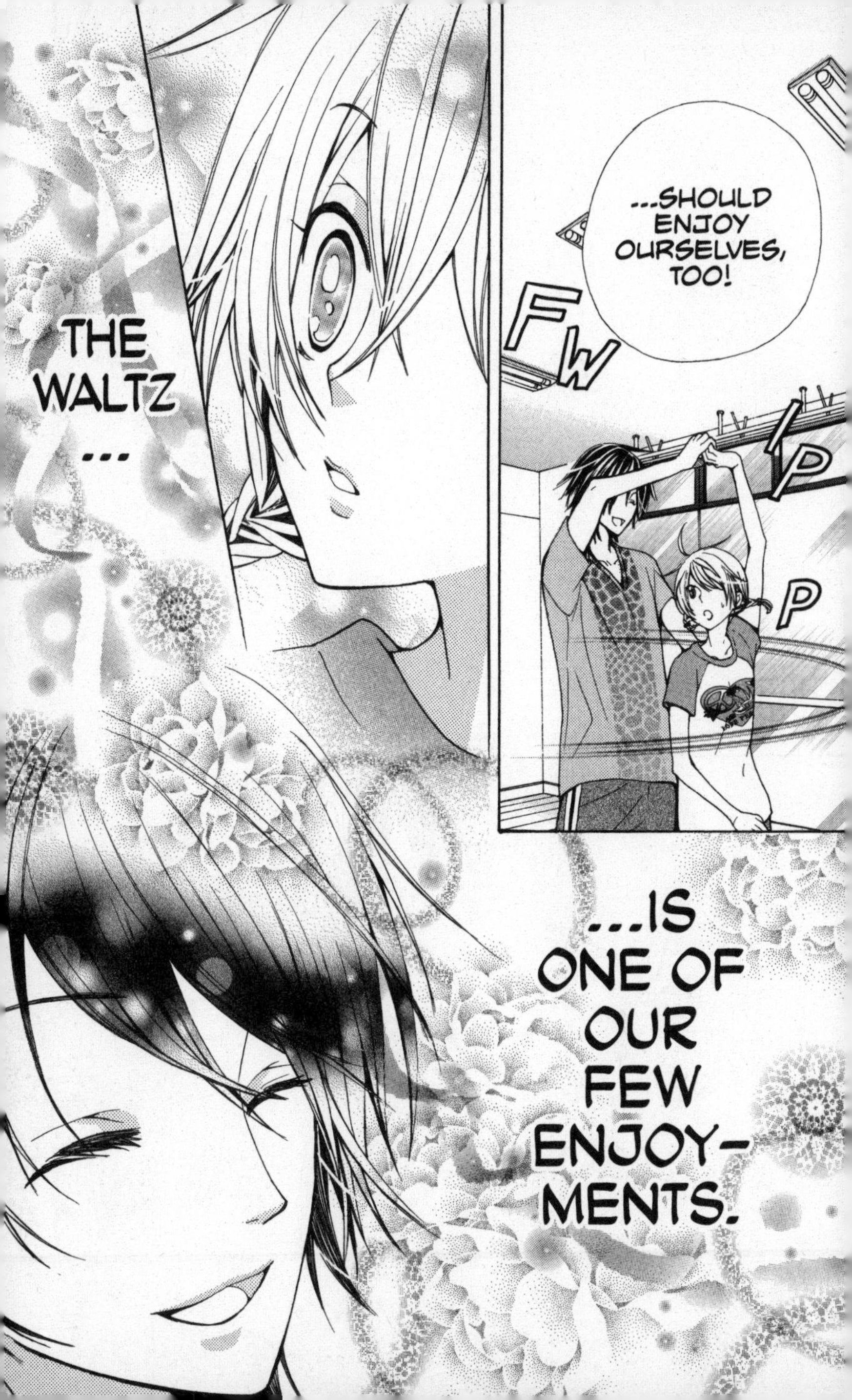
...SHOULD ENJOY OURSELVES, TOO!
FWIPP
THE WALTZ ...
...IS ONE OF OUR FEW ENJOY-MENTS.

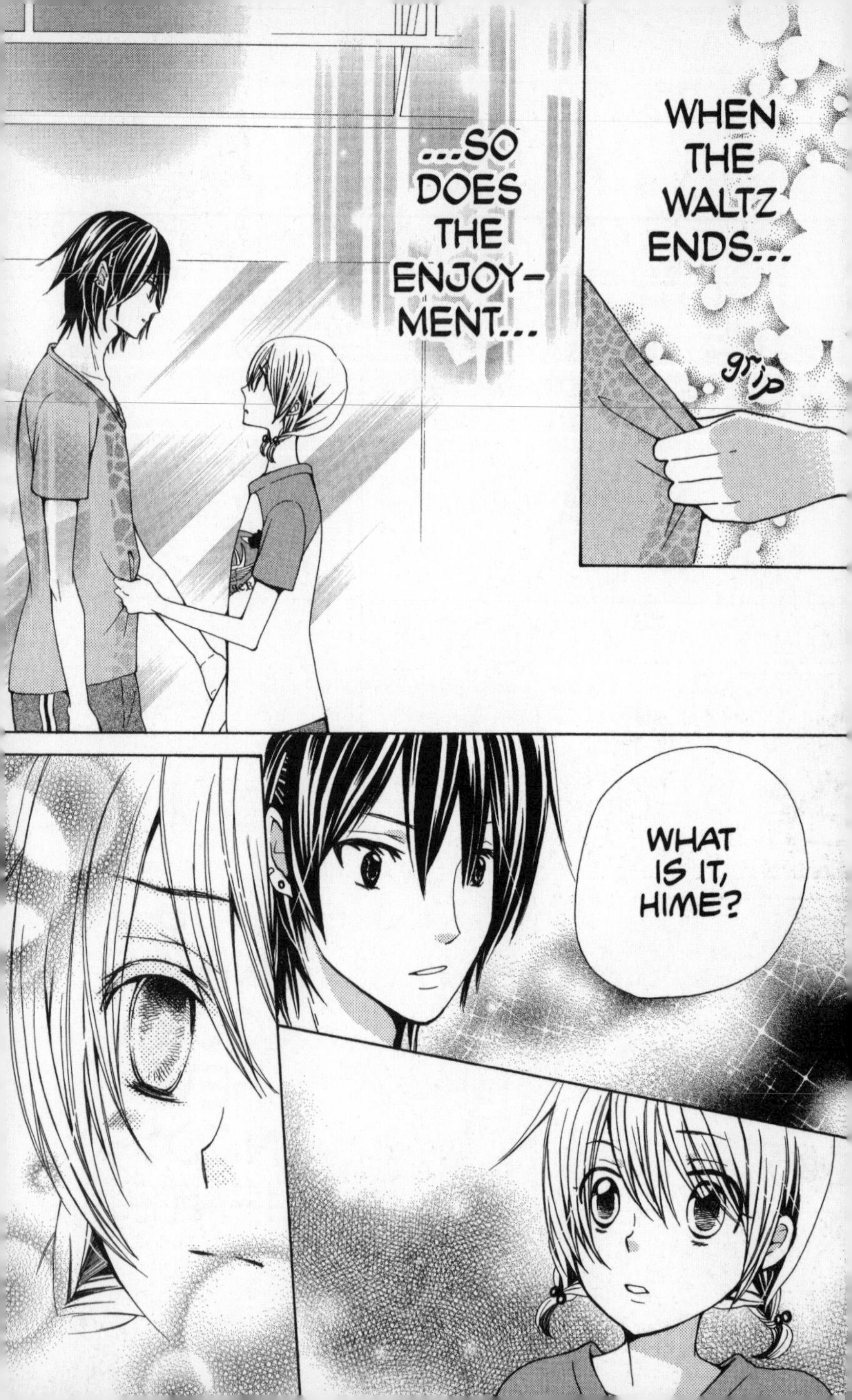
WHEN THE WALTZ ENDS...
grip
...SO DOES THE ENJOY-MENT...
WHAT IS IT, HIME?

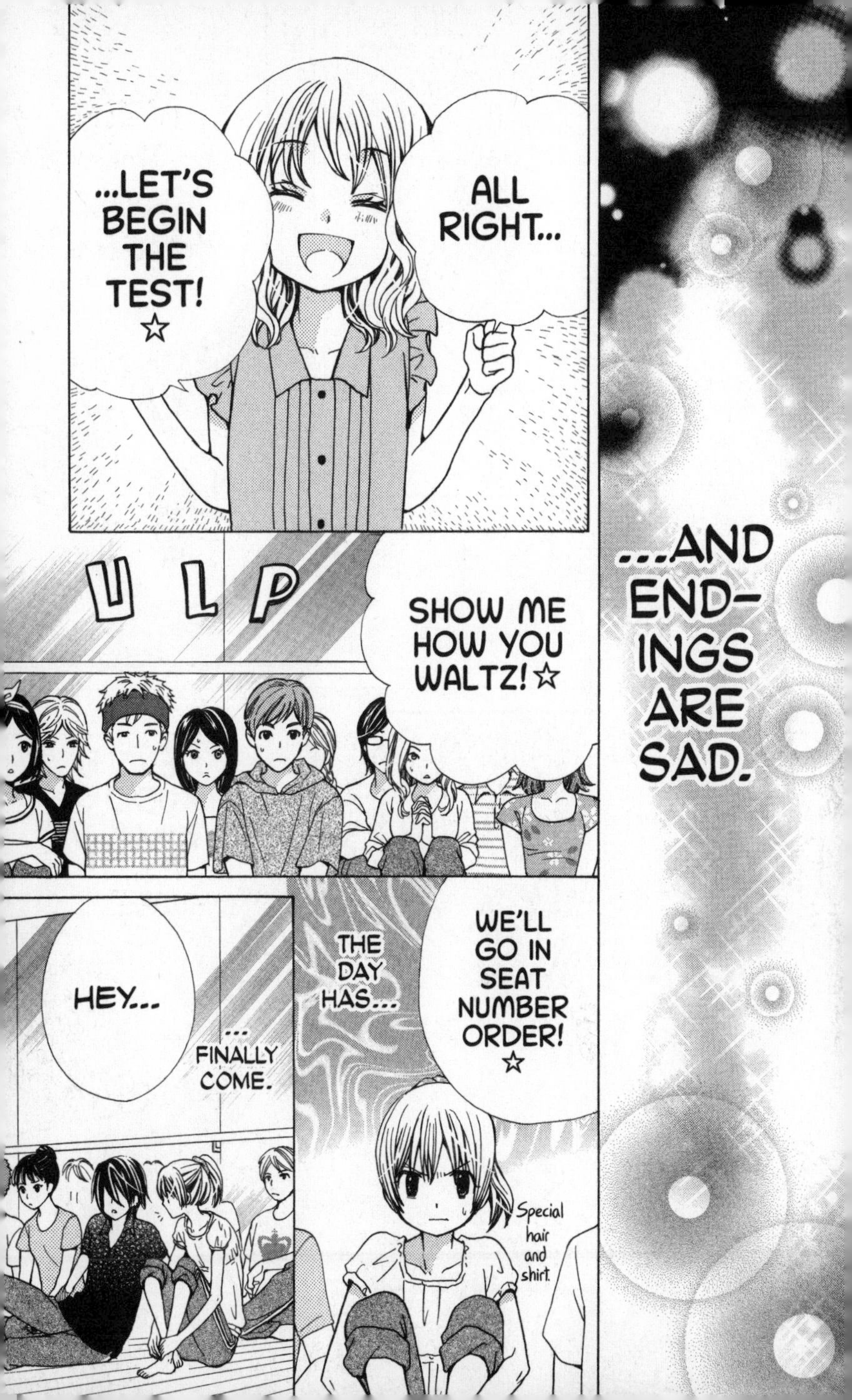
...AND END-INGS ARE SAD.
ALL RIGHT...
...LET'S BEGIN THE TEST! ☆
SHOW ME HOW YOU WALTZ! ☆
ULP
WE'LL GO IN SEAT NUMBER ORDER! ☆
THE DAY HAS...
Special hair and shirt.
...FINALLY COME.
HEY...

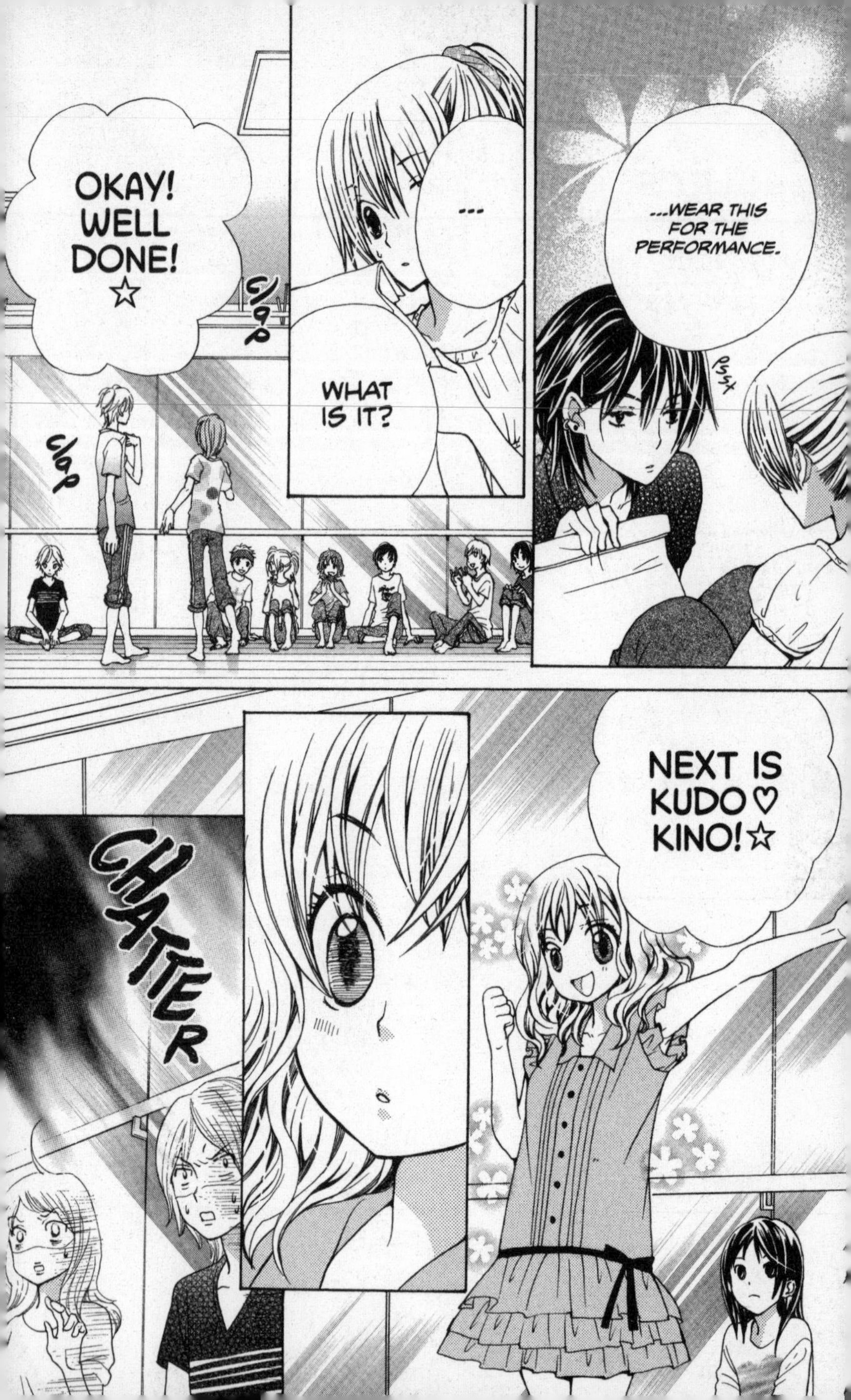
...WEAR THIS FOR THE PERFORMANCE.
pssst
...
WHAT IS IT?
OKAY! WELL DONE! ☆
clap
clap
NEXT IS KUDO ♡ KINO! ☆
CHATTER

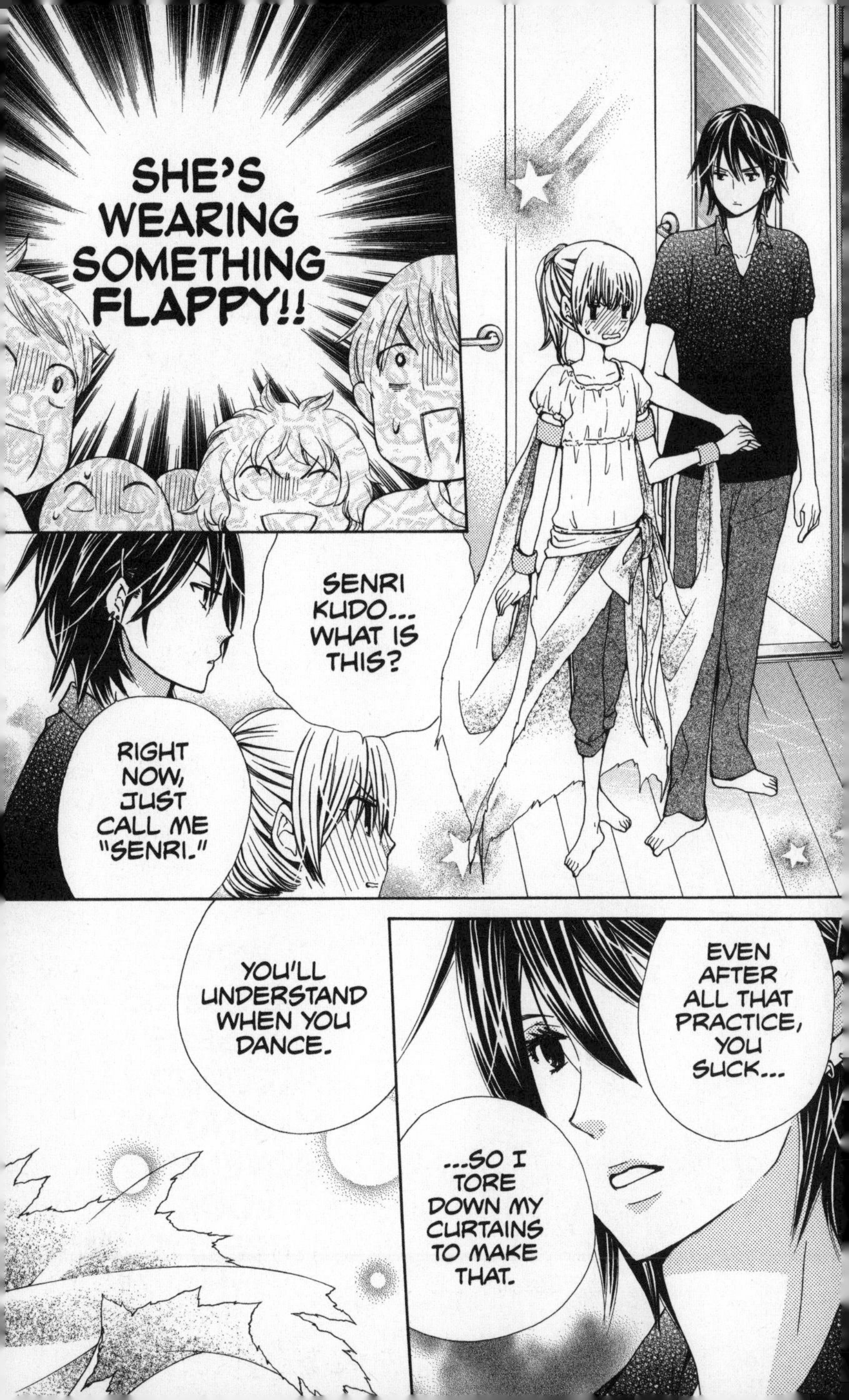
SHE'S WEARING SOMETHING FLAPPY!!
SENRI KUDO... WHAT IS THIS?
RIGHT NOW, JUST CALL ME "SENRI."
EVEN AFTER ALL THAT PRACTICE, YOU SUCK...
...SO I TORE DOWN MY CURTAINS TO MAKE THAT.
YOU'LL UNDERSTAND WHEN YOU DANCE.

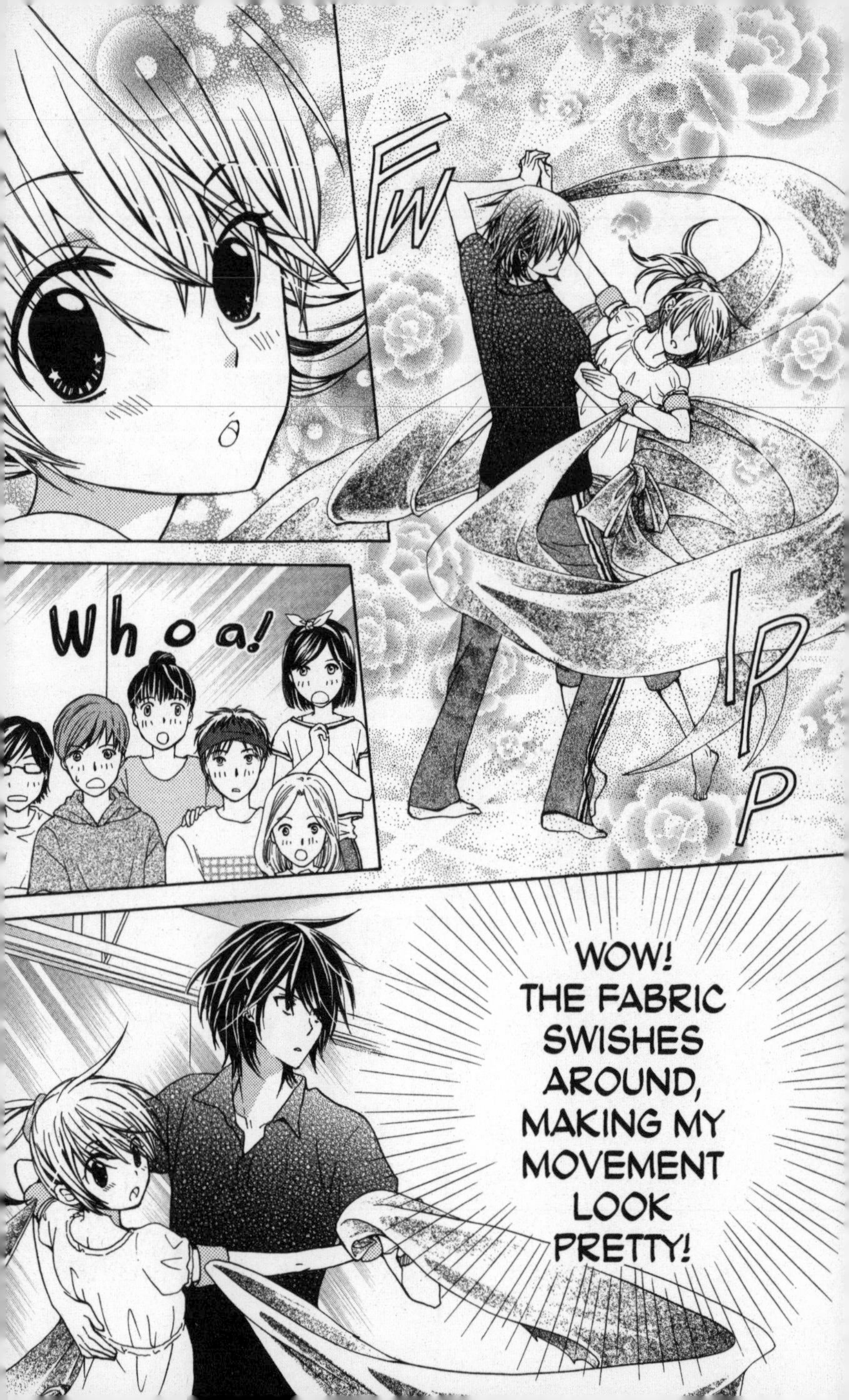
FW
IPP
Whoa!
WOW! THE FABRIC SWISHES AROUND, MAKING MY MOVEMENT LOOK PRETTY!

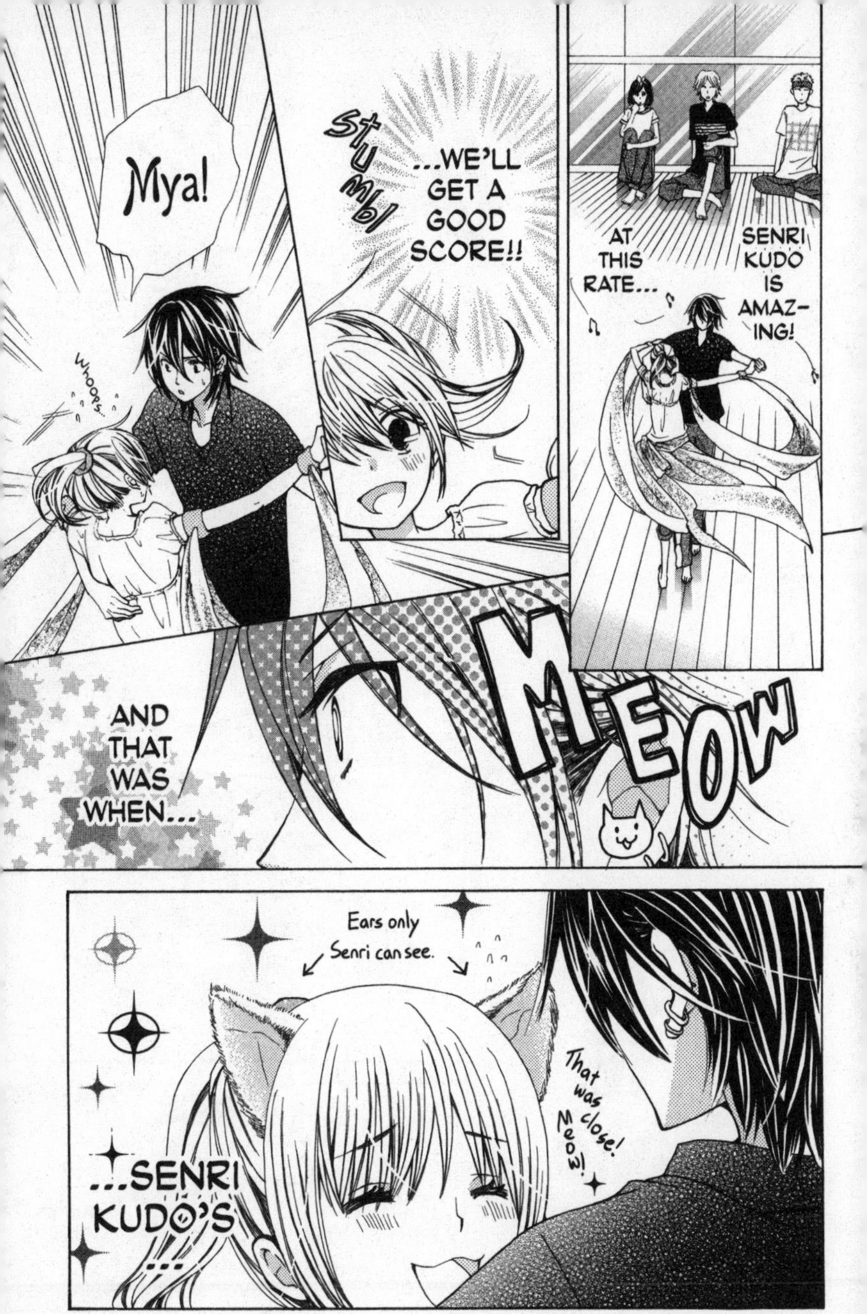
SENRI KUDO IS AMAZ-ING!
AT THIS RATE...
...WE'LL GET A GOOD SCORE!!
STUMBL
Mya!
Whoops...
MEOW
AND THAT WAS WHEN...
Ears only Senri can see.
That was close! Meow!
...SENRI KUDO'S ...

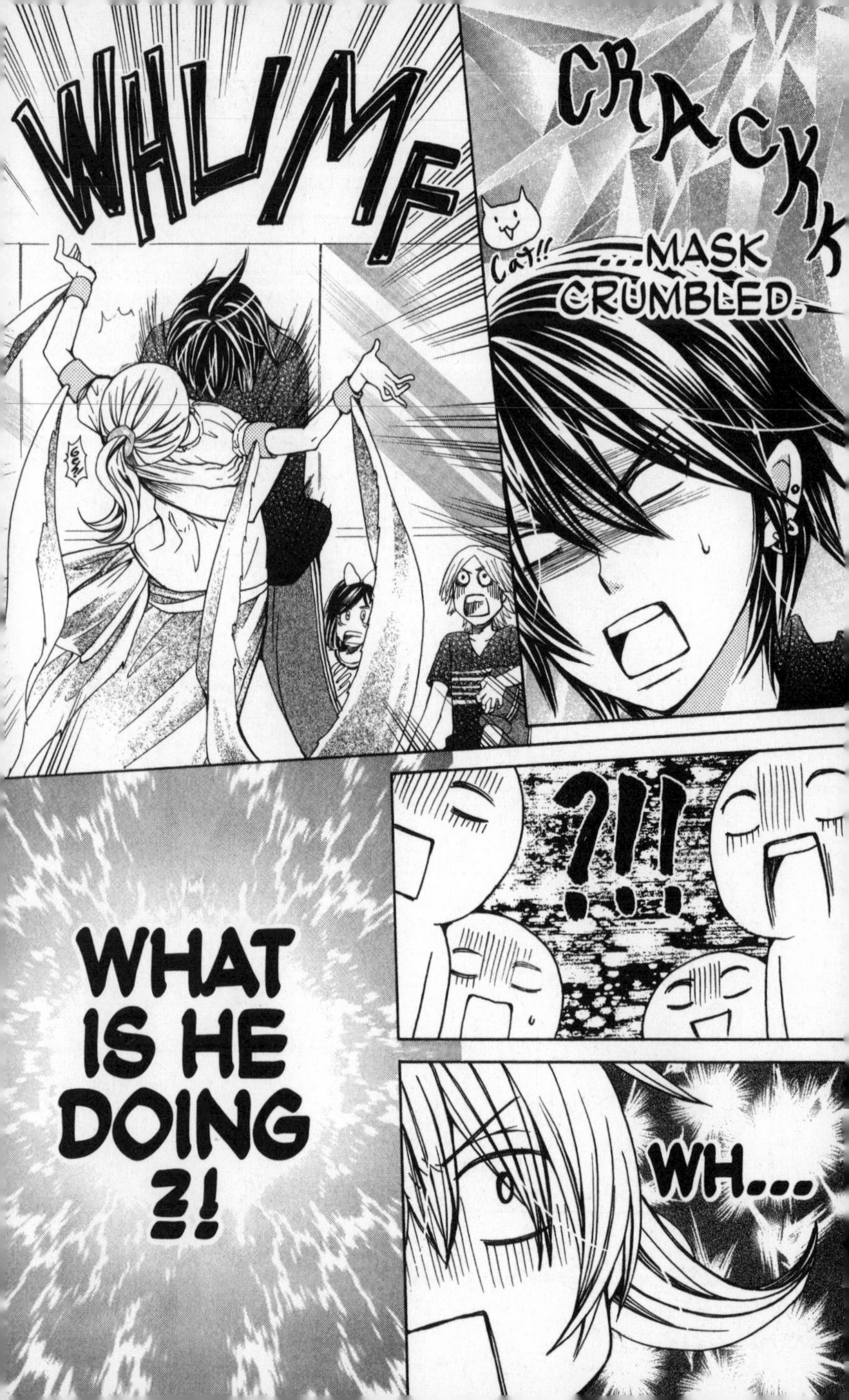
CRACKKK
Cat!!
...MASK CRUMBLED.
WHUMF
?!!
WH...
WHAT IS HE DOING?!

# Chapter 32

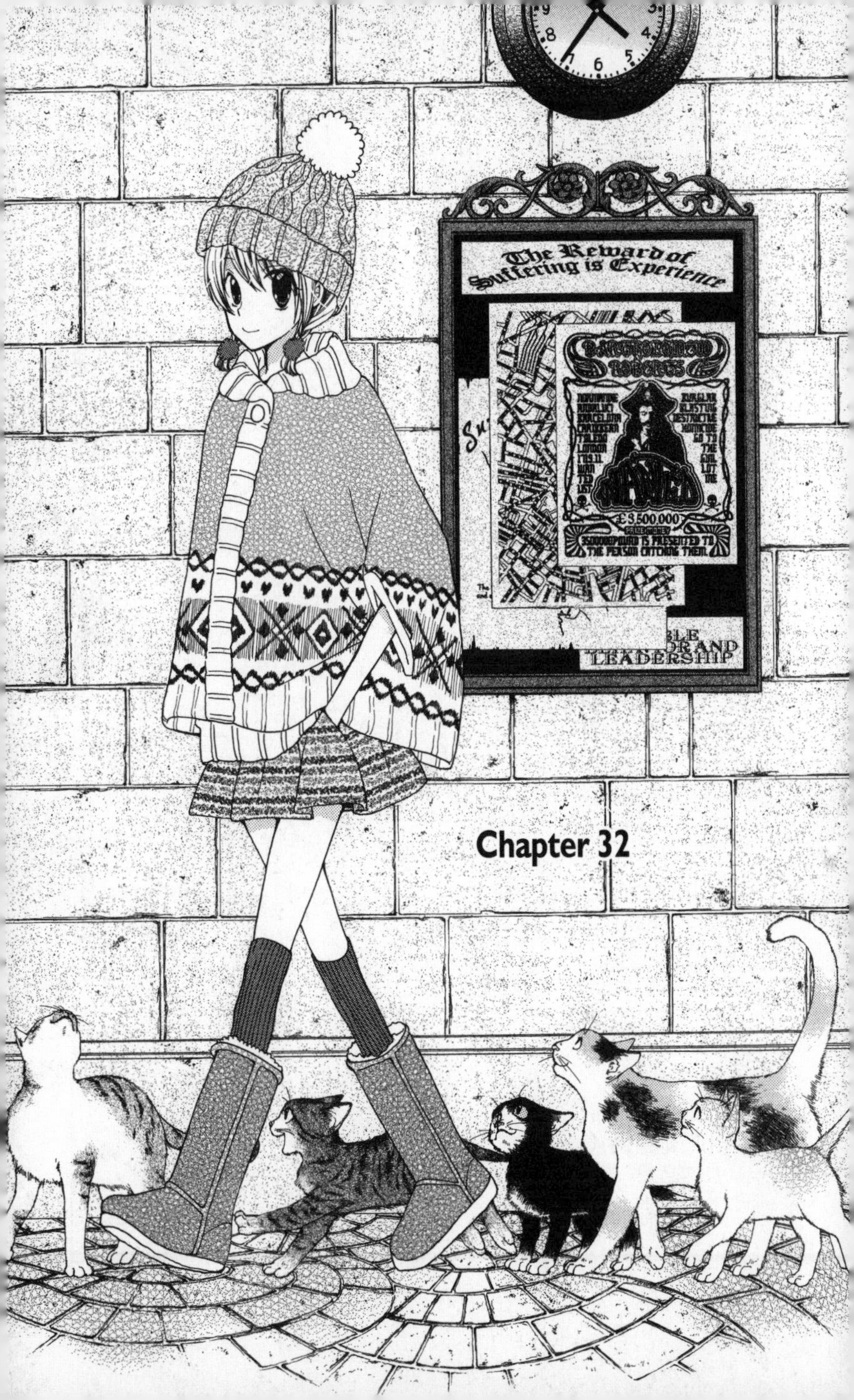
The Reward of Suffering is Experience
WANTED
£3,500,000
THE PERSON CATCHING THEM.
LEADERSHIP

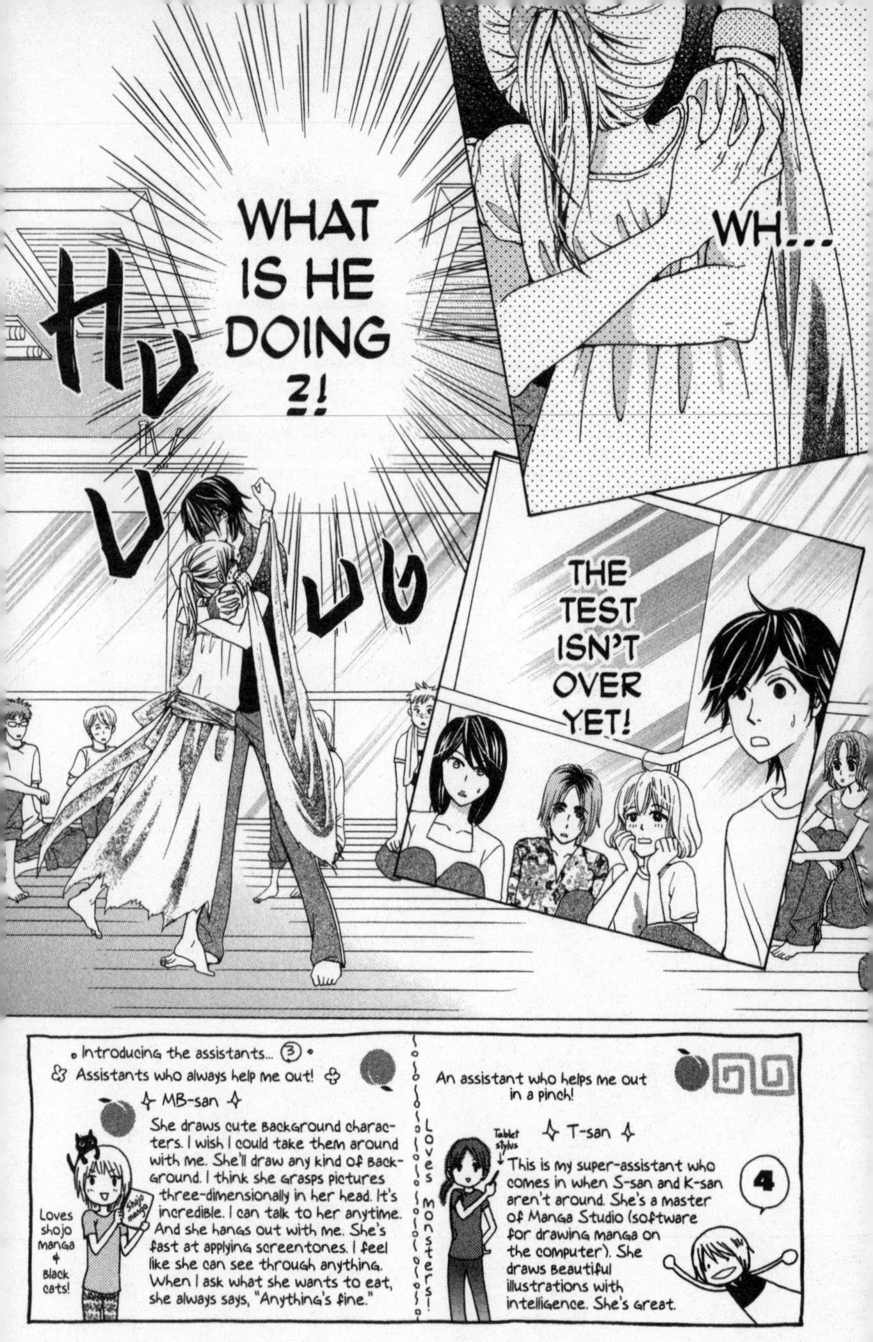
WH...
WHAT IS HE DOING?!
THE TEST ISN'T OVER YET!

• Introducing the assistants... ③ •

Assistants who always help me out!

✧ MB-san ✧

She draws cute background characters. I wish I could take them around with me. She'll draw any kind of background. I think she grasps pictures three-dimensionally in her head. It's incredible. I can talk to her anytime. And she hangs out with me. She's fast at applying screentones. I feel like she can see through anything. When I ask what she wants to eat, she always says, "Anything's fine."

Loves shojo manga & Black cats!

Shojo manga

Loves Monsters!

An assistant who helps me out in a pinch!

✧ T-san ✧

Tablet stylus

This is my super-assistant who comes in when S-san and K-san aren't around. She's a master of Manga Studio (software for drawing manga on the computer). She draws beautiful illustrations with intelligence. She's great.

4

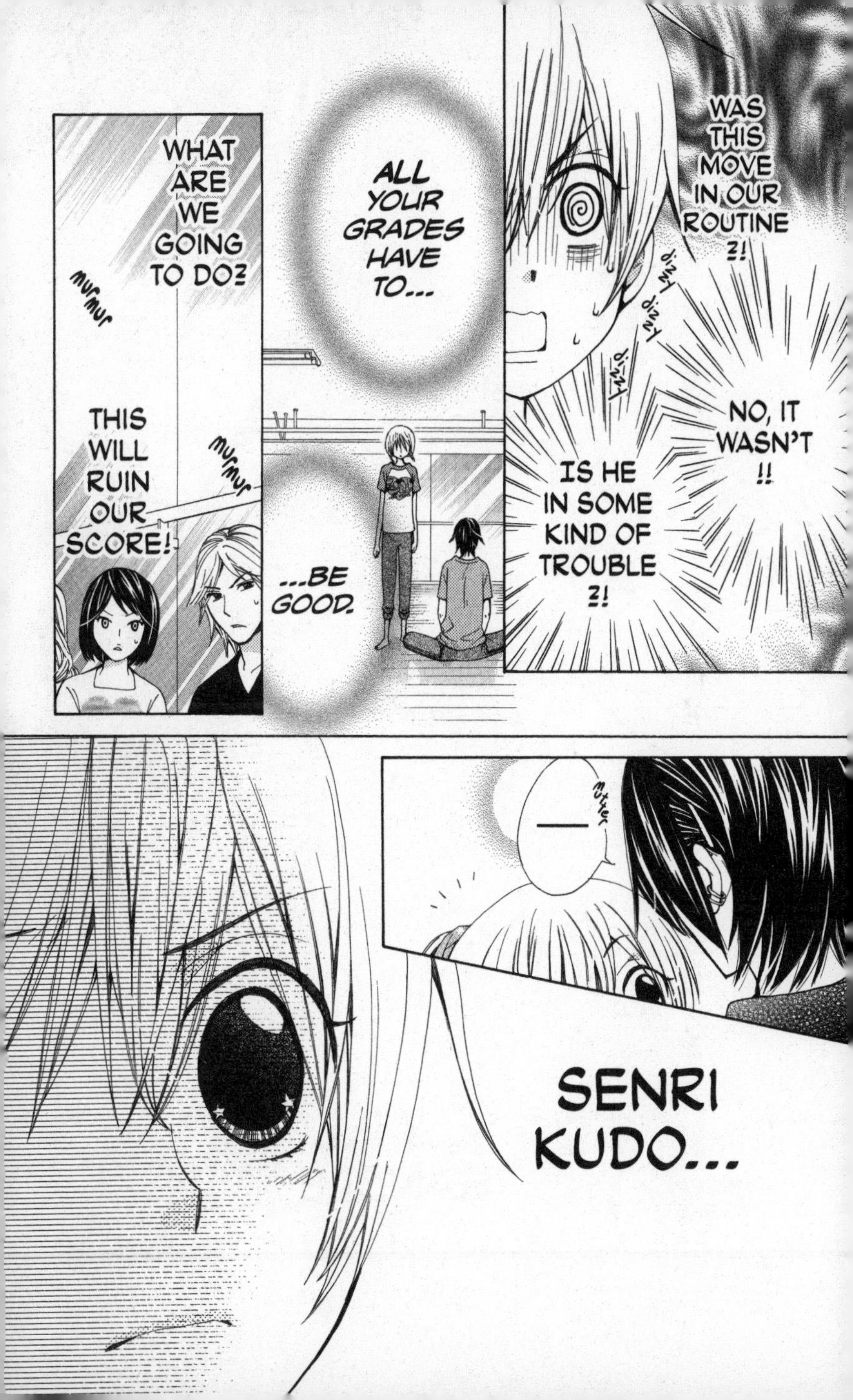
WAS THIS MOVE IN OUR ROUTINE?!
dizzy dizzy dizzy dizzy
NO, IT WASN'T!!
IS HE IN SOME KIND OF TROUBLE?!
ALL YOUR GRADES HAVE TO...
...BE GOOD.
WHAT ARE WE GOING TO DO?
murmur
THIS WILL RUIN OUR SCORE!
murmur
mutter
—
SENRI KUDO...

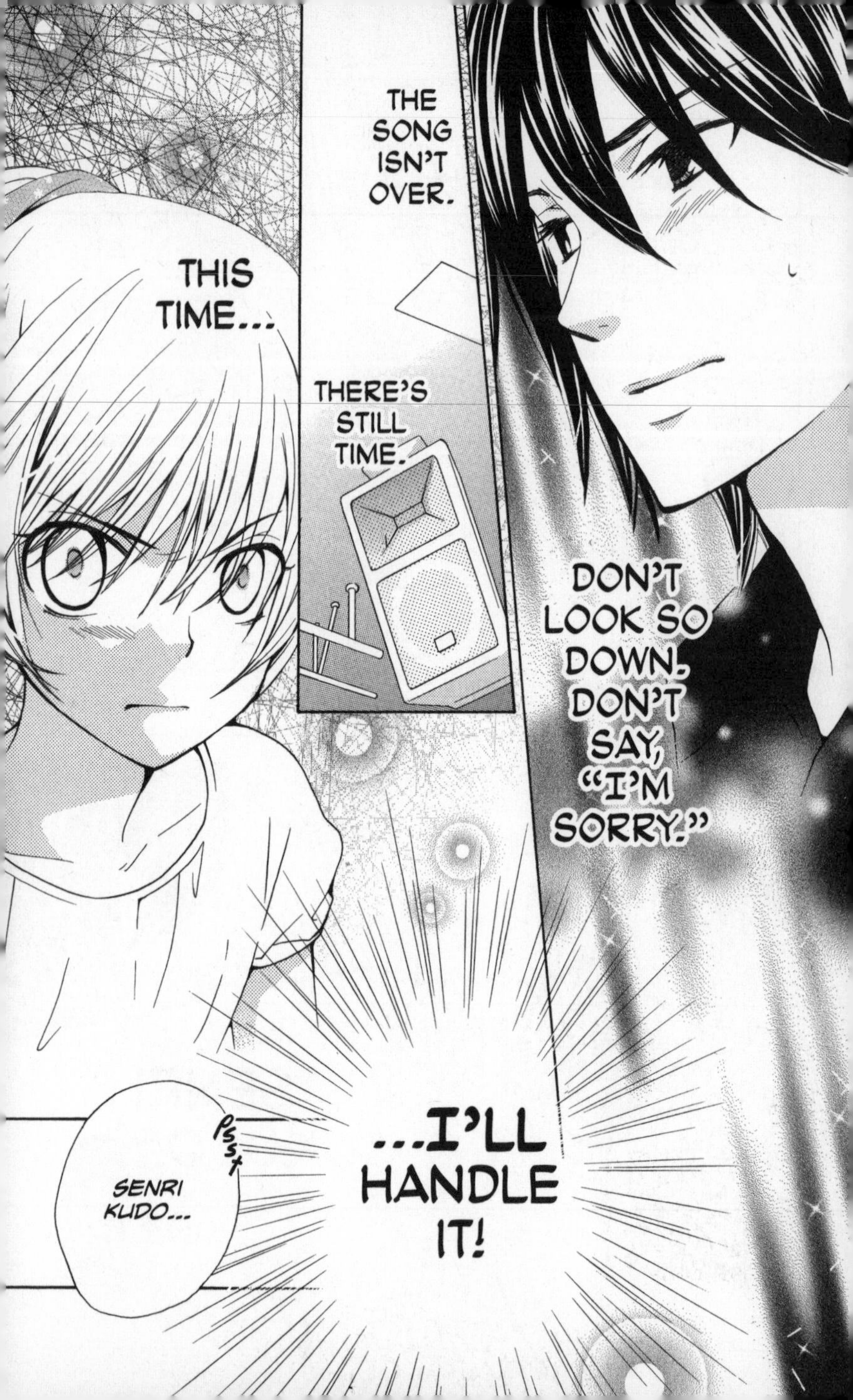
THE SONG ISN'T OVER.
THERE'S STILL TIME.
DON'T LOOK SO DOWN. DON'T SAY, "I'M SORRY."
THIS TIME...
...I'LL HANDLE IT!
SENRI KUDO...
Psst

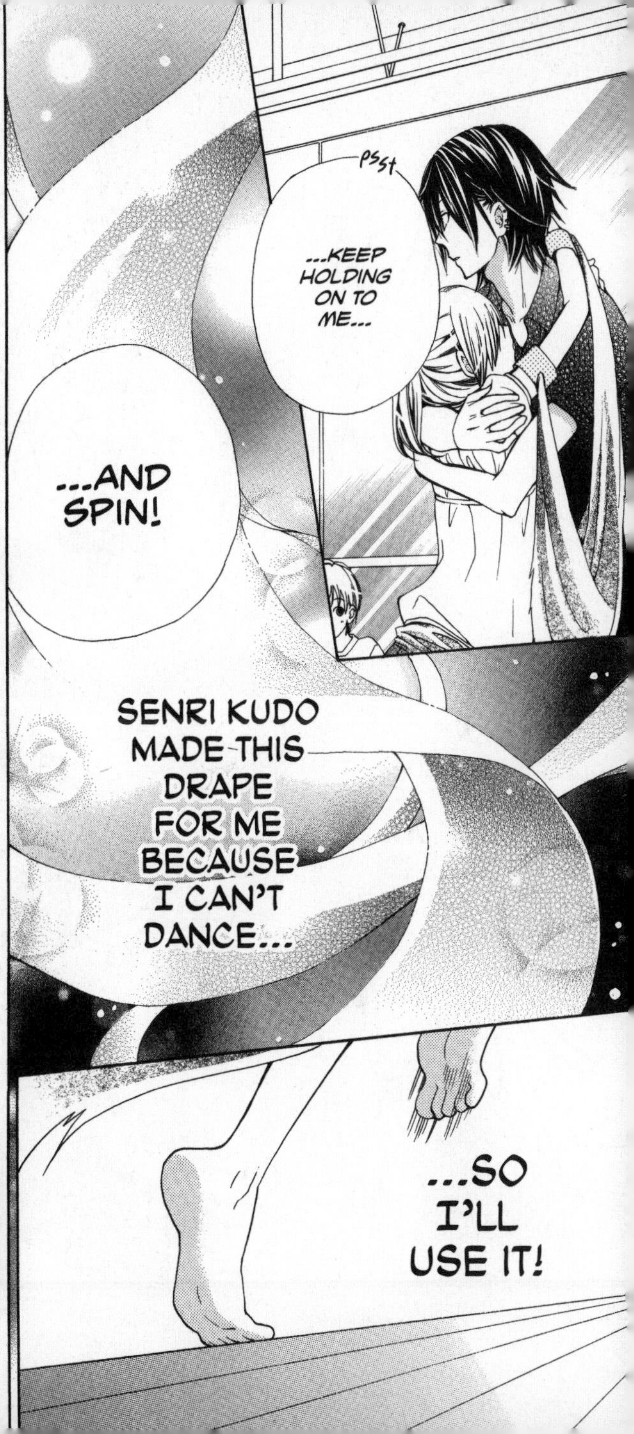
PSST
...KEEP HOLDING ON TO ME...
...AND SPIN!
SENRI KUDO MADE THIS DRAPE FOR ME BECAUSE I CAN'T DANCE...
...SO I'LL USE IT!

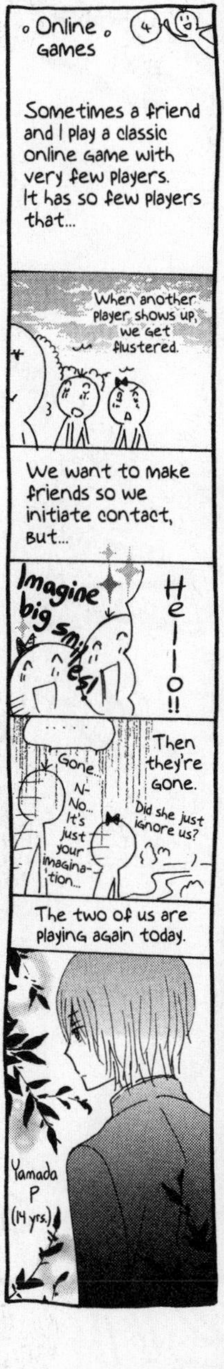
Online Games
4
Sometimes a friend and I play a classic online game with very few players. It has so few players that...
When another player shows up, we get flustered.
We want to make friends so we initiate contact, but...
Imagine big smiles!
Hello!!
.....
Then they're gone.
Gone
N-No... It's just your imagination...
Did she just ignore us?
The two of us are playing again today.
Yamada P (14 yrs.)

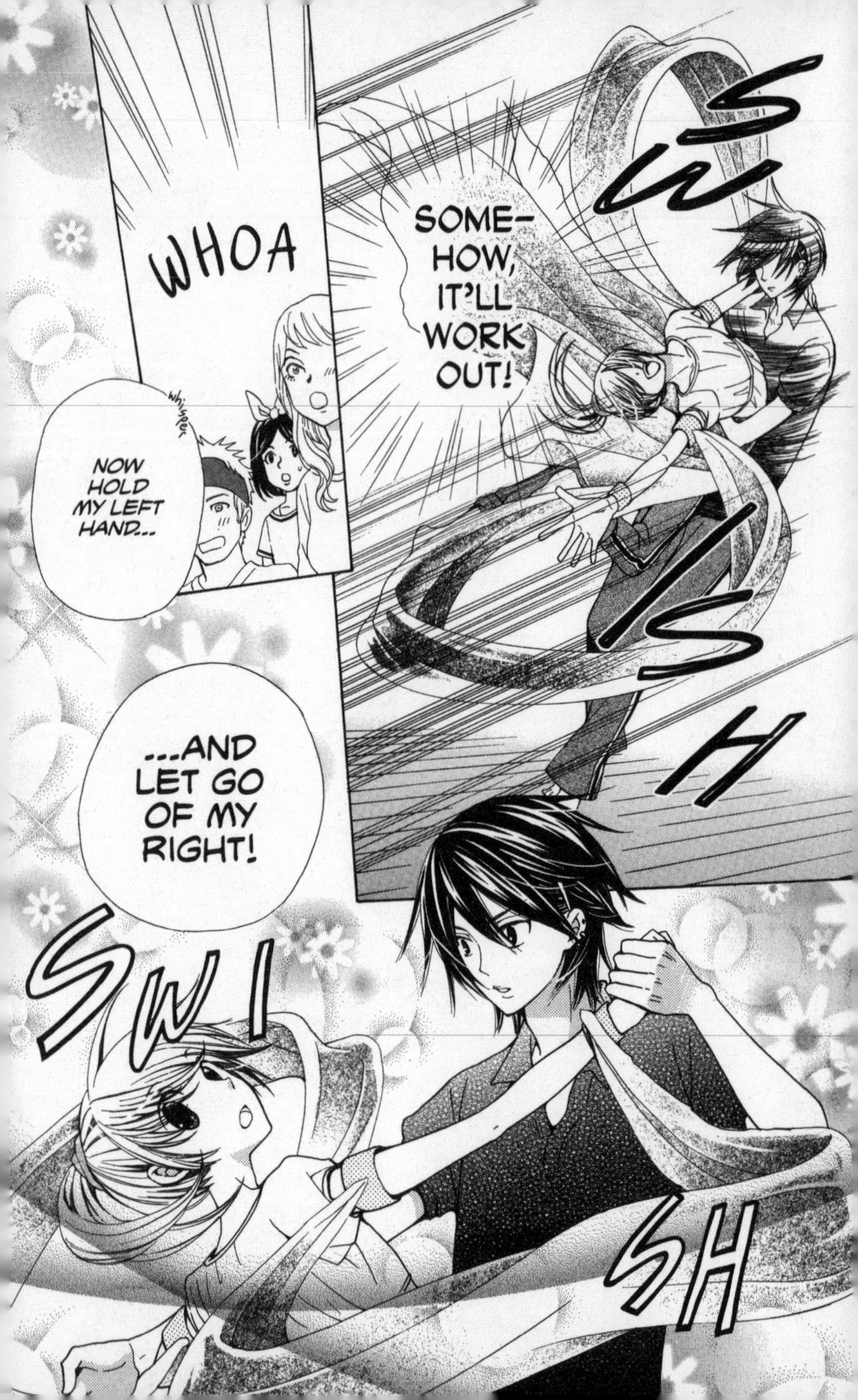
SWISH
SOME-HOW, IT'LL WORK OUT!
WHOA
whisper
NOW HOLD MY LEFT HAND...
...AND LET GO OF MY RIGHT!
SWISH

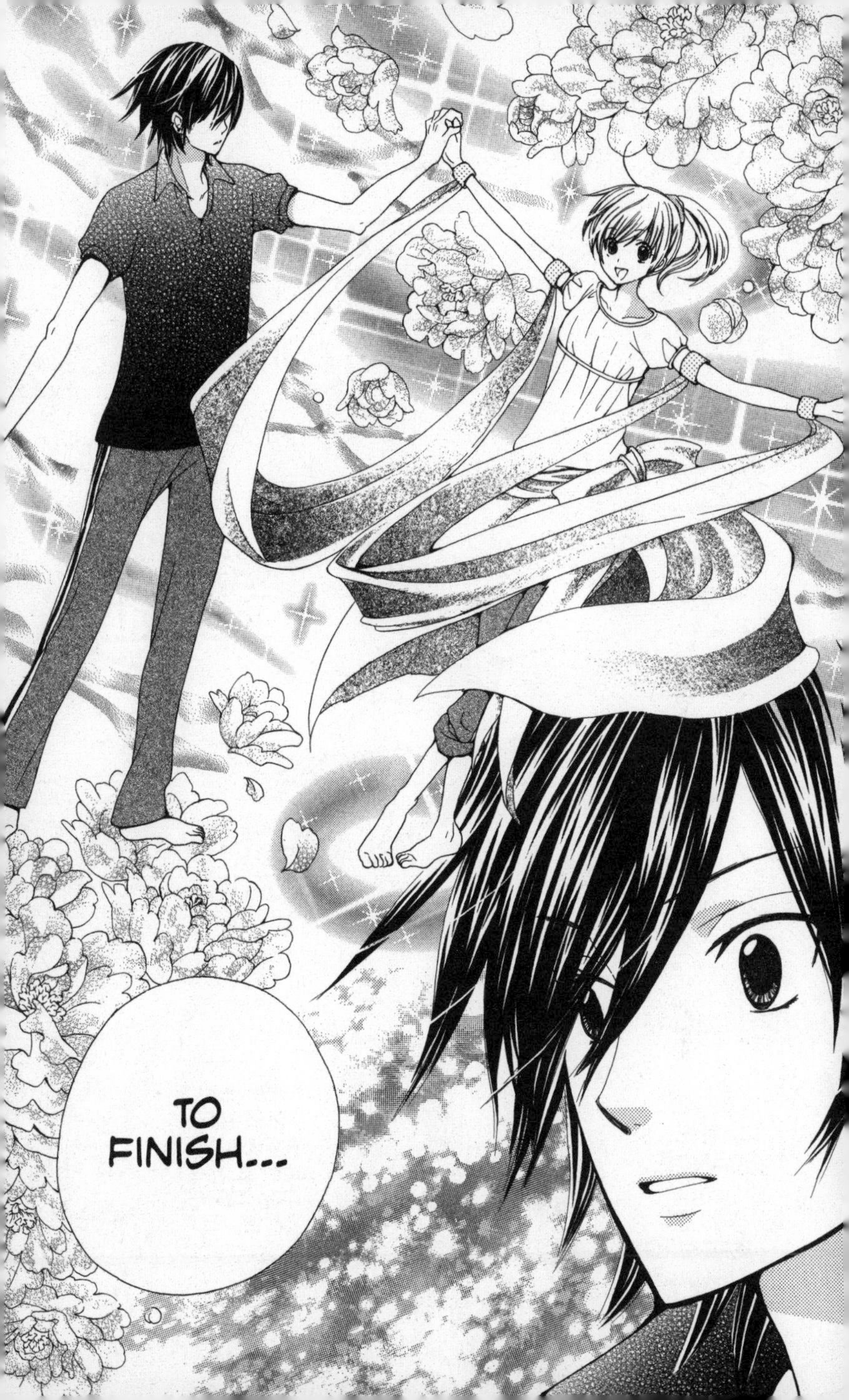
TO FINISH...

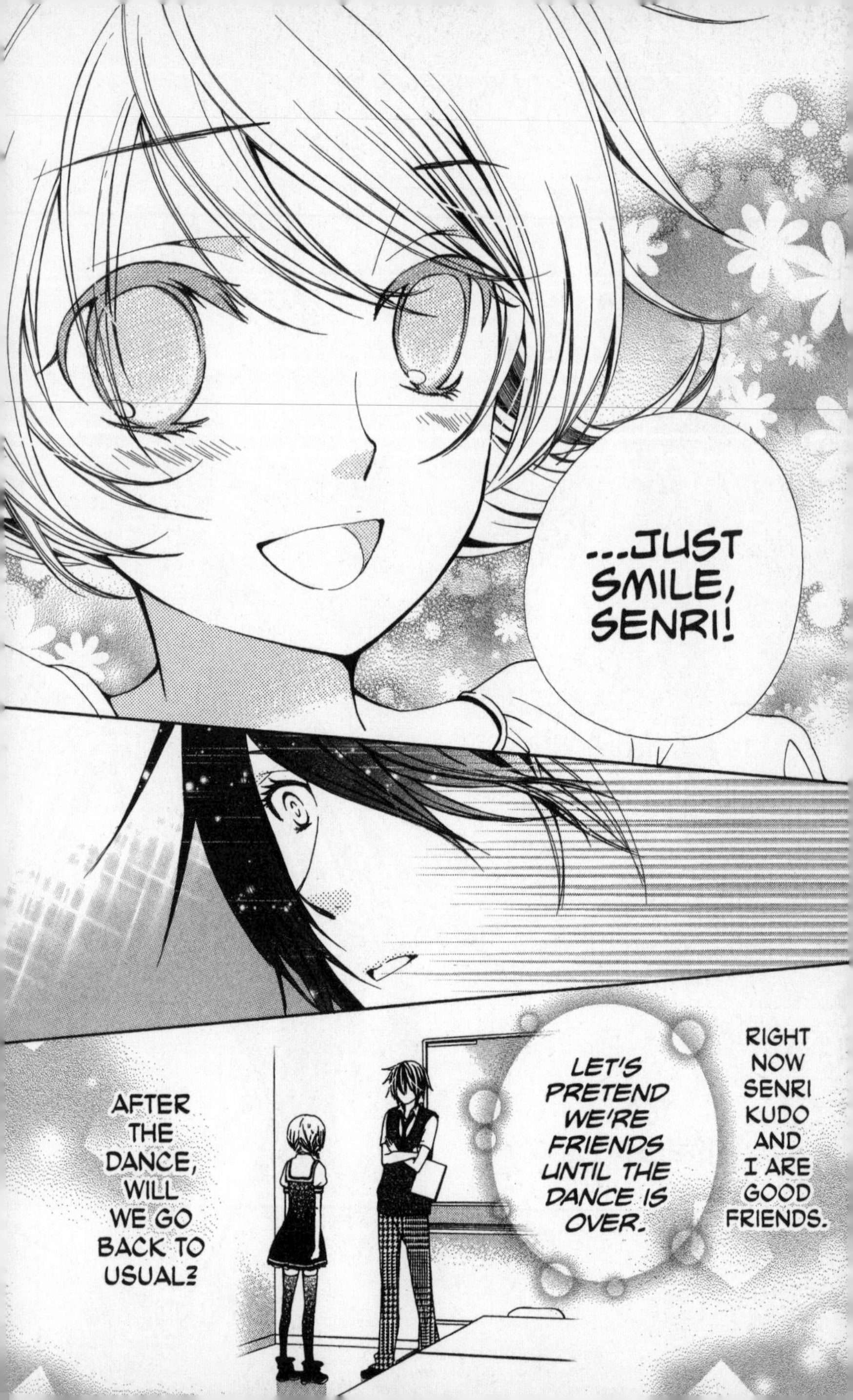
...JUST SMILE, SENRI!
RIGHT NOW SENRI KUDO AND I ARE GOOD FRIENDS.
LET'S PRETEND WE'RE FRIENDS UNTIL THE DANCE IS OVER.
AFTER THE DANCE, WILL WE GO BACK TO USUAL?

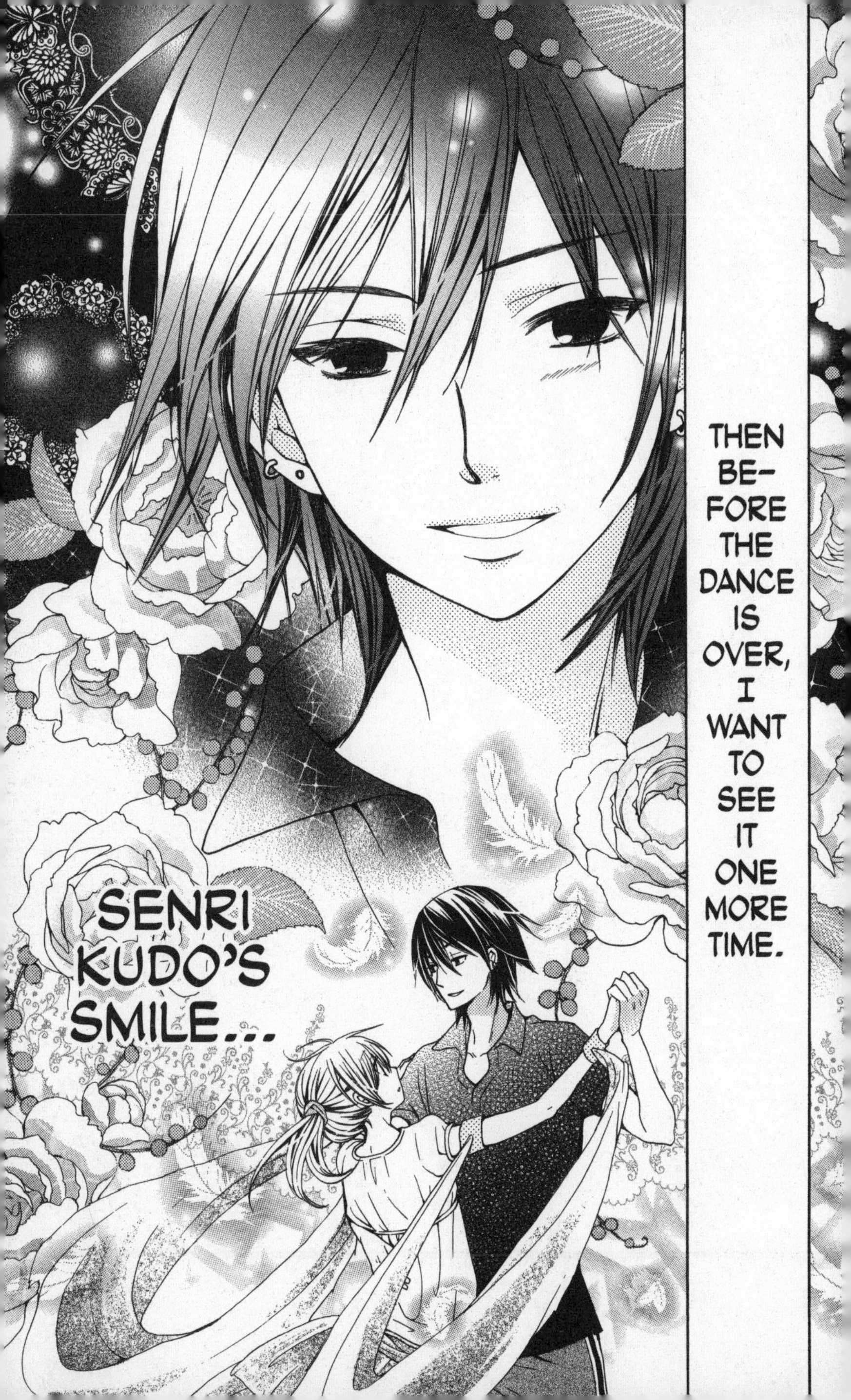
THEN BE-FORE THE DANCE IS OVER, I WANT TO SEE IT ONE MORE TIME.
SENRI KUDO'S SMILE...

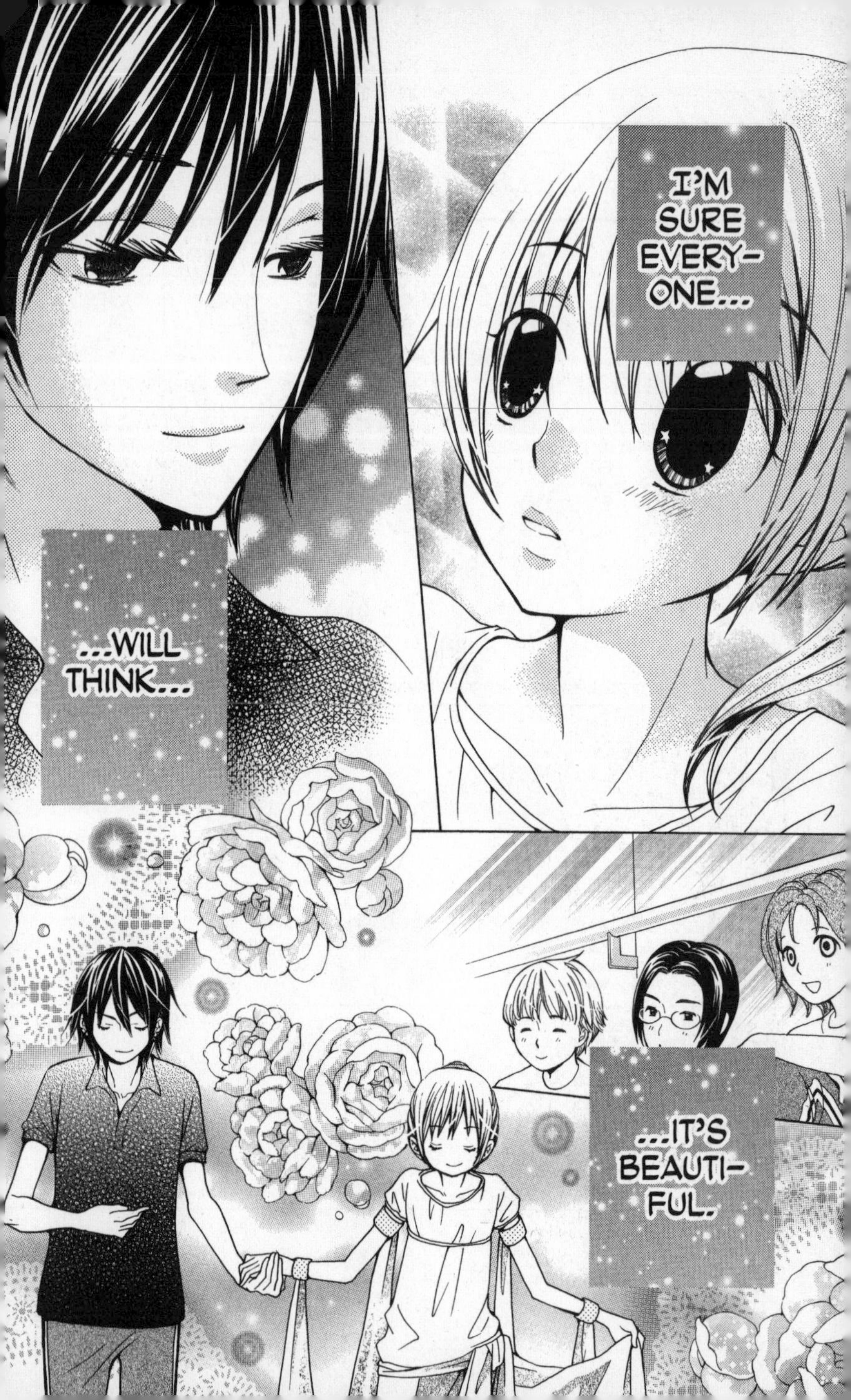
I'M SURE EVERY-ONE...
...WILL THINK...
...IT'S BEAUTI-FUL.

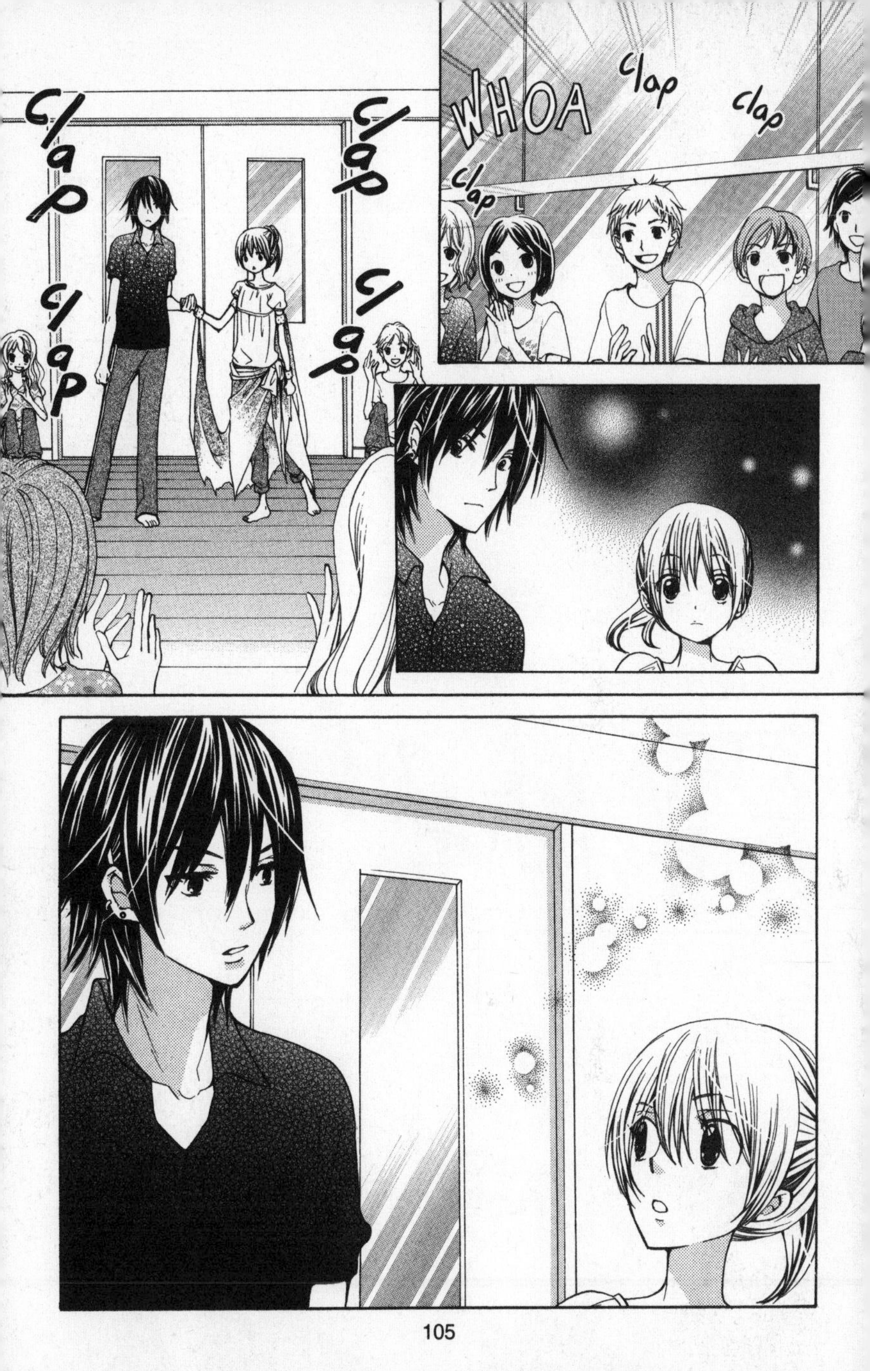
WHOA
clap
clap
clap
clap
clap
clap
clap
clap

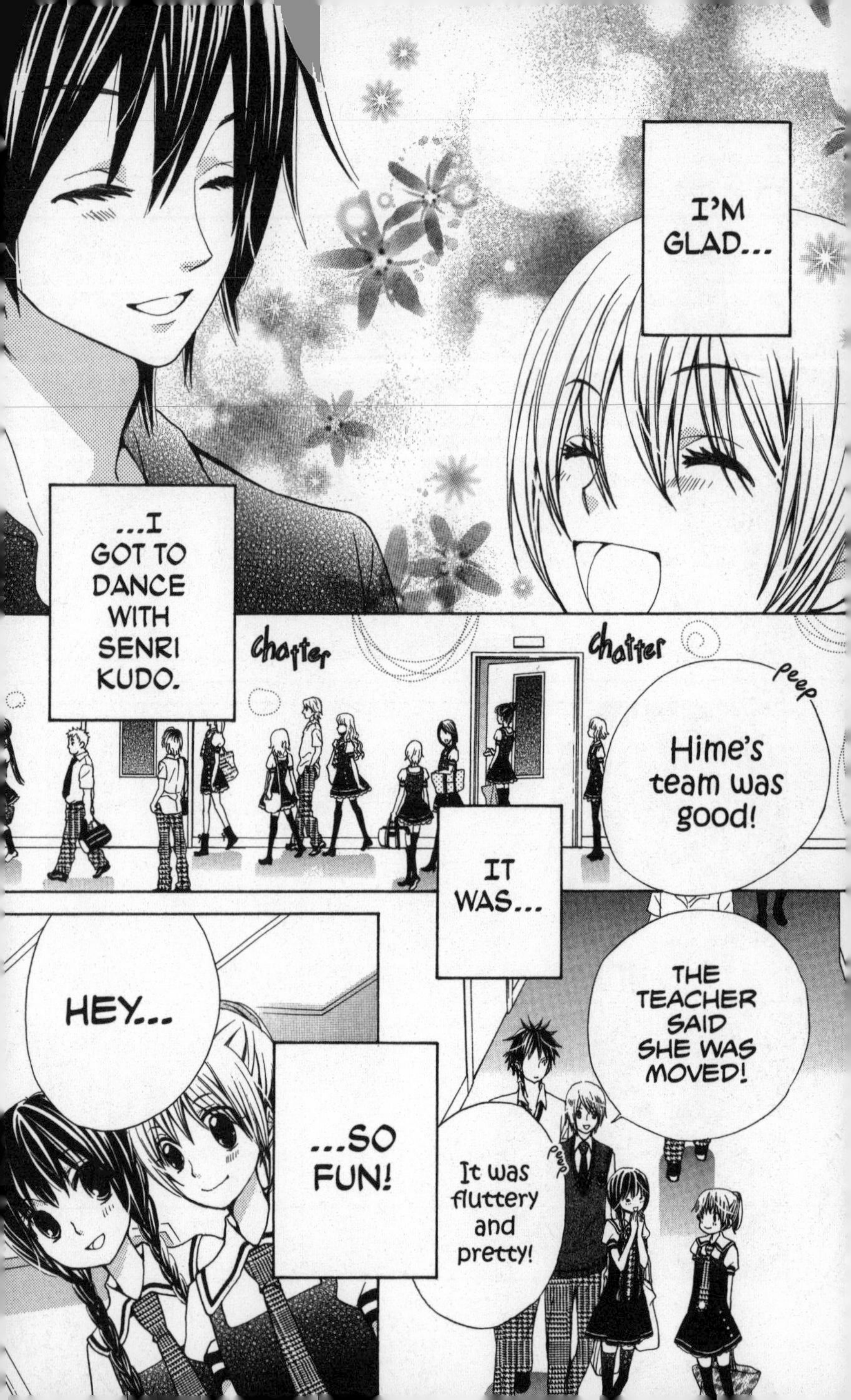
I'M GLAD...
...I GOT TO DANCE WITH SENRI KUDO.
chatter
chatter
peep
Hime's team was good!
IT WAS...
THE TEACHER SAID SHE WAS MOVED!
peep
It was fluttery and pretty!
...SO FUN!
HEY...

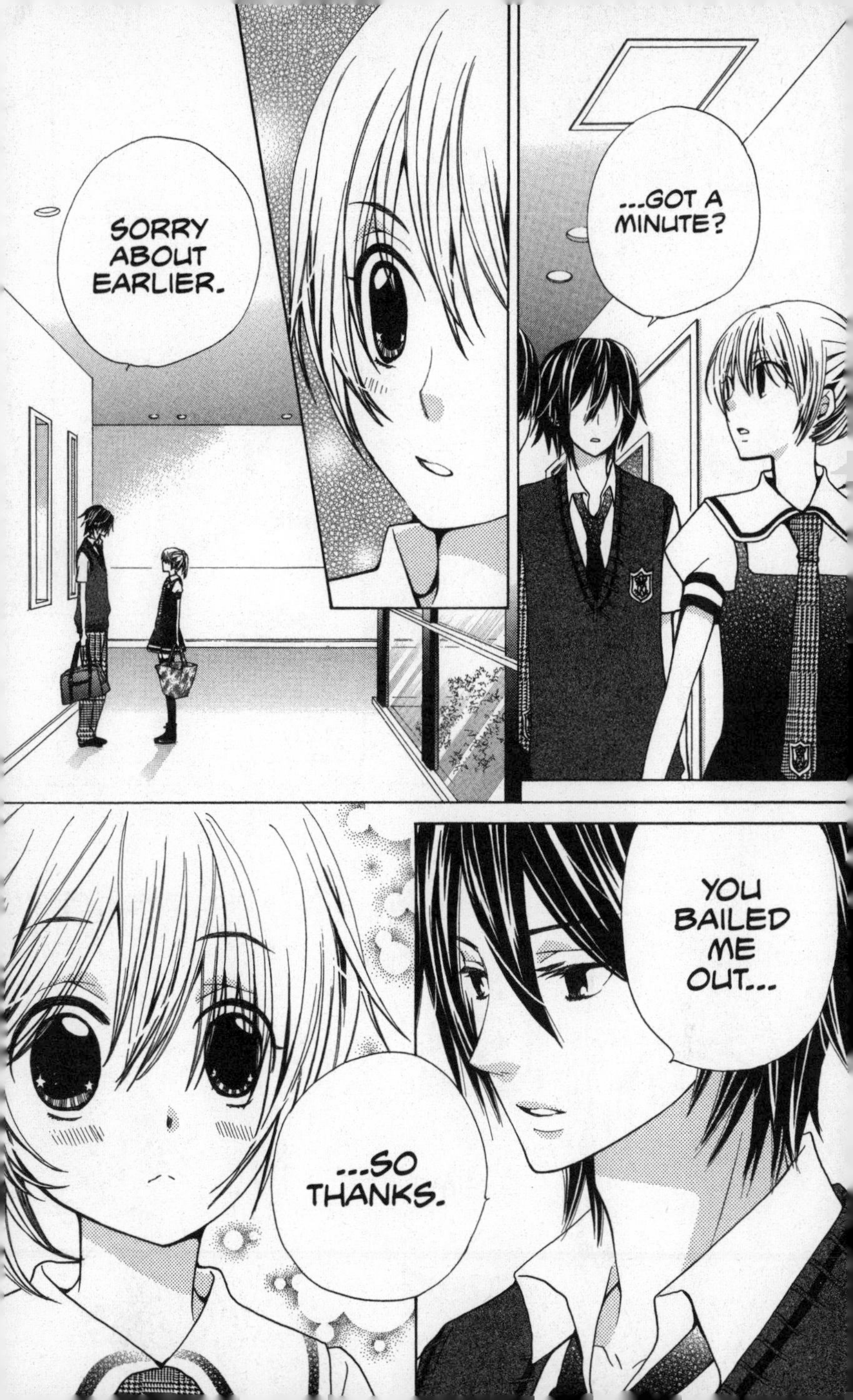
...GOT A MINUTE?
SORRY ABOUT EARLIER.
YOU BAILED ME OUT...
...SO THANKS.

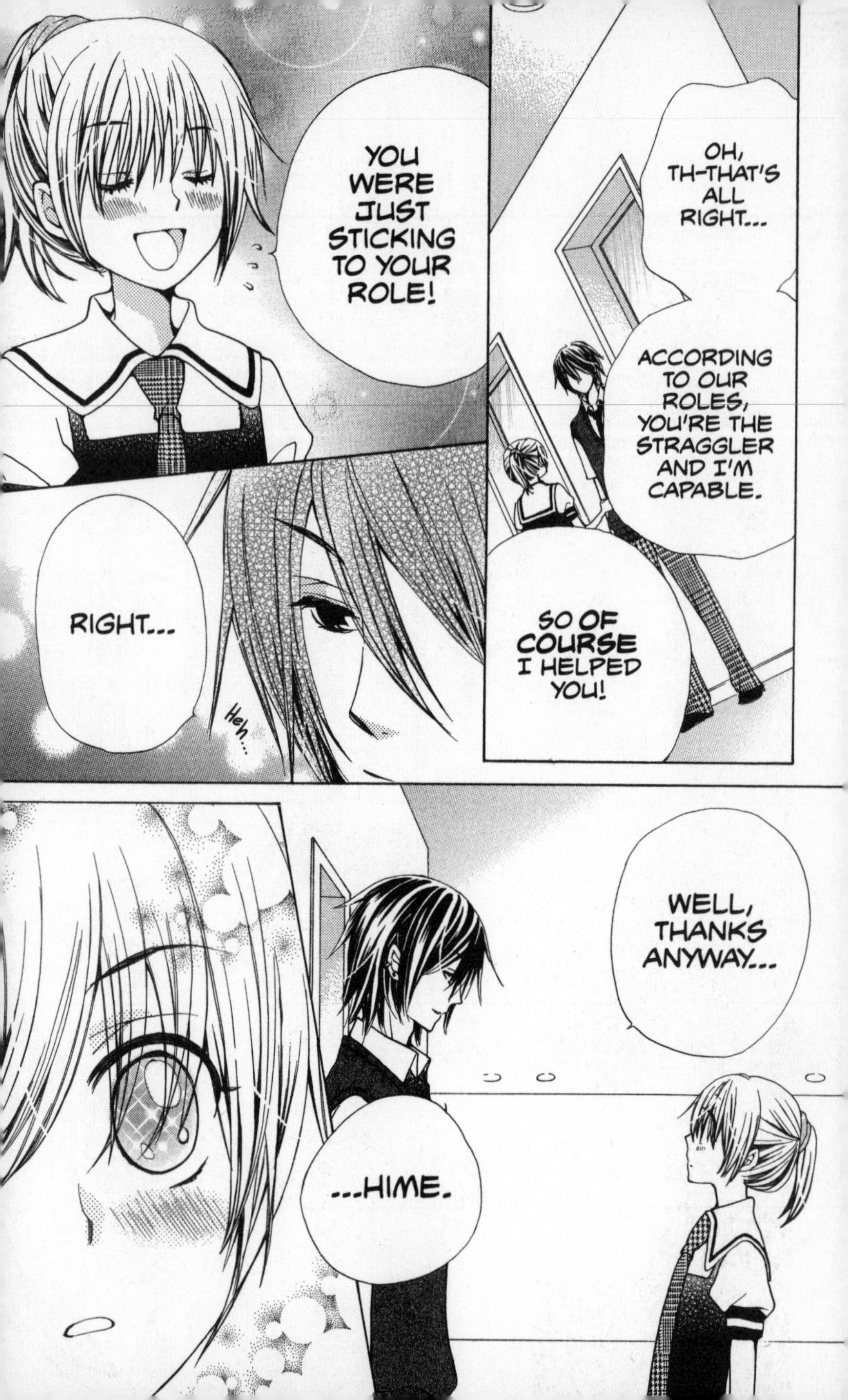
OH, TH-THAT'S ALL RIGHT...
ACCORDING TO OUR ROLES, YOU'RE THE STRAGGLER AND I'M CAPABLE.
SO OF COURSE I HELPED YOU!
YOU WERE JUST STICKING TO YOUR ROLE!
RIGHT...
Heh...
WELL, THANKS ANYWAY...
...HIME.

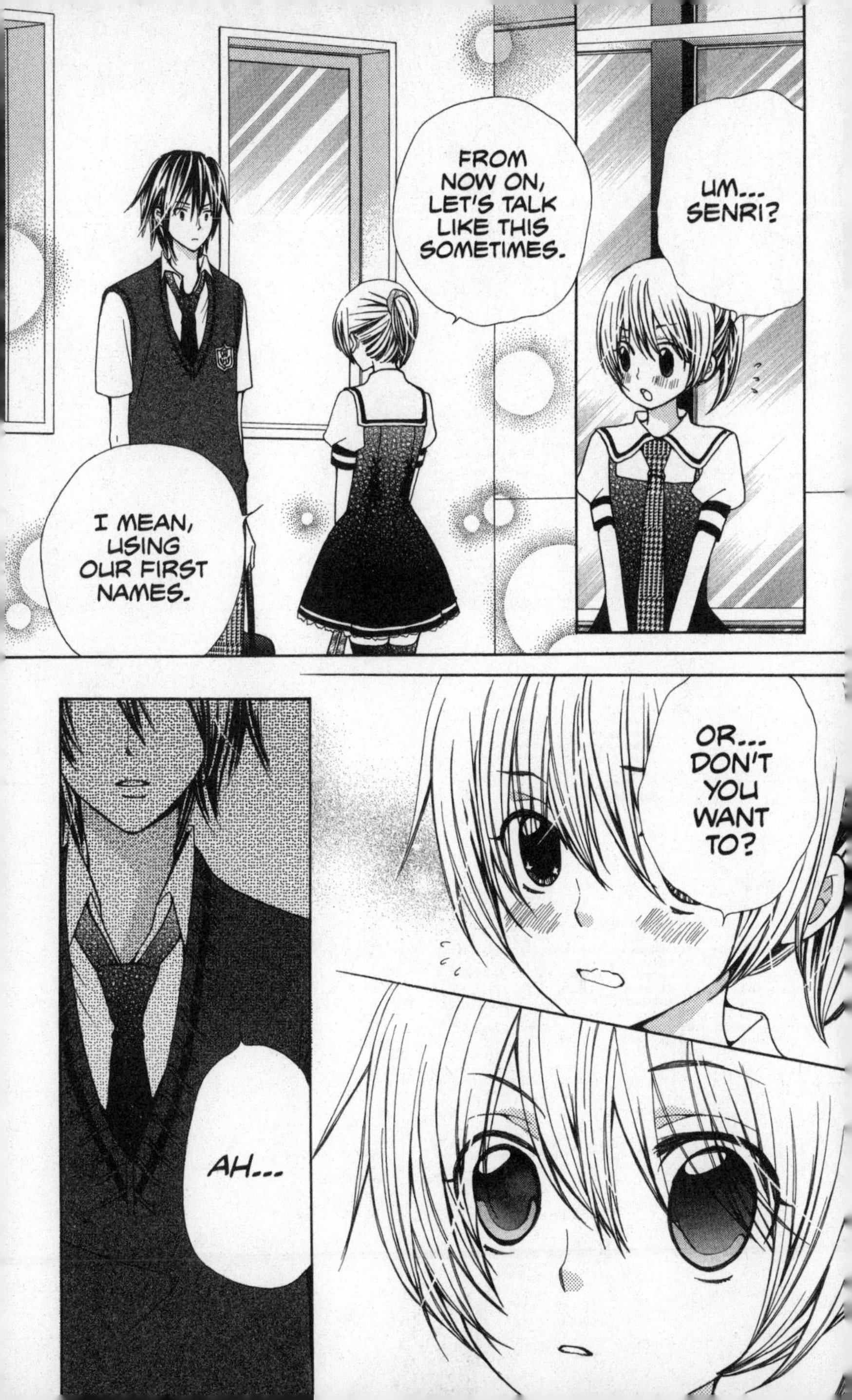
UM... SENRI?
FROM NOW ON, LET'S TALK LIKE THIS SOMETIMES.
I MEAN, USING OUR FIRST NAMES.
OR... DON'T YOU WANT TO?
AH...

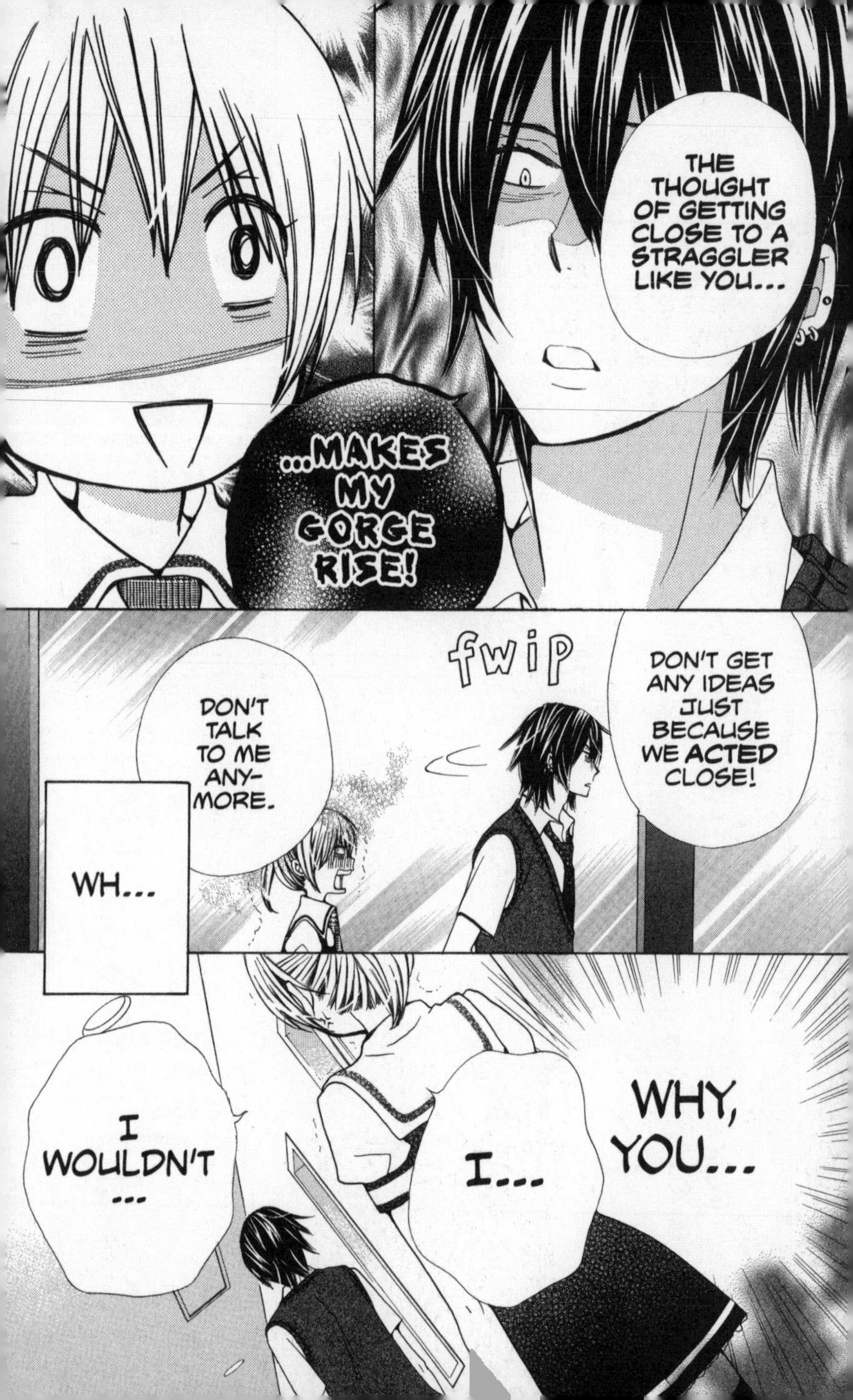
THE THOUGHT OF GETTING CLOSE TO A STRAGGLER LIKE YOU...
...MAKES MY GORGE RISE!
DON'T GET ANY IDEAS JUST BECAUSE WE ACTED CLOSE!
fwip
DON'T TALK TO ME ANYMORE.
WH...
WHY, YOU...
I...
I WOULDN'T ...

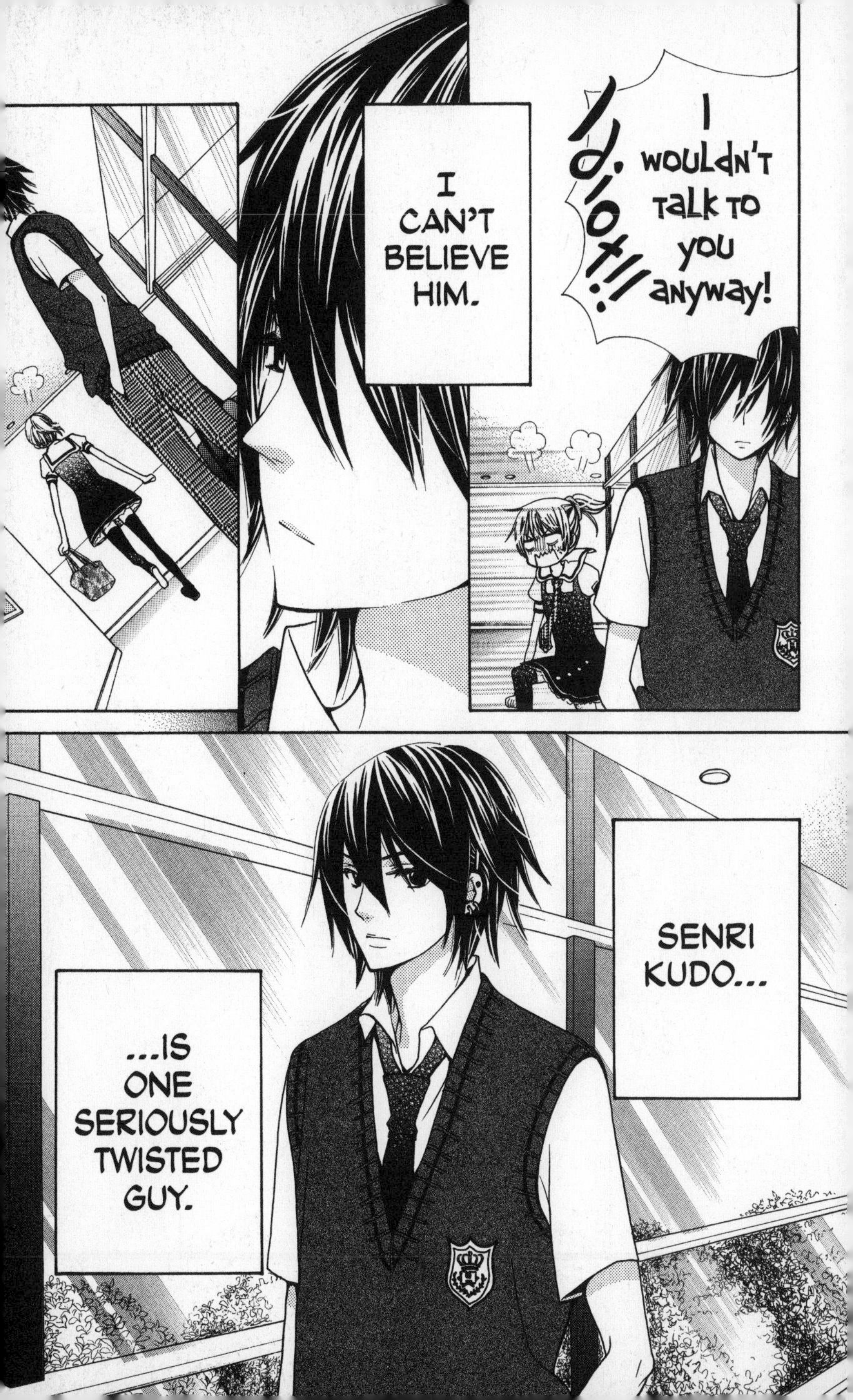
I wouldn't talk to you anyway!
Idiot!!!
I CAN'T BELIEVE HIM.
SENRI KUDO...
...IS ONE SERIOUSLY TWISTED GUY.

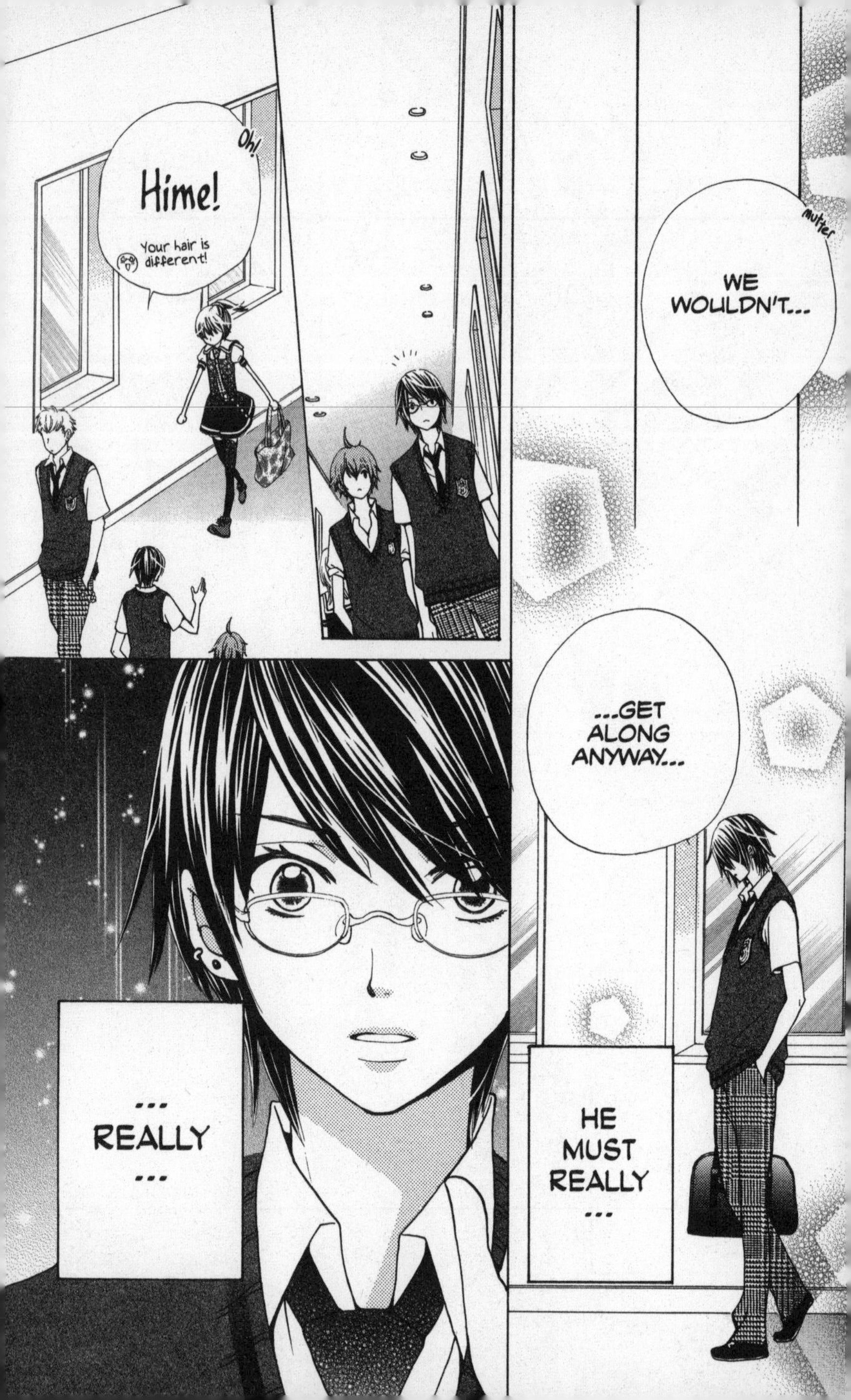
mutter
WE WOULDN'T...
...GET ALONG ANYWAY...
HE MUST REALLY ...
Oh!
Hime!
Your hair is different!
... REALLY ...

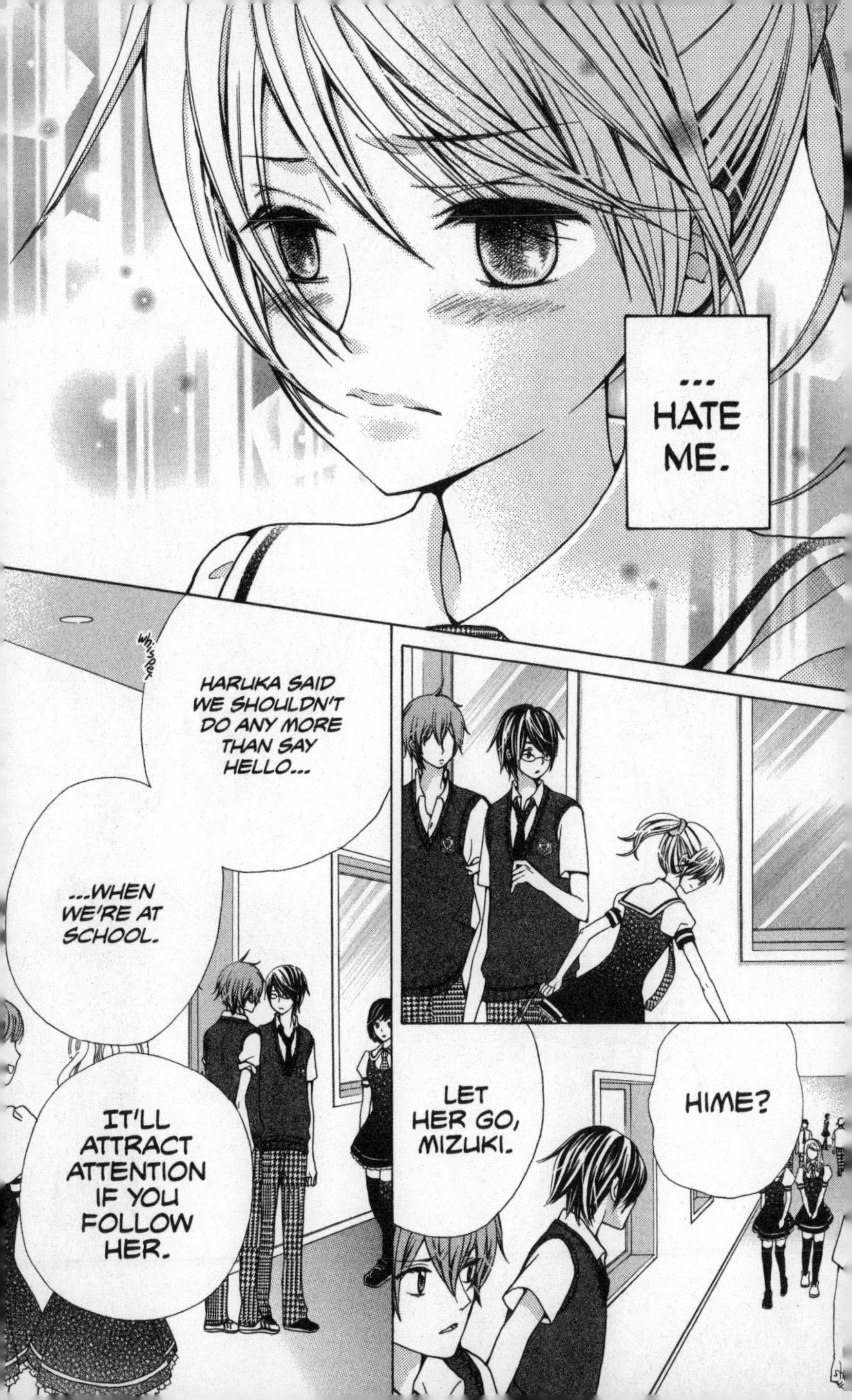

... HATE ME.
HIME?
LET HER GO, MIZUKI.
whisper
HARUKA SAID WE SHOULDN'T DO ANY MORE THAN SAY HELLO...
...WHEN WE'RE AT SCHOOL.
IT'LL ATTRACT ATTENTION IF YOU FOLLOW HER.

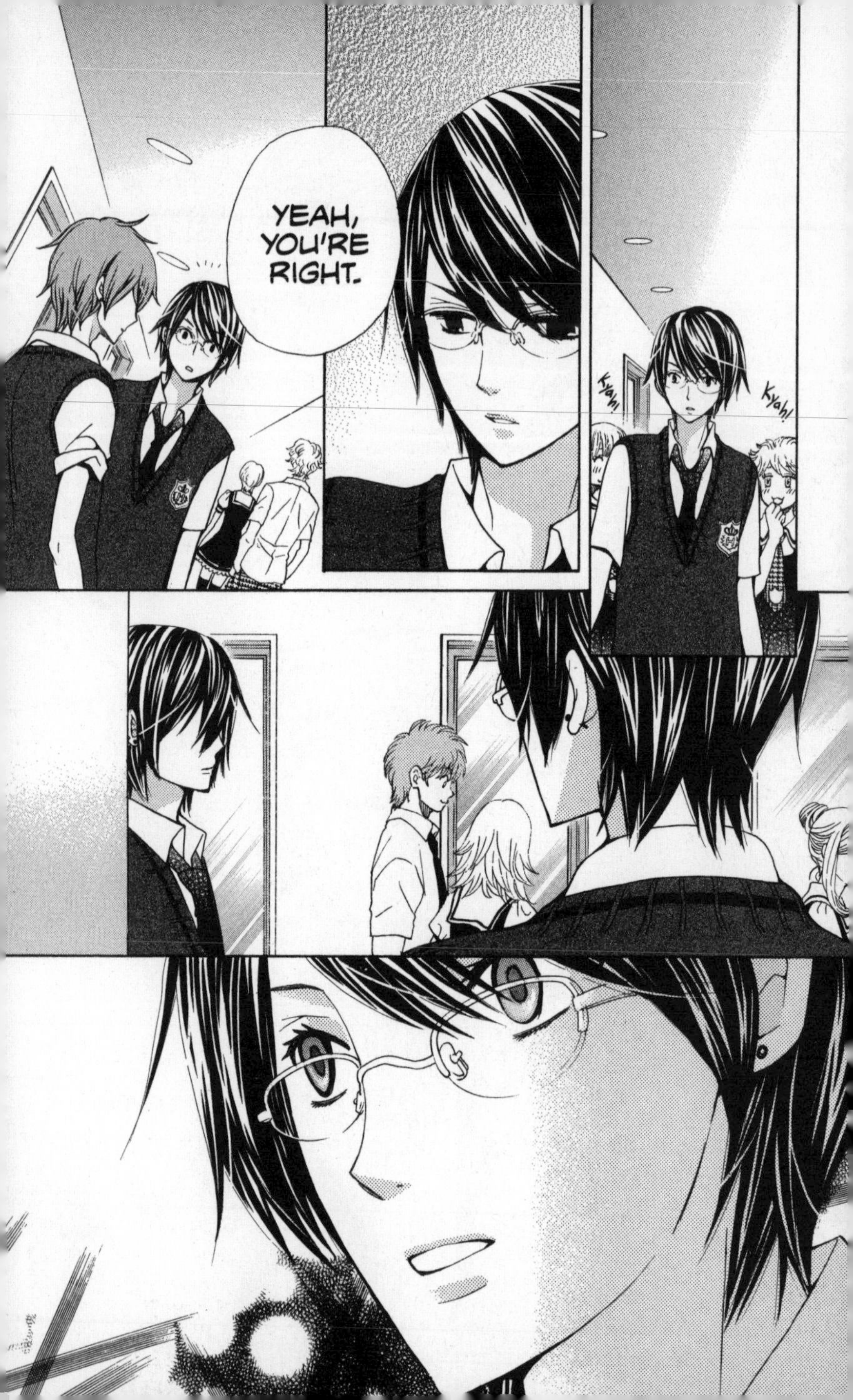
Kyah!
Kyah!
YEAH, YOU'RE RIGHT.

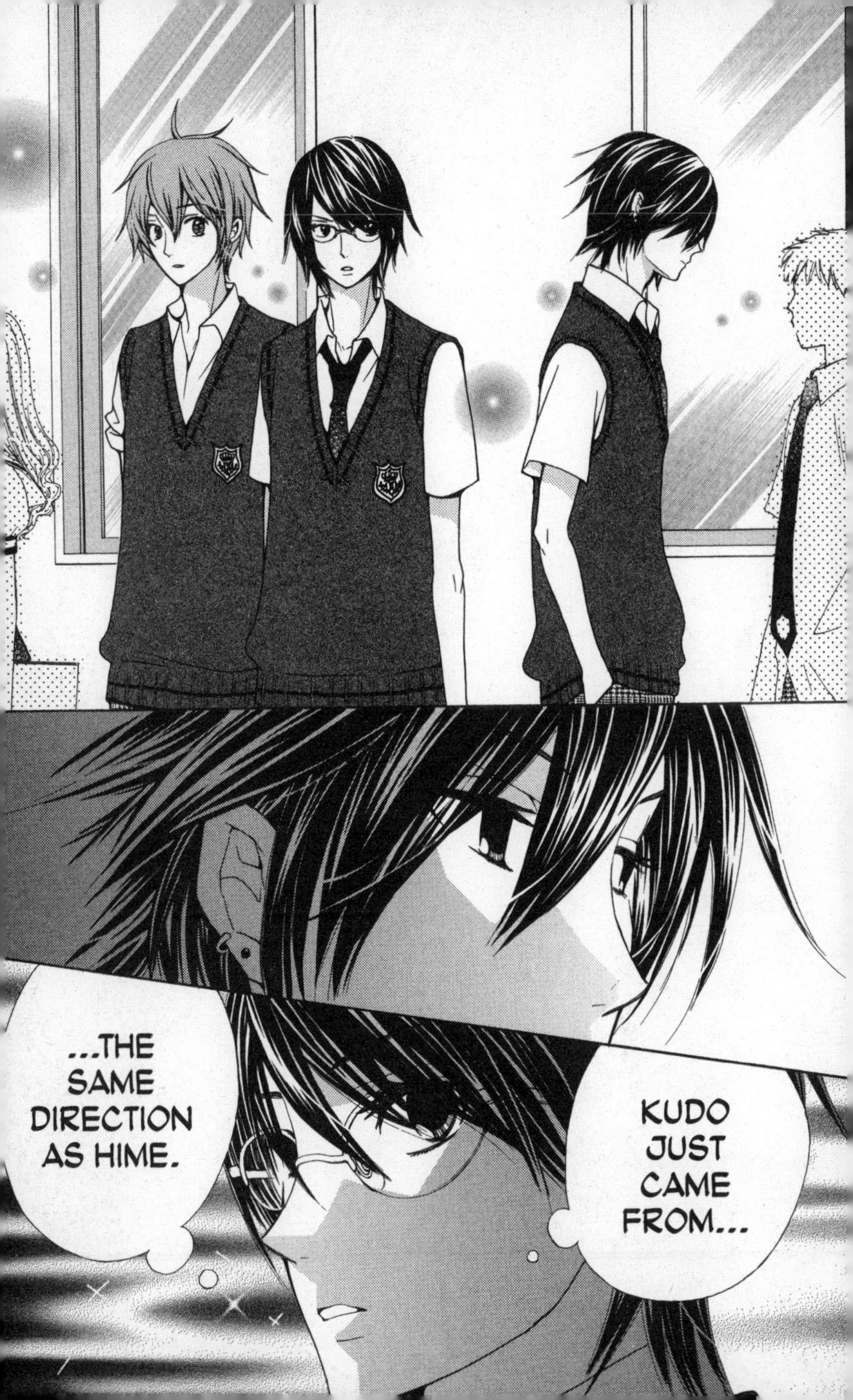
KUDO JUST CAME FROM...
...THE SAME DIRECTION AS HIME.

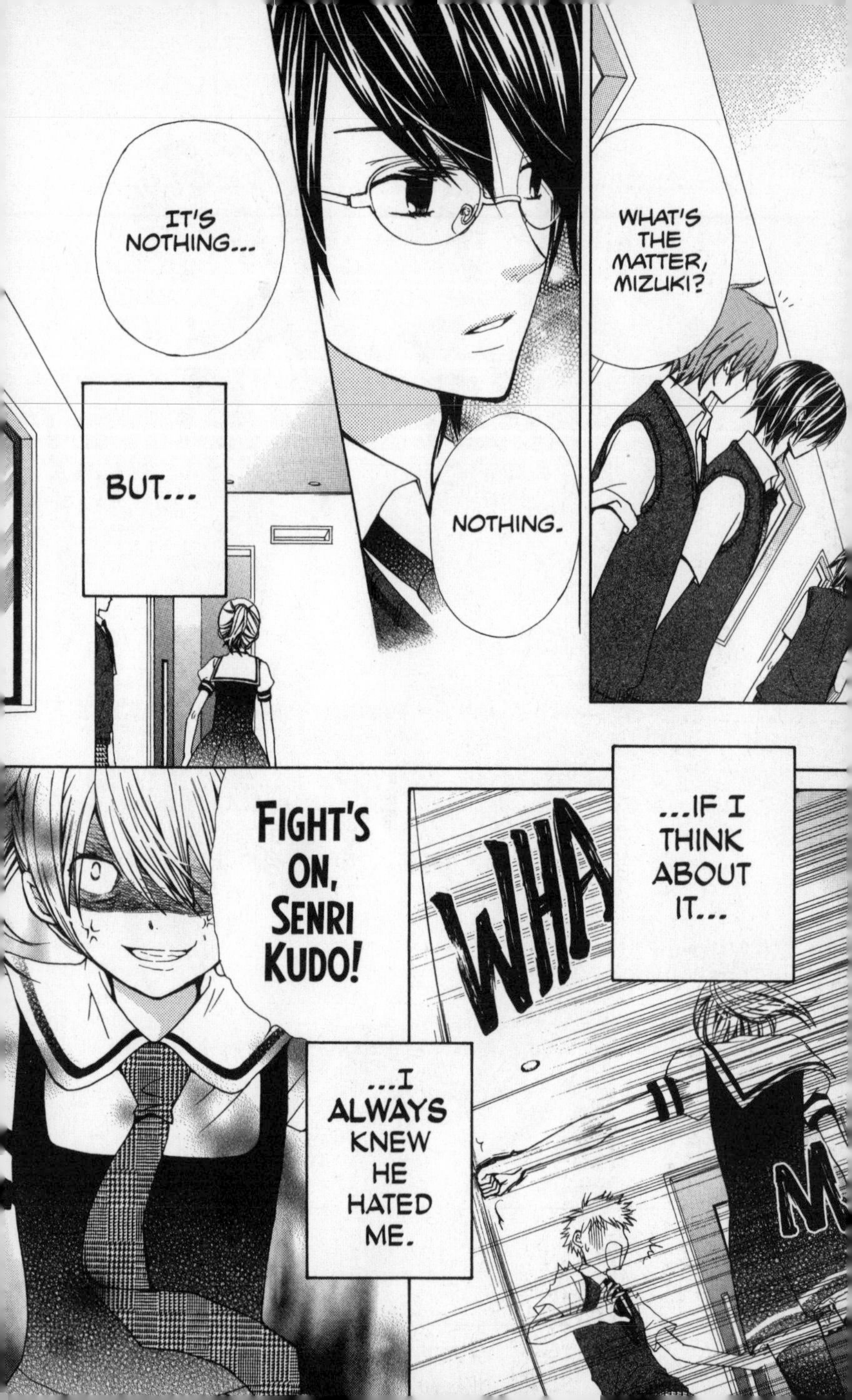
WHAT'S THE MATTER, MIZUKI?
NOTHING.
IT'S NOTHING...
BUT...
...IF I THINK ABOUT IT...
WHA
...I ALWAYS KNEW HE HATED ME.
FIGHT'S ON, SENRI KUDO!

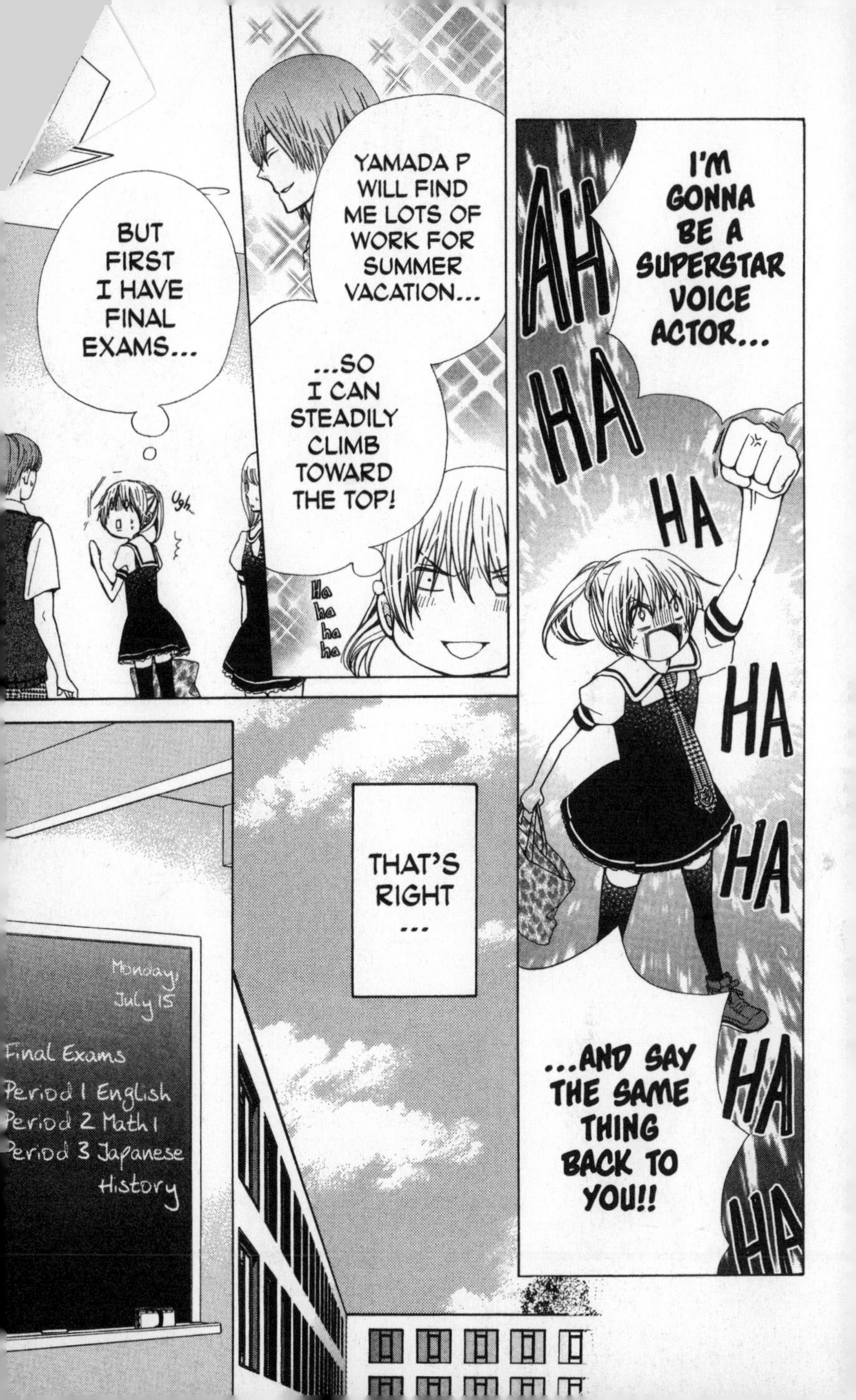

I'M GONNA BE A SUPERSTAR VOICE ACTOR...
AH HA HA HA HA HA HA HA
...AND SAY THE SAME THING BACK TO YOU!!
YAMADA P WILL FIND ME LOTS OF WORK FOR SUMMER VACATION...
...SO I CAN STEADILY CLIMB TOWARD THE TOP!
Ha ha ha ha ha
BUT FIRST I HAVE FINAL EXAMS...
Ugh...
THAT'S RIGHT...
Monday, July 15
Final Exams
Period 1 English
Period 2 Math I
Period 3 Japanese History

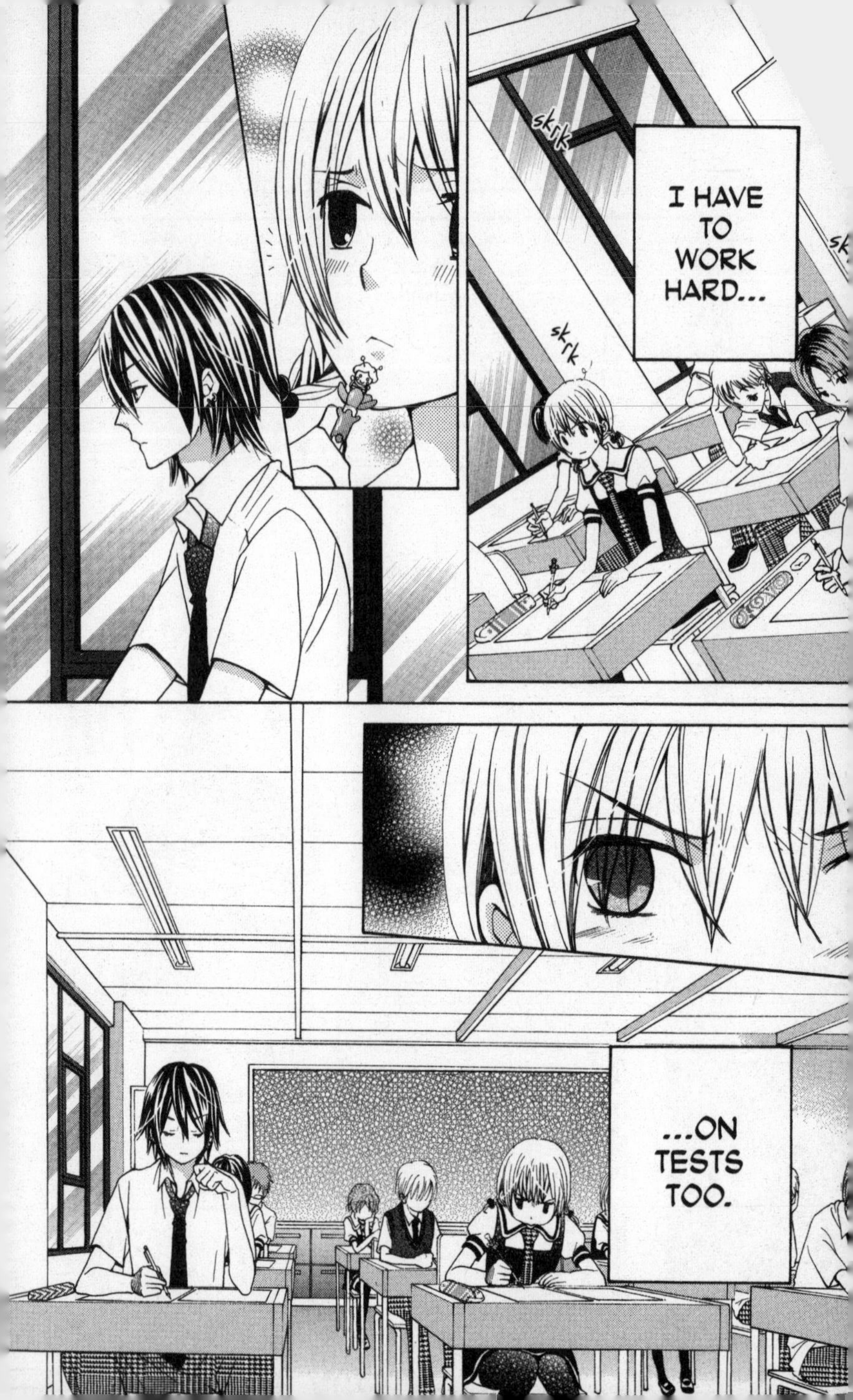
skrk
I HAVE TO WORK HARD...
skrk
sk
...ON TESTS TOO.

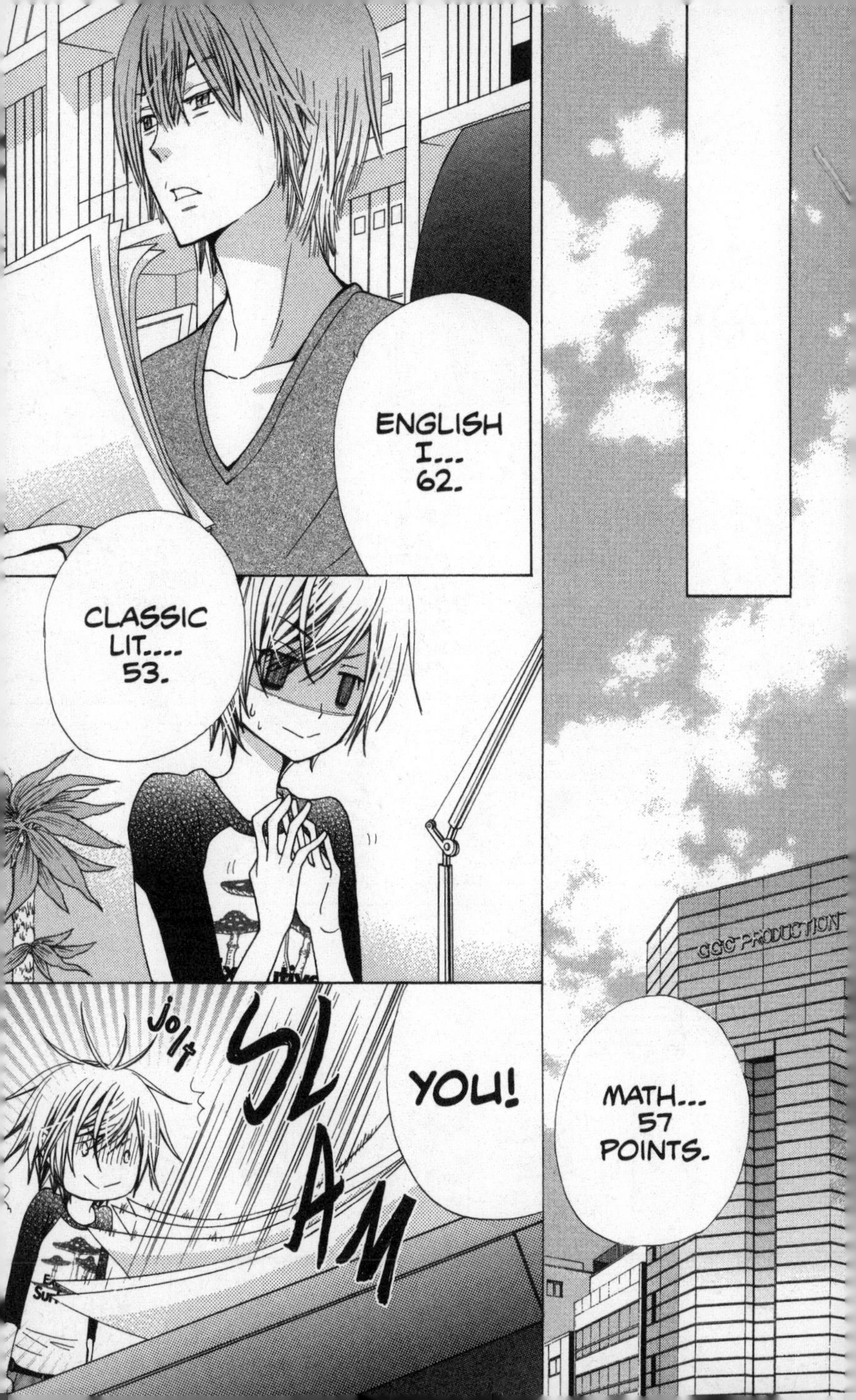
MATH... 57 POINTS.
ENGLISH I... 62.
CLASSIC LIT..... 53.
YOU!
SLAM
jolt

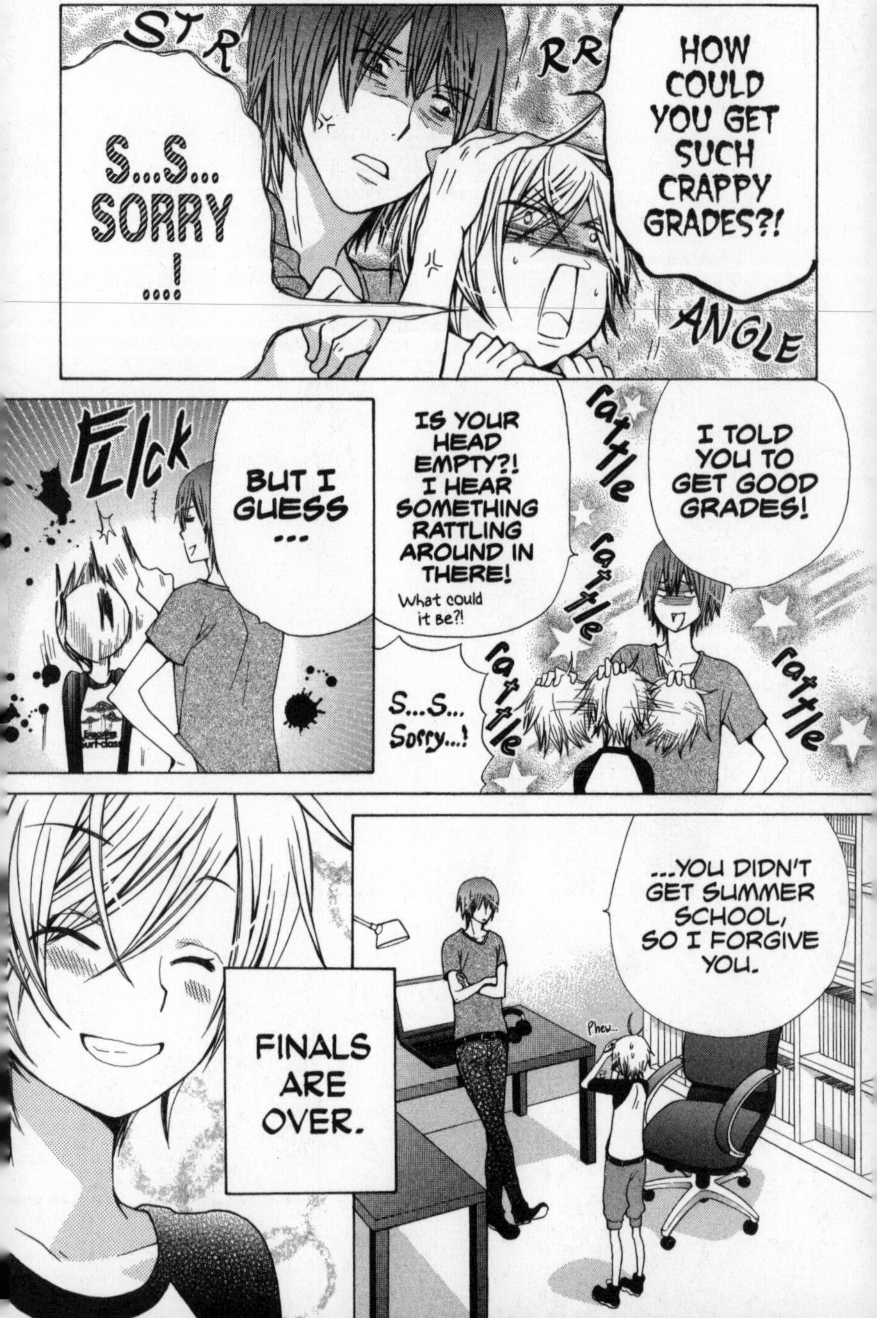
HOW COULD YOU GET SUCH CRAPPY GRADES?!
STR
RR
S...S... SORRY...!
ANGLE
I TOLD YOU TO GET GOOD GRADES!
rattle
rattle
rattle
rattle
IS YOUR HEAD EMPTY?! I HEAR SOMETHING RATTLING AROUND IN THERE!
What could it be?!
S...S... Sorry...!
BUT I GUESS ...
FLIck
...YOU DIDN'T GET SUMMER SCHOOL, SO I FORGIVE YOU.
Phew...
FINALS ARE OVER.

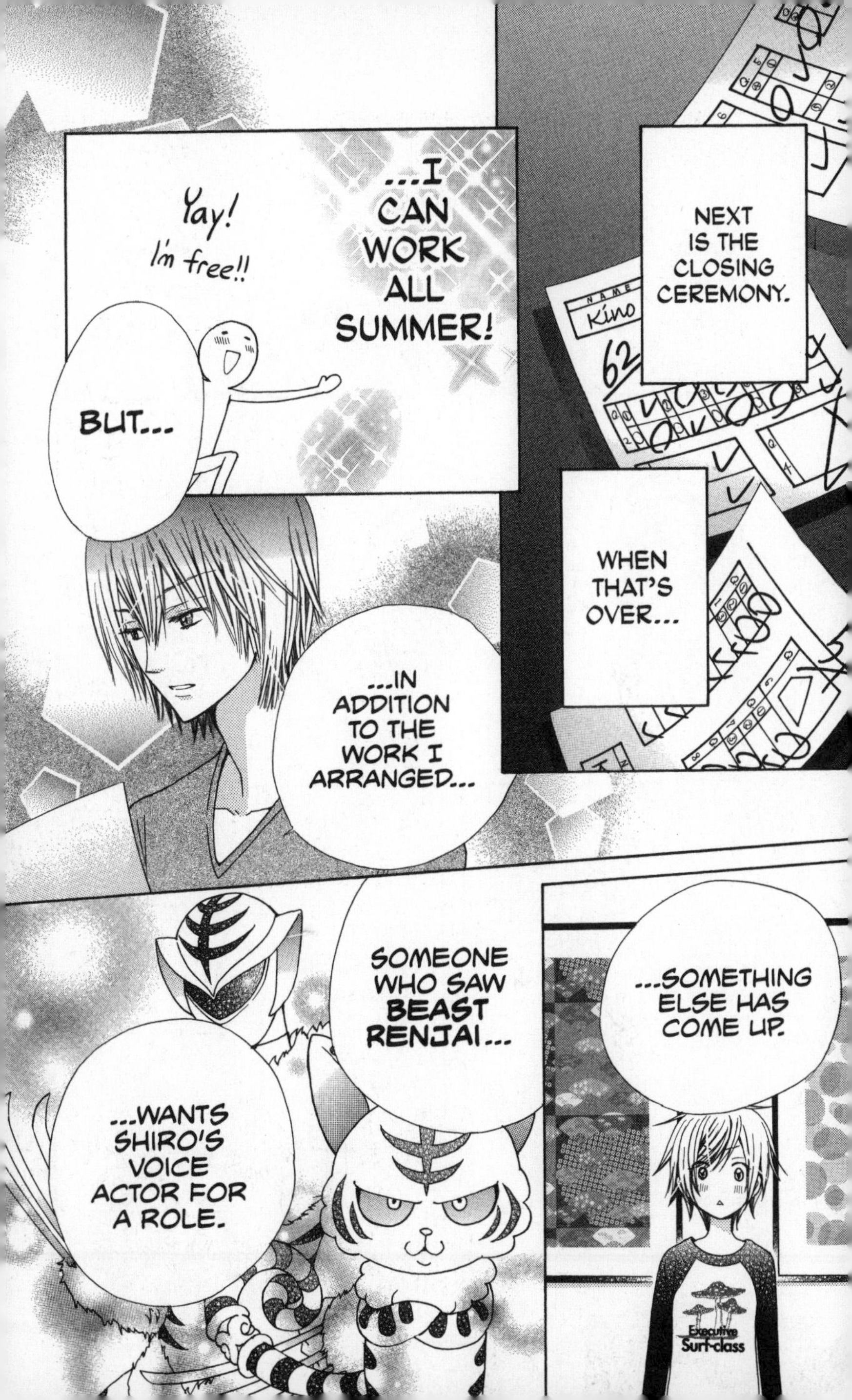
NEXT IS THE CLOSING CEREMONY.
NAME
Kino
62
WHEN THAT'S OVER...
...I CAN WORK ALL SUMMER!
Yay! I'm free!!
BUT...
...IN ADDITION TO THE WORK I ARRANGED...
...SOMETHING ELSE HAS COME UP.
Executive Surf-class
SOMEONE WHO SAW BEAST RENJAI...
...WANTS SHIRO'S VOICE ACTOR FOR A ROLE.

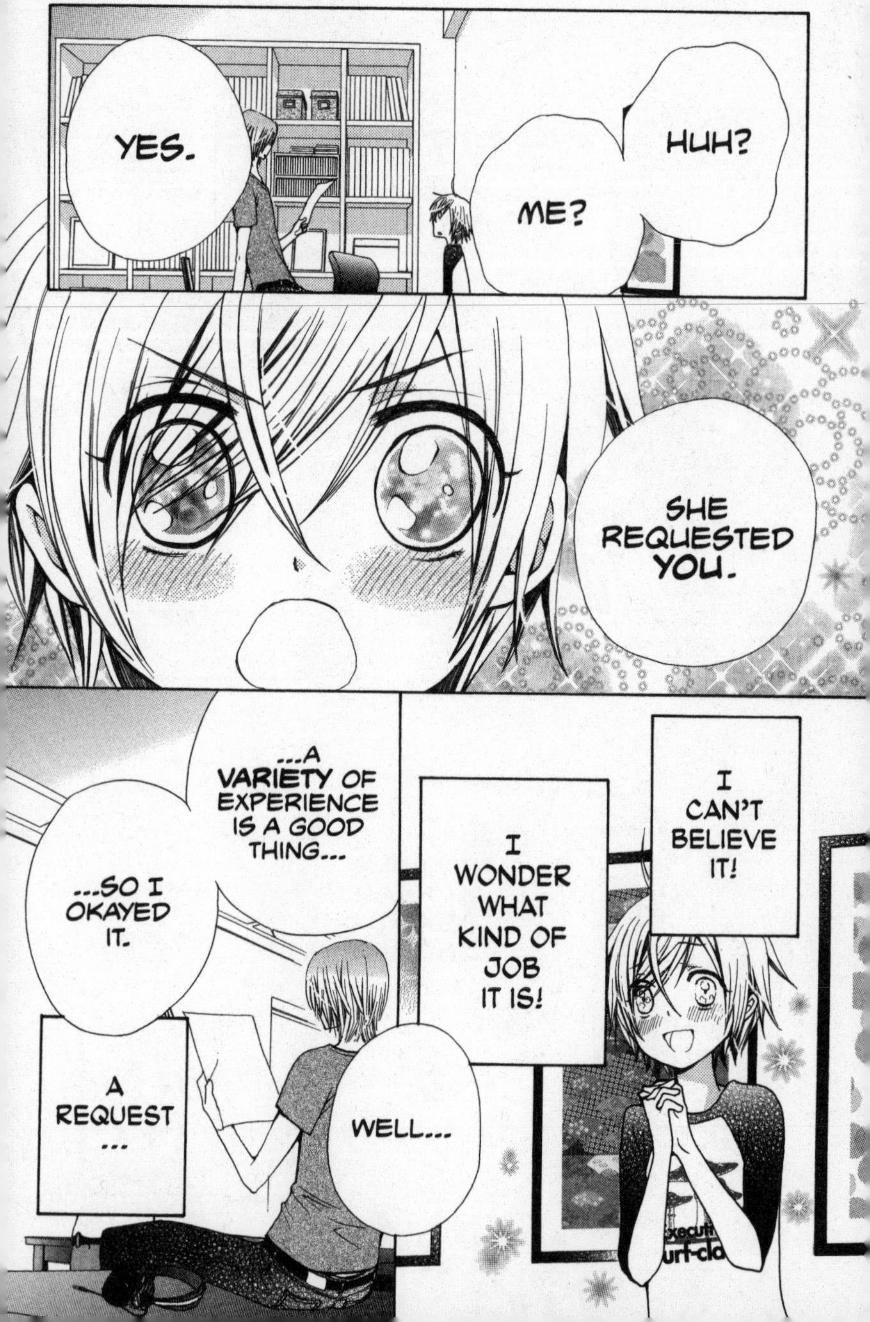
HUH?
ME?
YES.
SHE REQUESTED YOU.
I CAN'T BELIEVE IT!
I WONDER WHAT KIND OF JOB IT IS!
...A VARIETY OF EXPERIENCE IS A GOOD THING...
...SO I OKAYED IT.
WELL...
A REQUEST...

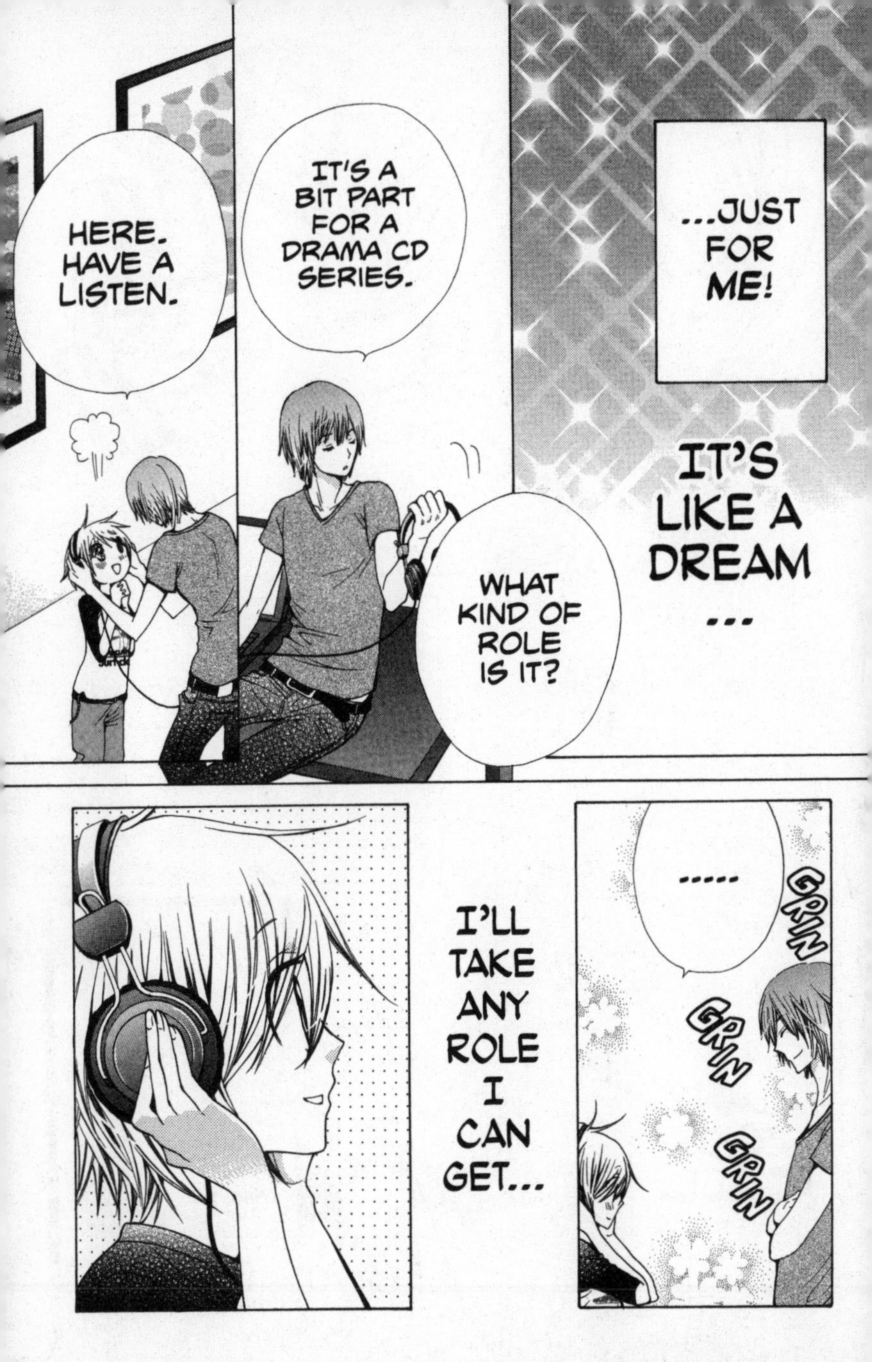

...JUST FOR ME!
IT'S LIKE A DREAM ...
WHAT KIND OF ROLE IS IT?
IT'S A BIT PART FOR A DRAMA CD SERIES.
HERE. HAVE A LISTEN.
.....
GRIN GRIN GRIN
I'LL TAKE ANY ROLE I CAN GET...

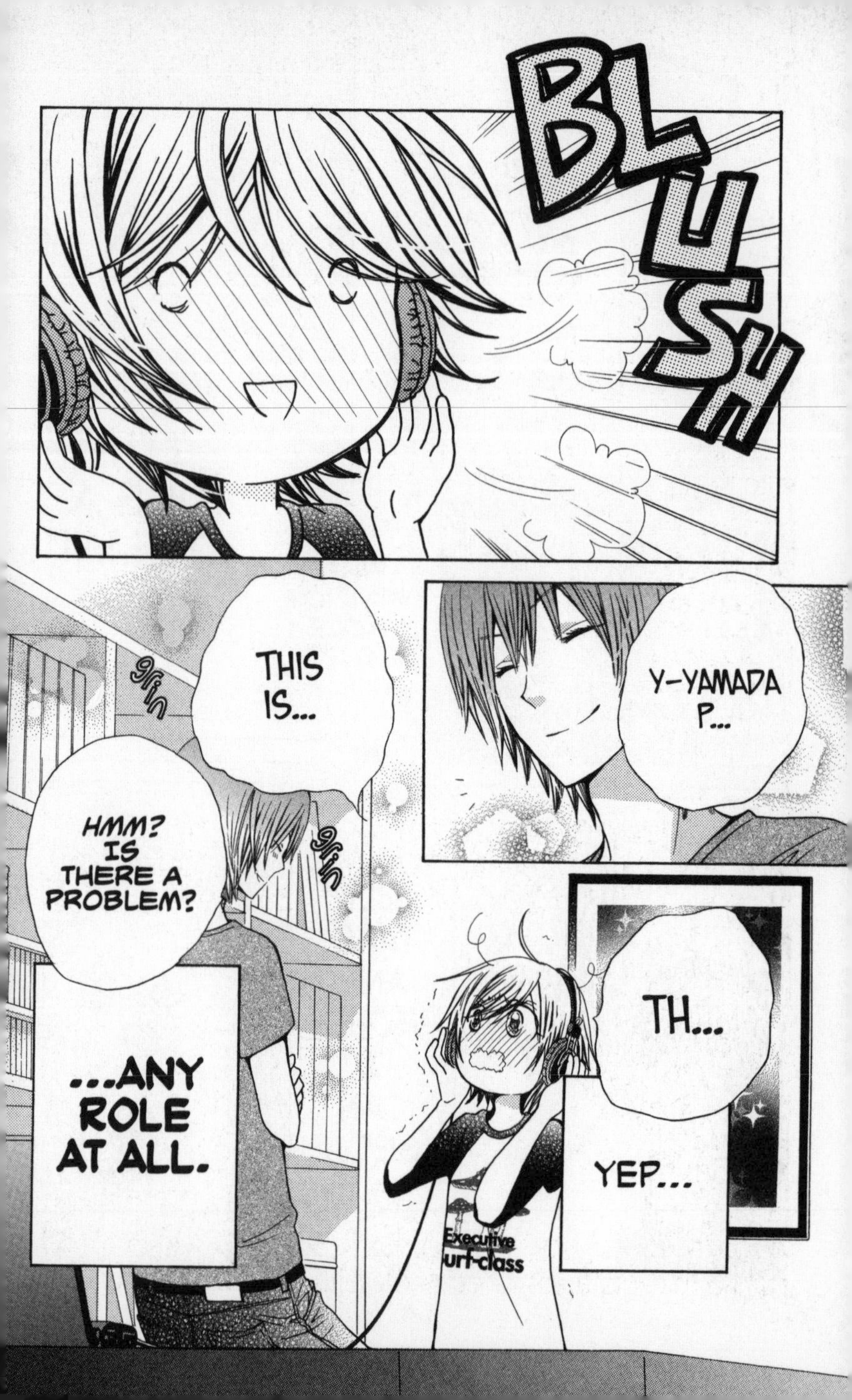
BLUSH
Y-YAMADA P...
THIS IS...
grin
HMM? IS THERE A PROBLEM?
grin
TH...
...ANY ROLE AT ALL.
YEP...
Executive
Surf-class

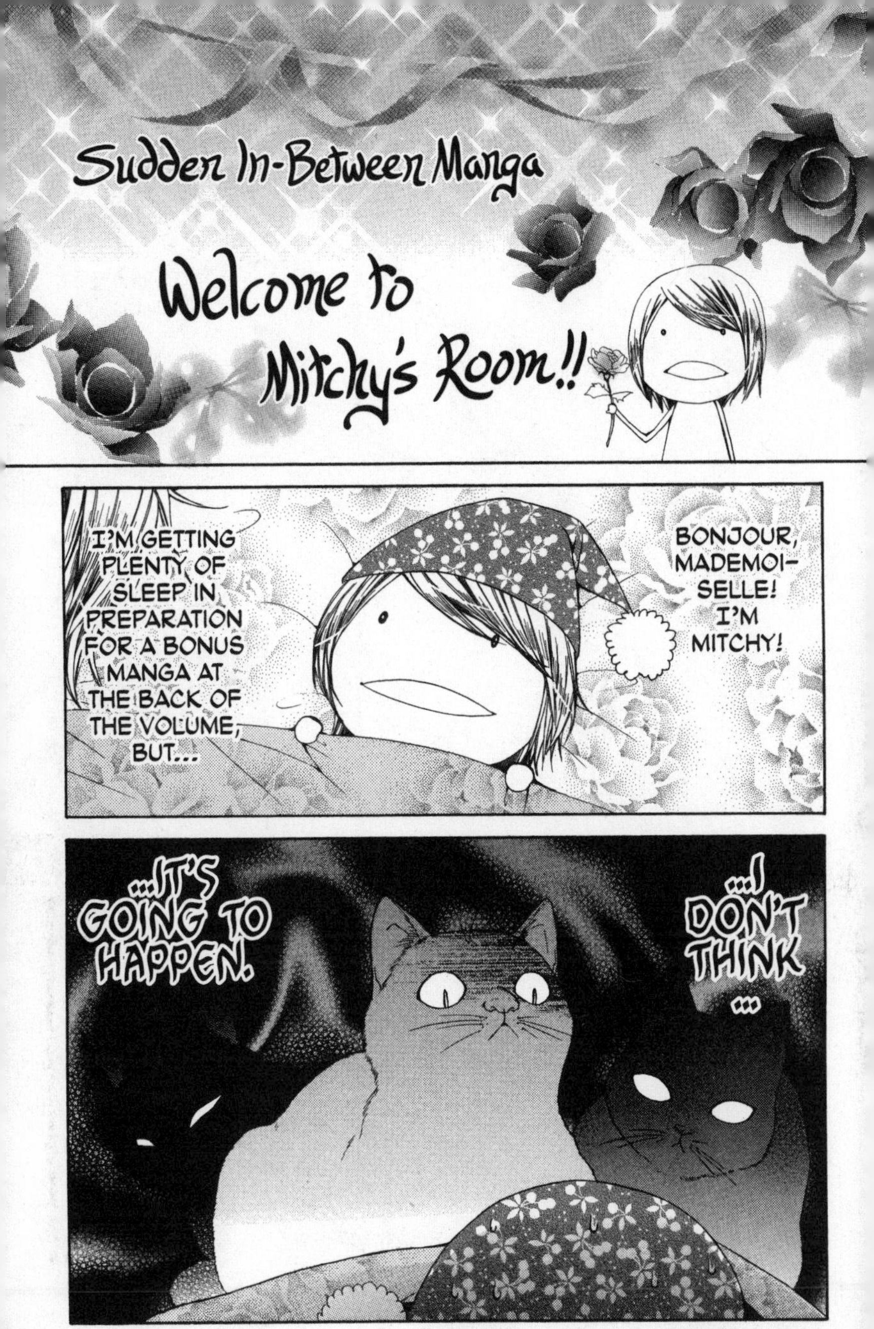
Sudden In-Between Manga
Welcome to Mitchy's Room!!
BONJOUR, MADEMOI-SELLE! I'M MITCHY!
I'M GETTING PLENTY OF SLEEP IN PREPARATION FOR A BONUS MANGA AT THE BACK OF THE VOLUME, BUT...
...I DON'T THINK...
...IT'S GOING TO HAPPEN.

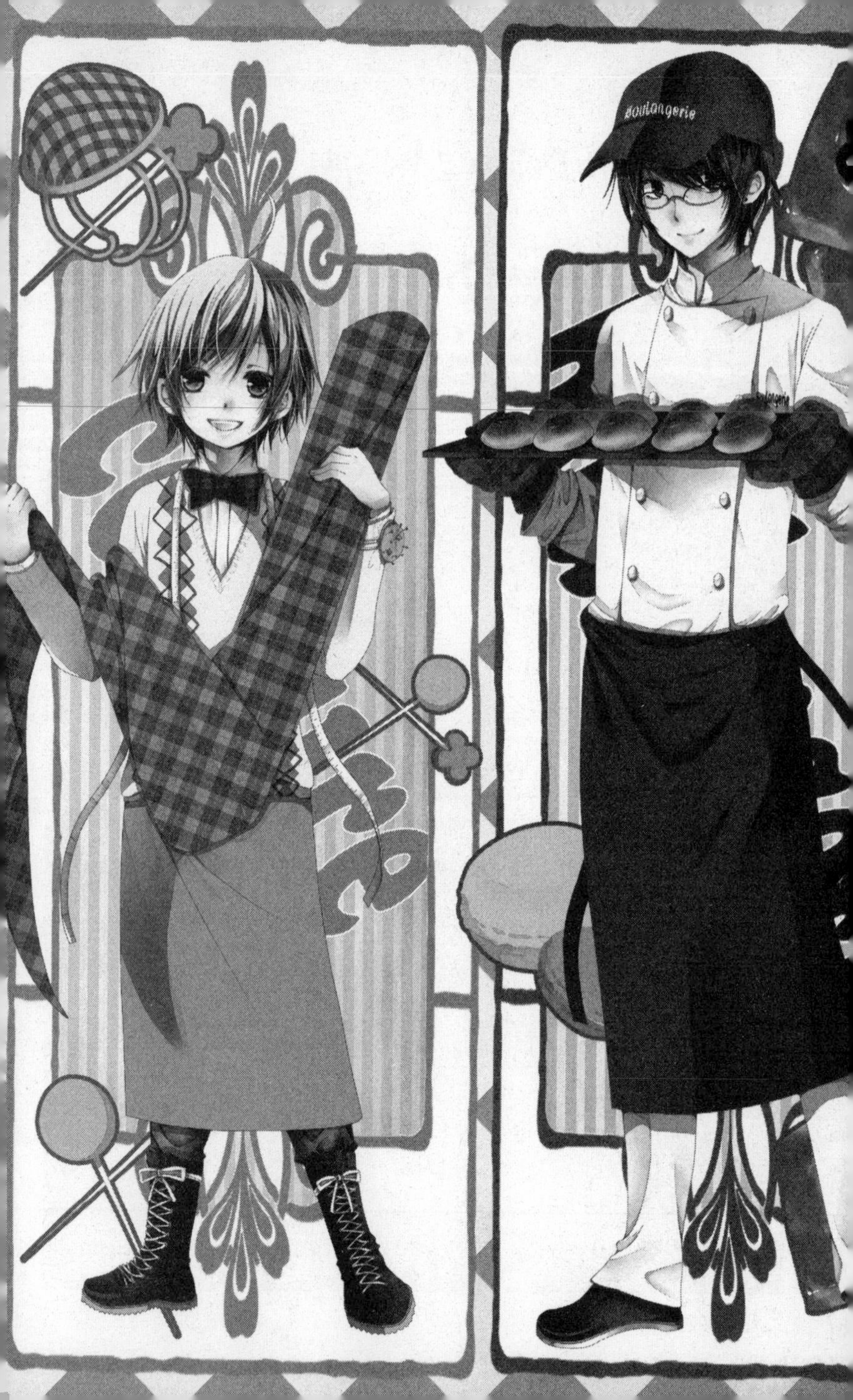
Boulangerie

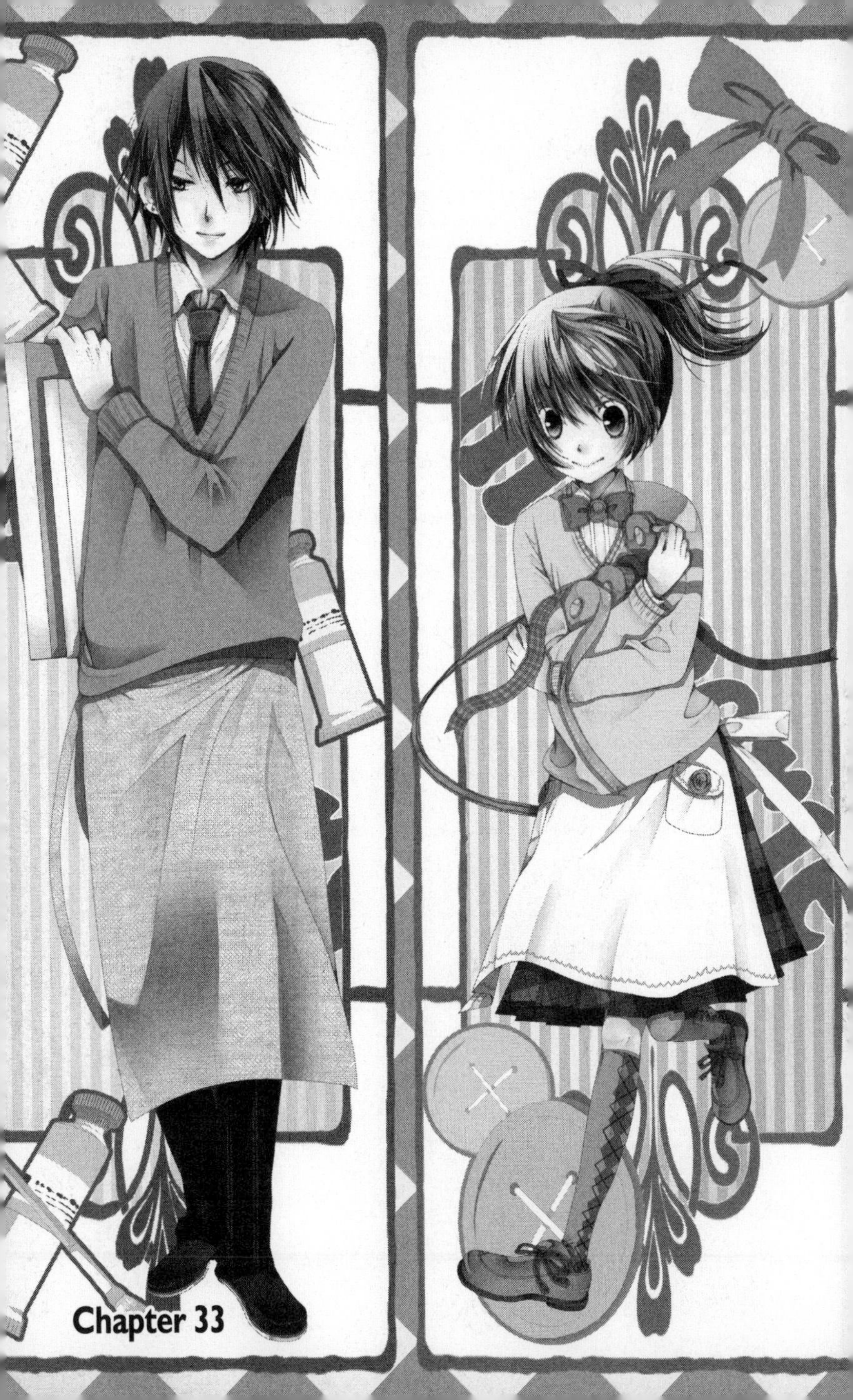
Chapter 33

~Skip this if boys' love isn't for you!!~

{Sudden Bonus Materials Corner!!}

## *Pale Blue Eyes, Crimson Tears*

Written by Yuki Isoguchi
Art by Kazumi Sano

"Can't you do it?"

Under Takato's harsh gaze, Fujitani shrank back.

"Takato... But...if we do that, then their relationship will..."

The words Fujitani had prepared so carefully were suddenly blocked by Takato's lips.

"...!"

As Takato toyed with his lips, first deeply and then just light brushes against his mouth, Fujitani's vision wavered.

Takato suddenly let him go, and an impassioned sigh passed between them.

"Takato..."

Seeing surprise and even more joy in Fujitani's moist eyes, Takato snickered to himself.

*He's mine.*

He gently ran his finger along Fujitani's cheek to his kiss-wet lips.

"Just do what I say."

In response to Takato's quiet, merciless words, all Fujitani could do was nod.

"I...I understand."

"Good boy," Takato whispered before slowly kissing Fujitani's trembling lips.

Smitten and drunk on sensation, Fujitani surrendered himself.

"I...will do whatever you say. So...take me."

At the faint, supplicatory sound of Fujitani's voice, Takato laughed softly, full of satisfaction.

"That depends on you."

The molten red sun slowly descended to the west, casting two shadows in sharp relief.

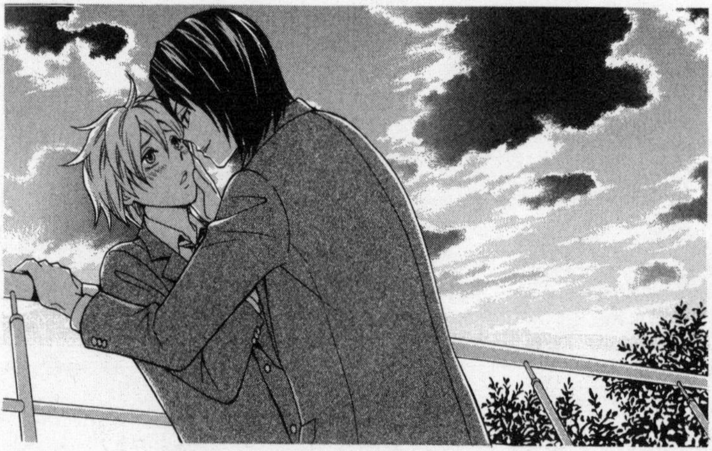

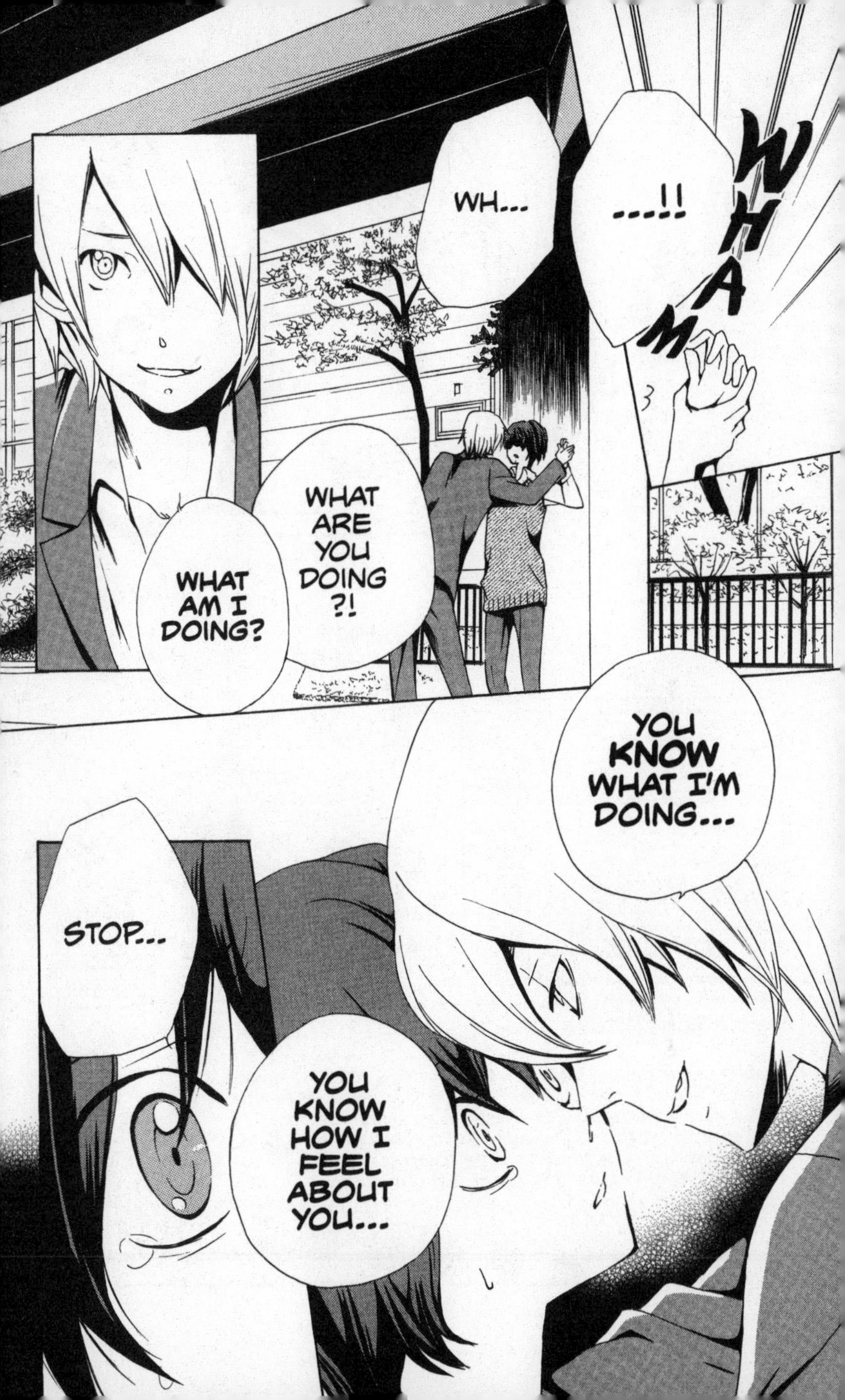
WHAM
...!!
WH...
WHAT ARE YOU DOING?!
WHAT AM I DOING?
YOU KNOW WHAT I'M DOING...
YOU KNOW HOW I FEEL ABOUT YOU...
STOP...

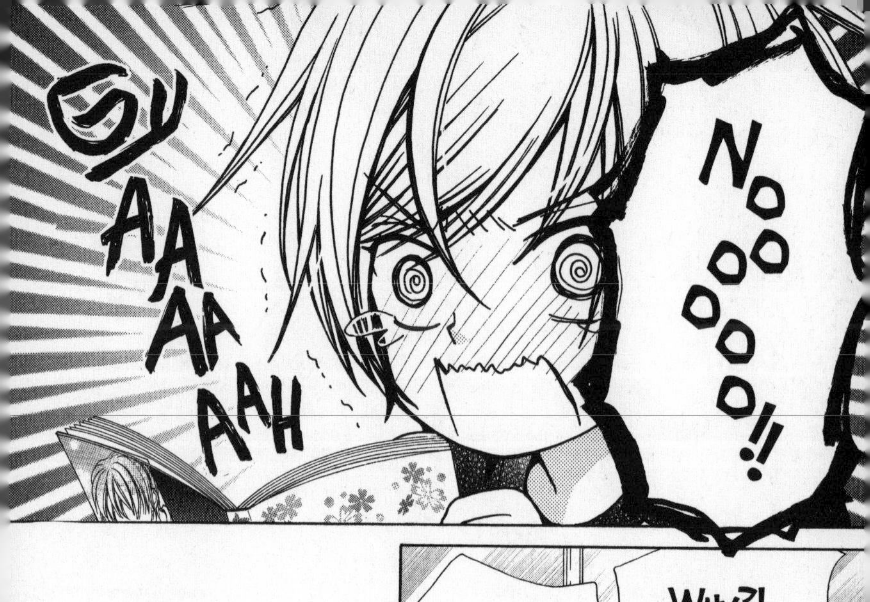
NOOOOOOO!!
GYAAAAAAAH
WHY?! THE WORLD HAS TONS OF GIRLS...
...BUT ALL THESE BOYS FALL FOR BOYS!!
trmbl
trmbl
Hmm? No! Don't do that!! Gyaaah!
YOU GUESSED IT.

◦ Sudden Bonus Materials Corner ◦

Apologies to anyone who doesn't go in for boys' & love novels and manga. It's just a script that Shiro does in the manga. My assistant I-san drew a gorgeous insert. The previous two pages look like a completely different manga!! The craftsmanship of the novel almost made me spit out my green tea! I tried to pull off something like a BL manga, but I didn't think I could beat her.

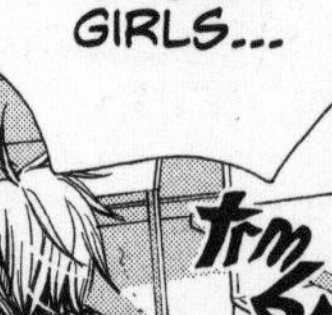
5

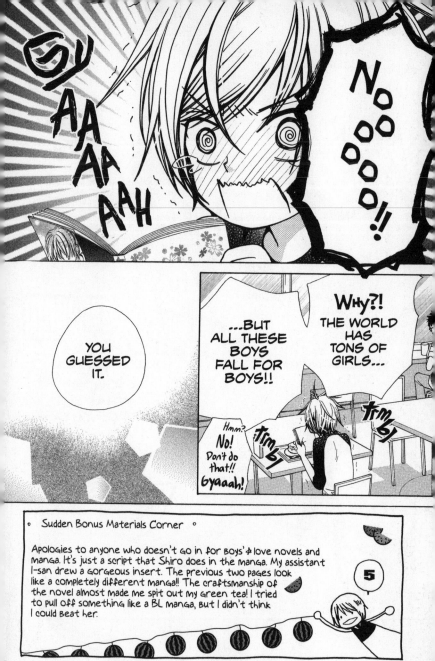

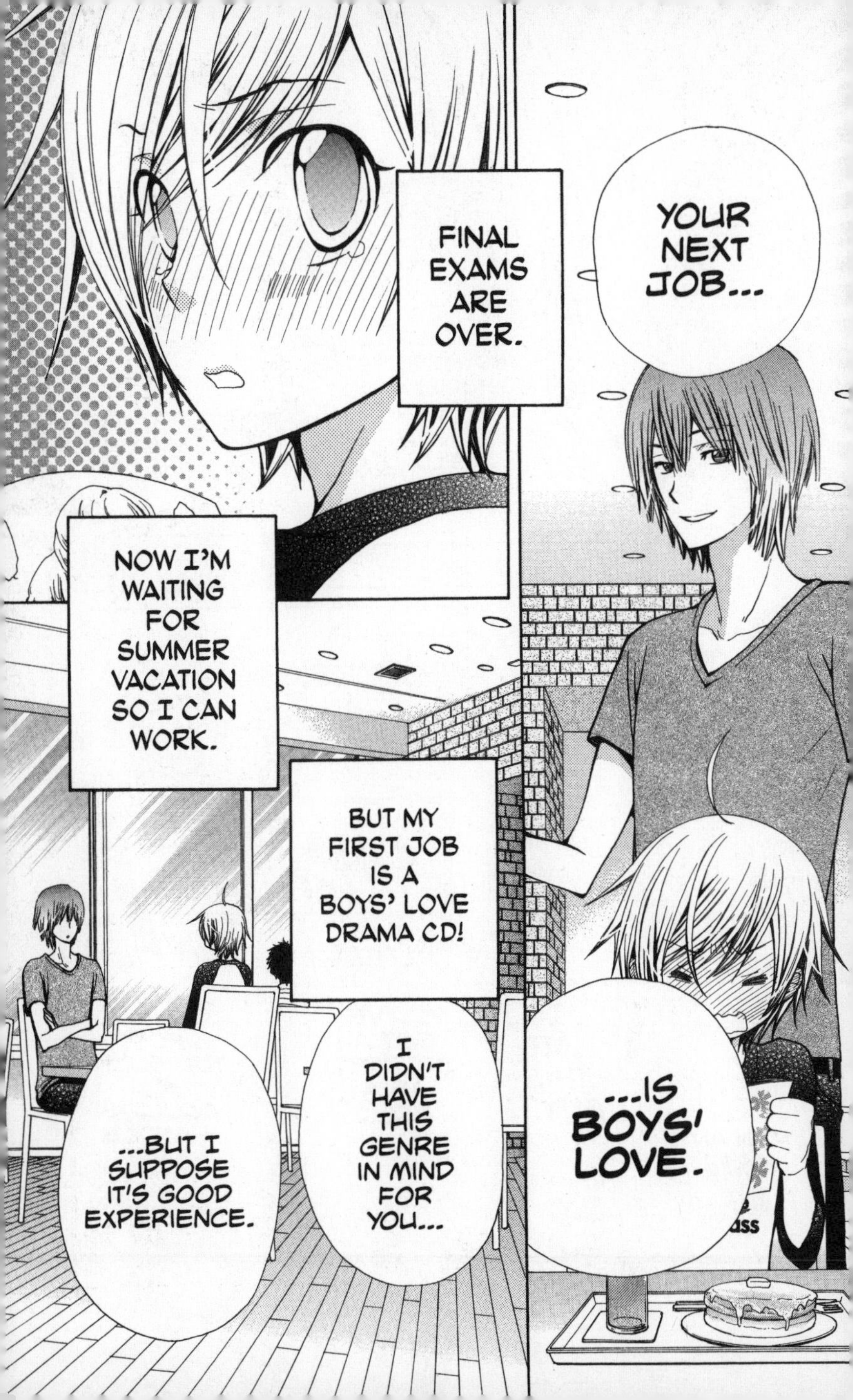
YOUR NEXT JOB...
...IS BOYS' LOVE.
FINAL EXAMS ARE OVER.
NOW I'M WAITING FOR SUMMER VACATION SO I CAN WORK.
BUT MY FIRST JOB IS A BOYS' LOVE DRAMA CD!
I DIDN'T HAVE THIS GENRE IN MIND FOR YOU...
...BUT I SUPPOSE IT'S GOOD EXPERIENCE.

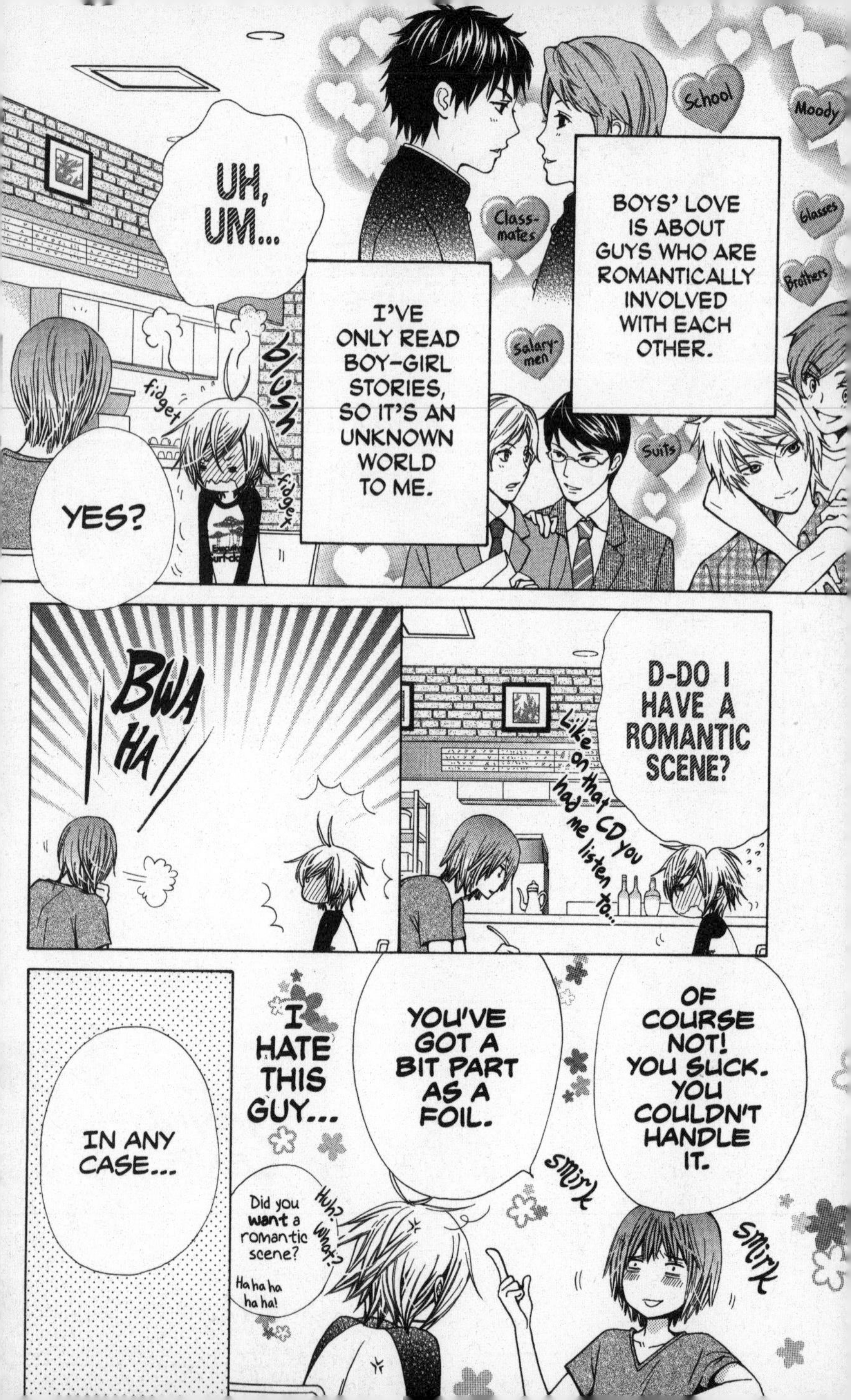
School
Moody
BOYS' LOVE IS ABOUT GUYS WHO ARE ROMANTICALLY INVOLVED WITH EACH OTHER.
Glasses
Class-mates
Brothers
I'VE ONLY READ BOY-GIRL STORIES, SO IT'S AN UNKNOWN WORLD TO ME.
Salary-men
Suits
UH, UM...
blush
fidget
fidget
YES?
D-DO I HAVE A ROMANTIC SCENE?
Like on that CD you had me listen to...
BWA HA
OF COURSE NOT! YOU SUCK. YOU COULDN'T HANDLE IT.
YOU'VE GOT A BIT PART AS A FOIL.
smirk
smirk
I HATE THIS GUY...
Huh? What?
Did you want a romantic scene?
Ha ha ha ha ha!
IN ANY CASE...

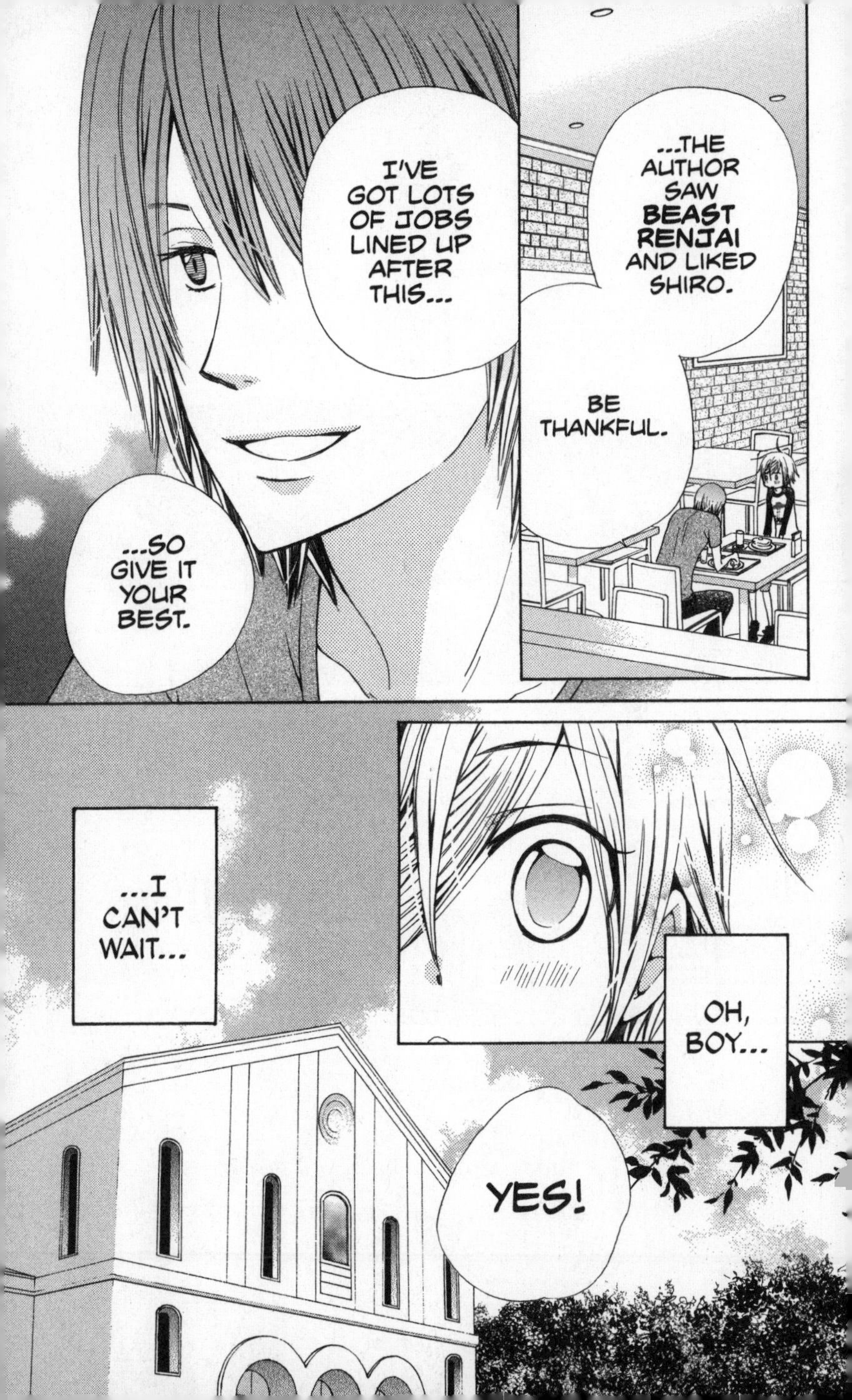
...THE AUTHOR SAW BEAST RENJAI AND LIKED SHIRO.
BE THANKFUL.
I'VE GOT LOTS OF JOBS LINED UP AFTER THIS...
...SO GIVE IT YOUR BEST.
OH, BOY...
YES!
...I CAN'T WAIT...

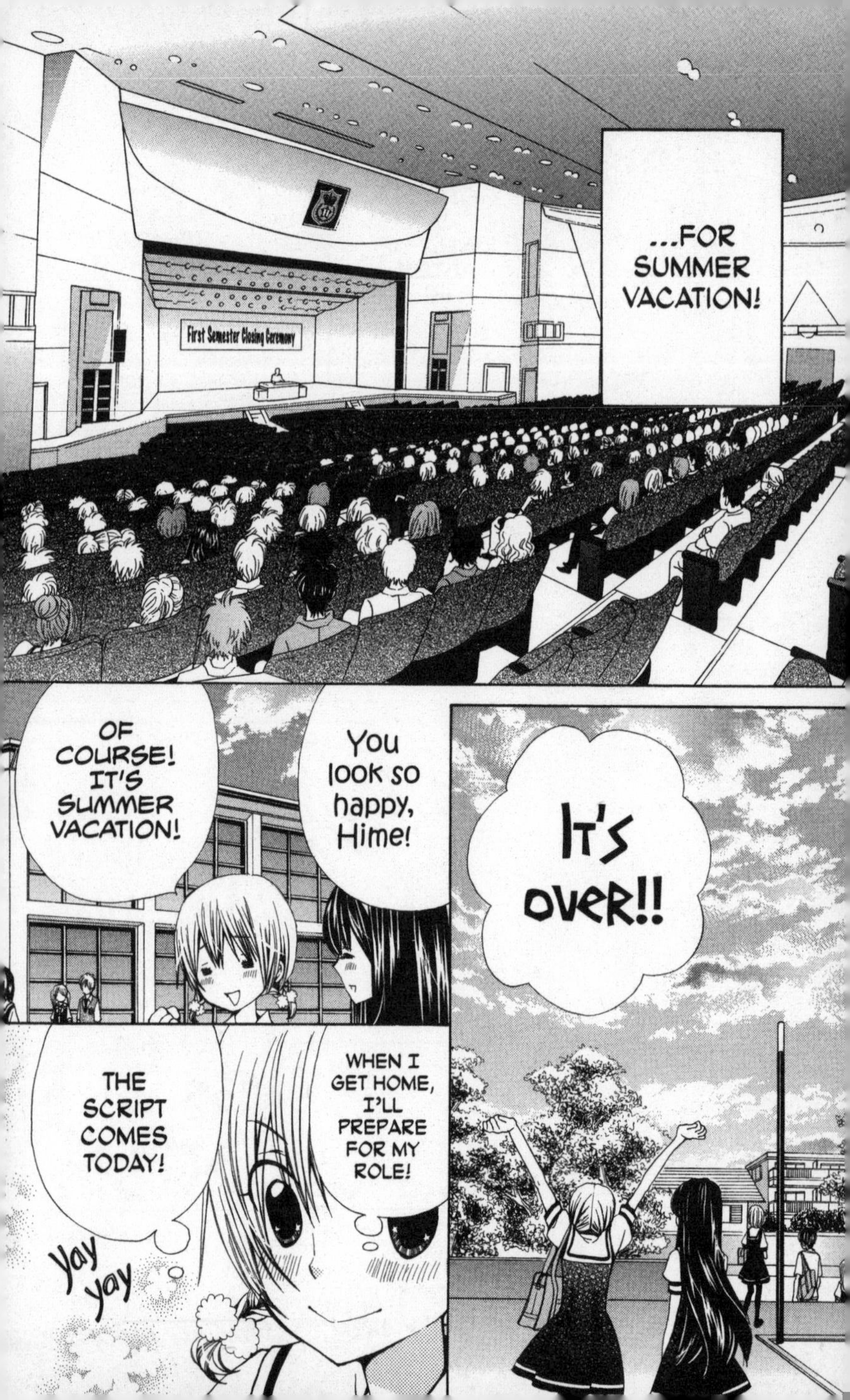
First Semester Closing Ceremony
...FOR SUMMER VACATION!
It's over!!
You look so happy, Hime!
OF COURSE! IT'S SUMMER VACATION!
WHEN I GET HOME, I'LL PREPARE FOR MY ROLE!
THE SCRIPT COMES TODAY!
yay yay

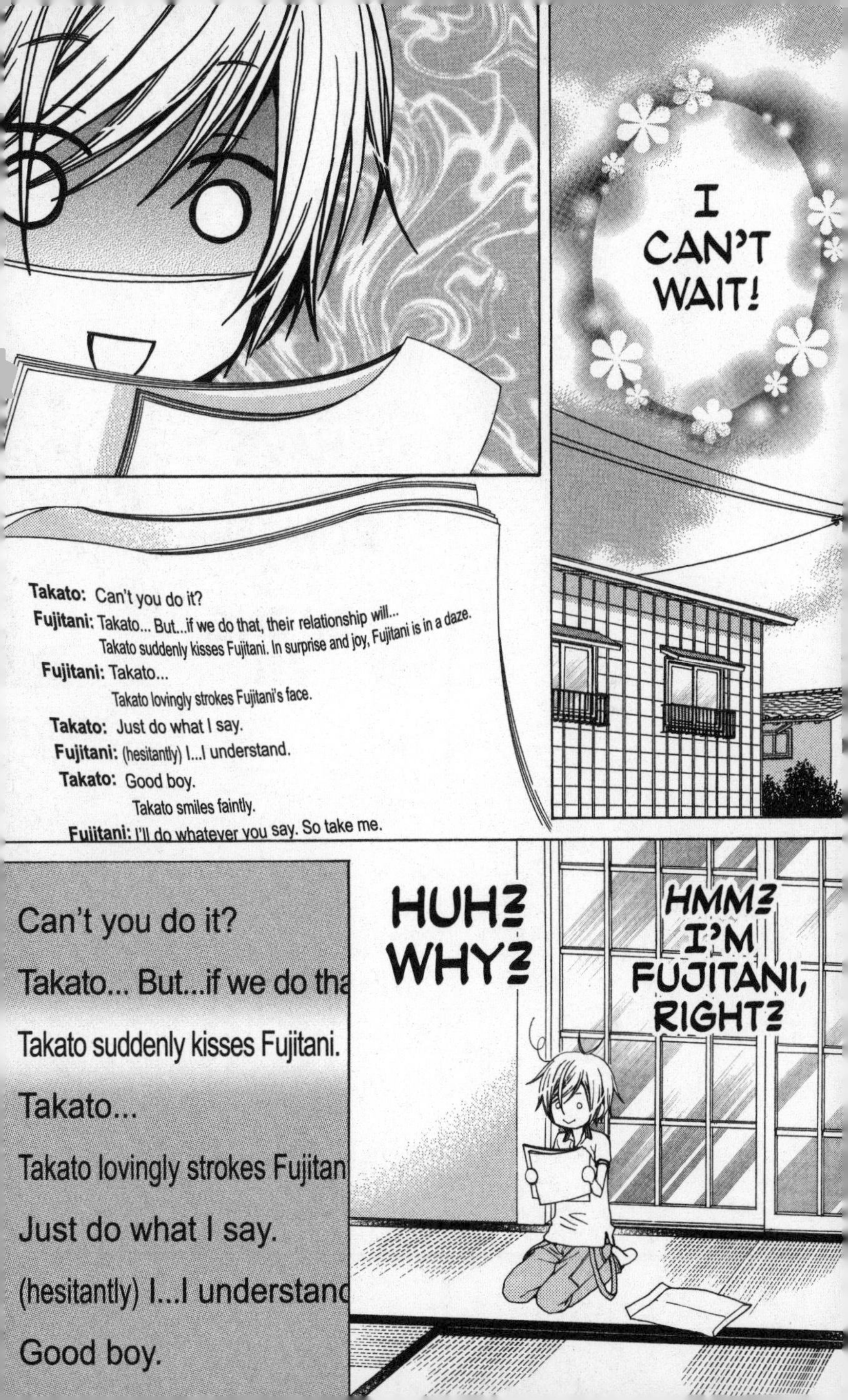
I CAN'T WAIT!
Takato: Can't you do it?
Fujitani: Takato... But...if we do that, their relationship will...
Takato suddenly kisses Fujitani. In surprise and joy, Fujitani is in a daze.
Fujitani: Takato...
Takato lovingly strokes Fujitani's face.
Takato: Just do what I say.
Fujitani: (hesitantly) I...I understand.
Takato: Good boy.
Takato smiles faintly.
Fujitani: I'll do whatever you say. So take me.
HMM? I'M FUJITANI, RIGHT?
HUH? WHY?
Can't you do it?
Takato... But...if we do tha
Takato suddenly kisses Fujitani.
Takato...
Takato lovingly strokes Fujitan
Just do what I say.
(hesitantly) I...I understand
Good boy.

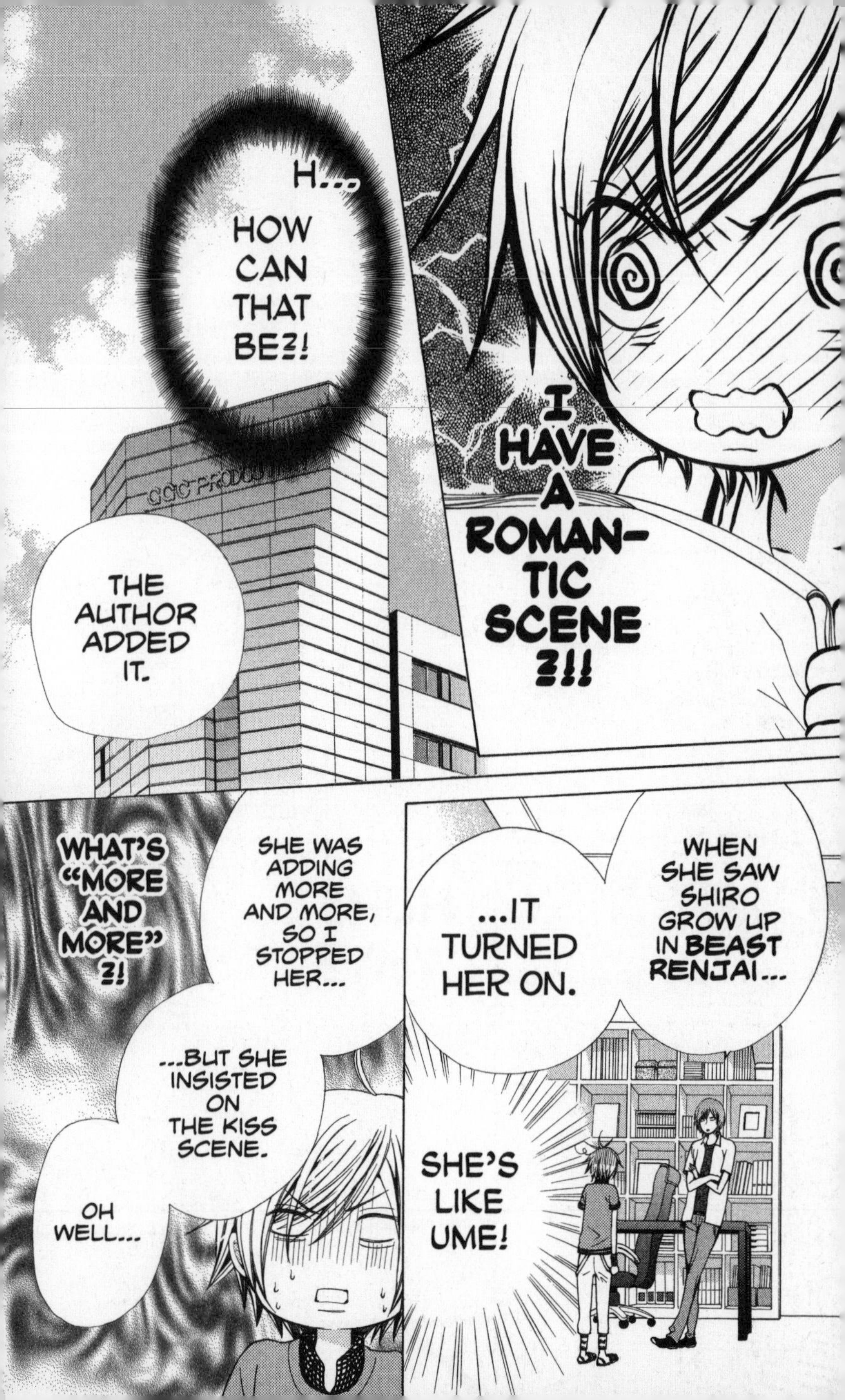
I HAVE A ROMANTIC SCENE?!!
H... HOW CAN THAT BE?!
THE AUTHOR ADDED IT.
WHEN SHE SAW SHIRO GROW UP IN BEAST RENJAI...
...IT TURNED HER ON.
SHE'S LIKE UME!
SHE WAS ADDING MORE AND MORE, SO I STOPPED HER...
WHAT'S "MORE AND MORE"?!
...BUT SHE INSISTED ON THE KISS SCENE.
OH WELL...

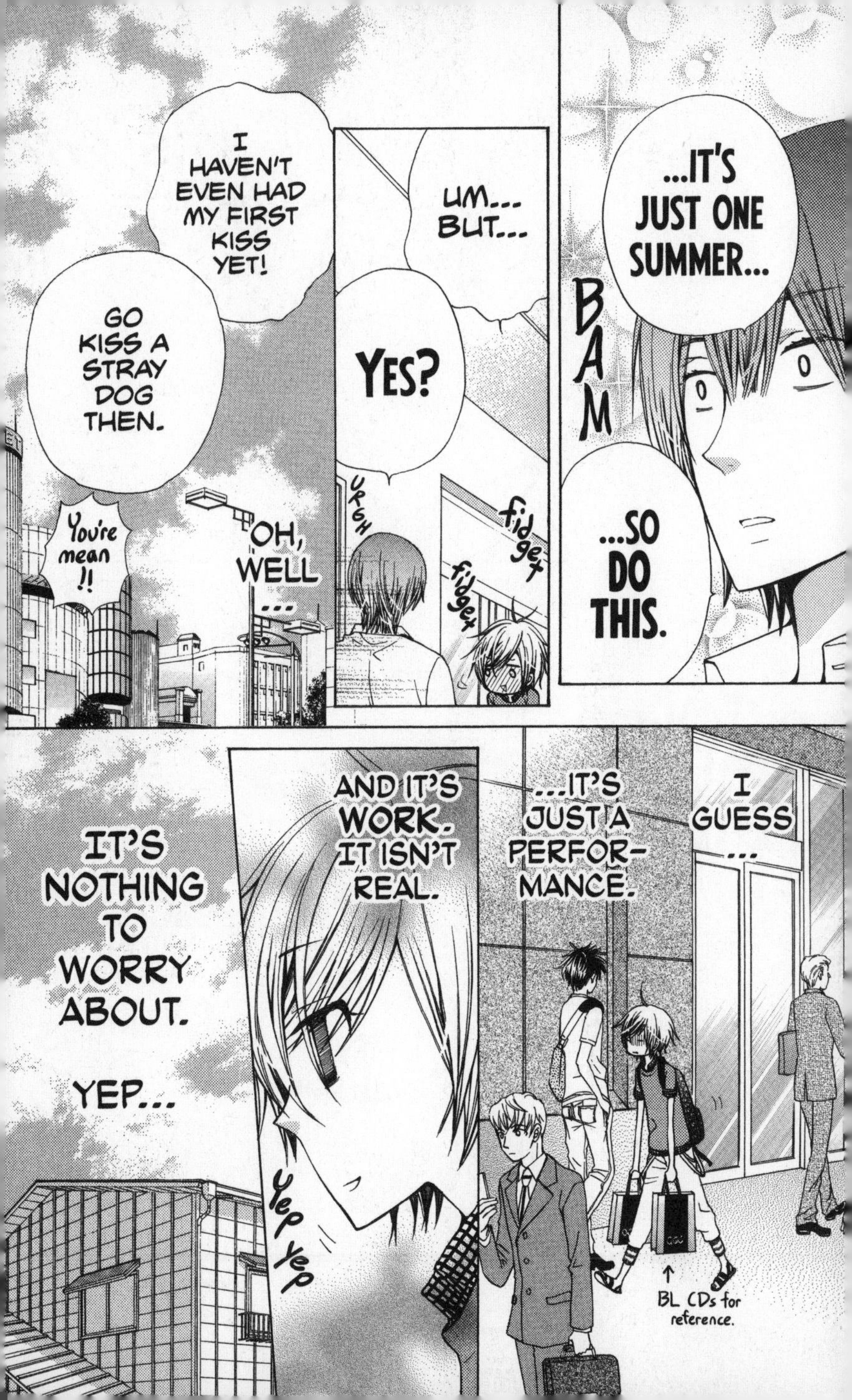
...IT'S JUST ONE SUMMER...
BAM
...SO DO THIS.
UM... BUT...
YES?
URGH
fidget
fidget
I HAVEN'T EVEN HAD MY FIRST KISS YET!
GO KISS A STRAY DOG THEN.
You're mean!!
OH, WELL...
I GUESS...
...IT'S JUST A PERFORMANCE.
AND IT'S WORK. IT ISN'T REAL.
IT'S NOTHING TO WORRY ABOUT.
YEP...
Yep yep
BL CDs for reference.

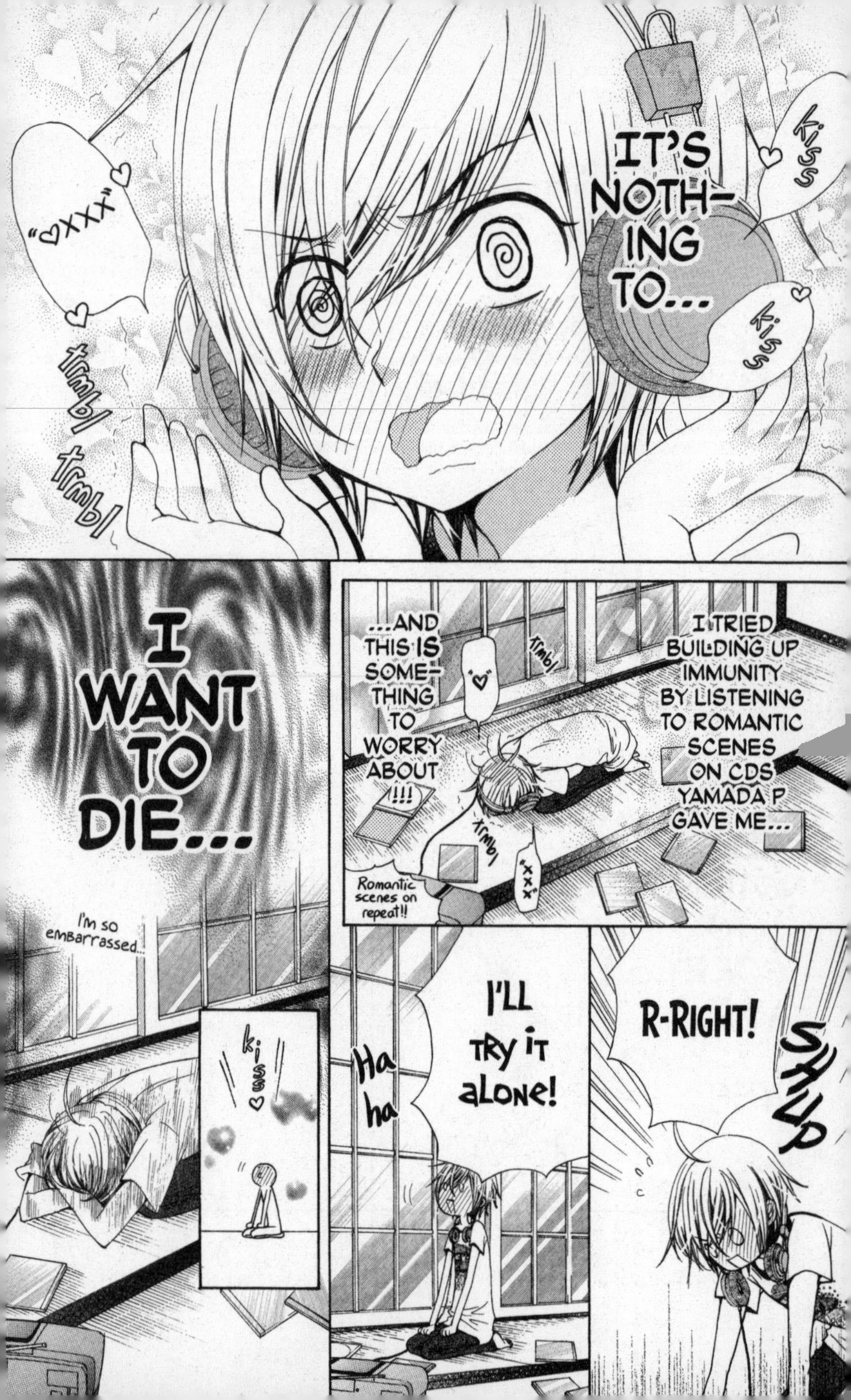
kiss
IT'S NOTHING TO...
kiss
"♡xxx"
trmbl trmbl
I TRIED BUILDING UP IMMUNITY BY LISTENING TO ROMANTIC SCENES ON CDS YAMADA P GAVE ME...
trmbl
"♡"
...AND THIS IS SOMETHING TO WORRY ABOUT!!!
trmbl
"xxx"
Romantic scenes on repeat!!
R-RIGHT!
SHLP
I'LL TRY IT ALONE!
Ha ha
I WANT TO DIE...
I'm so embarrassed...
kiss♡

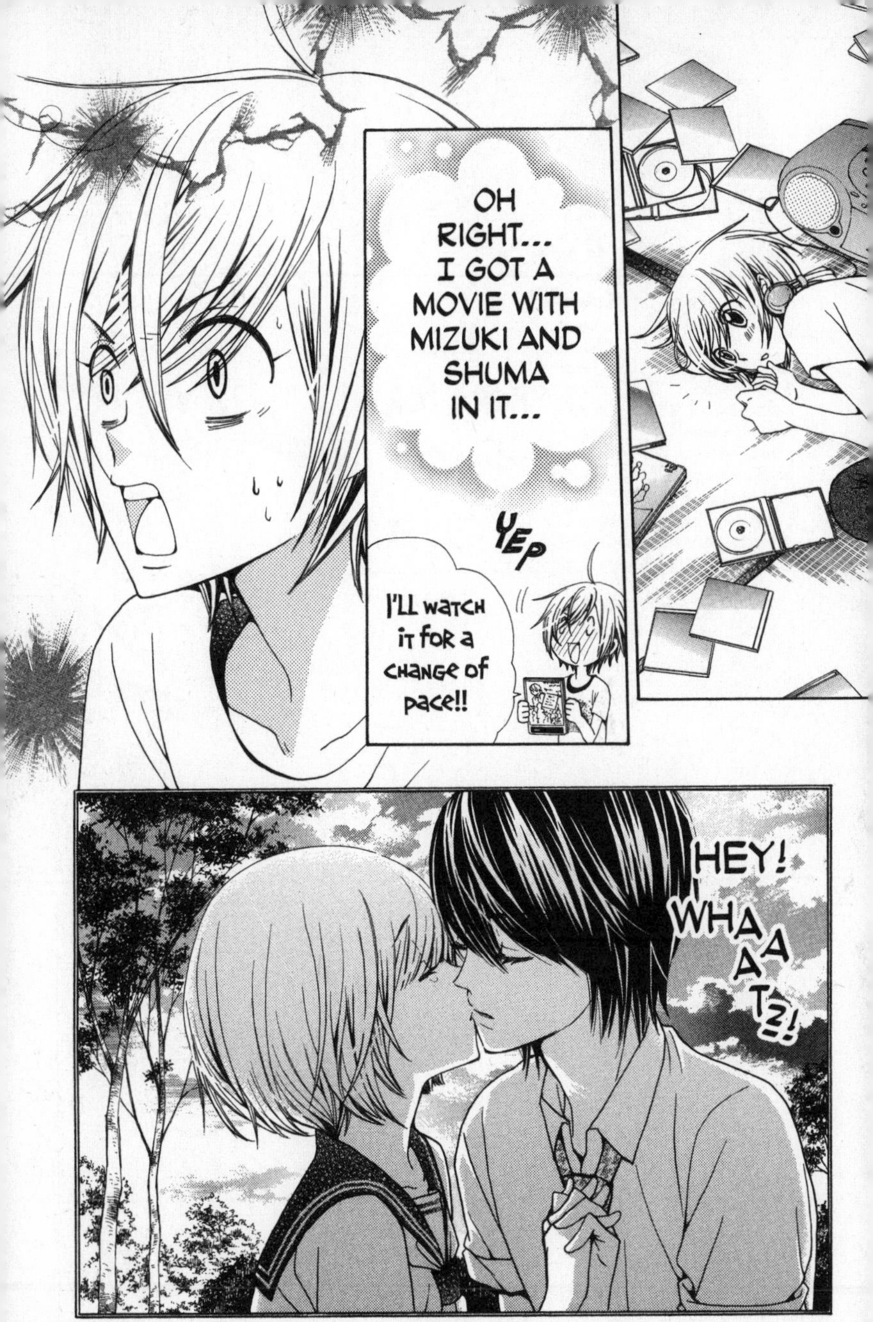
OH RIGHT... I GOT A MOVIE WITH MIZUKI AND SHUMA IN IT...
YEP
I'LL watch it for a change of pace!!
HEY! WHAAAT?!

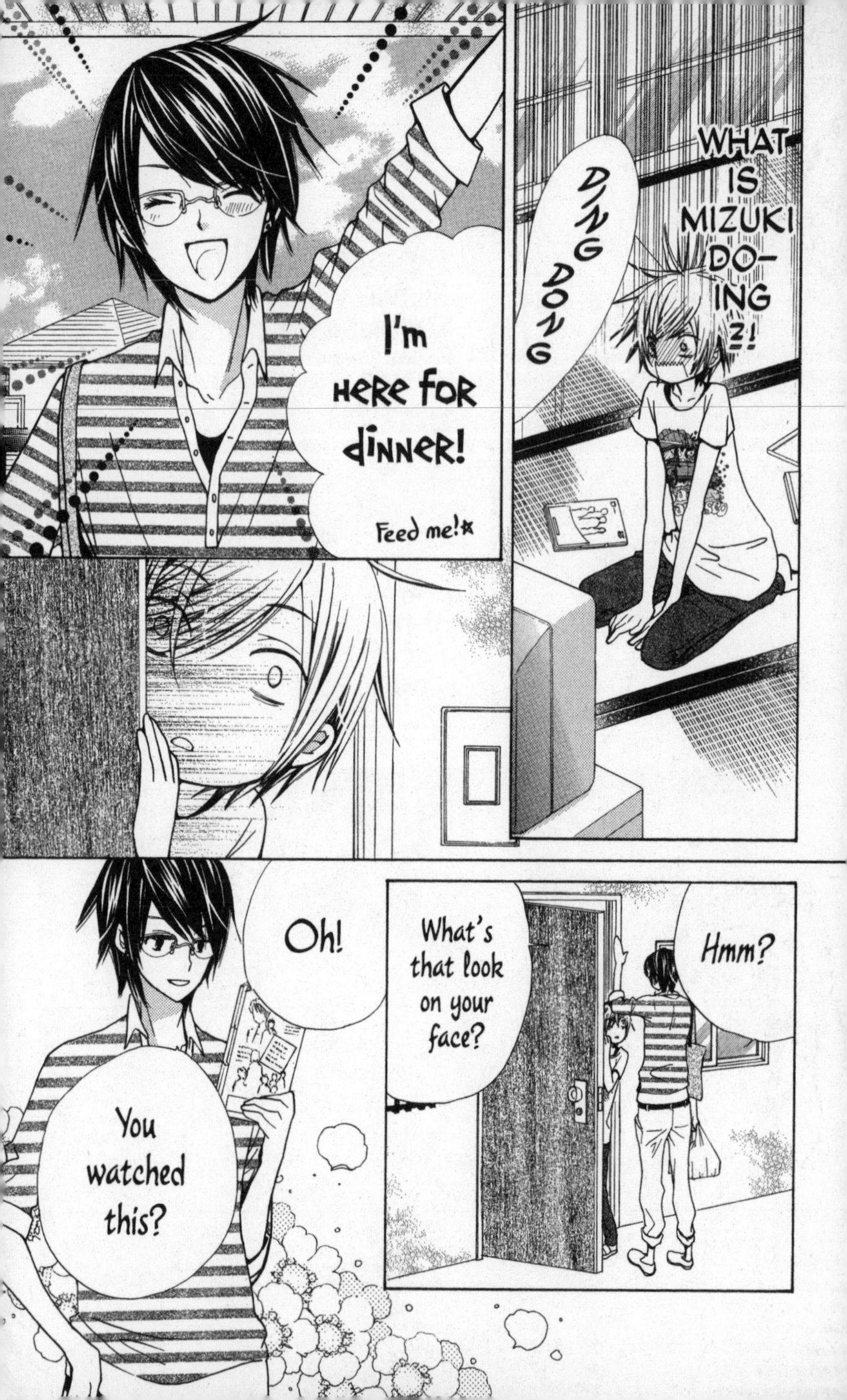
DING DONG
WHAT IS MIZUKI DO-ING?!
I'm here for dinner!
Feed me!☆
Hmm?
What's that look on your face?
Oh!
You watched this?

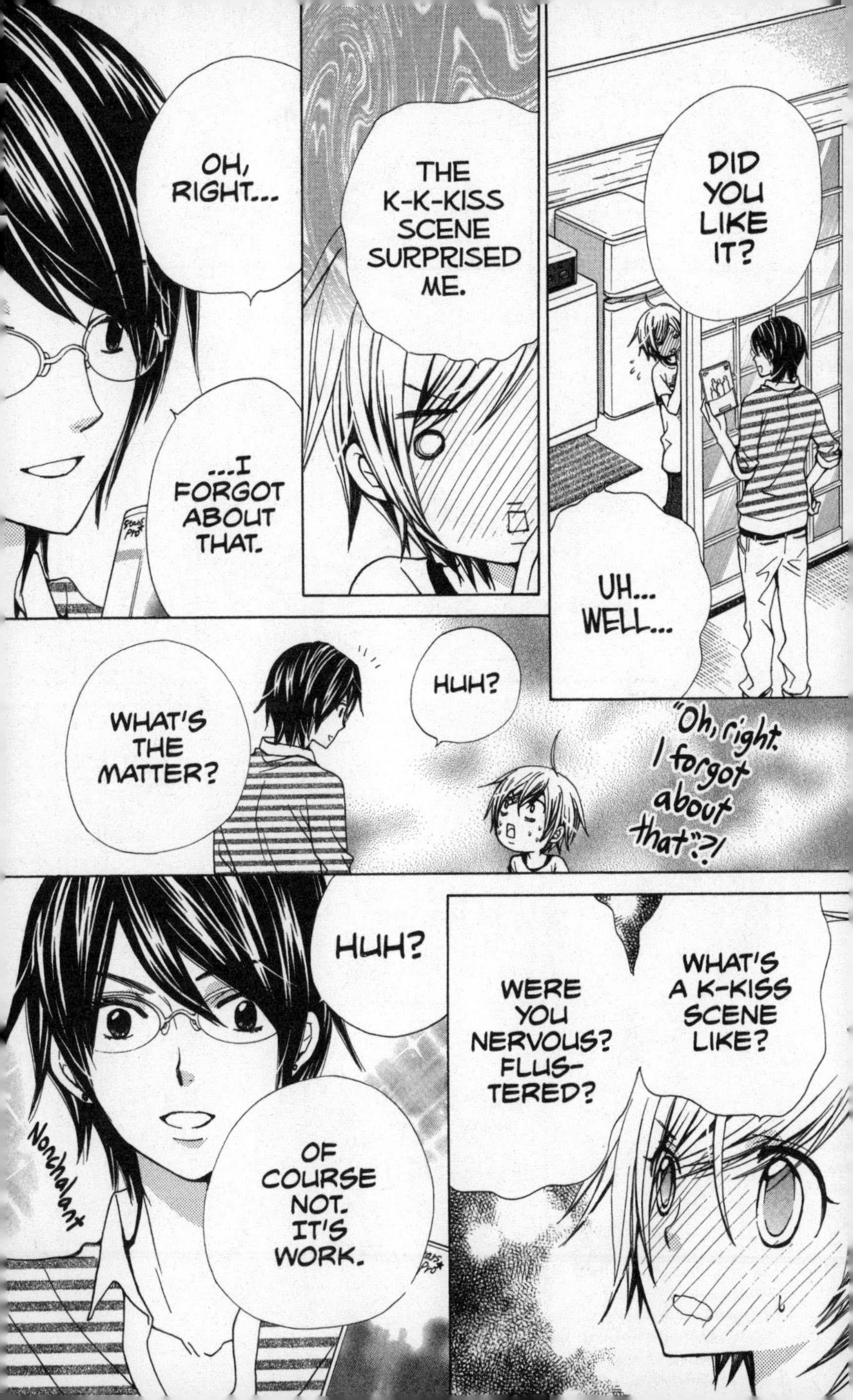
DID YOU LIKE IT?
UH... WELL...
THE K-K-KISS SCENE SURPRISED ME.
OH, RIGHT...
...I FORGOT ABOUT THAT.
"Oh, right. I forgot about that"?!
HUH?
WHAT'S THE MATTER?
WHAT'S A K-KISS SCENE LIKE?
WERE YOU NERVOUS? FLUS-TERED?
HUH?
OF COURSE NOT. IT'S WORK.
Nonchalant

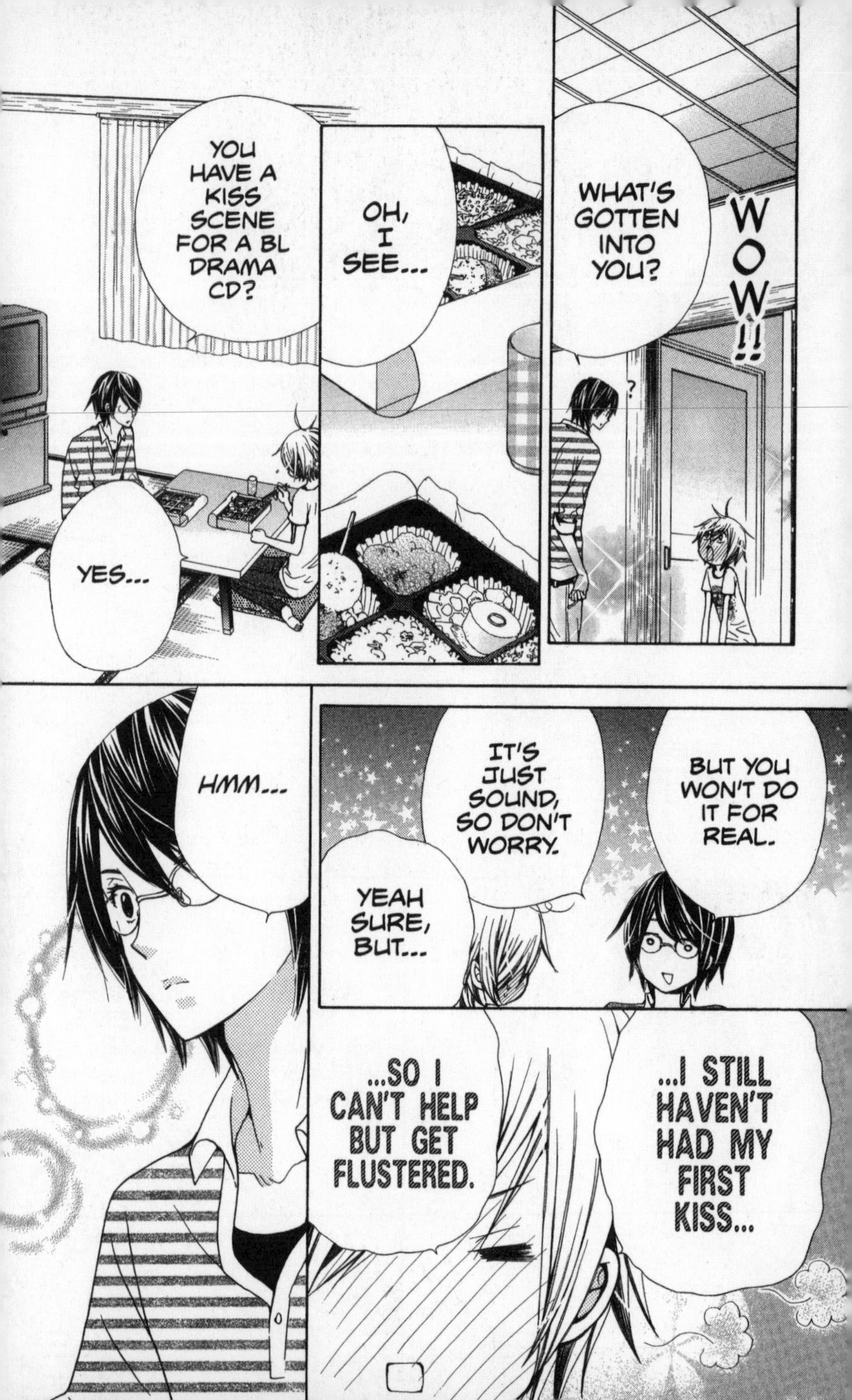
WOW!!
WHAT'S GOTTEN INTO YOU?
?
OH, I SEE...
YOU HAVE A KISS SCENE FOR A BL DRAMA CD?
YES...
BUT YOU WON'T DO IT FOR REAL.
IT'S JUST SOUND, SO DON'T WORRY.
YEAH SURE, BUT...
...I STILL HAVEN'T HAD MY FIRST KISS...
...SO I CAN'T HELP BUT GET FLUSTERED.
HMM...

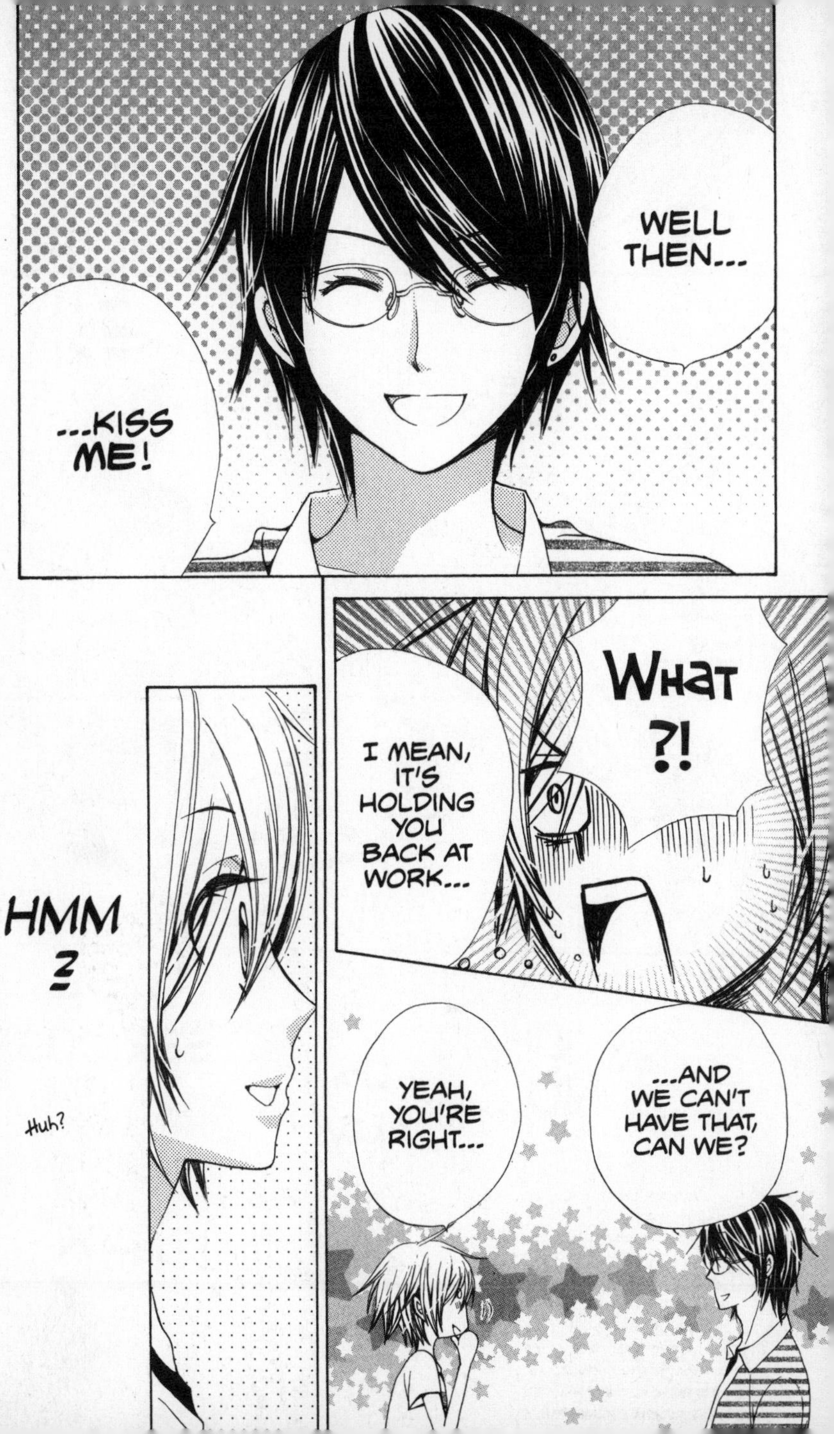
WELL THEN...
...KISS ME!
WHAT ?!
I MEAN, IT'S HOLDING YOU BACK AT WORK...
...AND WE CAN'T HAVE THAT, CAN WE?
YEAH, YOU'RE RIGHT...
HMM?
Huh?

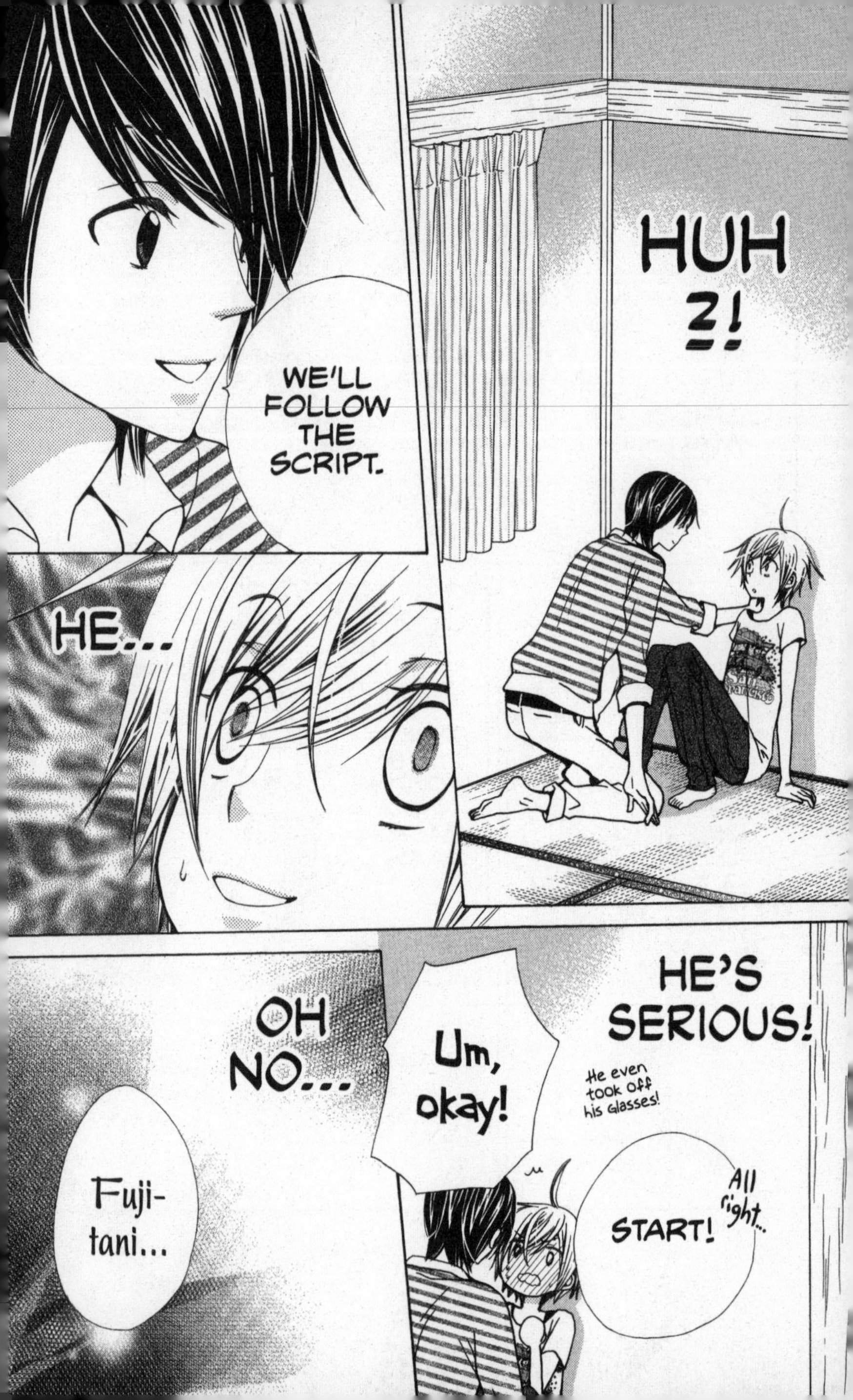
HUH ?!
WE'LL FOLLOW THE SCRIPT.
HE...
HE'S SERIOUS!
He even took off his glasses!
Um, okay!
All right...
START!
OH NO...
Fuji-tani...

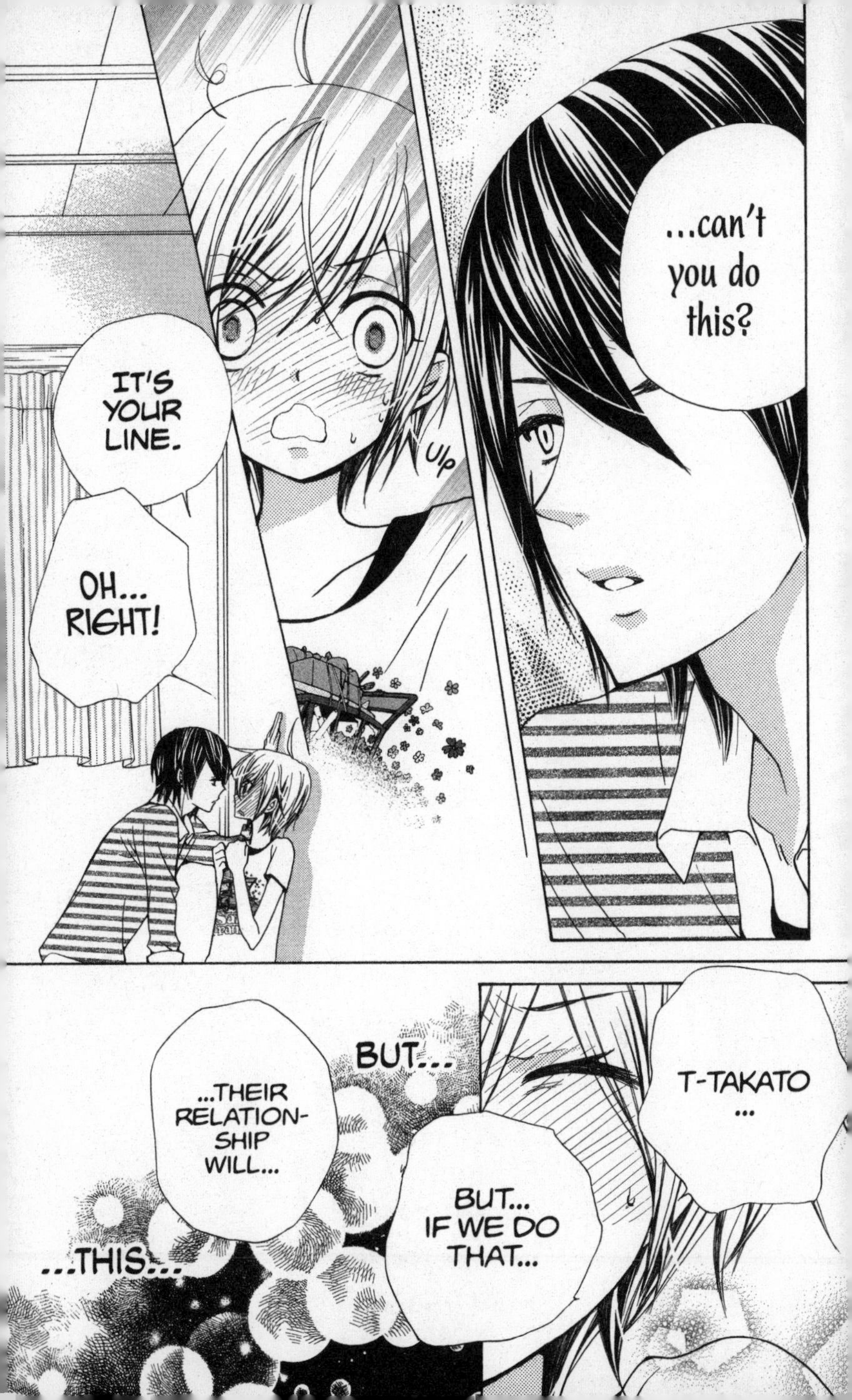
...can't you do this?
ULP
IT'S YOUR LINE.
OH... RIGHT!
T-TAKATO...
BUT... IF WE DO THAT...
BUT...
...THEIR RELATIONSHIP WILL...
...THIS...

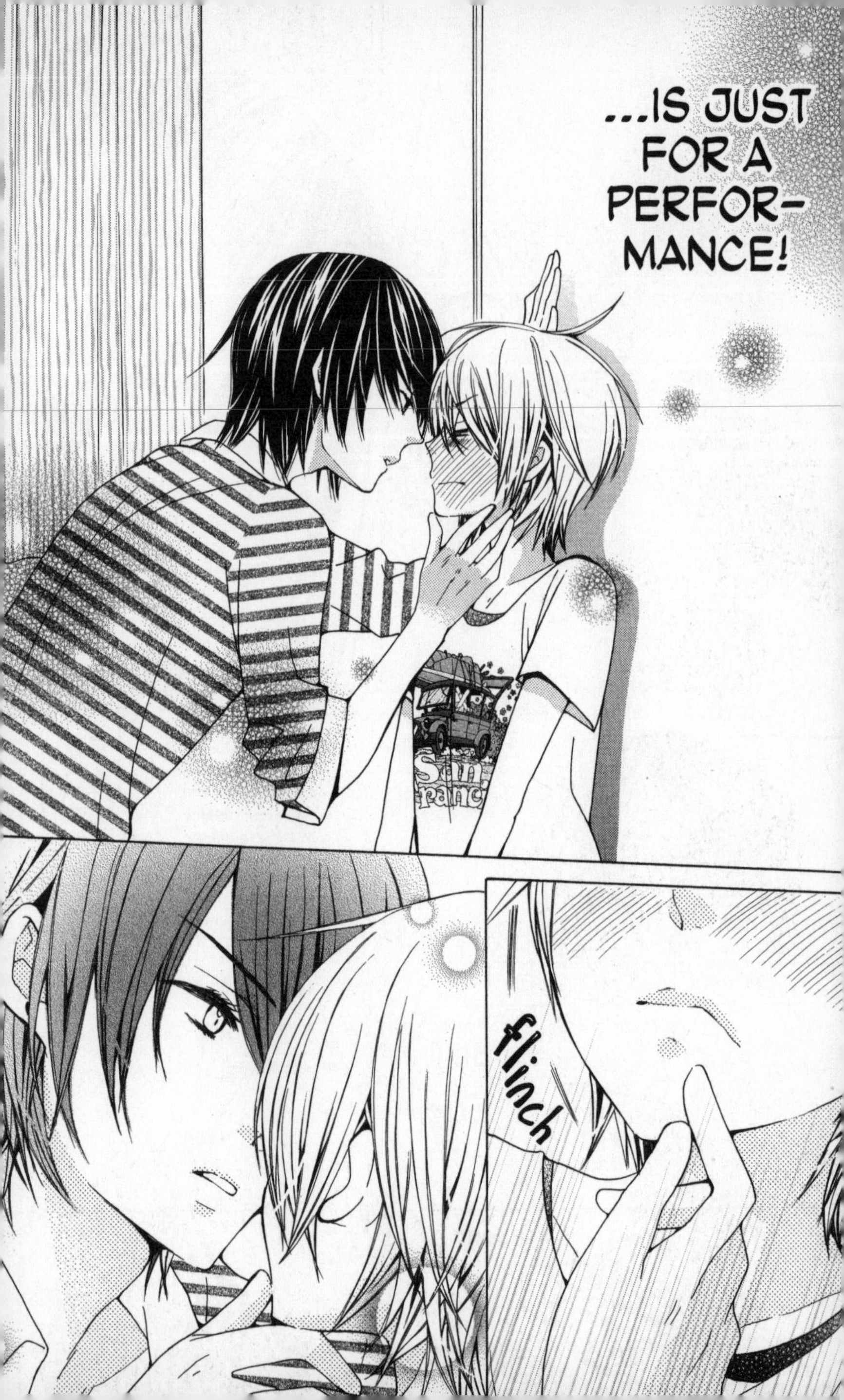
...IS JUST FOR A PERFOR-MANCE!
flinch

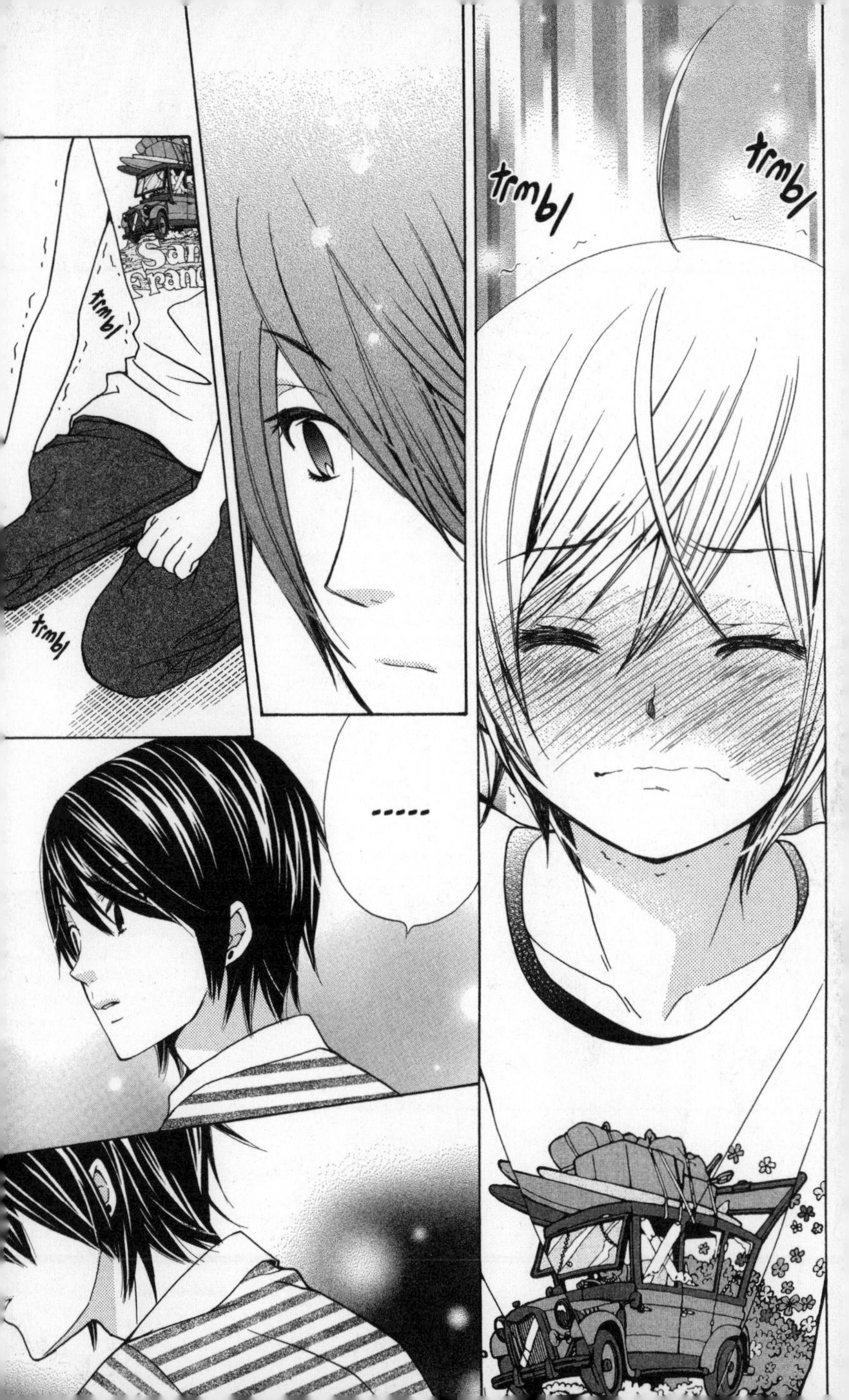
trmbl
trmbl
trmbl
trmbl
-----

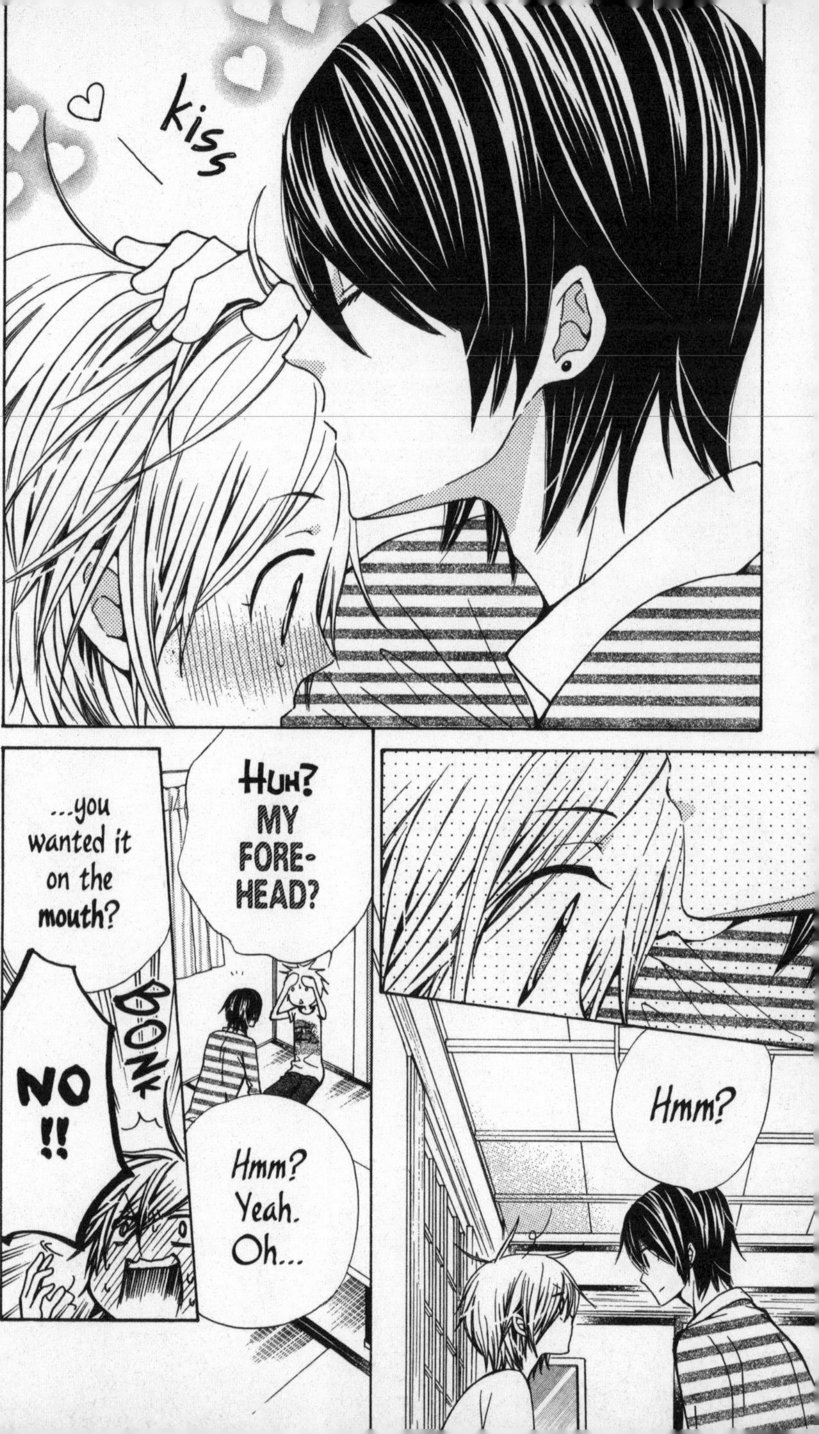
kiss
Hmm?
HUH? MY FORE-HEAD?
...you wanted it on the mouth?
Hmm? Yeah. Oh...
BONK
NO!!

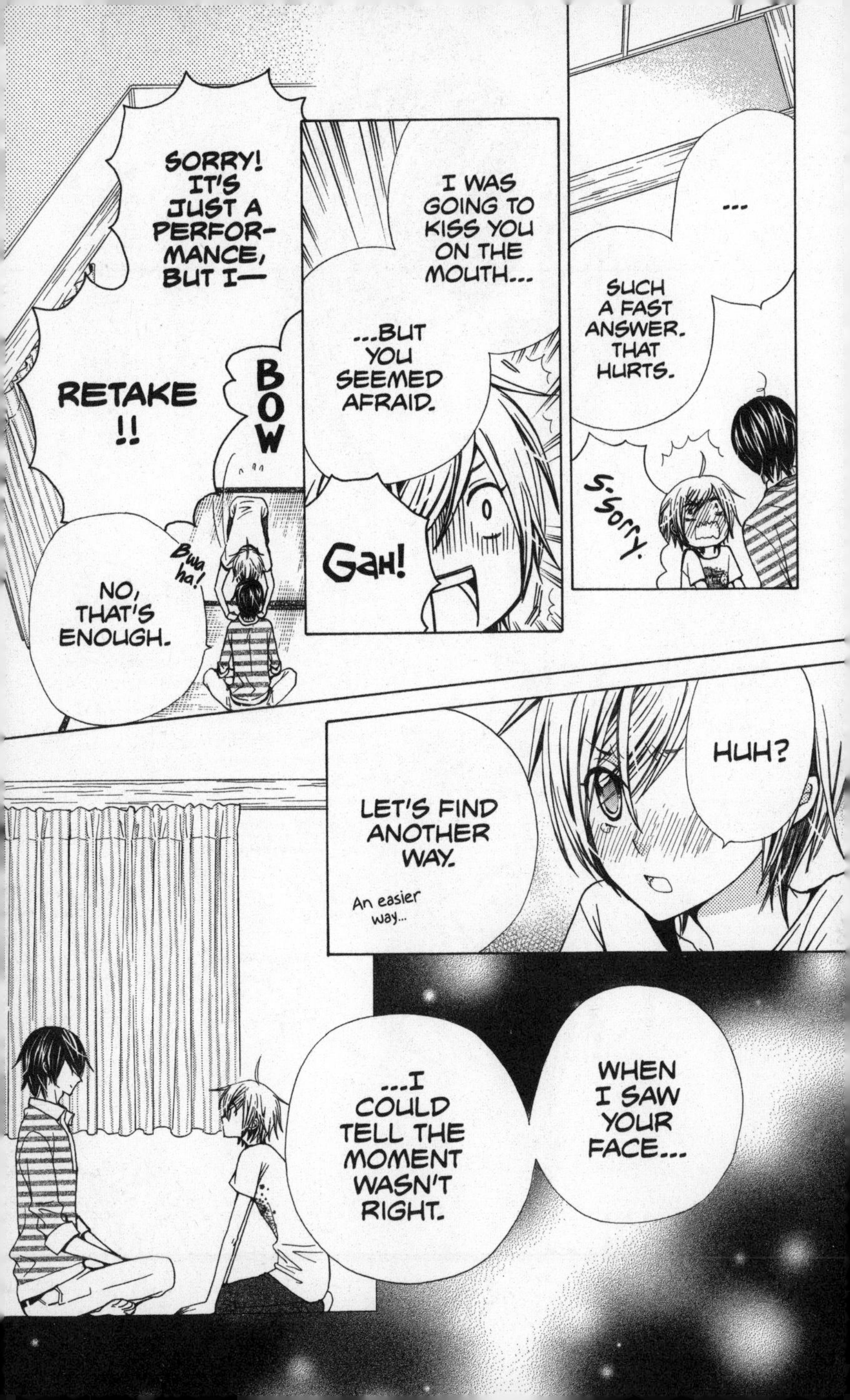
...
SUCH A FAST ANSWER. THAT HURTS.
S-SORRY.
I WAS GOING TO KISS YOU ON THE MOUTH...
...BUT YOU SEEMED AFRAID.
GAH!
SORRY! IT'S JUST A PERFORMANCE, BUT I—
BOW
RETAKE!!
Bwa ha!
NO, THAT'S ENOUGH.
HUH?
LET'S FIND ANOTHER WAY.
An easier way...
WHEN I SAW YOUR FACE...
...I COULD TELL THE MOMENT WASN'T RIGHT.

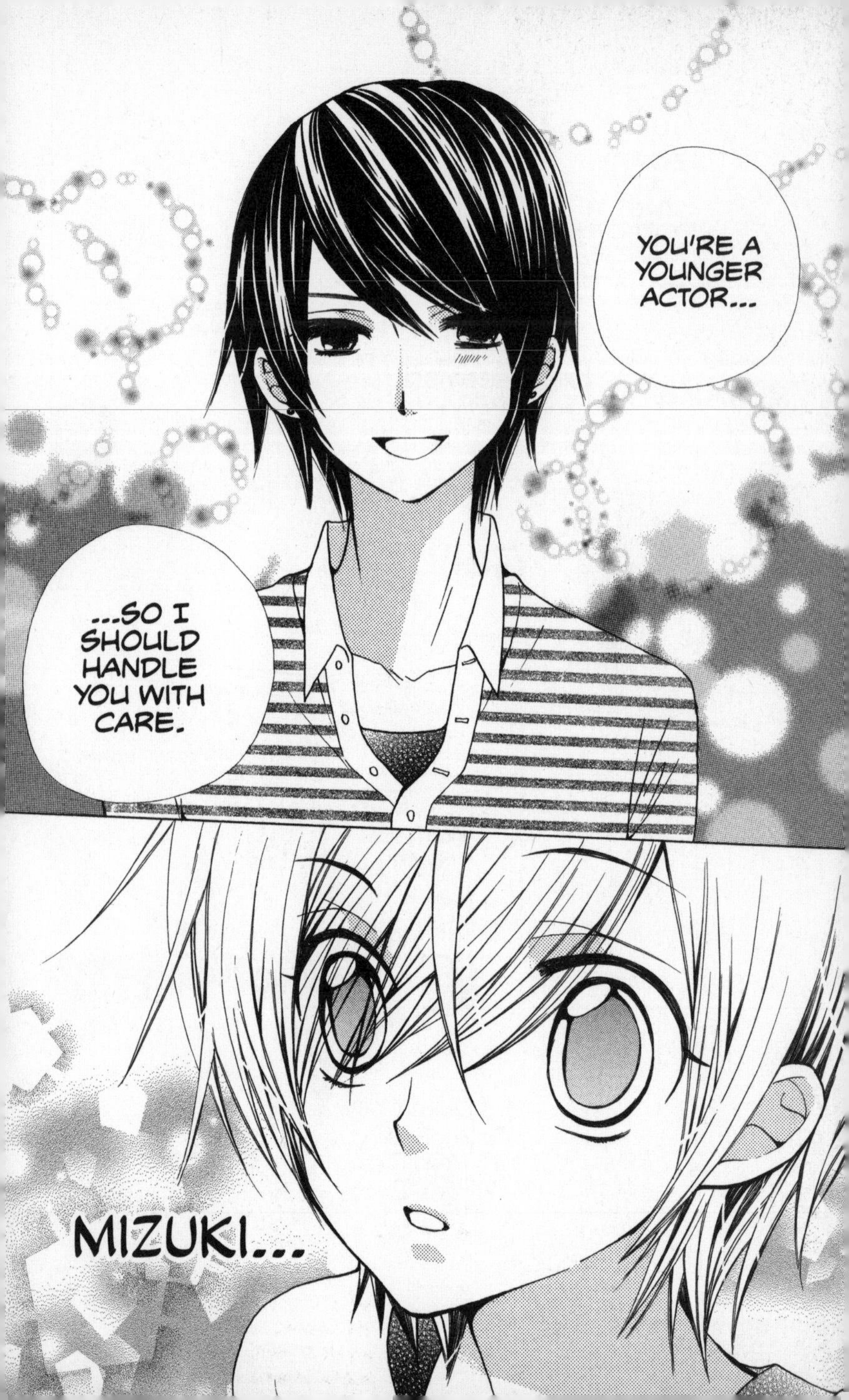
YOU'RE A YOUNGER ACTOR...
...SO I SHOULD HANDLE YOU WITH CARE.
MIZUKI...

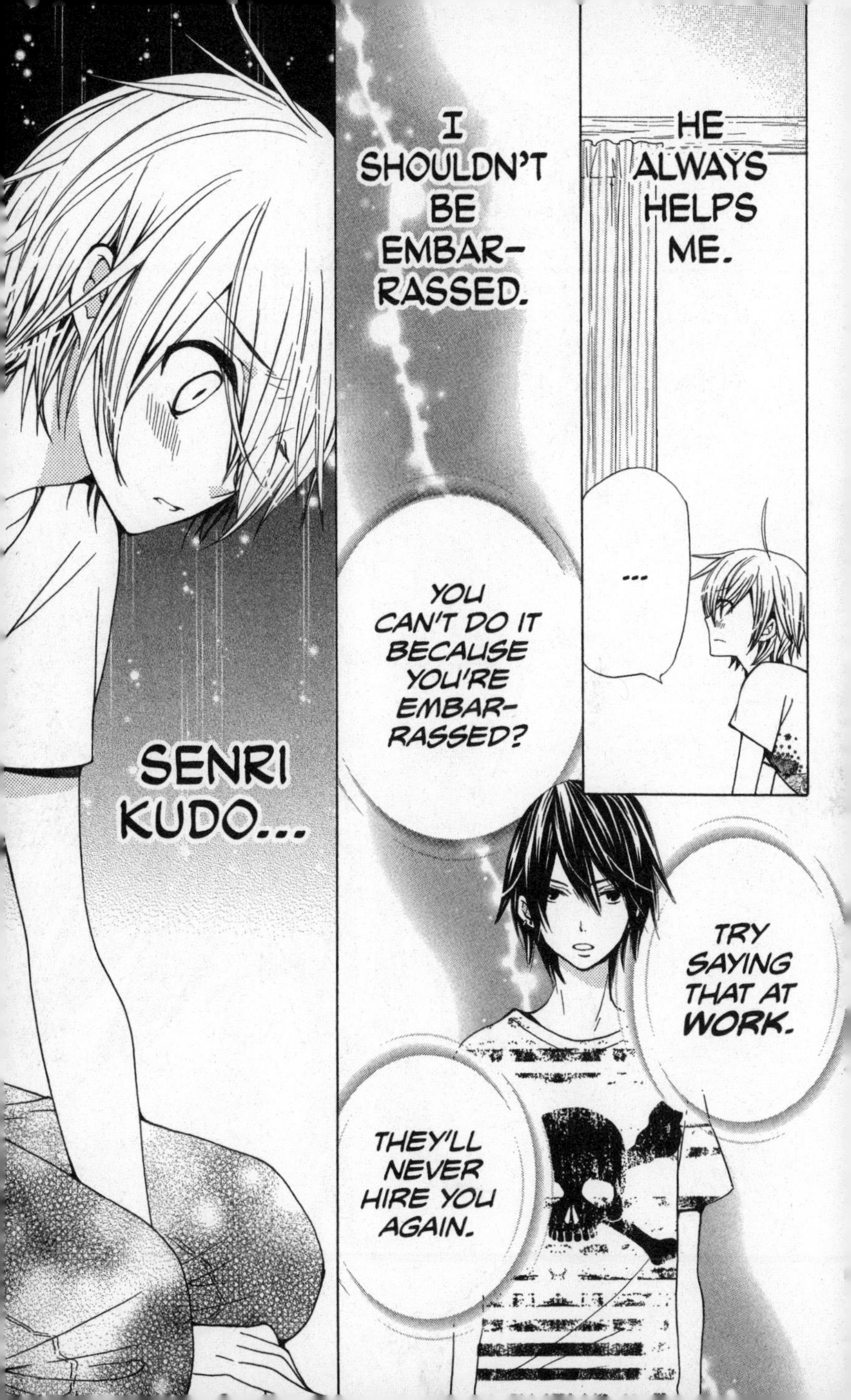
HE ALWAYS HELPS ME.
...
I SHOULDN'T BE EMBAR-RASSED.
YOU CAN'T DO IT BECAUSE YOU'RE EMBAR-RASSED?
TRY SAYING THAT AT WORK.
THEY'LL NEVER HIRE YOU AGAIN.
SENRI KUDO...

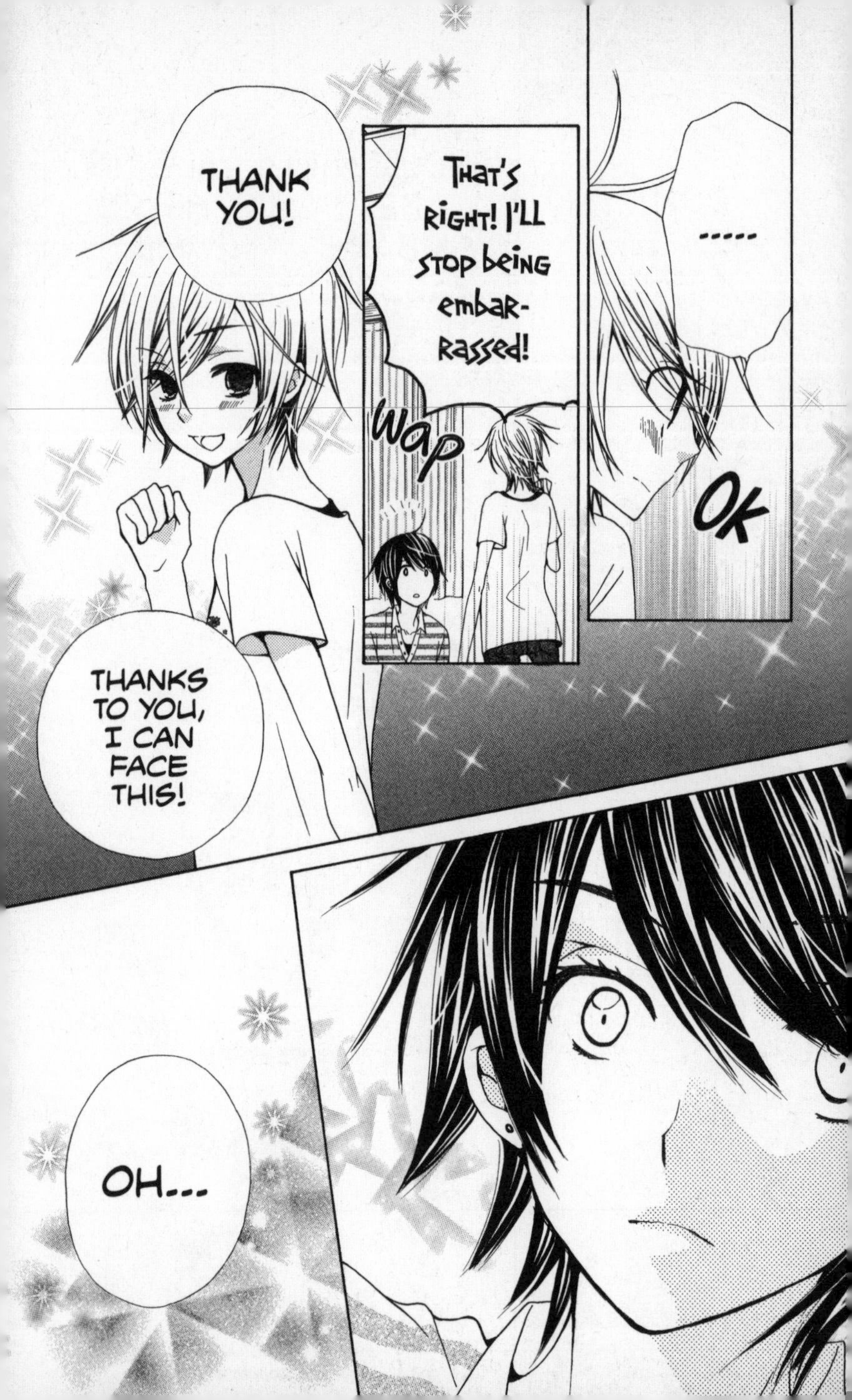
.....
OK
That's right! I'll stop being embarrassed!
WAP
THANK YOU!
THANKS TO YOU, I CAN FACE THIS!
OH...

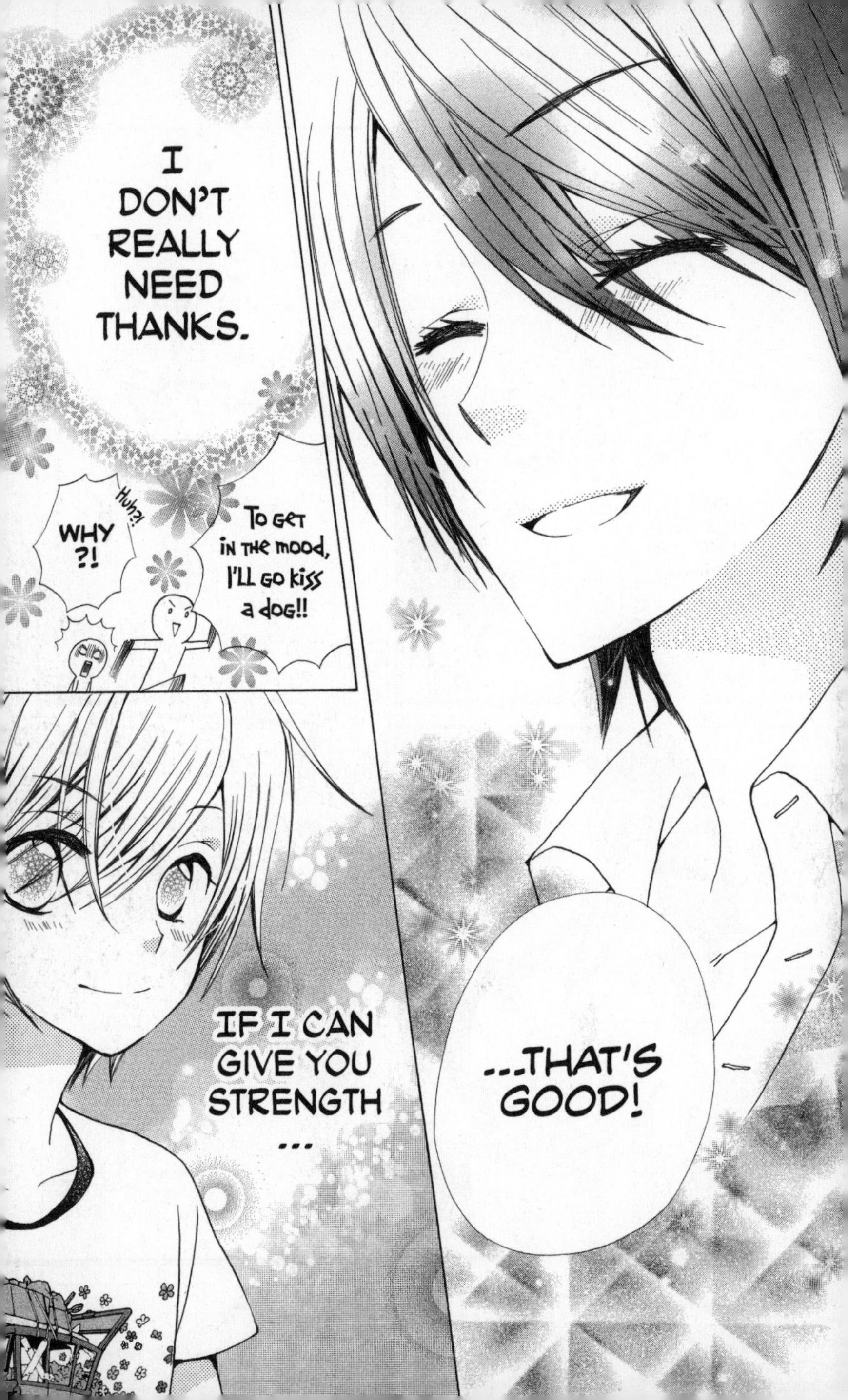
I DON'T REALLY NEED THANKS.
Huh?!
WHY ?!
To get in the mood, I'll go kiss a dog!!
IF I CAN GIVE YOU STRENGTH ...
...THAT'S GOOD!

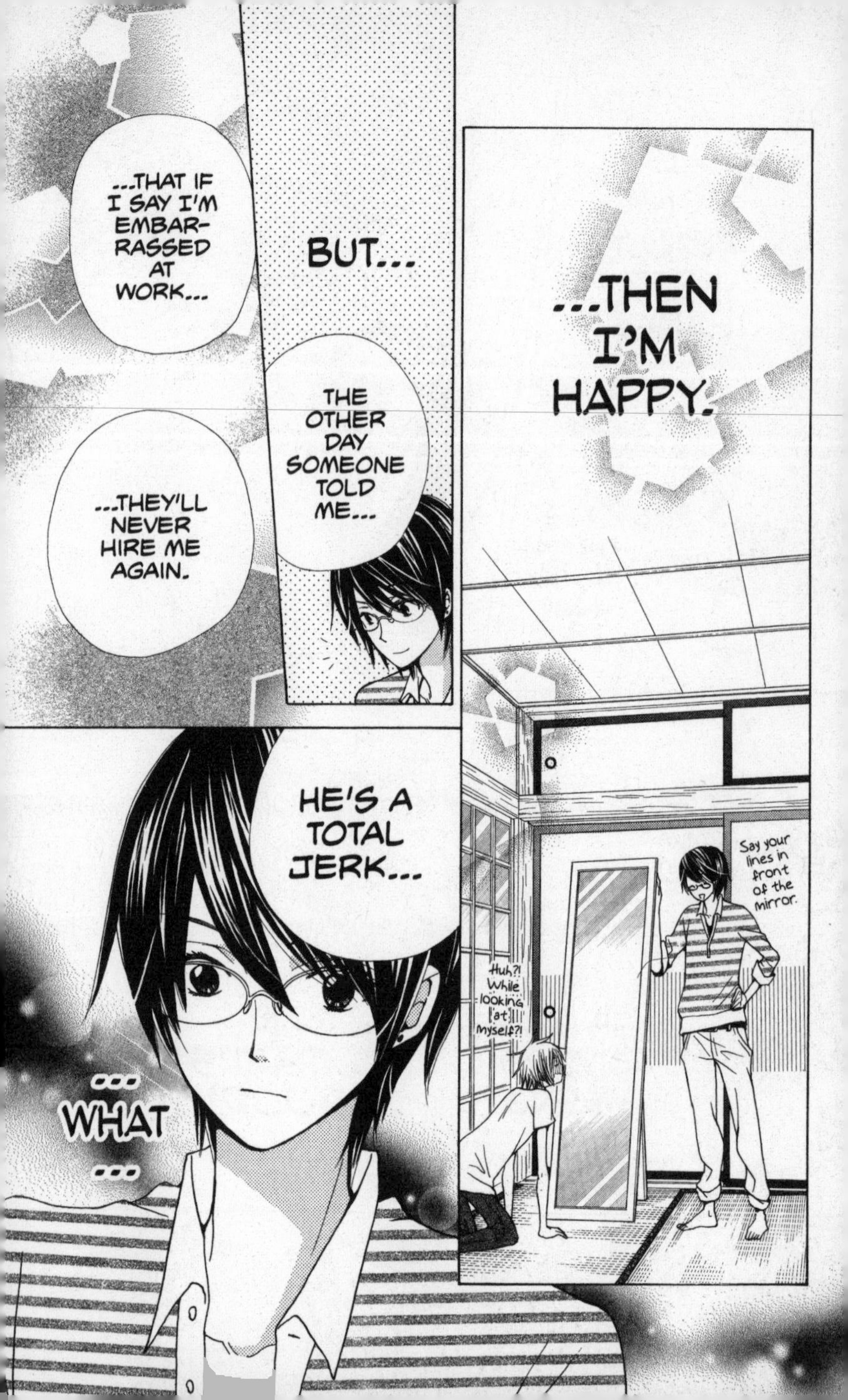
...THEN I'M HAPPY.
Say your lines in front of the mirror.
Huh?! While looking at myself?!
BUT...
THE OTHER DAY SOMEONE TOLD ME...
...THAT IF I SAY I'M EMBARRASSED AT WORK...
...THEY'LL NEVER HIRE ME AGAIN.
HE'S A TOTAL JERK...
...WHAT...

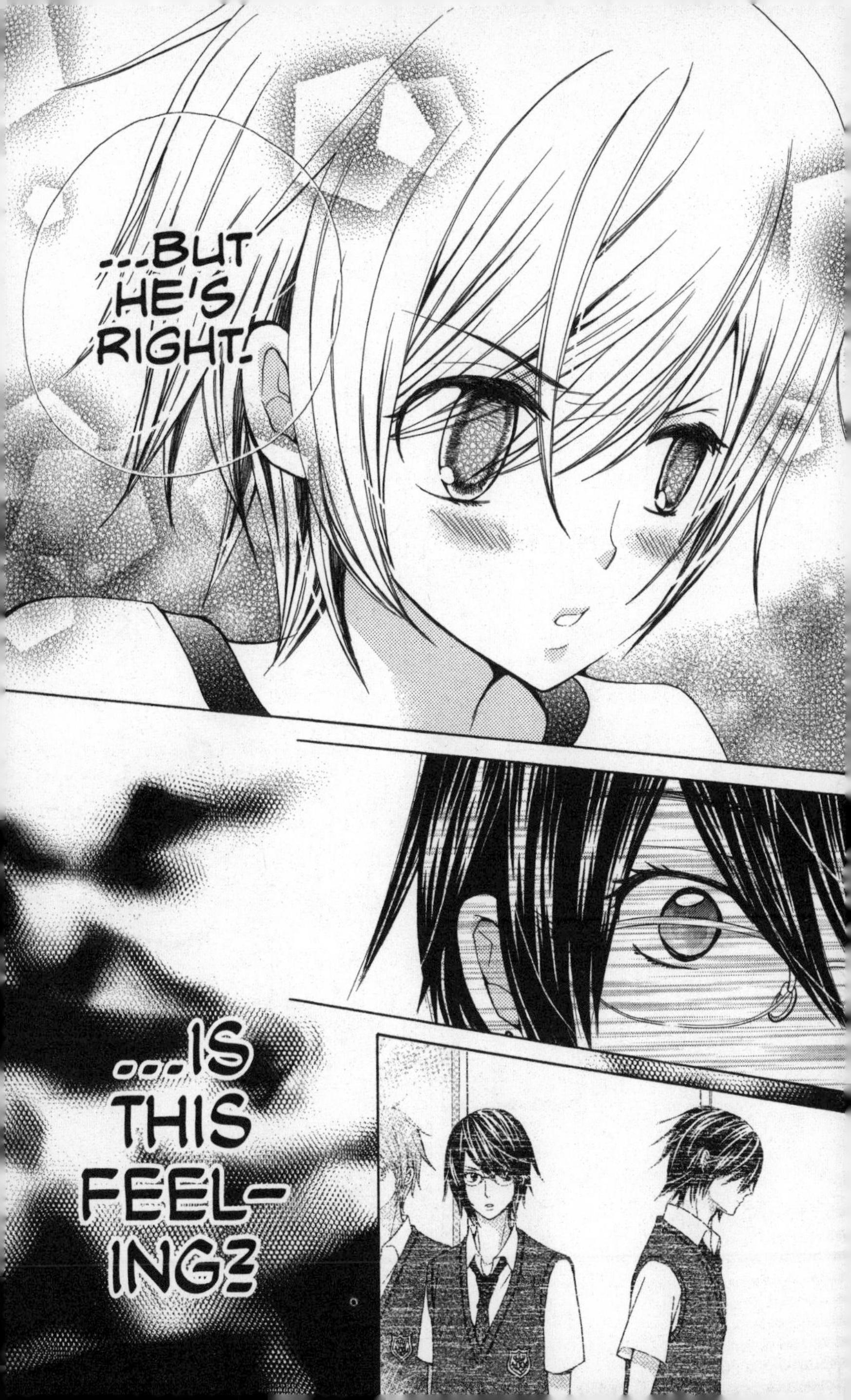
...BUT HE'S RIGHT.
...IS THIS FEEL-ING?

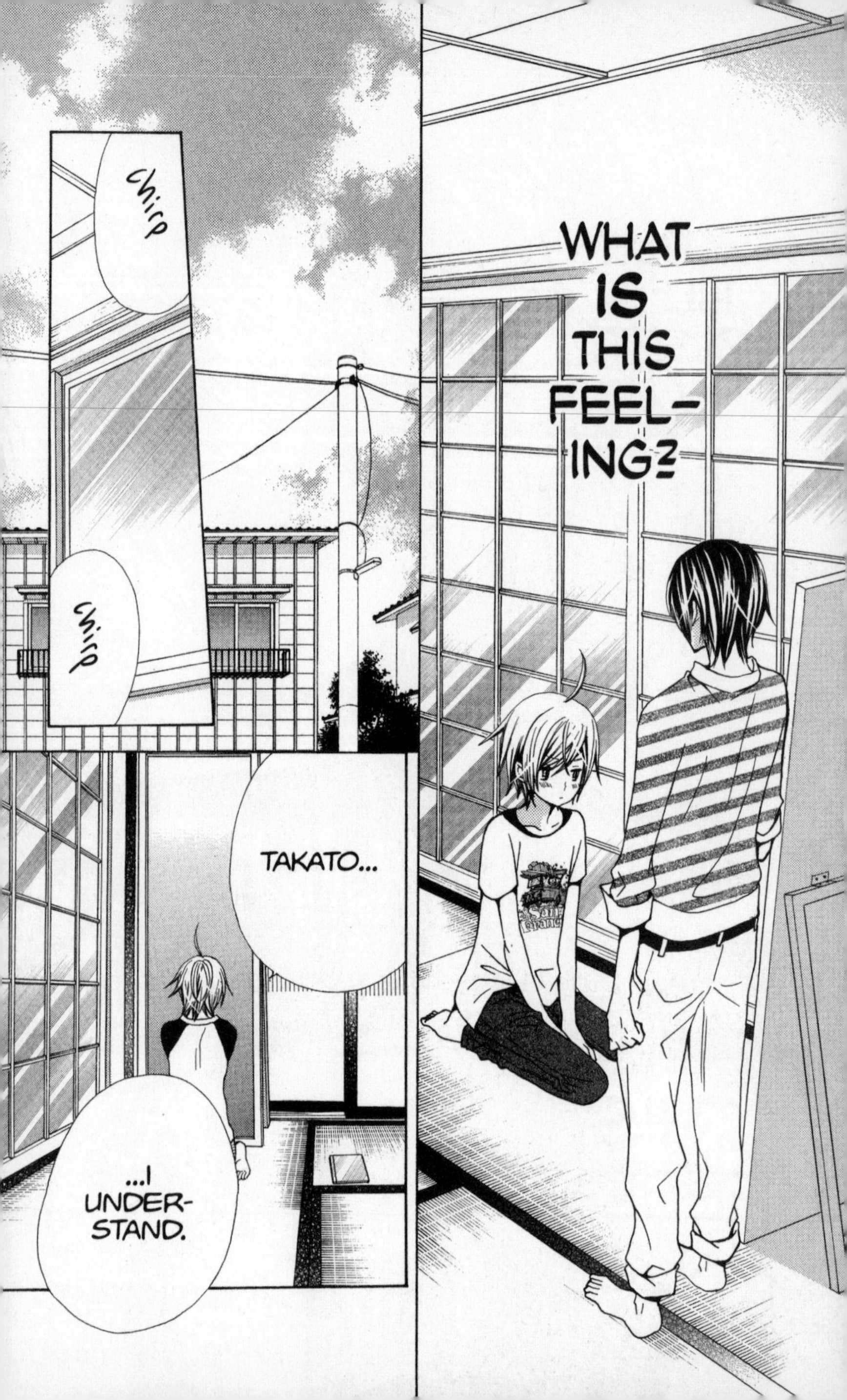
WHAT IS THIS FEELING?
chirp
chirp
TAKATO...
...I UNDERSTAND.

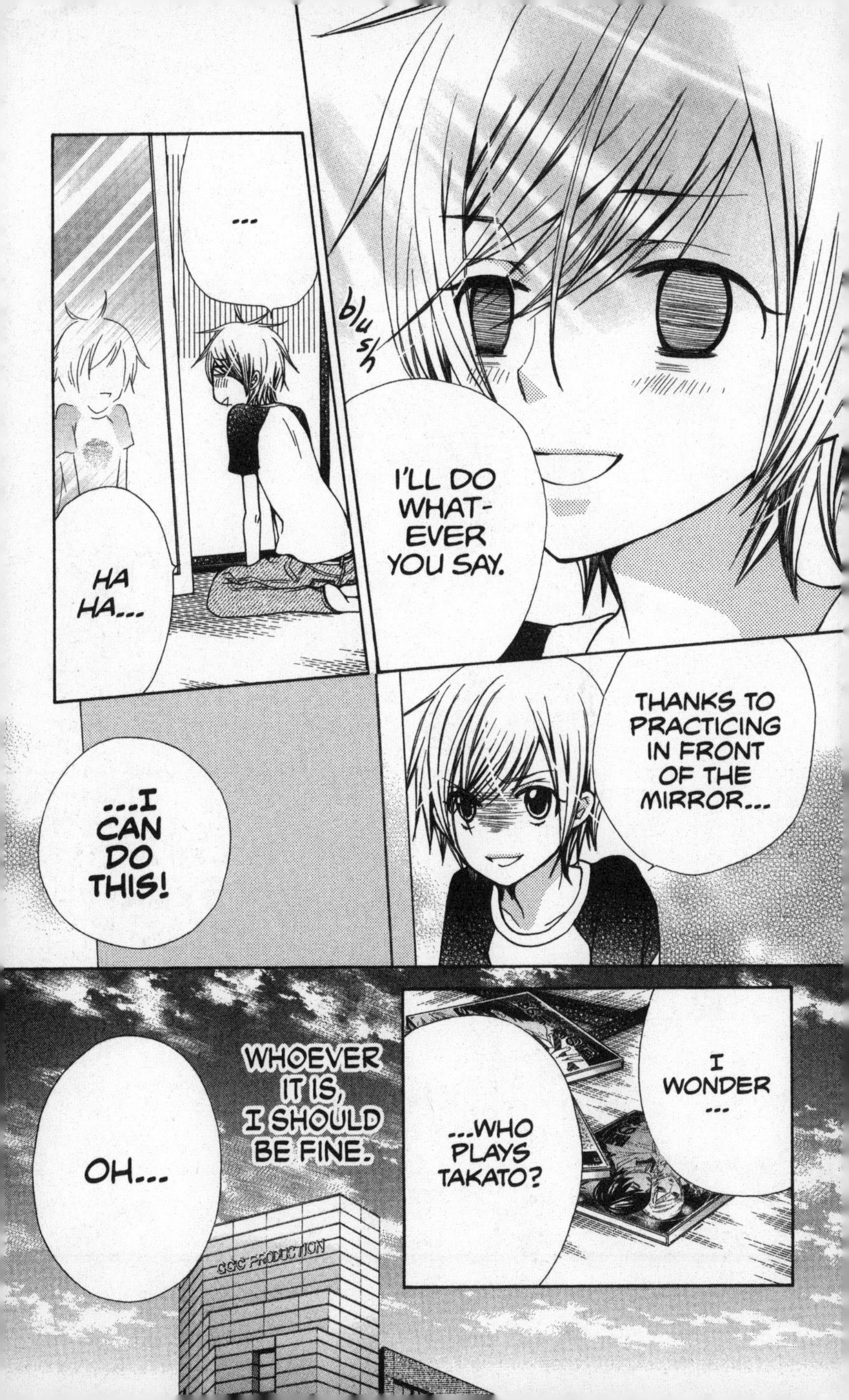
blush
I'LL DO WHATEVER YOU SAY.
...
HA HA...
THANKS TO PRACTICING IN FRONT OF THE MIRROR...
...I CAN DO THIS!
I WONDER...
...WHO PLAYS TAKATO?
WHOEVER IT IS, I SHOULD BE FINE.
OH...
GGC PRODUCTION

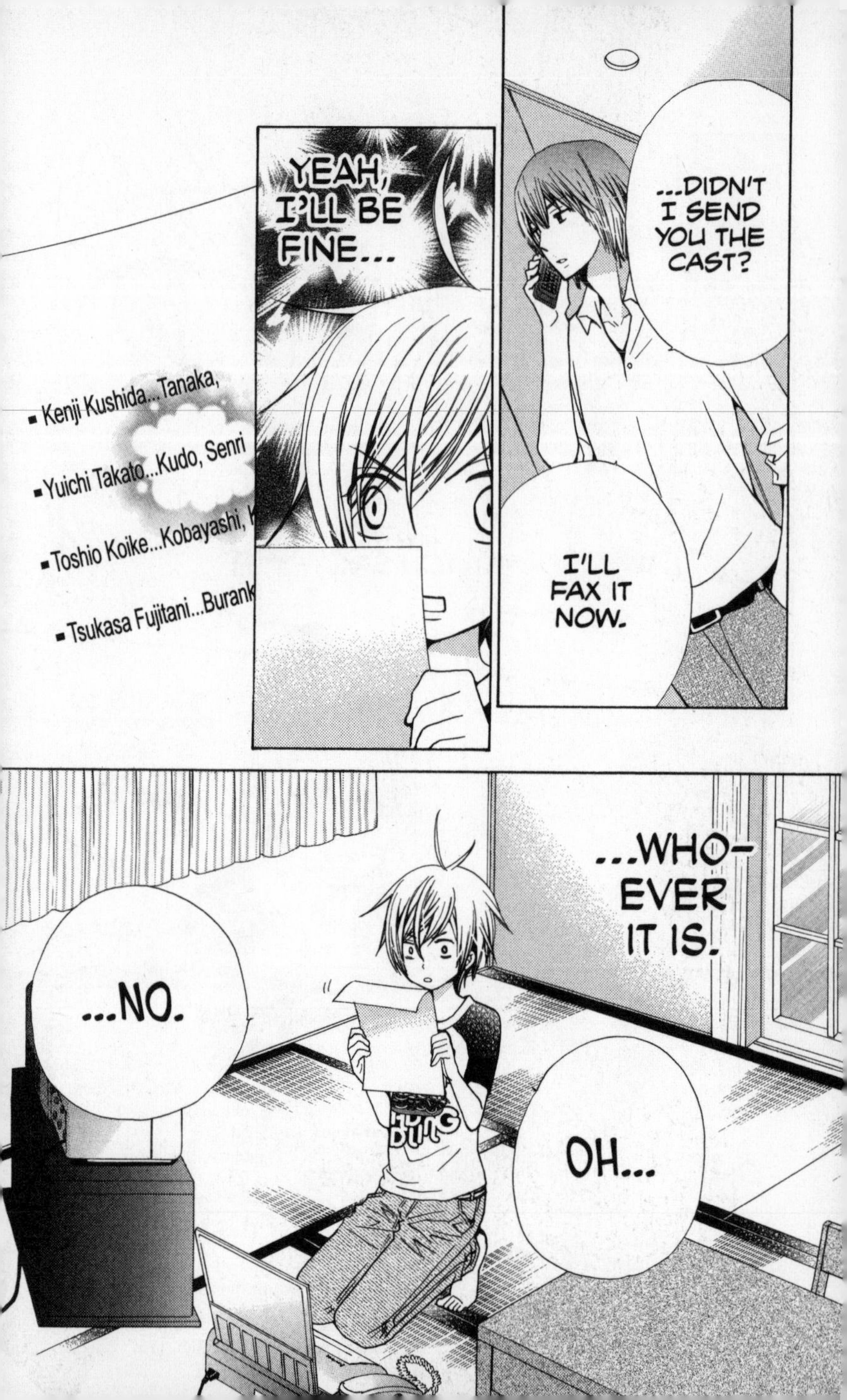
...DIDN'T I SEND YOU THE CAST?
I'LL FAX IT NOW.
YEAH, I'LL BE FINE...
■ Kenji Kushida...Tanaka,
■ Yuichi Takato...Kudo, Senri
■ Toshio Koike...Kobayashi,
■ Tsukasa Fujitani...Burank
...WHO-EVER IT IS.
OH...
...NO.

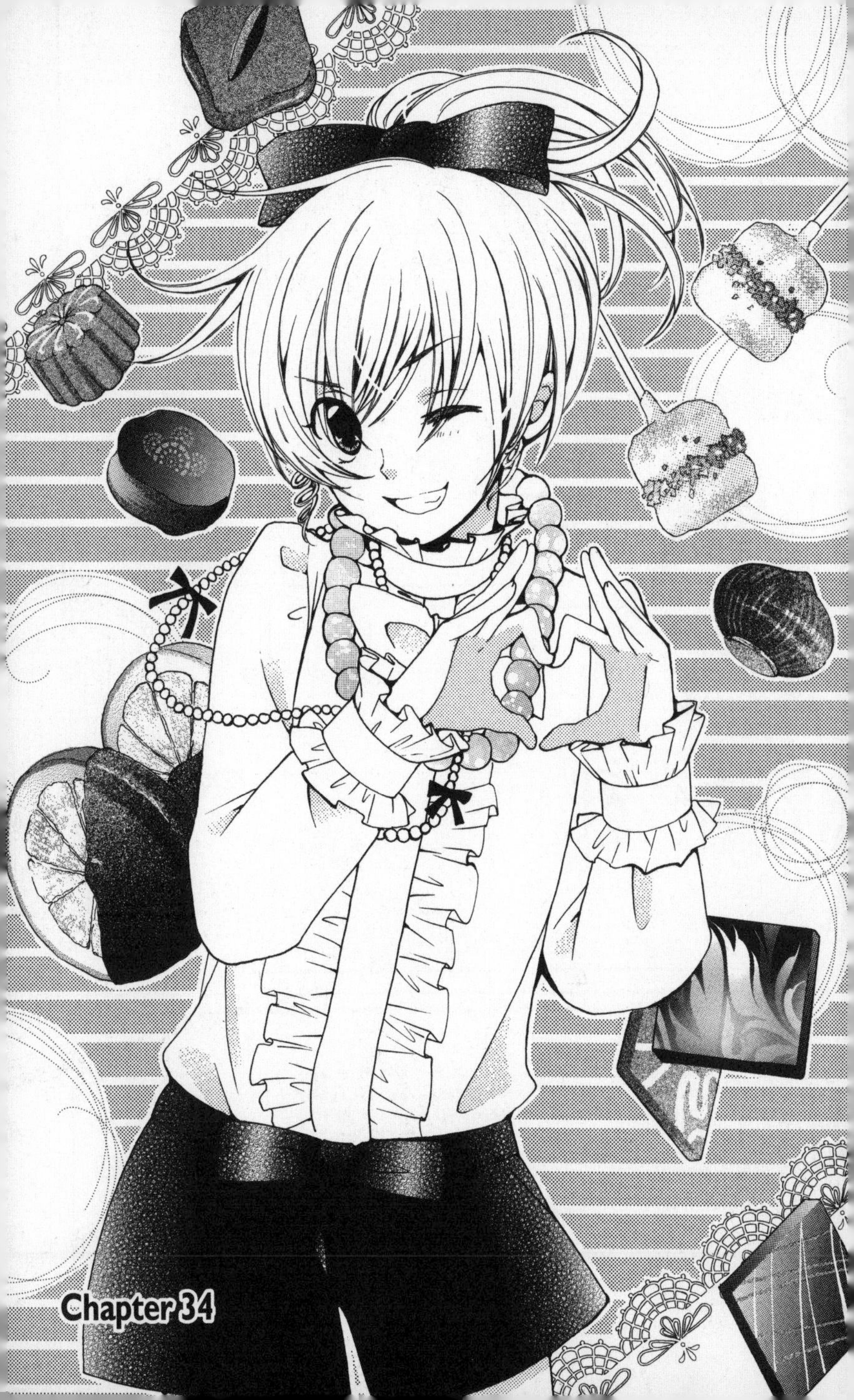
Chapter 34

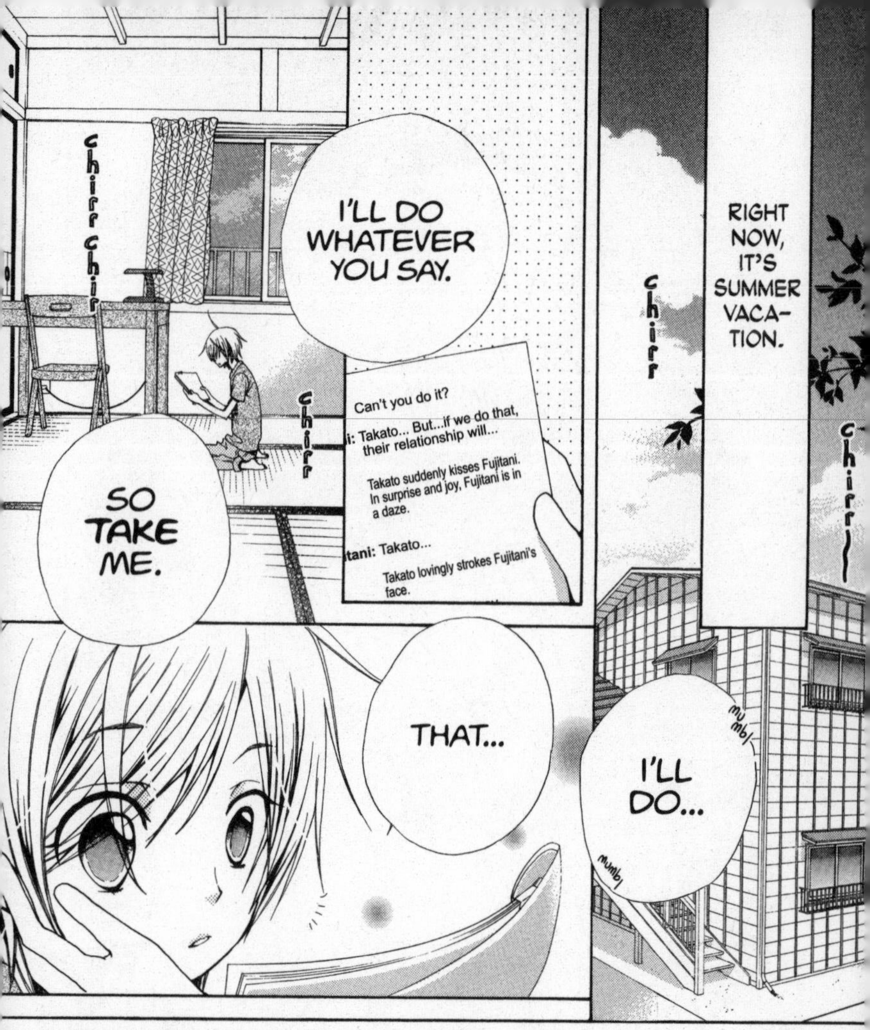
RIGHT NOW, IT'S SUMMER VACA-TION.
chirr
chirrr~
I'LL DO WHATEVER YOU SAY.
Can't you do it?
i: Takato... But...if we do that, their relationship will...
Takato suddenly kisses Fujitani. In surprise and joy, Fujitani is in a daze.
itani: Takato...
Takato lovingly strokes Fujitani's face.
SO TAKE ME.
chirr chirr
chirr
mumbl
I'LL DO...
mumbl
THAT...

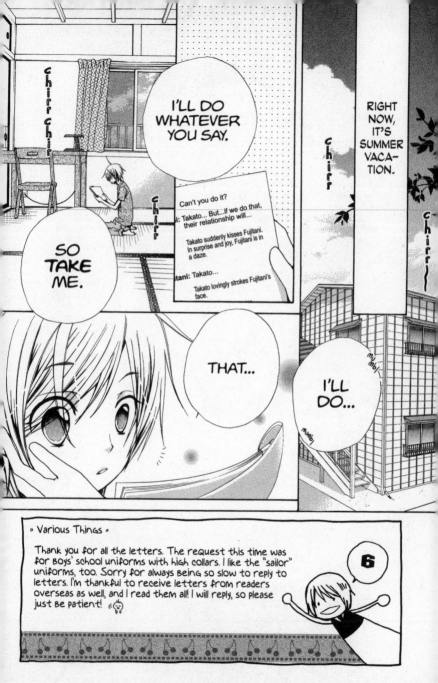

∘ Various Things ∘

Thank you for all the letters. The request this time was for boys' school uniforms with high collars. I like the "sailor" uniforms, too. Sorry for always being so slow to reply to letters. I'm thankful to receive letters from readers overseas as well, and I read them all! I will reply, so please just be patient!

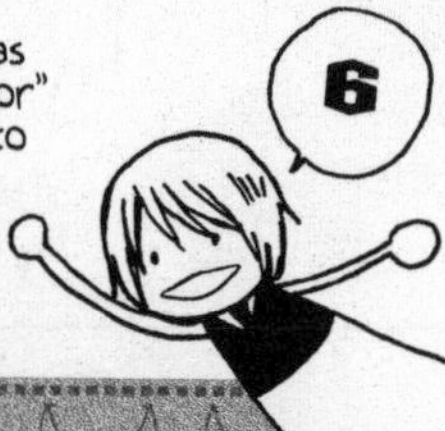
6

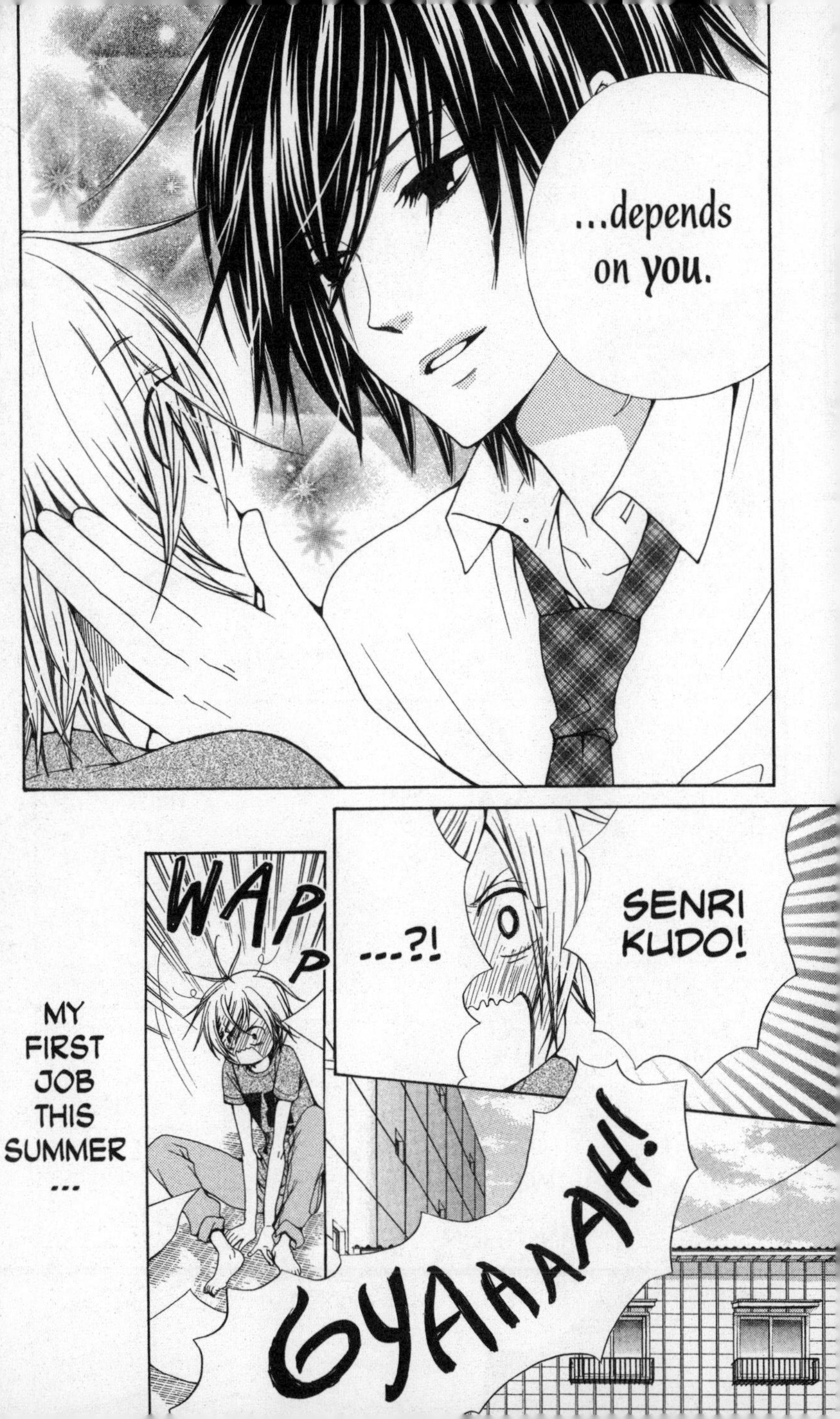
...depends on you.
SENRI KUDO!
---?!
GYAAAAH!
WAPP
MY FIRST JOB THIS SUMMER ...

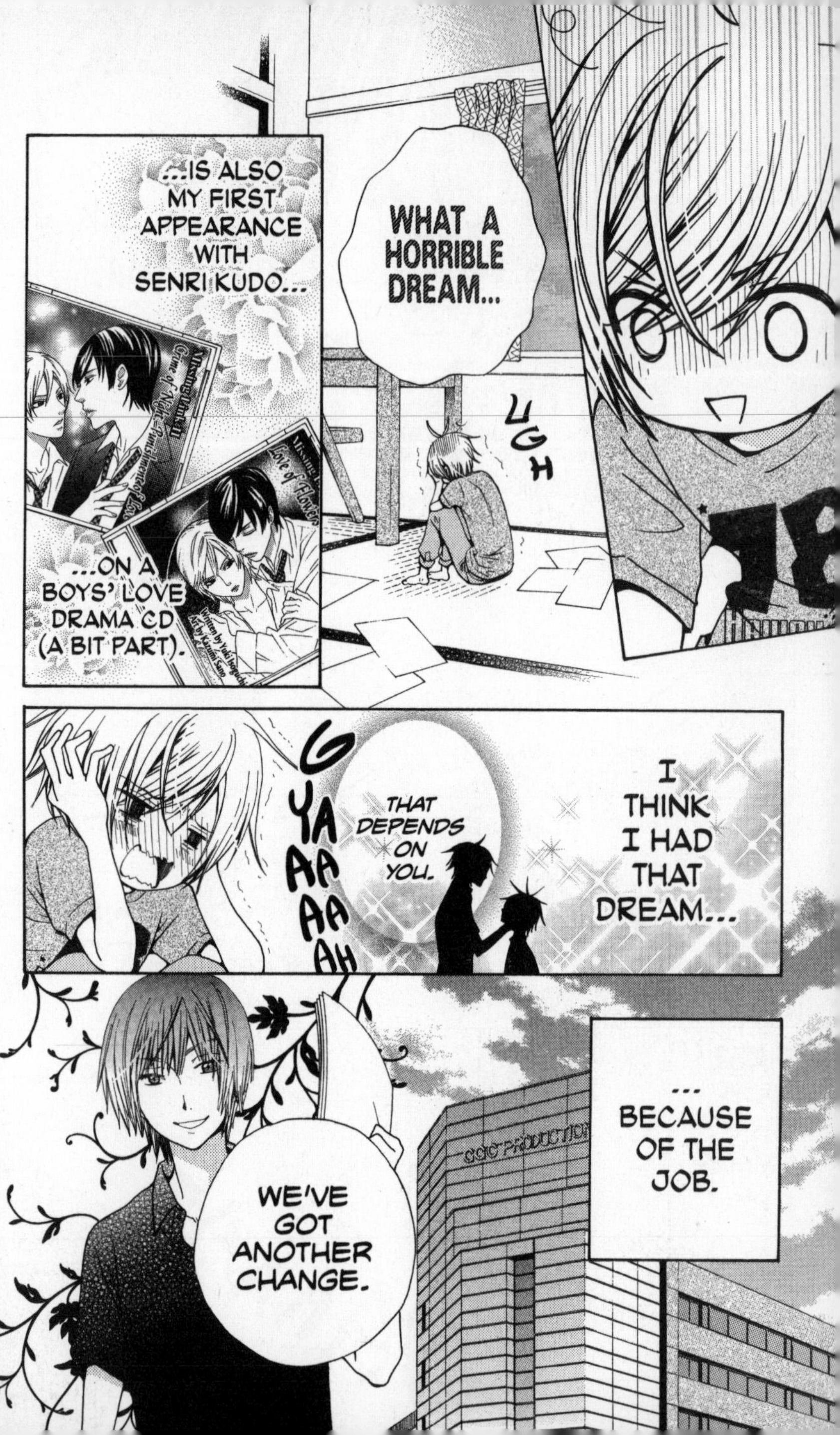
WHAT A HORRIBLE DREAM...
UGH
...IS ALSO MY FIRST APPEARANCE WITH SENRI KUDO...
...ON A BOYS' LOVE DRAMA CD (A BIT PART).
I THINK I HAD THAT DREAM...
THAT DEPENDS ON YOU.
GYAAAAAAAH
...BECAUSE OF THE JOB.
WE'VE GOT ANOTHER CHANGE.

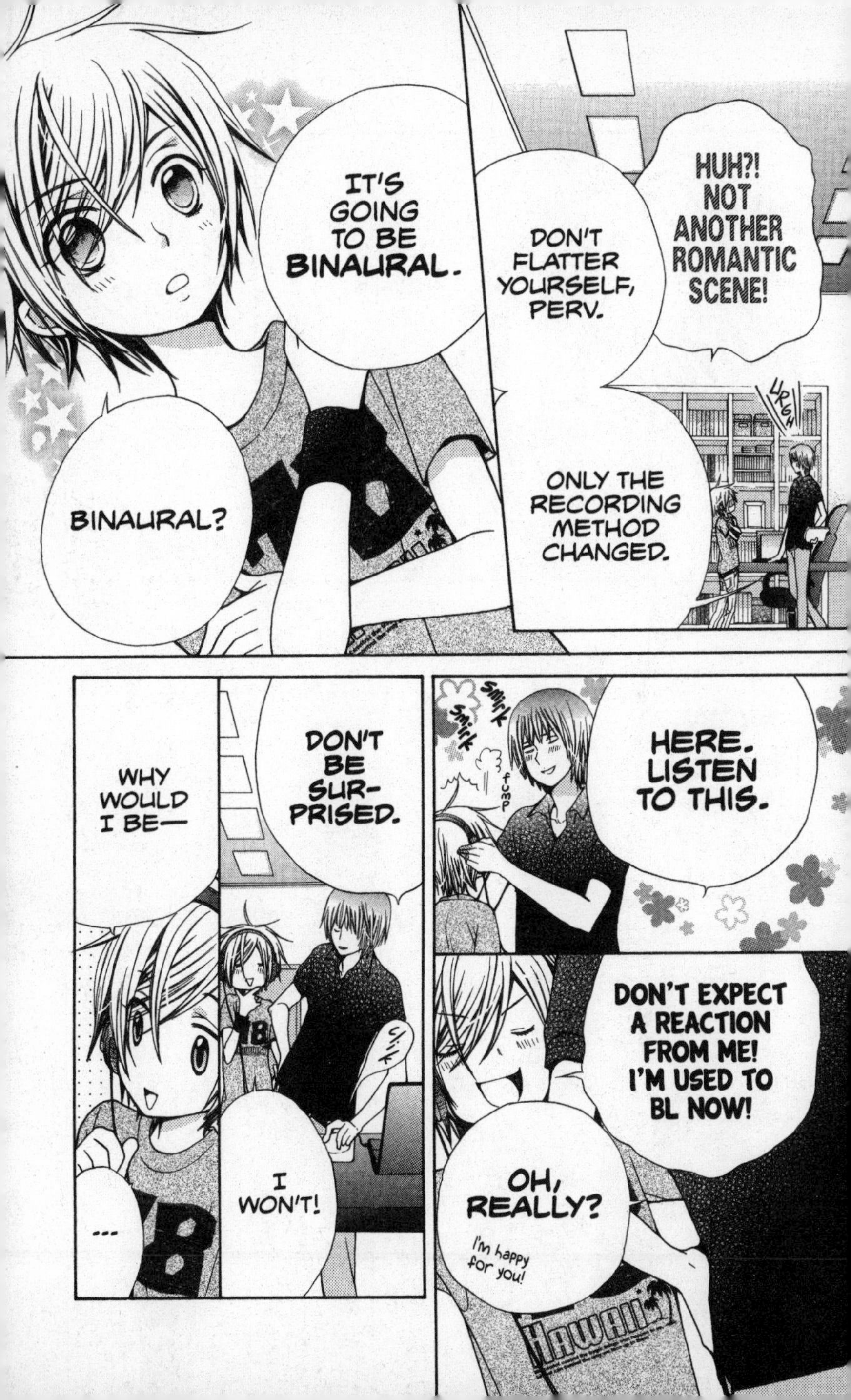
HUH?! NOT ANOTHER ROMANTIC SCENE!
URGH
DON'T FLATTER YOURSELF, PERV.
ONLY THE RECORDING METHOD CHANGED.
IT'S GOING TO BE BINAURAL.
BINAURAL?
HERE. LISTEN TO THIS.
Smirk Smirk
FUMP
DON'T EXPECT A REACTION FROM ME! I'M USED TO BL NOW!
OH, REALLY?
I'm happy for you!
DON'T BE SUR-PRISED.
I WON'T!
WHY WOULD I BE—
...

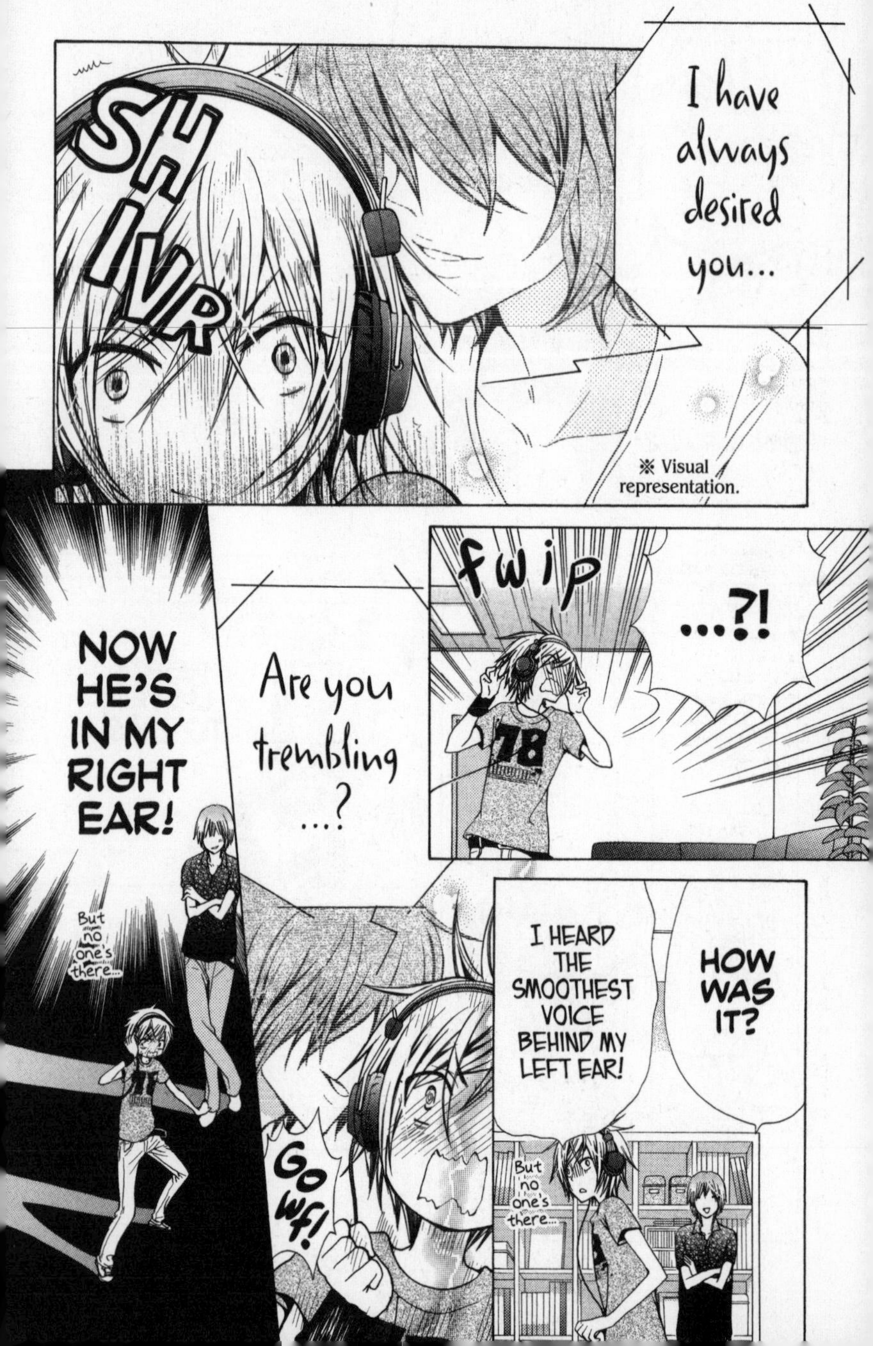

I have always desired you...
SHIVR
※ Visual representation.
fwip
...?!
HOW WAS IT?
I HEARD THE SMOOTHEST VOICE BEHIND MY LEFT EAR!
But no one's there...
GOWF!
Are you trembling...?
NOW HE'S IN MY RIGHT EAR!
But no one's there...

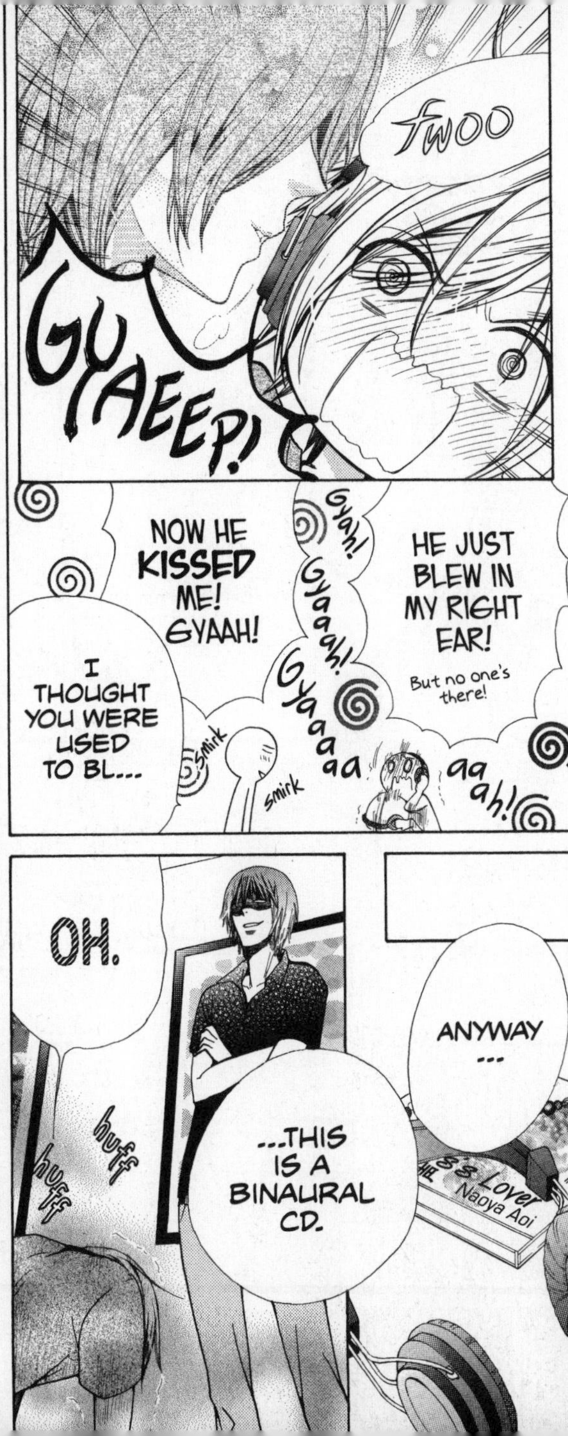
fwoo
GYAEEP!!
HE JUST BLEW IN MY RIGHT EAR!
But no one's there!
Gyah! Gyaaah! Gyaaaaaaaaah!
NOW HE KISSED ME! GYAAH!
I THOUGHT YOU WERE USED TO BL...
smirk
smirk
ANYWAY...
...THIS IS A BINAURAL CD.
Lover
Naoya Aoi
OH.
huff
huff

◦ End ◦

We've reached the end of the sidebars. Thank you for reading!! I bought an LCD tablet!! Yay!! It's really easy to draw on.

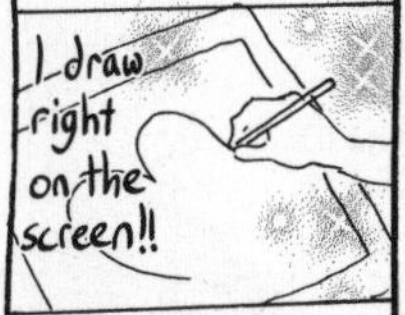
I draw right on the screen!!

And a heartfelt thanks to everyone who read this, everyone who helped with research, the graphic novel editor, my editor, my assistants, my friends and my family!!!

♡ If you want, let me hear your thoughts! ♡

Maki Minami c/o
Shojo Beat
P.O. Box 77010
San Francisco, CA 94107

Maki Minami
南マキ

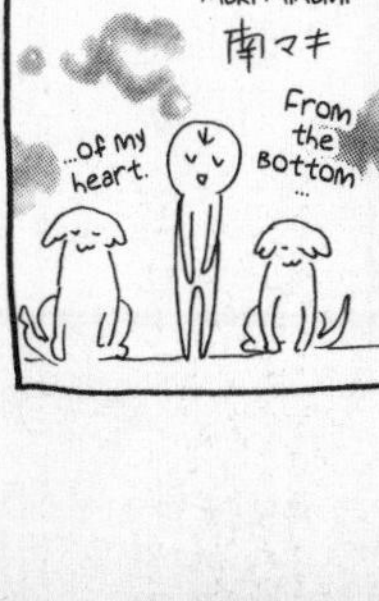
From the bottom...
...of my heart.

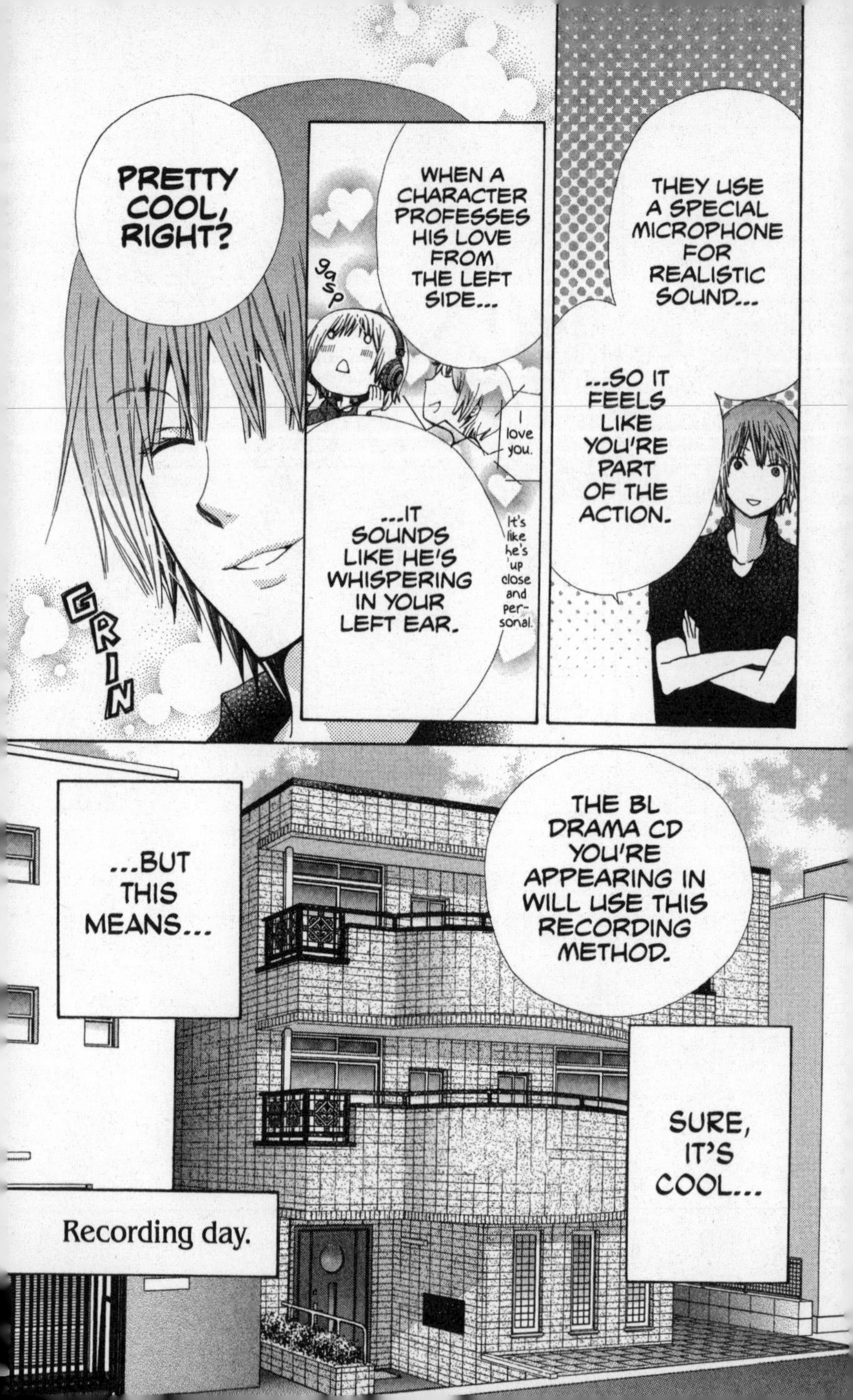
THEY USE A SPECIAL MICROPHONE FOR REALISTIC SOUND...
...SO IT FEELS LIKE YOU'RE PART OF THE ACTION.
WHEN A CHARACTER PROFESSES HIS LOVE FROM THE LEFT SIDE...
gasp
I love you.
...IT SOUNDS LIKE HE'S WHISPERING IN YOUR LEFT EAR.
It's like he's up close and per-sonal.
PRETTY COOL, RIGHT?
GRIN
THE BL DRAMA CD YOU'RE APPEARING IN WILL USE THIS RECORDING METHOD.
SURE, IT'S COOL...
...BUT THIS MEANS...
Recording day.

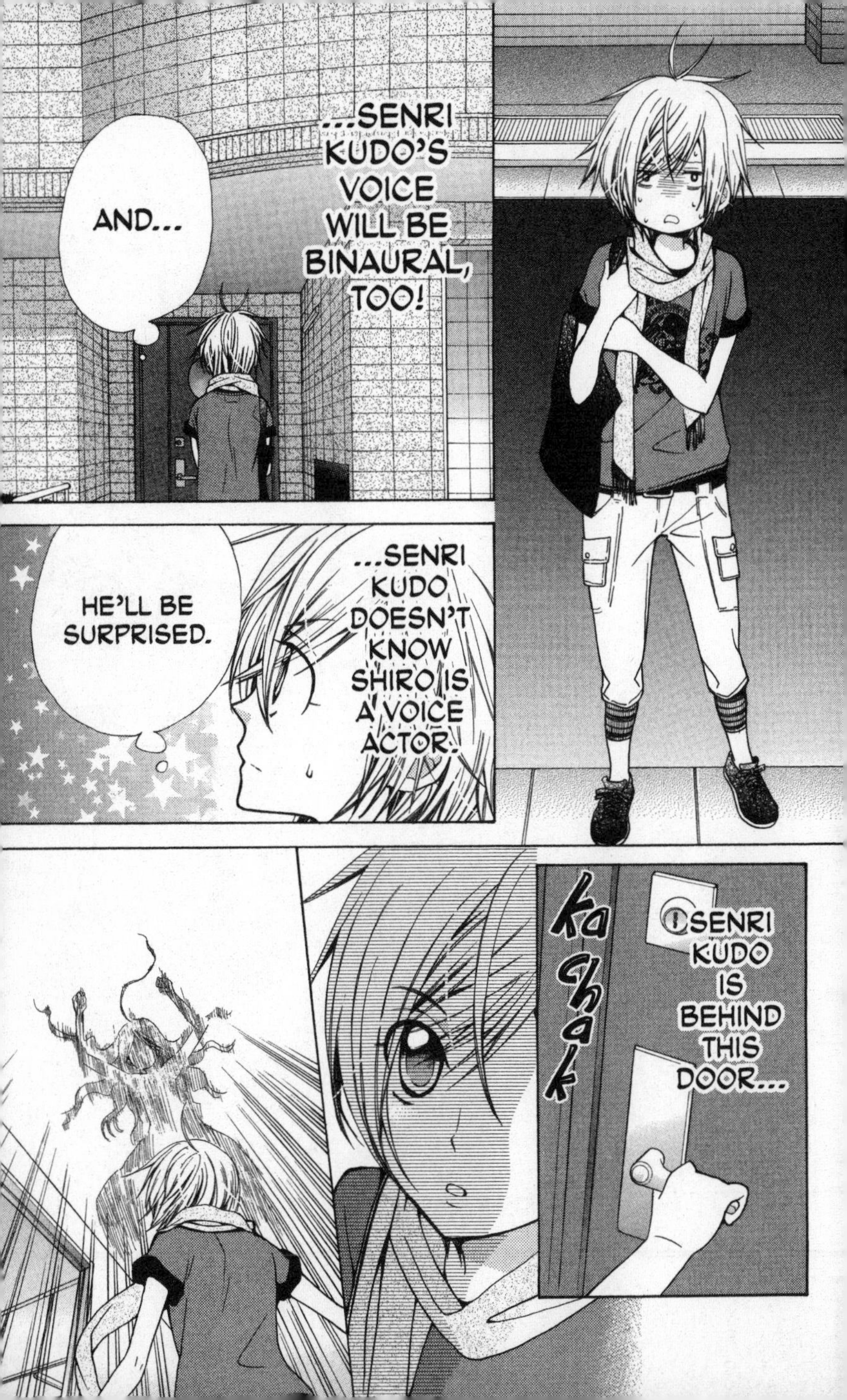
...SENRI KUDO'S VOICE WILL BE BINAURAL, TOO!
AND...
...SENRI KUDO DOESN'T KNOW SHIRO IS A VOICE ACTOR.
HE'LL BE SURPRISED.
SENRI KUDO IS BEHIND THIS DOOR...
Ka chak

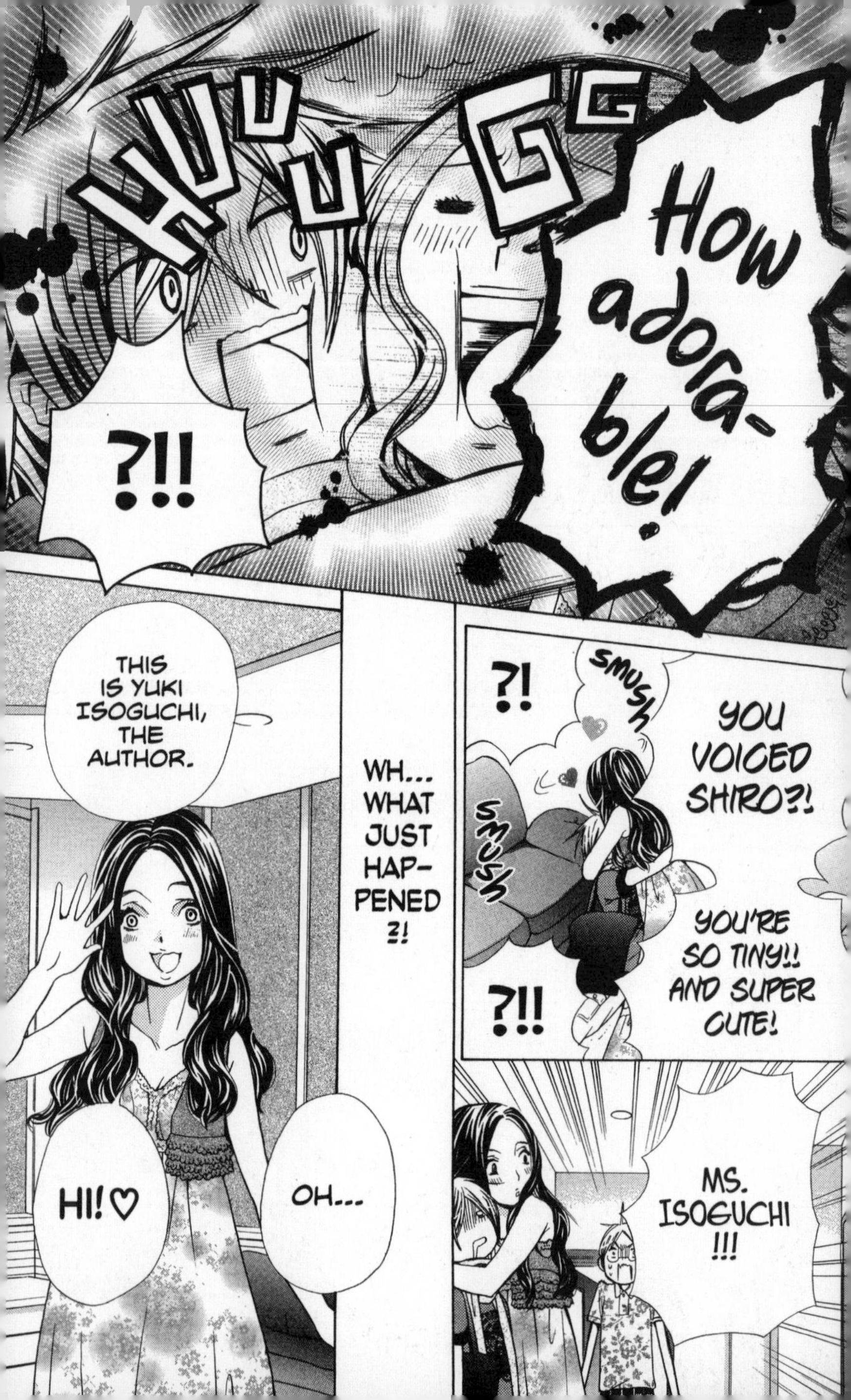
How adorable! ♥
HYUUGG
?!!
YOU VOICED SHIRO?!
SMUSH
?!
YOU'RE SO TINY!! AND SUPER CUTE!
SMUSH
?!!
MS. ISOGUCHI!!!
WH... WHAT JUST HAP-PENED?!
THIS IS YUKI ISOGUCHI, THE AUTHOR.
OH...
HI! ♡

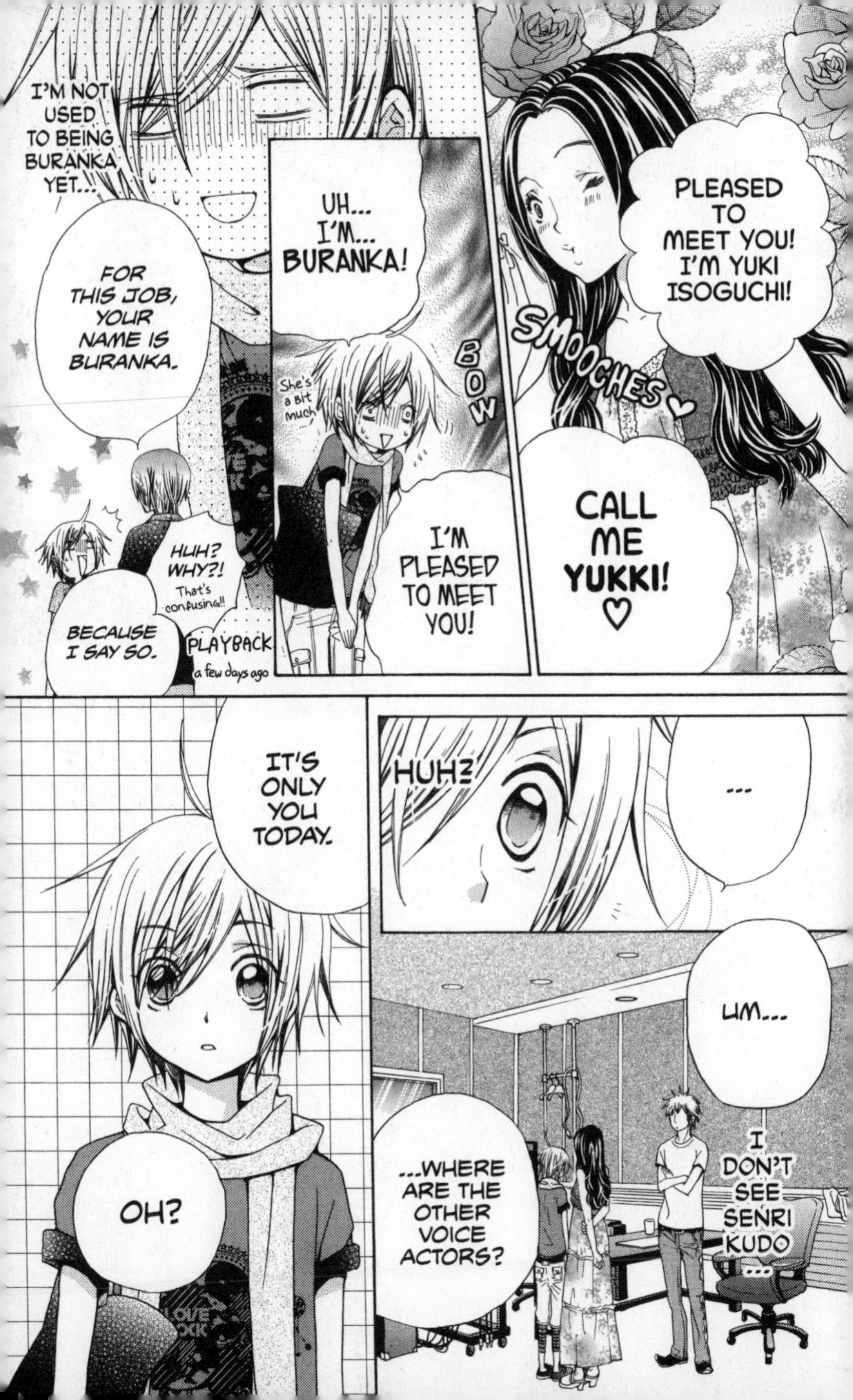
PLEASED TO MEET YOU! I'M YUKI ISOGUCHI!
SMOOCHES ♥
CALL ME YUKKI! ♡
UH... I'M... BURANKA!
BOW
She's a bit much...!
I'M PLEASED TO MEET YOU!
I'M NOT USED TO BEING BURANKA YET...!!
FOR THIS JOB, YOUR NAME IS BURANKA.
HUH? WHY?! That's confusing!!
BECAUSE I SAY SO.
PLAYBACK
a few days ago
...
HUH?
UM...
I DON'T SEE SENRI KUDO...
...WHERE ARE THE OTHER VOICE ACTORS?
IT'S ONLY YOU TODAY.
OH?

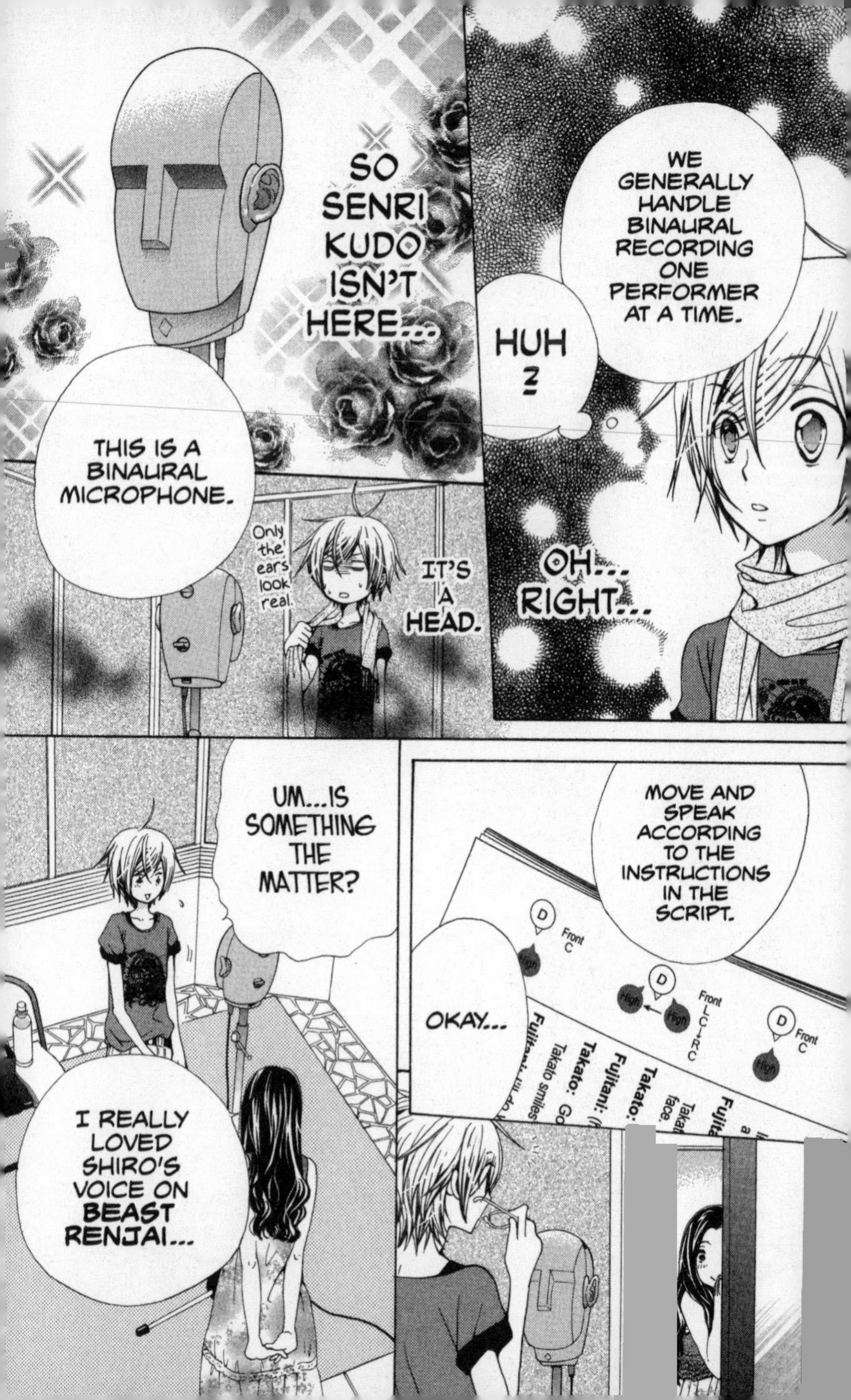

WE GENERALLY HANDLE BINAURAL RECORDING ONE PERFORMER AT A TIME.
HUH?
OH... RIGHT...
SO SENRI KUDO ISN'T HERE...
THIS IS A BINAURAL MICROPHONE.
IT'S A HEAD.
Only the ears look real.
MOVE AND SPEAK ACCORDING TO THE INSTRUCTIONS IN THE SCRIPT.
OKAY...
Front C
Front L C R C
Front C
Takato:
Takato:
Takato smiles
UM...IS SOMETHING THE MATTER?
I REALLY LOVED SHIRO'S VOICE ON BEAST RENJAI...

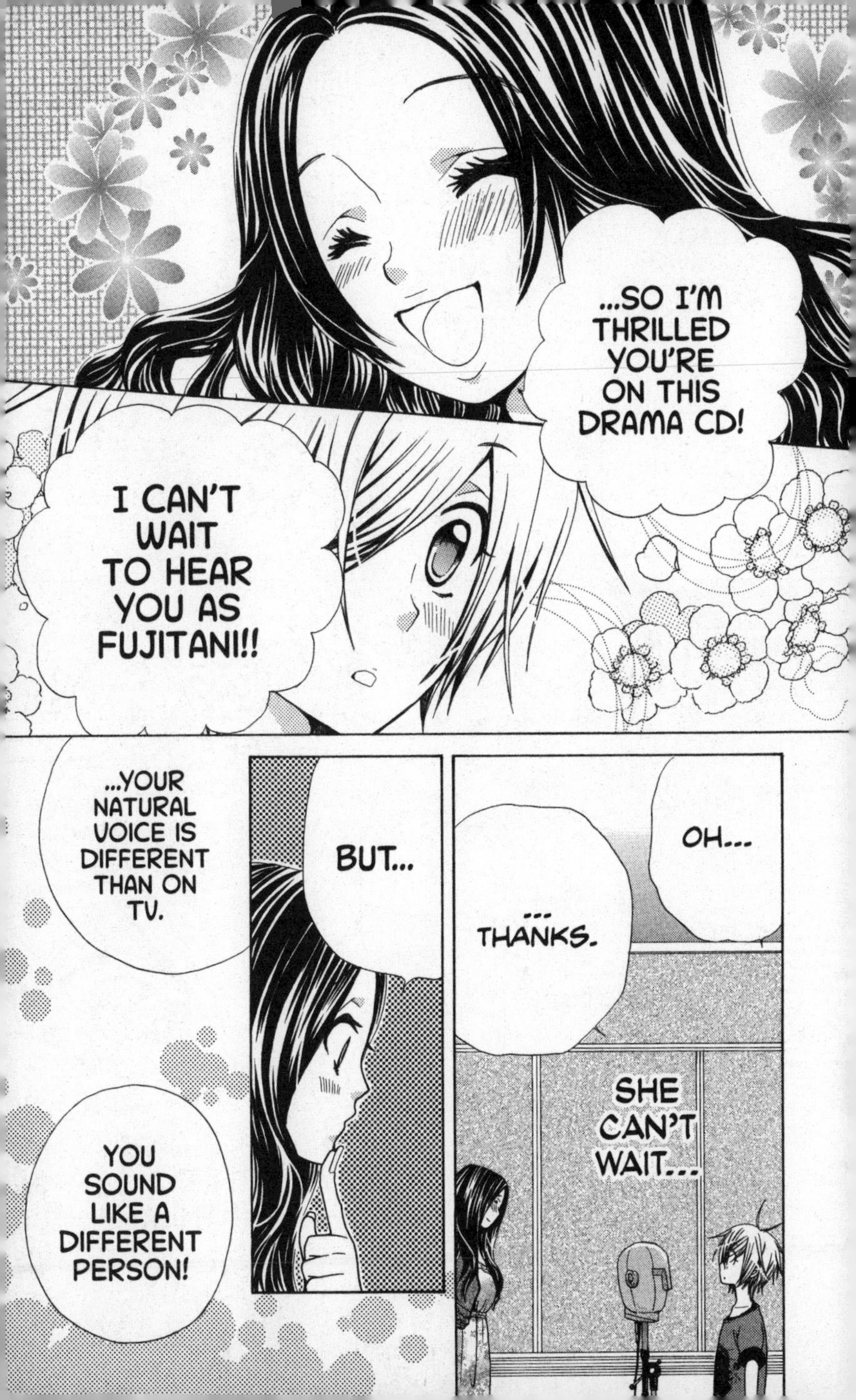
...SO I'M THRILLED YOU'RE ON THIS DRAMA CD!
I CAN'T WAIT TO HEAR YOU AS FUJITANI!!
OH...
... THANKS.
SHE CAN'T WAIT...
BUT...
...YOUR NATURAL VOICE IS DIFFERENT THAN ON TV.
YOU SOUND LIKE A DIFFERENT PERSON!

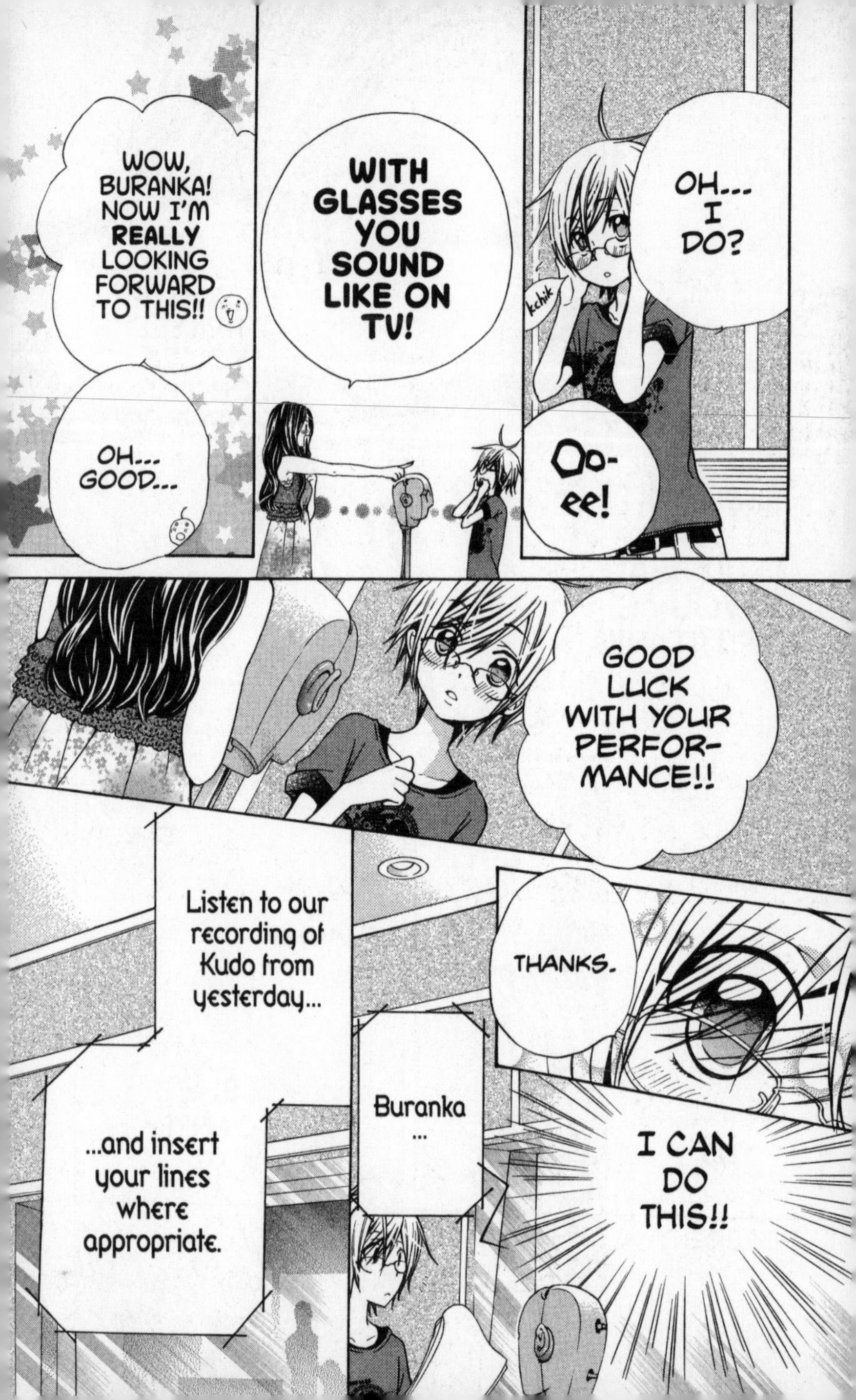
OH... I DO?
kchik
Oo-ee!
WITH GLASSES YOU SOUND LIKE ON TV!
WOW, BURANKA! NOW I'M REALLY LOOKING FORWARD TO THIS!!
OH... GOOD...
GOOD LUCK WITH YOUR PERFORMANCE!!
THANKS.
I CAN DO THIS!!
Listen to our recording of Kudo from yesterday...
Buranka...
...and insert your lines where appropriate.

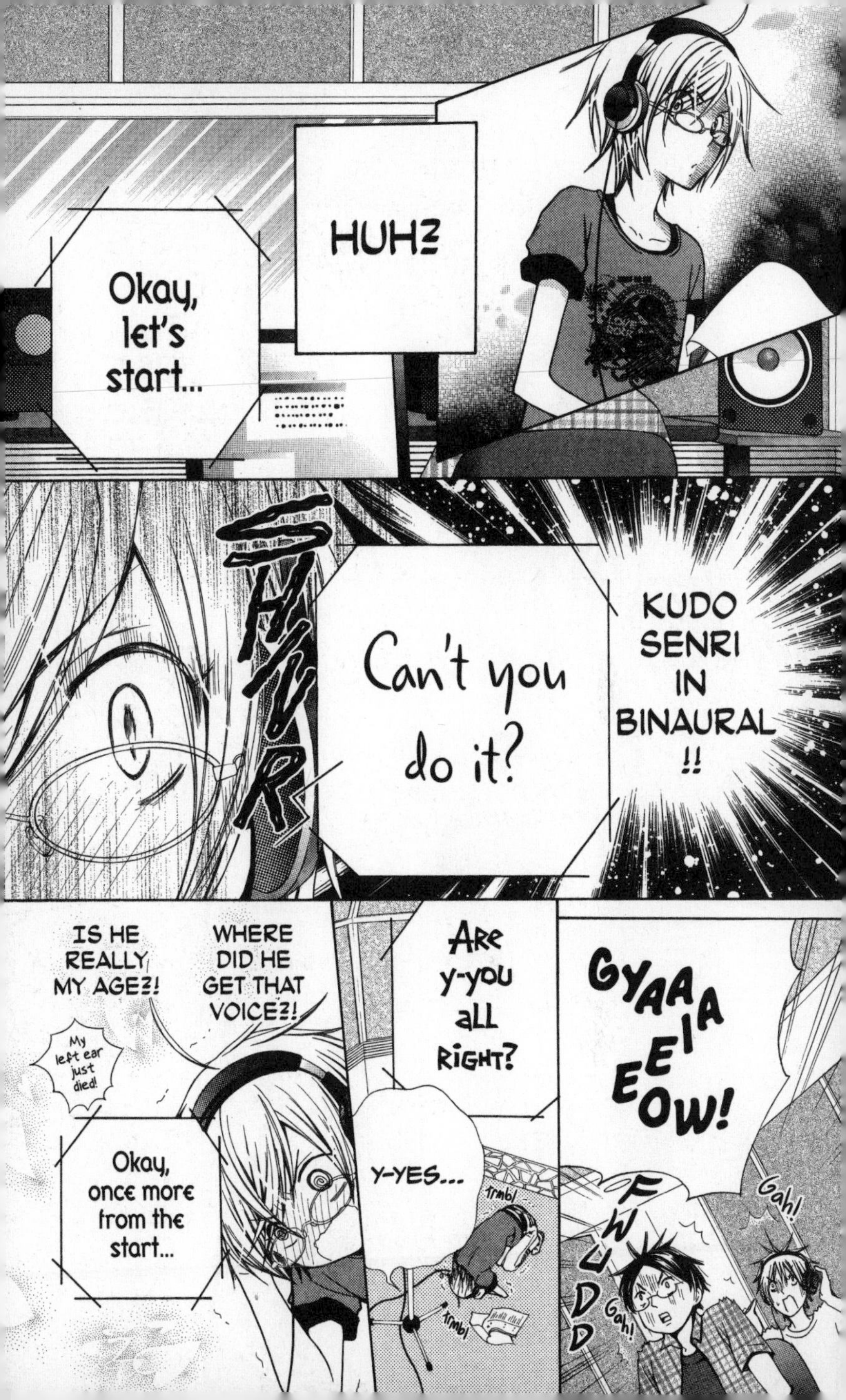
HUH?
Okay, let's start...
KUDO SENRI IN BINAURAL!!
Can't you do it?
SHIVR
GYAAAIAEEEOW!
FWUDD
Gah!
Gah!
Are y-you all right?
Y-YES...
trmbl
trmbl
WHERE DID HE GET THAT VOICE?!
IS HE REALLY MY AGE?!
My left ear just died!
Okay, once more from the start...

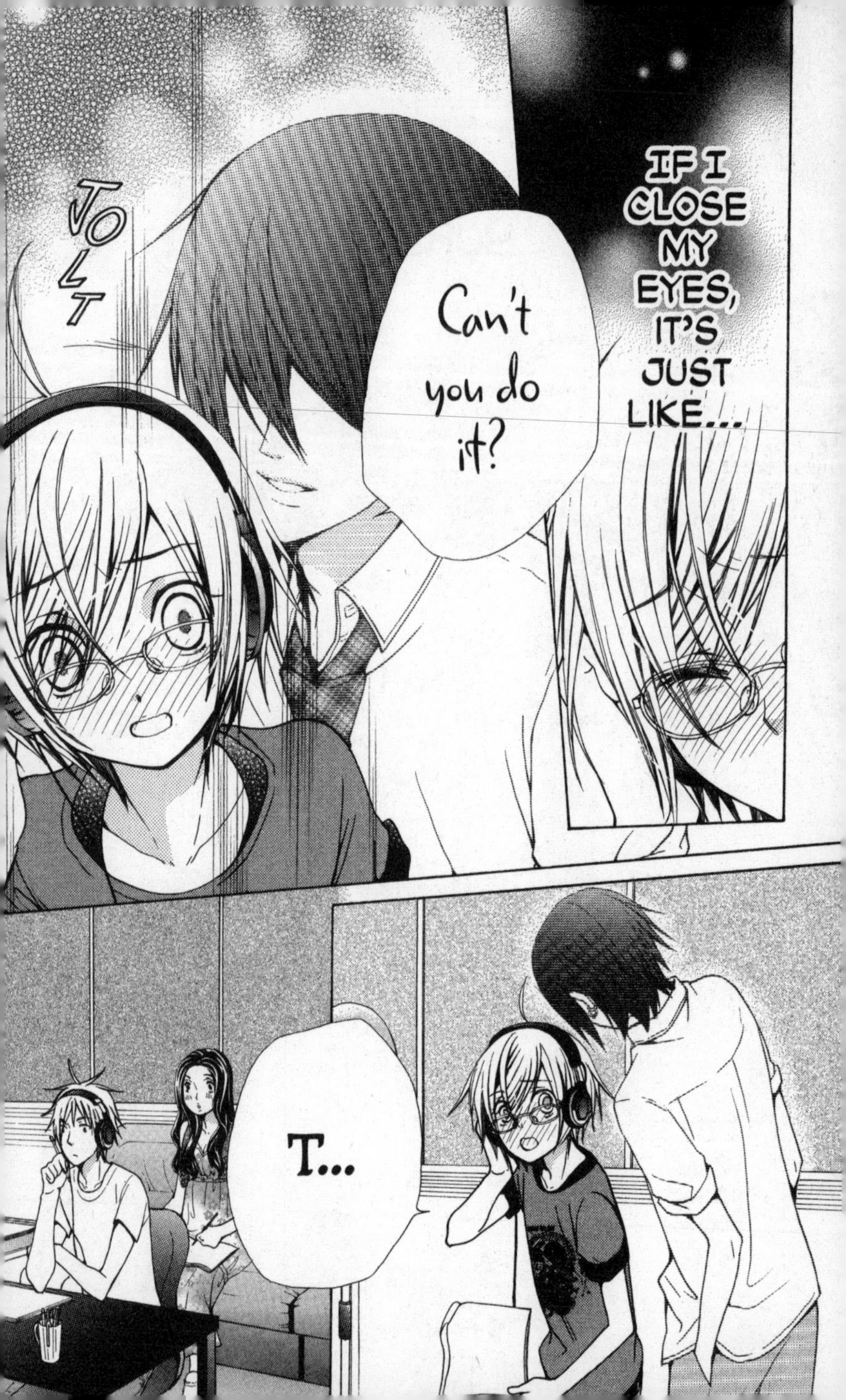
IF I CLOSE MY EYES, IT'S JUST LIKE...
Can't you do it?
JOLT
T...

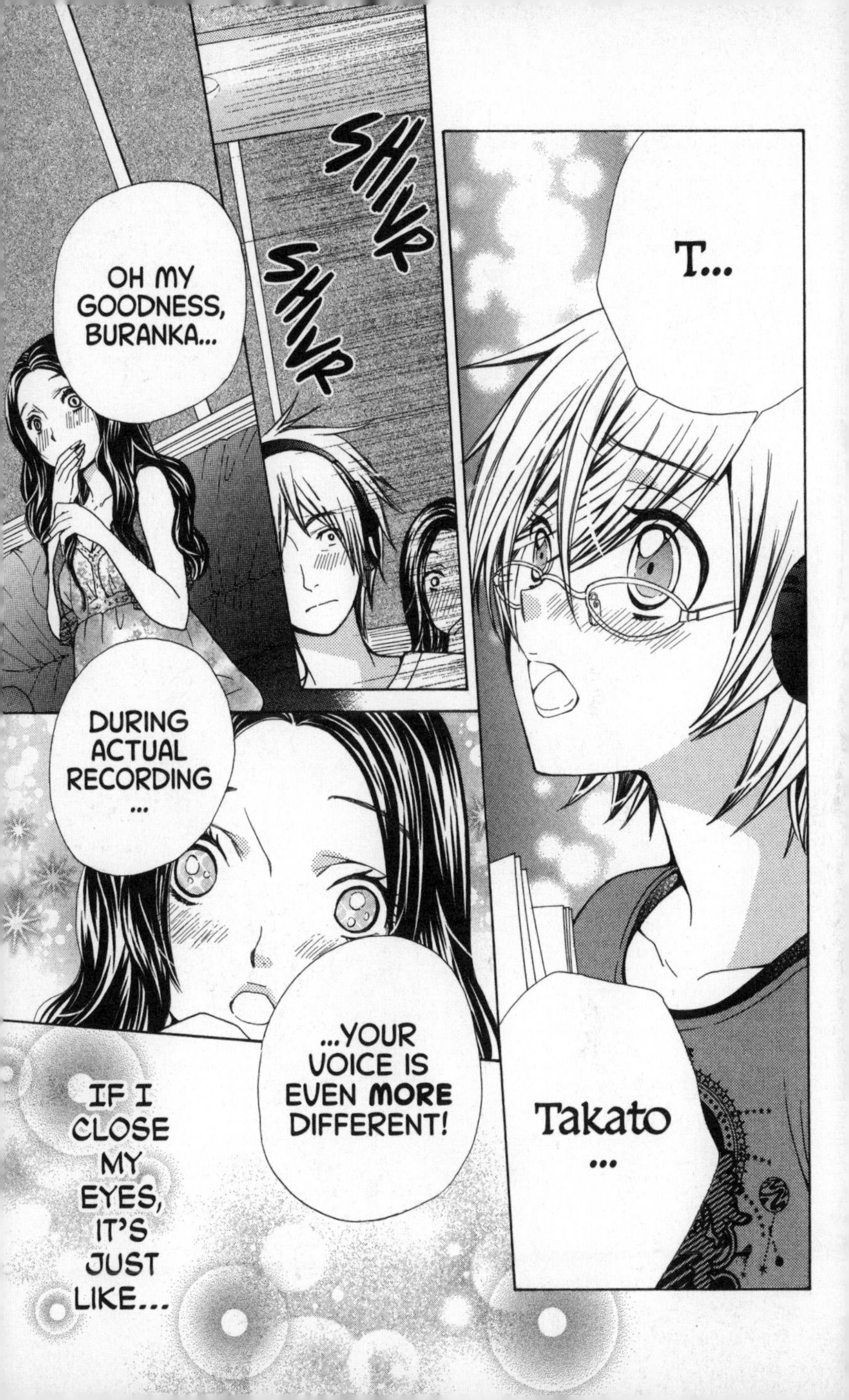
T...
Takato ...
SHIVR
SHIVR
OH MY GOODNESS, BURANKA...
DURING ACTUAL RECORDING ...
...YOUR VOICE IS EVEN MORE DIFFERENT!
IF I CLOSE MY EYES, IT'S JUST LIKE...

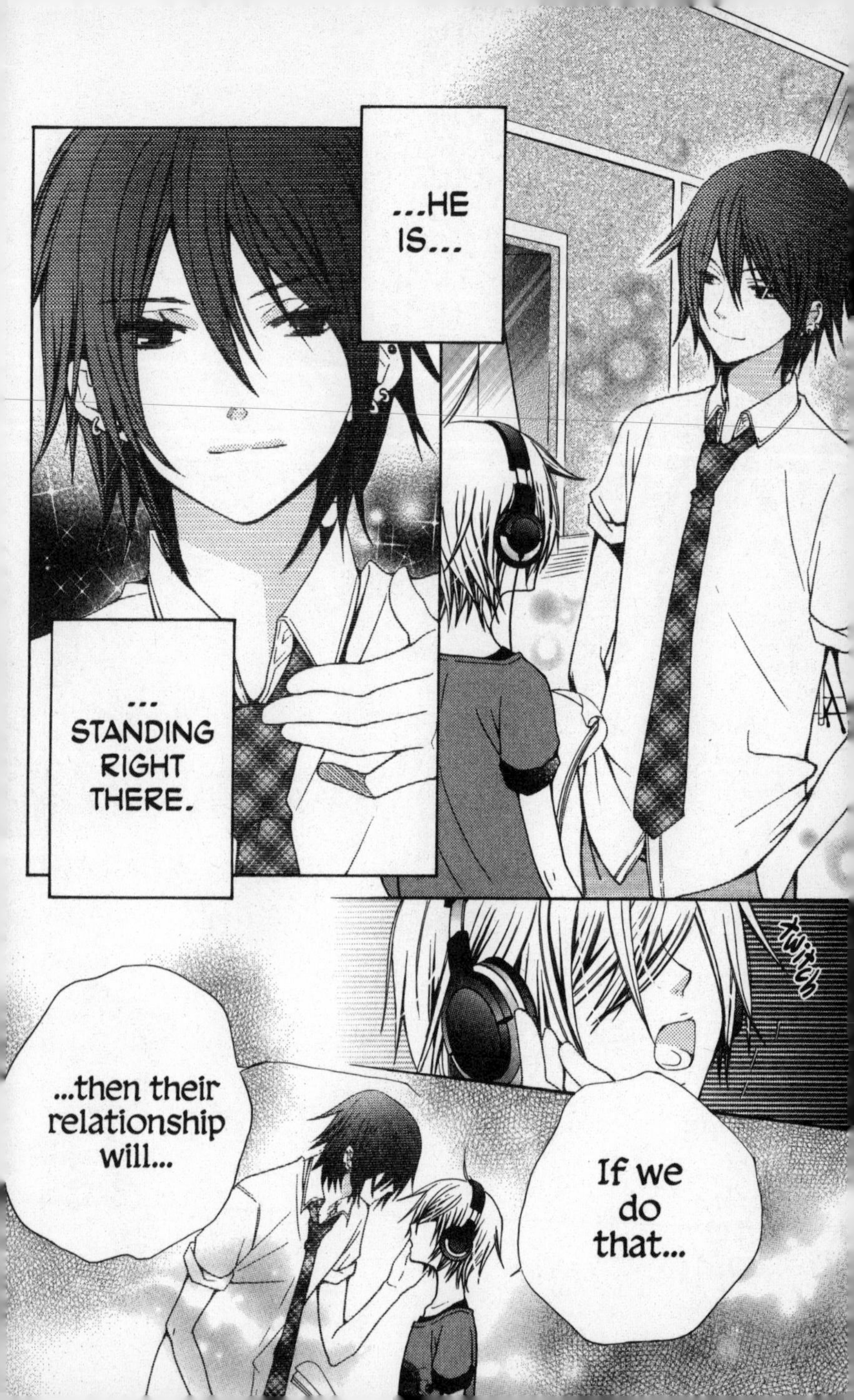
...HE IS...
... STANDING RIGHT THERE.
twitch
If we do that...
...then their relationship will...

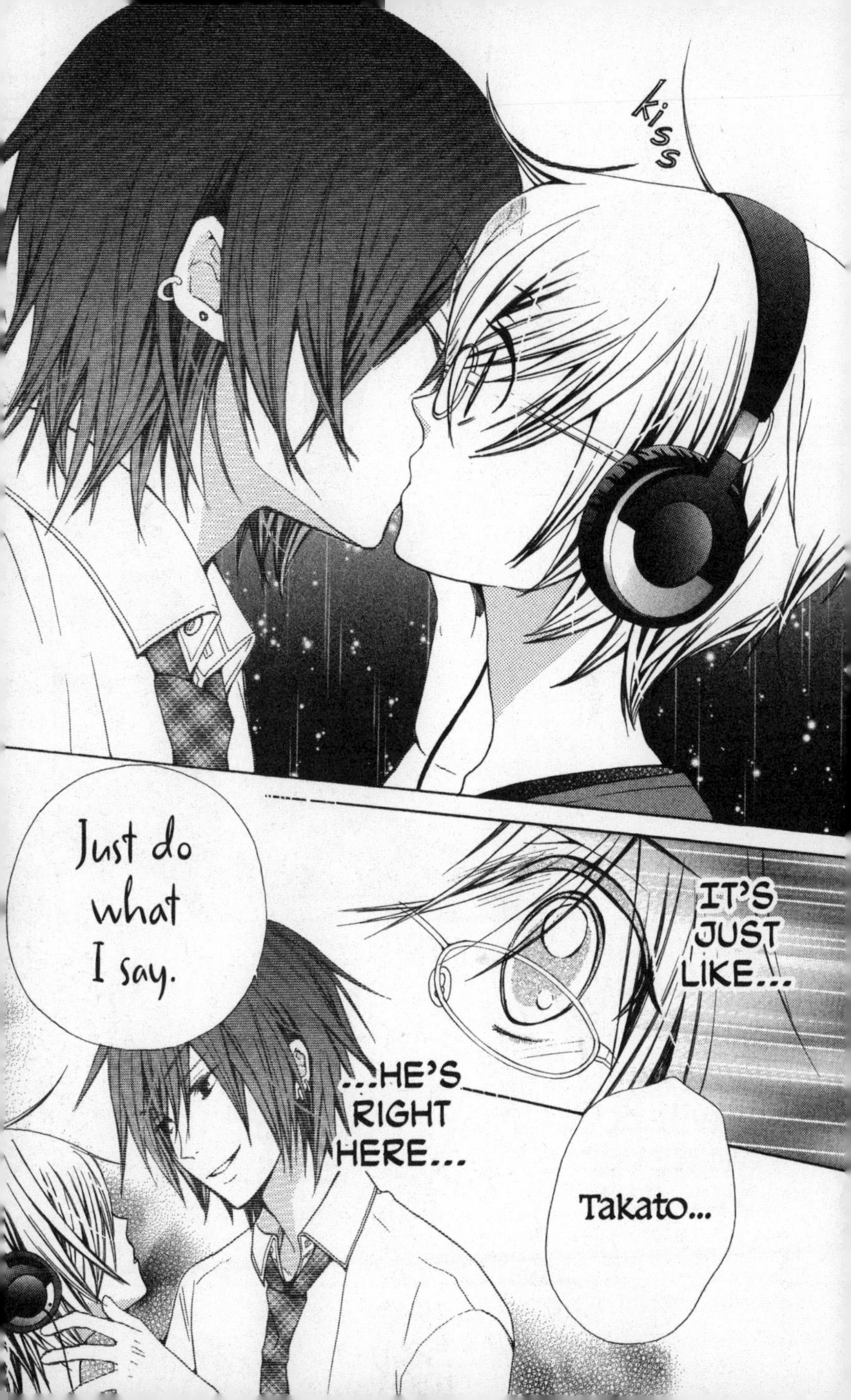
kiss
IT'S JUST LIKE...
...HE'S RIGHT HERE...
Takato...
Just do what I say.

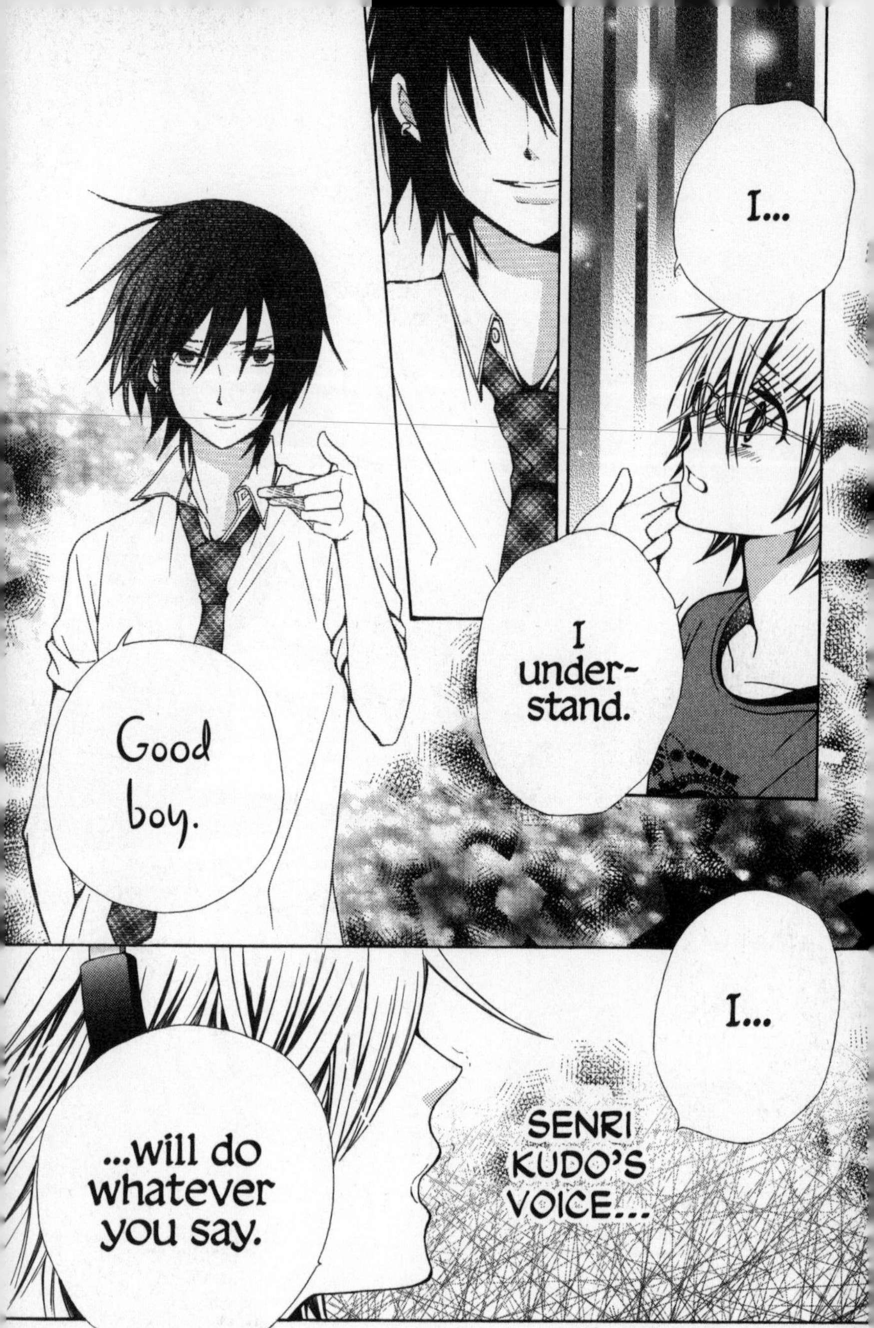
I...
I understand.
Good boy.
I...
SENRI KUDO'S VOICE...
...will do whatever you say.

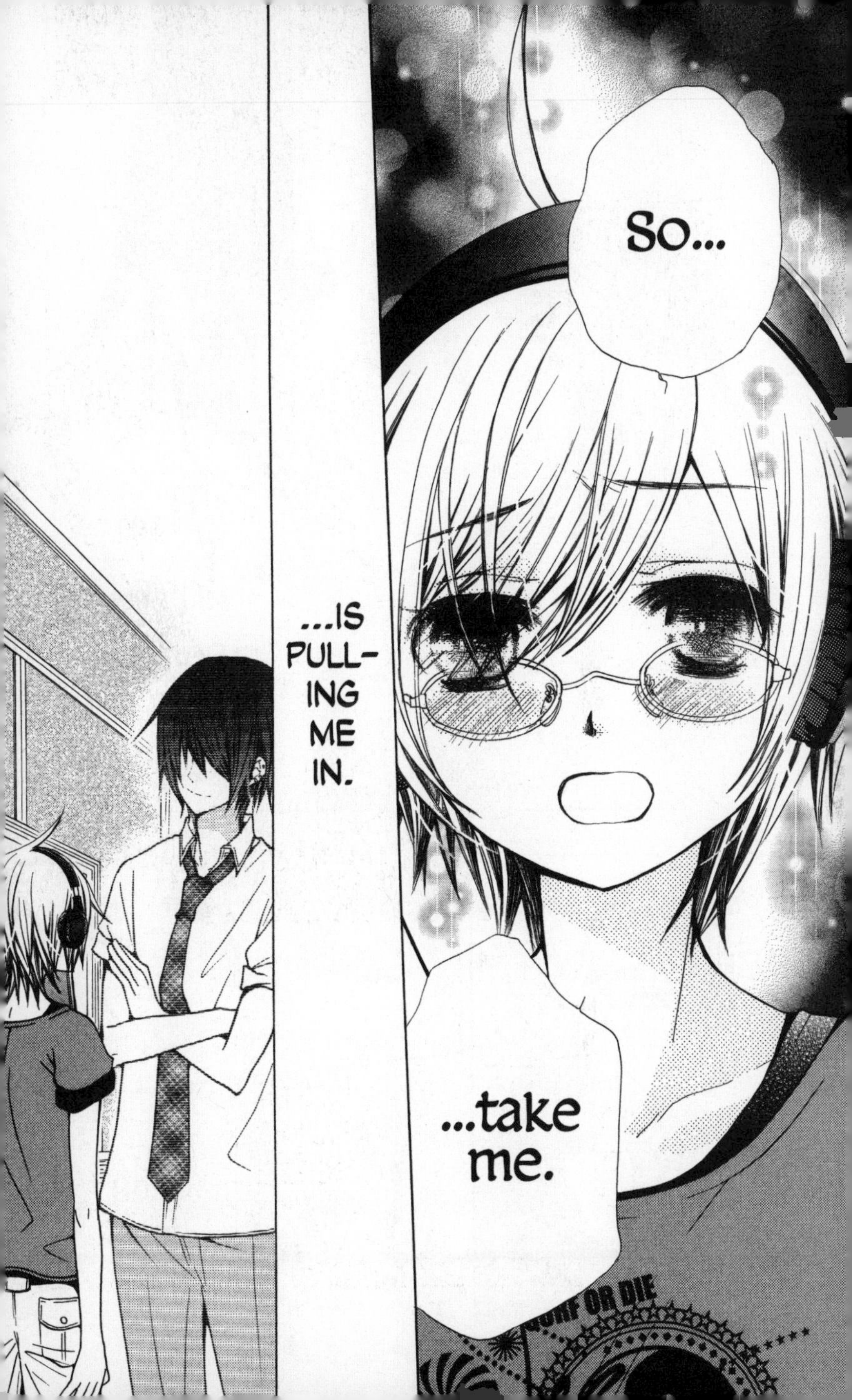
SO...
...take me.
...IS PULLING ME IN.

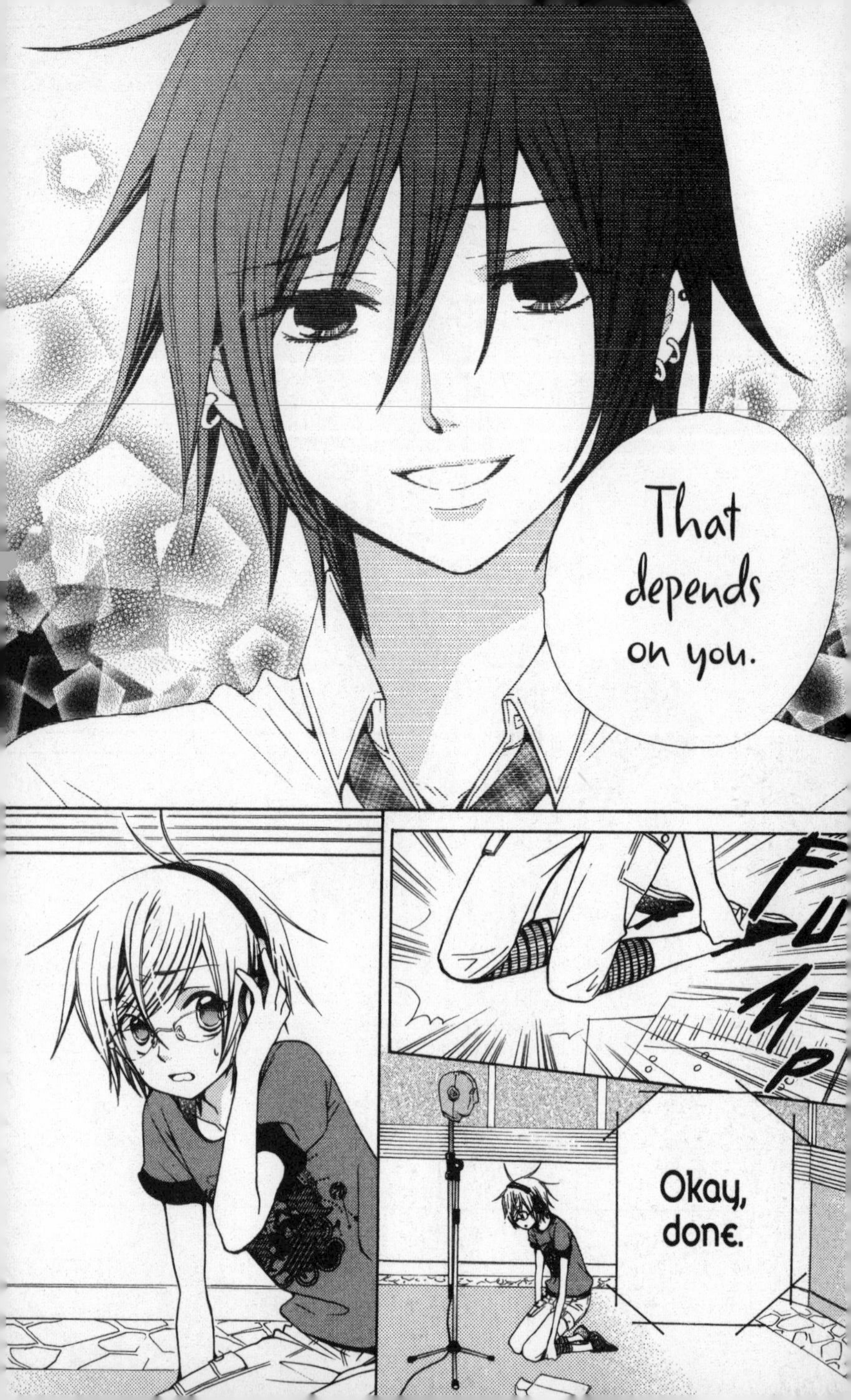
That depends on you.
FUMP
Okay, done.

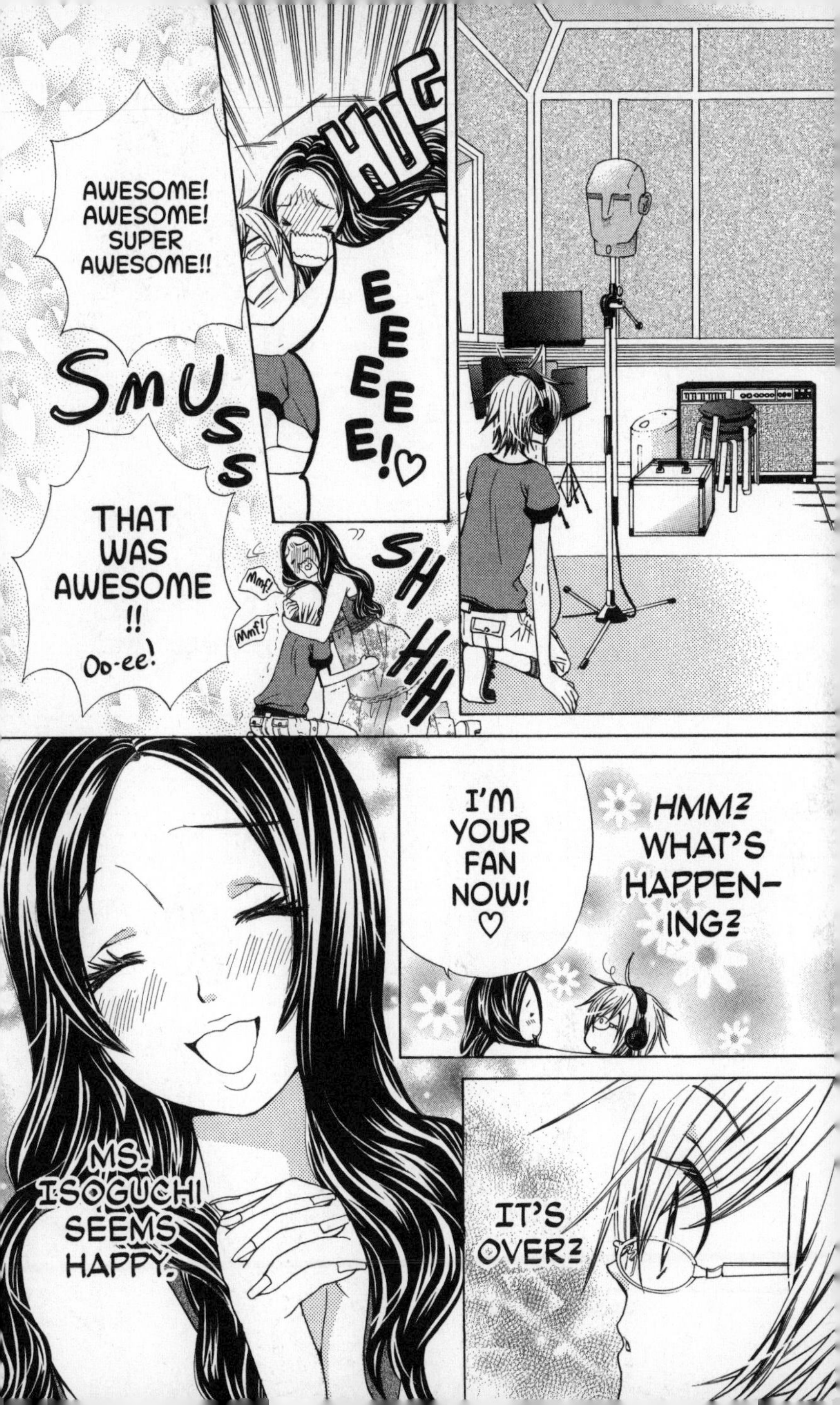
HUG
EEEEE!♡
AWESOME! AWESOME! SUPER AWESOME!!
SMUSS
SHHHH
Mmf!
Mmf!
THAT WAS AWESOME!!
Oo-ee!
HMM? WHAT'S HAPPEN-ING?
I'M YOUR FAN NOW! ♡
IT'S OVER?
MS. ISOGUCHI SEEMS HAPPY.

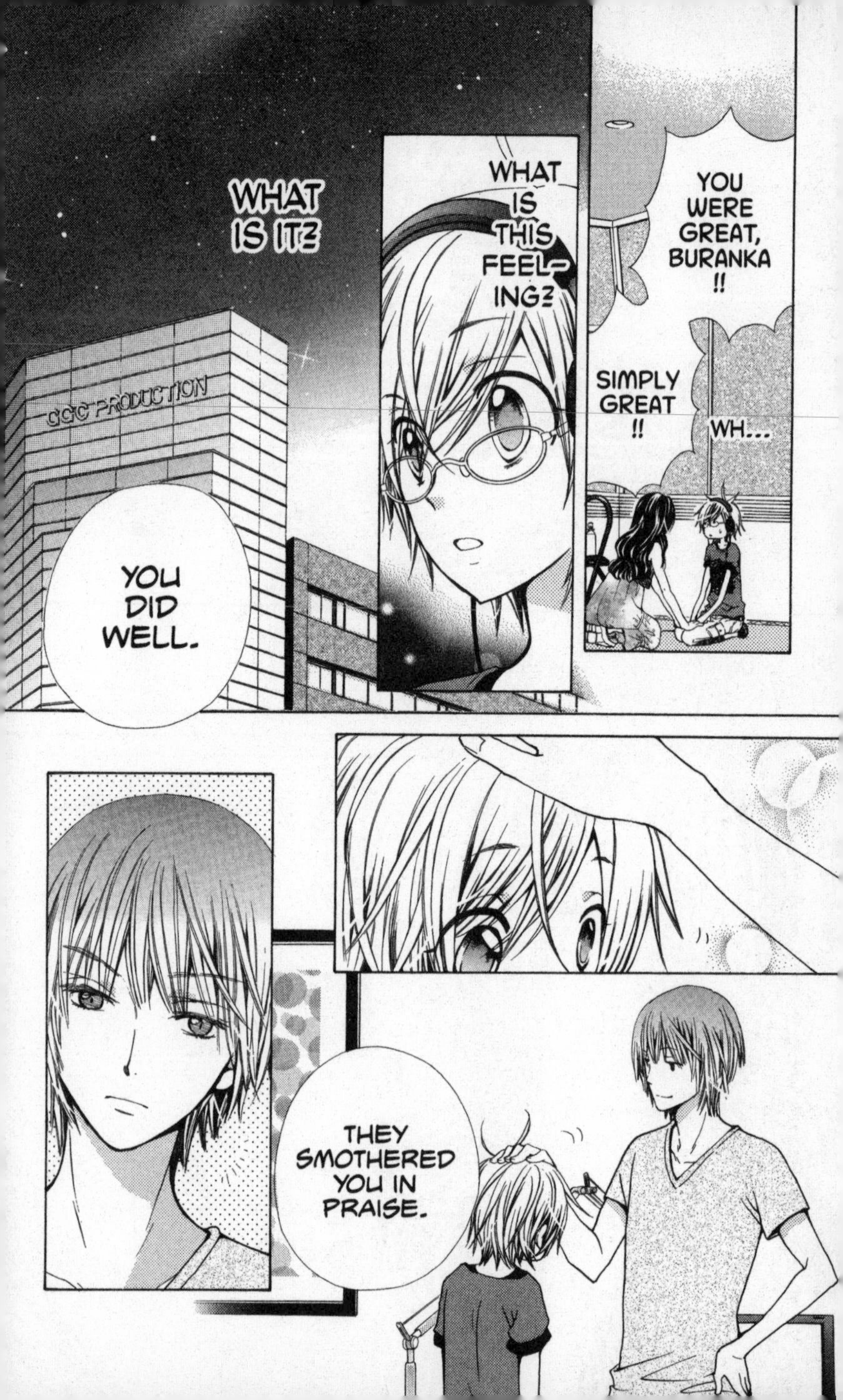
YOU WERE GREAT, BURANKA!!
SIMPLY GREAT!!
WH...
WHAT IS THIS FEELING?
WHAT IS IT?
GCC PRODUCTION
YOU DID WELL.
THEY SMOTHERED YOU IN PRAISE.

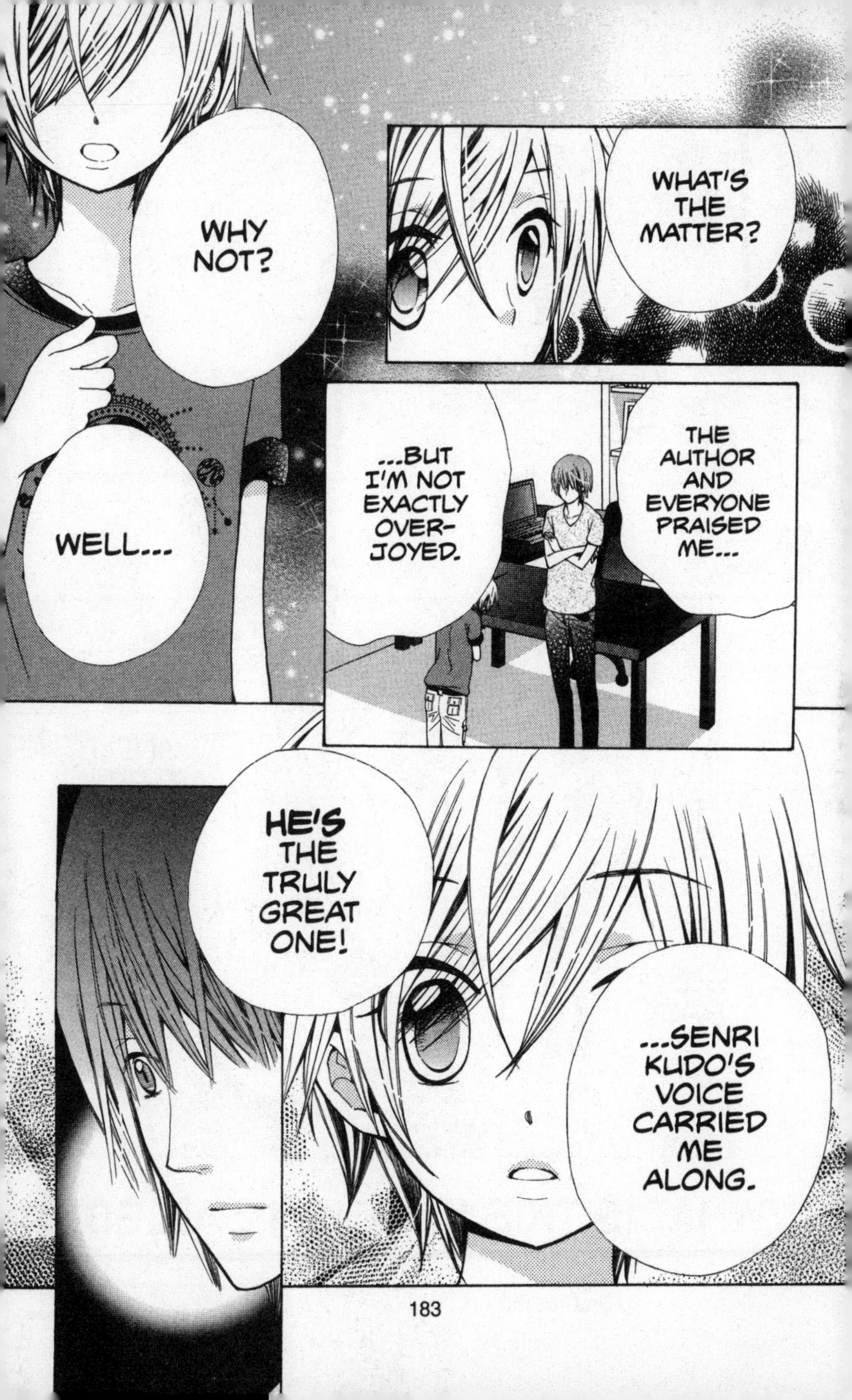
WHAT'S THE MATTER?
THE AUTHOR AND EVERYONE PRAISED ME...
...BUT I'M NOT EXACTLY OVER-JOYED.
WHY NOT?
WELL...
...SENRI KUDO'S VOICE CARRIED ME ALONG.
HE'S THE TRULY GREAT ONE!

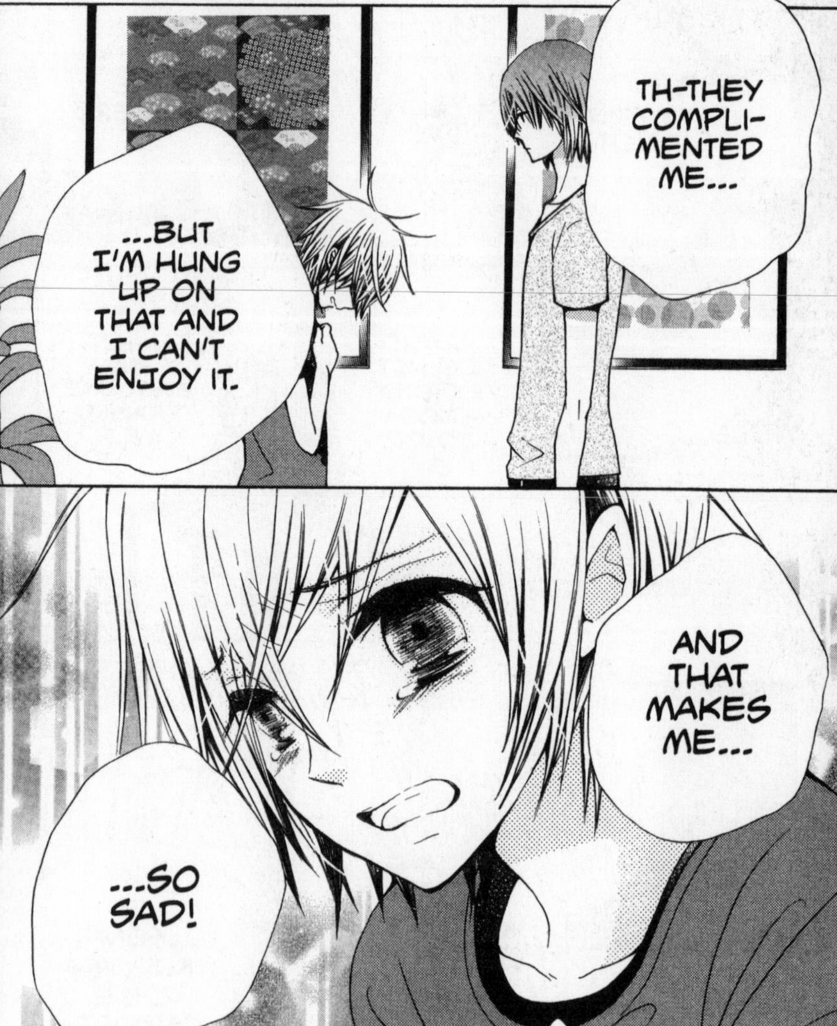
TH-THEY COMPLI-MENTED ME...
...BUT I'M HUNG UP ON THAT AND I CAN'T ENJOY IT.
AND THAT MAKES ME...
...SO SAD!

WHAT IS THIS EMOTION CALLED?

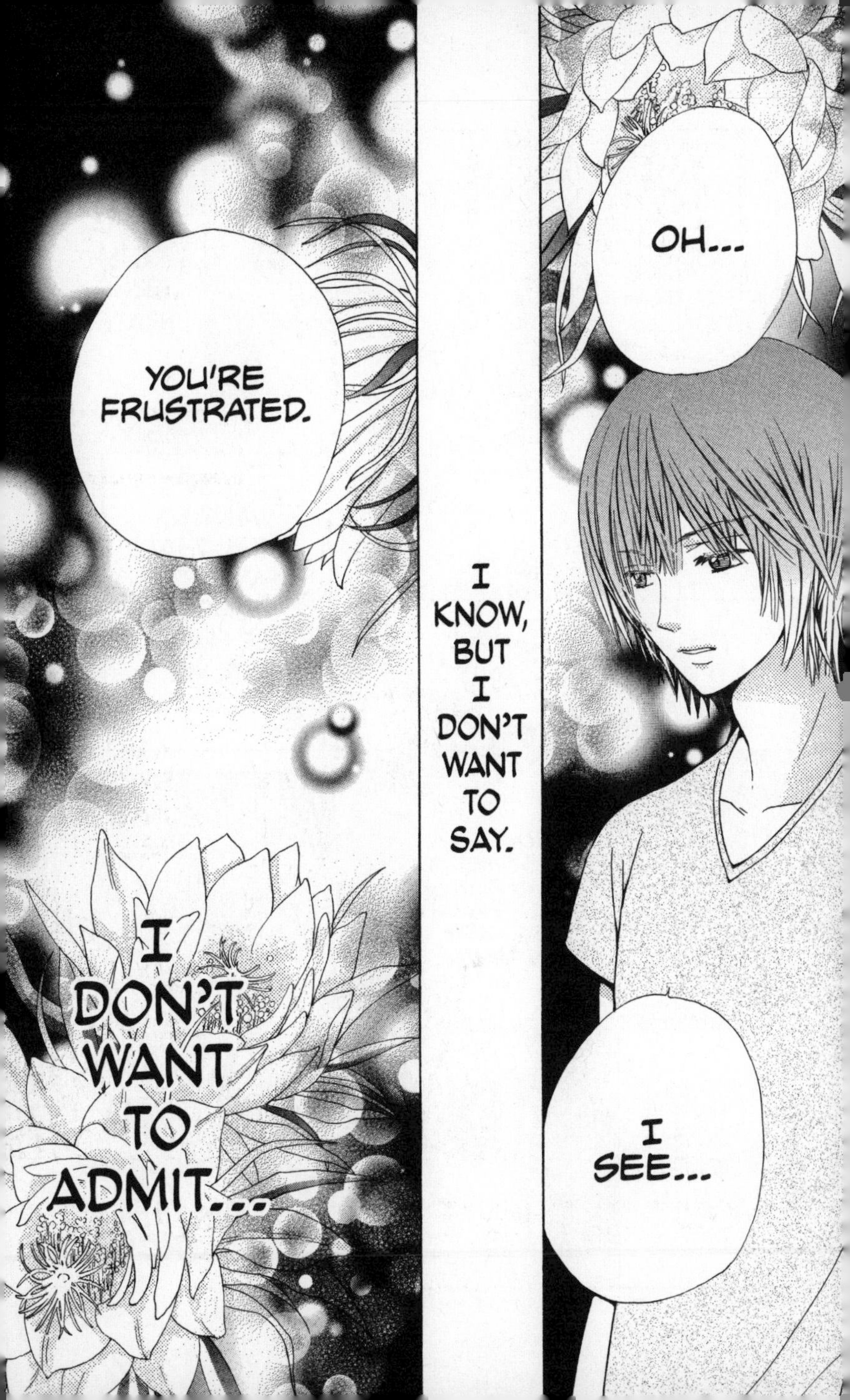
OH...
I SEE...
I KNOW, BUT I DON'T WANT TO SAY.
YOU'RE FRUSTRATED.
I DON'T WANT TO ADMIT...

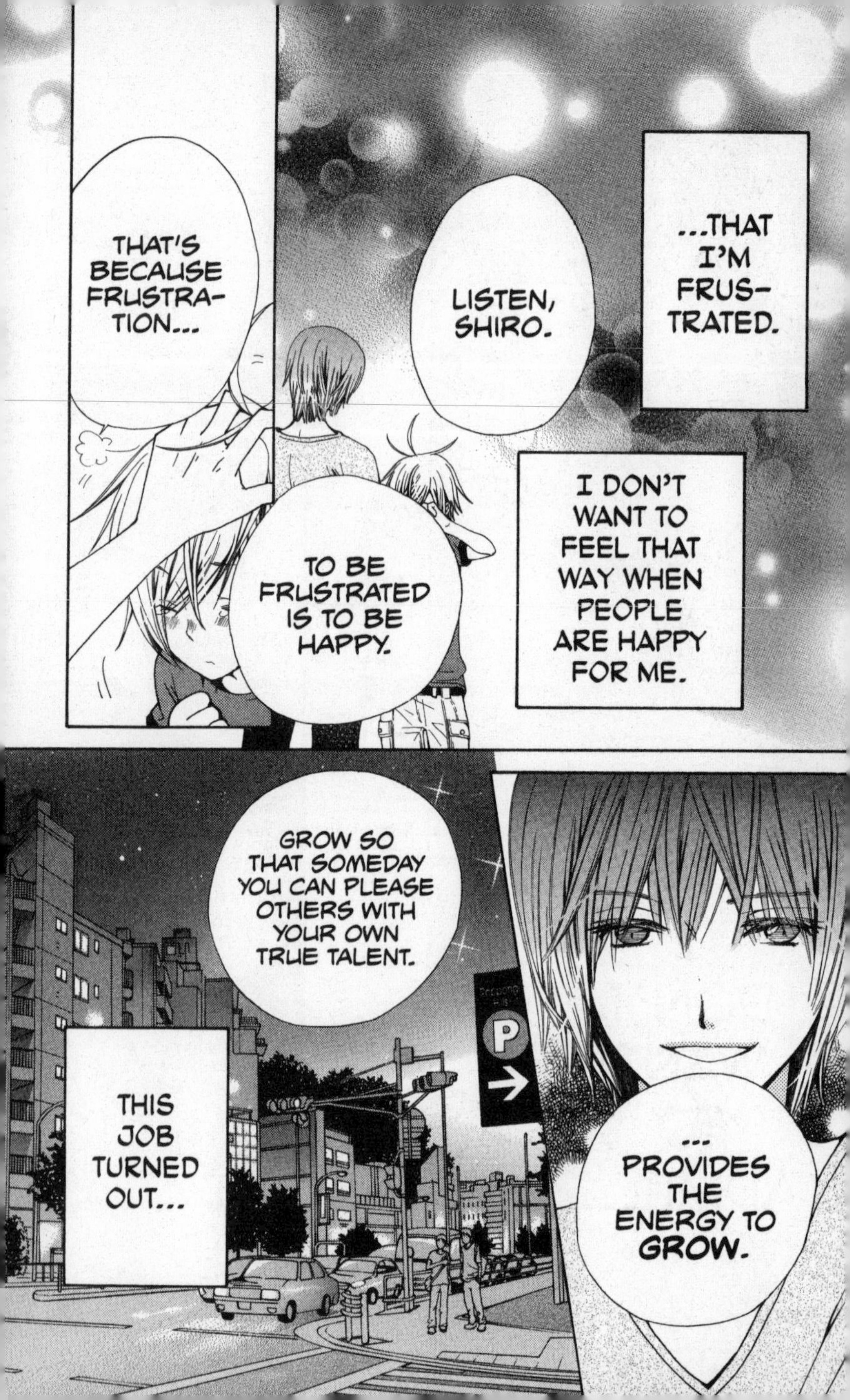

...THAT I'M FRUS-TRATED.
I DON'T WANT TO FEEL THAT WAY WHEN PEOPLE ARE HAPPY FOR ME.
LISTEN, SHIRO.
TO BE FRUSTRATED IS TO BE HAPPY.
THAT'S BECAUSE FRUSTRA-TION...
...PROVIDES THE ENERGY TO GROW.
GROW SO THAT SOMEDAY YOU CAN PLEASE OTHERS WITH YOUR OWN TRUE TALENT.
THIS JOB TURNED OUT...

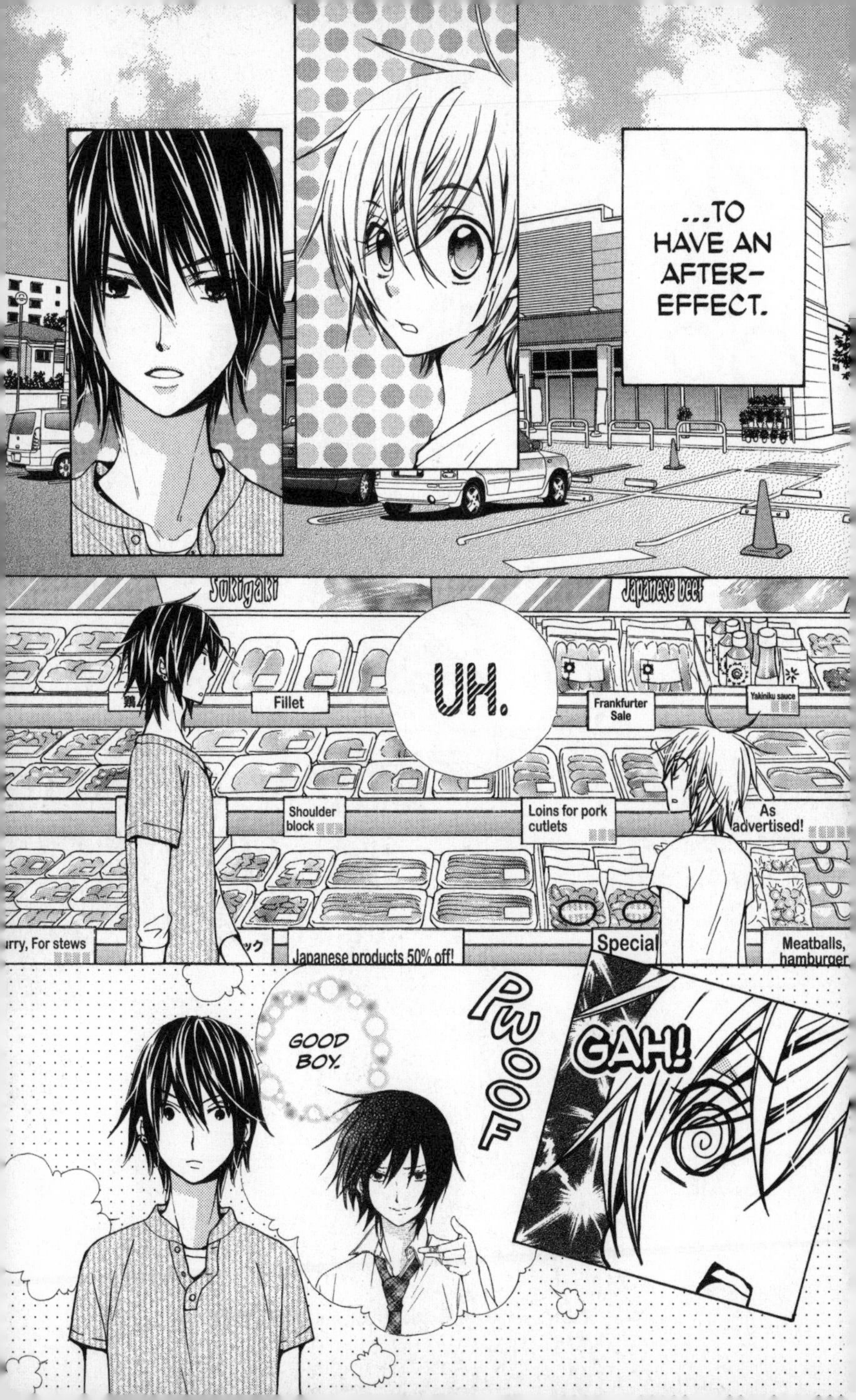
...TO HAVE AN AFTER-EFFECT.
Japanese beef
Sukiyaki
UH.
Yakiniku sauce
Frankfurter Sale
Fillet
As advertised!
Loins for pork cutlets
Shoulder block
Meatballs, hamburger
Special
Japanese products 50% off!
urry, For stews
GAH!
PWOOF
GOOD BOY.

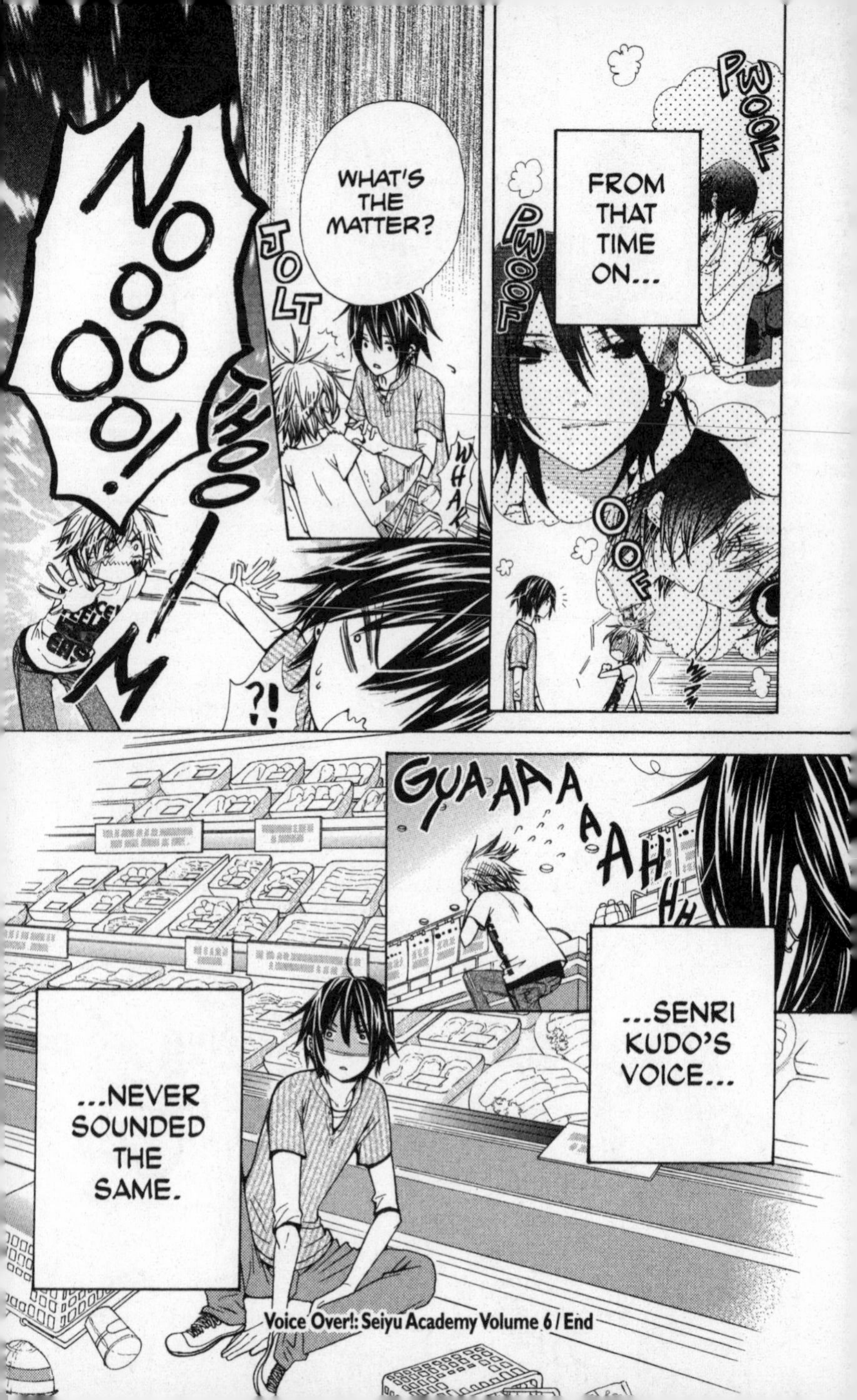
PWOOF
FROM THAT TIME ON...
PWOOF
OOOF
WHAT'S THE MATTER?
JOLT
WHAK
NOOOOOO!
THOOM
?!
GYAAAAAAHHH
...SENRI KUDO'S VOICE...
...NEVER SOUNDED THE SAME.
Voice Over!: Seiyu Academy Volume 6 / End

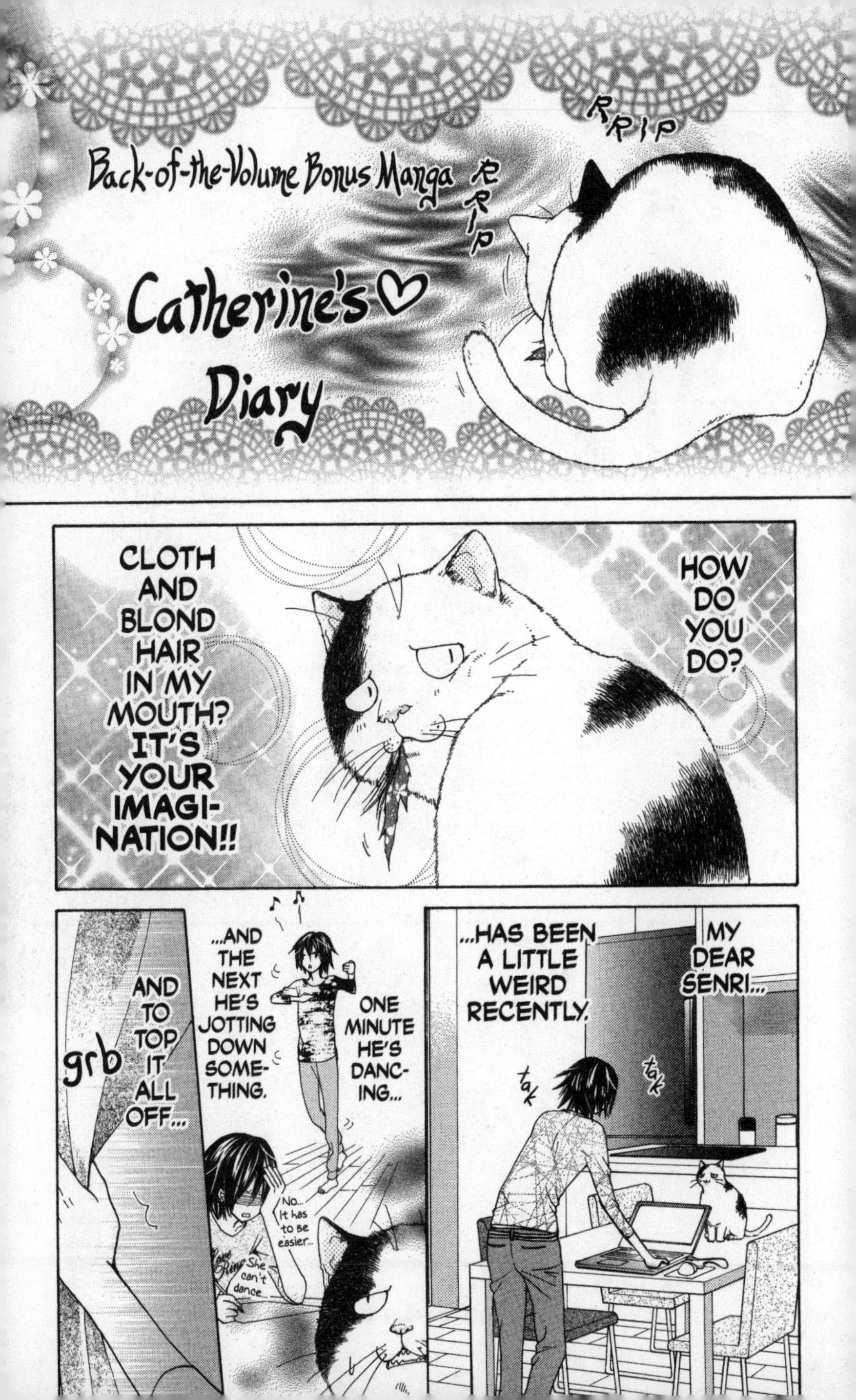
Back-of-the-Volume Bonus Manga
Catherine's ♡ Diary
RRIP
RRIP
HOW DO YOU DO?
CLOTH AND BLOND HAIR IN MY MOUTH? IT'S YOUR IMAGINATION!!
MY DEAR SENRI...
...HAS BEEN A LITTLE WEIRD RECENTLY.
tak
tak
ONE MINUTE HE'S DANCING...
...AND THE NEXT HE'S JOTTING DOWN SOMETHING.
No... It has to be easier...
She can't dance...
AND TO TOP IT ALL OFF...
grb

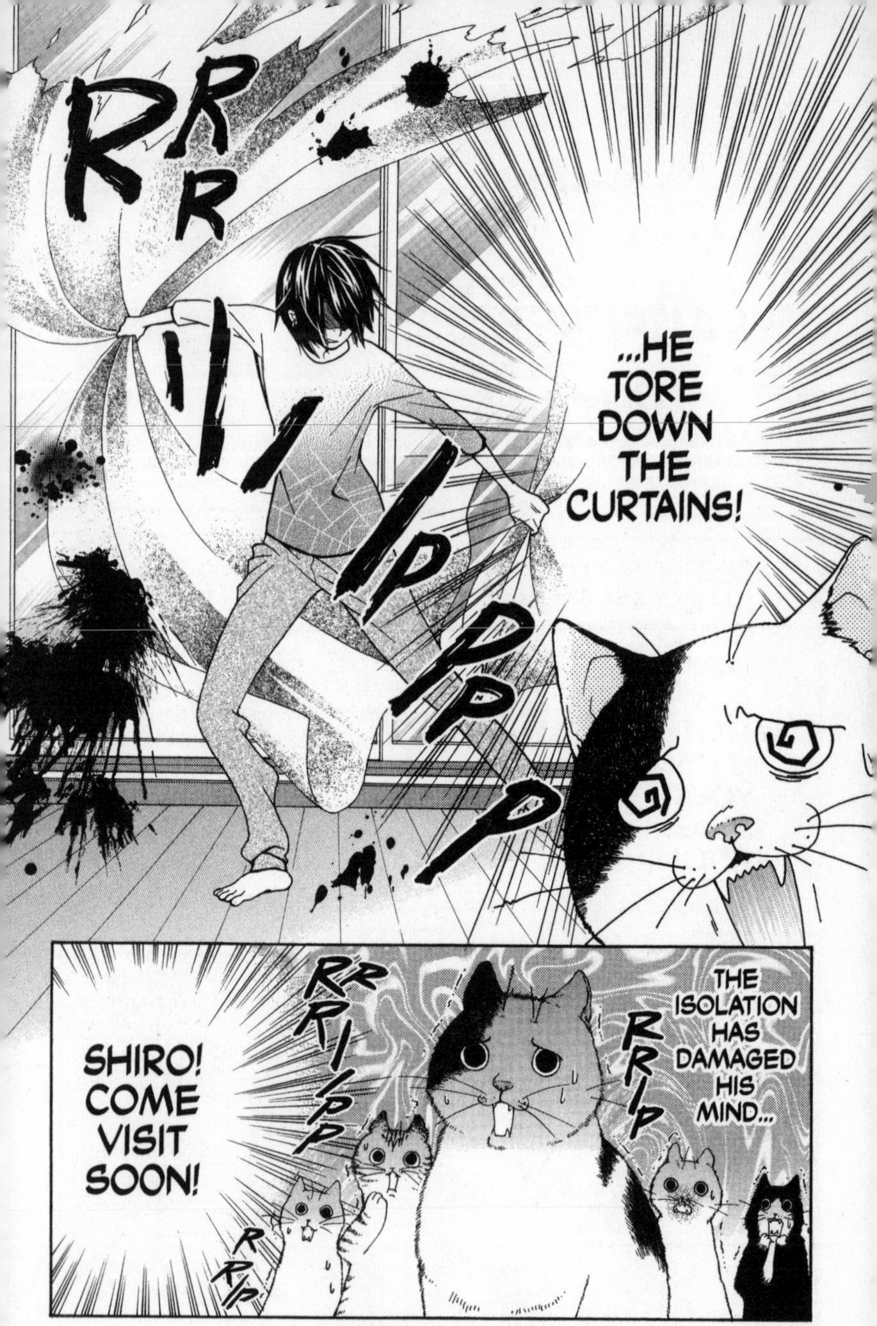
RRR
IIIPPPP
...HE TORE DOWN THE CURTAINS!
THE ISOLATION HAS DAMAGED HIS MIND...
RRIP
RRRIIPP
SHIRO! COME VISIT SOON!
RRIP

Bonus Pages / The End